THE STRUCTURE OF CONFLICT

SOCIAL PSYCHOLOGY

A series of monographs, treatises, and texts

Editors

Leon Festinger and Stanley Schachter

The Structure of Conflict

Edited by PAUL SWINGLE
Department of Psychology
McMaster University
Hamilton, Ontario, Canada

1970

A C A D E M I C   P R E S S   New York and London

ACADEMIC PRESS, INC.
111 Fifth Avenue, New York, New York 10003

United Kingdom Edition published by
ACADEMIC PRESS, INC. (LONDON) LTD.
Berkeley Square House, London W1X 6BA

LIBRARY OF CONGRESS CATALOG CARD NUMBER: 75-117079

PRINTED IN THE UNITED STATES OF AMERICA

CONTENTS

5. Threats and Promises
James T. Tedeschi

6. The Effects of Personality in Cooperation and Conflict
Kenneth W. Terhune

7. Dangerous Games
Paul G. Swingle

8. Deterrence Games: From Academic Casebook to Military Codebook
Irving Louis Horowitz

LIST OF CONTRIBUTORS

Numbers in parentheses indicate the pages on which the authors' contributions begin.

OTOMAR BARTOS (45),[*] Department of Sociology, University of Pittsburgh, Pittsburgh, Pennsylvania

CHARLES L. GRUDER (111), Department of Psychology, University of Illinois at Chicago Circle, Chicago, Illinois

IRVING LOUIS HOROWITZ (277), Department of Sociology, Livingston College, Rutgers University, New Brunswick, New Jersey

ARIE W. KRUGLANSKI (69),[†] Department of Psychology, University of California, Los Angeles, California

ANATOL RAPOPORT (1), Department of Psychiatry, Mental Health Research Institute, University of Michigan, Ann Arbor, Michigan

BERTRAM H. RAVEN (69),[‡] Department of Psychology, University of California, Los Angeles, California

PAUL G. SWINGLE (235), Department of Psychology, McMaster University, Hamilton, Ontario, Canada

JAMES T. TEDESCHI (155),[§] United States International University, San Diego, California

KENNETH W. TERHUNE (193), Cornell Aeronautical Laboratory, Buffalo, New York

*Present address: Department of Sociology, Dartmouth College, Hanover, New Hampshire.
†Present address: Department of Psychology, Tel Aviv University, Ramat Aviv, Israel.
‡Present address: Department of Social Psychology, London School of Economics, Aldwych, London, England.
§Present address: Department of Psychology, State University of New York, Albany, New York.

PREFACE

It is my feeling that some interpersonal friction is an inevitable product of the negotiation process. The principal factor affecting conflict is the protagonists' perception of the structure of the situation in which they find themselves. Implicit in this assumption is that dealing with conflict necessitates an understanding of the structural dimensions which affect the negotiation process. The contributors to the present volume are not in complete agreement as to the relative importance of structural vs. predispositional variables as determinants of conflict.

Although conflict may arise from many different sources, a prominent source is the struggle to acquire distribution prerogatives over scarce resources. Although all resources such as status, success, authority, money, publicity recognition, territory, time, and materials derive from scarcity, only conflicts over nonsocial resources can be reduced by increasing the resource pool. Competition for tangible resources such as money can presumably be made less fierce by increasing the amount of money available to the group. Competition for status, success, and other intangible resources cannot be ameliorated by increasing the resource pool – in a two-person struggle there can be only one winner, if winning is to have any value. A major factor maintaining conflict at a high level of violence is that of the protagonists defining negotiable conflict (focal issue a devisible resource) as nonnegotiable (focal issue a nondivisible resource such as "winning," and "not yielding").

Frequently, conflicts which develop over negotiable issues escalate rapidly and are accompanied by changes in the attitudes of the protagonists from concern over the initial issues to concern over not yielding. Once on the threat–counterthreat escalator, the bidding in violence becomes rapid, and each step becomes increasingly larger such that without bargaining traditions to limit the violence, insensate acts occur. University upheavals frequently seem to begin with conflicts over negotiable issues which are redefined in nonnegotiable terms and, due to a paucity of bargaining norms in universities, there are few if any limiters to slow down the tempo of the violence spiral.

The study of human conflict as an academic discipline is tragically young; by comparison, however, experimental gaming is in the zygotic stage, and, therefore, researchers have little in the form of concrete principles to show to the world. As Rapoport (1968) states, however, history shows that not every science born in the laboratory can be dismissed as irrelevant to the real world's problems prior to the development of "concepts of proven theoretical power." "The laboratory phase . . . [is] . . . the incubation period of a science."

Psychological gamers are always under great pressure to generalize from laboratory to real world or, when they refuse, to speculate as to the future contribution of game research to the settlement of the world's woes. When the gamer makes wildly enthusiastic statements about the isolation of the structural elements affecting the conflict process with the hope of formulating theories which will prove useful in the understanding conflict, he is accused of subjugating his science to his entertainment. It is interesting, however, that the demands made of psychological gamers are not of the order of resolving sibling rivalry but rather that of preventing thermonuclear war.

A different criticism is usually directed at gamers who attempt to deal with complex "real" situations in formal terms. The criticism is that the reductions of such complex situations are not only unrepresentative but misrepresentative of the actual situation. This reduction to a formal model frequently obscures the many avenues toward negotiation in the real situation with the result that attention is focused upon belligerent methods of influence which encourages the development of unpleasant concepts such as countercity negotiation (thermo-nuclear knockout of one US and one USSR city). A major concern of many critics of "strategic thinking" is that it may discourage less violent forms of settlement such as rhetoric directed at establishing legitimate spheres of influence by encouraging a dependence upon threat of violence to influence other parties to the conflict.

The contribution of game research hopefully will be the development of a discursive nomenclature for describing the structural dimensions in bargaining situations and perhaps provide the basis for the development of a robust theory of interpersonal conflict. The chapters included in this volume represent an oblique slice through the conflict literature, the major emphasis being on psychological gaming and the structure of conflict.

Chapter 1

CONFLICT RESOLUTION IN THE LIGHT OF GAME THEORY AND BEYOND

Anatol Rapoport

I. INTRODUCTION

Students of conflict and those concerned with conflict resolution look to diverse sources for information or inspiration: to ethology for the light it may shed on the biological underpinnings of aggression, to psychology for the roots of conflict in personality and for its motivational aspects, to sociology for the institutional settings, and to history for evidence of evolutionary trends.

Two theoretical frameworks of recent origin have provided additional vantage points for the development of theories of conflict. Both view conflict as a phenomenon *sui generis*, regardless of its origin or content. One is system theory, which, applied to the study of large organized social aggregates, views conflict as an interplay of forces, pressures, or stresses inherent in the structure and dynamics of such aggregates. The other is game theory, concerned with strategic aspects of conflict.

In a way, these two are poles apart. For system theory abstracts completely from the long-term goals of the actors in a conflict, in fact, ignores

1

actors as conscious agents. For example, Richardson (1939, 1948) developed his mathematical models of arms races and of war moods from this point of view. Game theory, on the contrary, focuses attention on the actor, a participant in a conflict, his interests, and his evaluations of the situations in which he finds himself.

Of all these approaches, only the last treats conflict theory as a branch of a theory of rational decision. Understandably, many students of conflict and of conflict resolution look to game theory as a source of insight into typically *human* conflicts based on the assumption that human beings are, at least in part, rational. These expectations may be justified, but only if the methods of game theory and the meaning of its results are clearly understood. Unfortunately, many misconceptions have arisen about these methods and results. We shall attempt first to dispel the misconceptions and to clarify the meaning of the results. Then we shall state what, in our opinion, is the true significance of game theory and how it is relevant to theories of human conflict and conflict resolution.

As has been said, game theory is concerned only with rationally conducted conflicts. Rationality in this context implies, first of all, the existence of well defined interests pursued by the conflicting parties (who will now be called players), and, second, the existence of alternative courses of action, among which each player can choose. No time pressure or any other limitation is put on the player's ability to choose the most suitable course of action. Thus, in analyzing the conflict represented by, say, the game of chess, the game theoretician assumes that a player can think through the consequences of his and his opponent's choices of moves to the very end of the game. No human player has this capacity, but game theory is not concerned with human players and their psychological characteristics but only with the logic of the game. Already at this point the limited relevance of game theory to a theory of behavior of real players should be apparent. However, this relevance, although limited, is not nil, inasmuch as the logic of the game does have some relevance to how it is played.

II. GAMES OF STRATEGY

The name "game theory" derives from its original preoccupation with *games of strategy*. These are distinguished from games of pure chance (e.g., craps) and from contests of skill (e.g., discus throwing). A strategy involves a player's *conditional* choices—conditional, that is, on the choices made by the other players. Chance may, however, be involved in a game of strategy. If so, chance is conceptualized as just another player, who also makes "choices" (e.g., how a die will fall or in what order cards will arrange themselves). But Chance has no "interests" and is not endowed with strategic skills. She chooses among the given alternatives purely randomly. A game of pure chance is one where

Chance is the *only* player that makes choices. Only if the players (besides Chance) have real choices among well-defined alternatives and are guided in their choices by considerations relevant to their interests, do we have a situation of interest to the game theoretician.

Games of strategy so defined are classified in game theory in various ways. The most important distinctions are those between games with only two players (two-person games), and those with more than two players (*n*-person games); also between two-person games in which the interests of the players are diametrically opposed (constant-sum games) and those where the interests are partially opposed and partially coincident (nonconstant sum games).[1] The latter category, as well as *n*-person games, are further differentiated according to whether players can agree on joint strategies (cooperative games) or not (noncooperative games).

A coalition, by definition of the term, involves an agreement among the players that have formed it to pursue a joint strategy. The agreement may (and often does) involve provisions as to how the gains or losses that accrue jointly to the members of the coalition shall be apportioned among them. These provisions can be viewed as results of *bargaining* among the members of the prospective coalition. Thus, game theory, to the extent that it deals with games in which coalitions can form, includes also a theory of bargaining. If we view agreements arrived at in the process of bargaining as instances of *conflict resolution,* then game theory can be said to treat instances of conflict resolution also. It is important to note, however, that the principles of conflict resolution as they emerge in game-theoretic analysis have nothing to do with such matters as reduction of hostility, redefinition of goals or interests, or the like. Certain "equity" principles are, to be sure, invoked in bargaining theory but only to the extent that they reflect symmetries in the strategic positions of the players— hence, purely structural features of the game itself, not the psychological characteristics of the players. In short, game theory is a "depsychologized" decision theory, dealing with situations controlled by more than one decision maker.

A game of strategy usually involves a *sequence* of decisions called the *moves* of the game. A game is defined by its rules. The rules specify which player has the move in each of the situations that may arise and what alternatives are open to him on each of his moves. They specify also the situations signifying that a play of the game is over. Depending on the terminal situation, each of the

---

[1] Constant-sum games are so-called because in them the sum of the payoffs to the two players is the same regardless of how the game ends. In particular, if this sum is zero, the game is called *zero-sum.* In all constant-sum games, the larger the payoff to one player, the smaller is the payoff to the other. This is the meaning of diametrically opposed interests. In nonconstant-sum games, the players have, in general, partially common, partially opposed interests. Such games are sometimes called *mixed-motive games.*

players gets a certain numerical *payoff* (positive or negative), i.e., a certain gain or loss accrues to him. A rational player is one who makes choices calculated to maximize his gains or minimize his losses under the constraints of the situation (that is, under the circumstance that not he alone decides in what situation the game will end).

It is shown in the theory of games that all of the choices made by a player (conditional on the others' choices) can be collapsed into a single choice of a *strategy*. A play of the game is thus determined by a simultaneous choice of a strategy by each of the players.

A strategy may be *pure* or *mixed*. A pure strategy is essentially a plan chosen by a player before a play of the game begins, which prescribes the choice of an alternative in each situation that may possibly arise in the course of the game. (Clearly the situations that may arise also depend on the choices of the other players.) A mixed strategy is essentially a prescription of a probability for each of the pure strategies available to a player. Imagine a wheel divided into (not necessarily equal) sectors and a fixed pointer. Then the probability that the spinning wheel will come to rest with the pointer in a particular sector will be proportional to the area of the sector. Let each sector represent one of the available strategies. Then a choice of a mixed strategy is represented by the apportionment of sectors of specified areas to strategies; the choice of a particular strategy in a given play amounts to letting the spinning wheel decide which strategy shall be chosen.

III. OPTIMAL STRATEGIES

We are now ready to state the principal result deduced in game theory concerning all two-person constant-sum games. In every such game, there is available to each player either a pure or a mixed strategy which guarantees that he will obtain the "best" payoff that he can get in this game, assuming that his opponent is rational, which means in this context that the opponent will also choose *his* "best" strategy (pure or mixed). Whether the best strategy is pure or mixed depends on the game. We thus have still another classification of games, namely two-person constant-sum games that admit optimal pure strategies and those that admit optimal mixed strategies.

This distinction is best elucidated by concrete examples. Consider the game tic-tac-toe (naughts and crosses). When two rational (i.e., competent) players play this game, the outcome is always a draw. This means that each player has a strategy that prevents the other from winning. Since both have such a strategy, neither can win.

Now, there is a variant of tic-tac-toe in which the player who moves first must always win. In this variant each player can place either a cross or a naught (instead of only one or the other) in a free space. A win is defined in the usual way, namely placing the last mark making three like marks in a row, column or diagonal. The first player's winning strategy can be described as follows: Place a cross in the central space. Thereafter, if three in a row can be completed, do so; if not, place the same mark that the opponent used last in a space symmetrical with the opponent's. This strategy guarantees a win to the first player. Assuming that all wins have the same payoff, it is the best strategy.

The use of a mixed strategy is illustrated by the ancient game of morra. The two players show simultaneously either one or two fingers each. At the same time each player guesses the sum of the fingers shown. If both guess or neither guesses, neither player wins. If only one guesses, he wins the sum of the fingers shown. It turns out that in this game each player has a best mixed strategy, namely: always guess "3" and randomize showing one or two fingers such that one finger is shown with a probability not smaller than 4/7 nor larger than 3/5. This strategy is best in the sense that it guarantees the player the *expectation* of breaking even. (It would be strange if this were not the case, since the positions of the two players are perfectly symmetrical in this game: neither moves first.) If a player chooses any other strategy (pure or mixed), it can be shown that his opponent can take advantage of it by choosing a strategy that guarantees him a positive expected gain. It is important to note that a best mixed strategy does not guarantee the largest possible gain (or smallest loss) on any *particular* play of the game but only in the sense of a statistical expectation. If the game is played many times, however, this expected gain will almost certainly become in the long run the average gain per play.

What sort of games admit optimal pure strategies? Game theory provides an answer to this question. Some games are so-called games of perfect information. In these games all the choices that have already been made in the course of a play are known to both (or all) players. This is so in most board games (e.g., chess, checkers, go, and tic-tac-toe). All of these games admit a best pure strategy for each player. It follows that if both players are rational (i.e., completely competent), the outcome of every play will be the same. We have seen that this is the case in both conventional tic-tac-toe (always a draw) and in the modified version (always a win for the first player).

Many games are not games of perfect information. Most card games, for example, begin with a shuffled deck, that is, a deck in which the arrangement of the cards is unknown to the players. We may consider the shuffling of the cards as a "choice" of a particular arrangement made by Chance (who, recall, is considered as one of the players). Since this choice is unknown to the other players, the game is not a game of perfect information. It may happen that a game of this sort admits optimal pure strategies, but in general it does not. In poker, for example, there is no optimal pure strategy. Good poker strategies are mixed in the sense that a player must sometimes bet a large amount when he holds a weak hand or a small amount when he holds a strong hand (bluffing). If he does not bluff, that is, if he bets amounts directly related to the strength of his hand, he will reveal the strength of his hand to the other players who can take advantage of this knowledge. It is easy to see that there is no best pure strategy in morra. For example, if a player guesses 3 and always shows 2 fingers, the other can always win by also showing two fingers. Note also that morra is not a game of perfect information. For if morra is depicted as a sequence of moves where one player moves at a time, then the rules imply that the second player does not know the first player's choice (for this is the case if they move simultaneously).

IV. NONCONSTANT-SUM GAMES

So far we have examined only two-person constant-sum games. As has been said, in every such game there is an optimal strategy (pure or mixed) available to each player. If he uses it, he will get the largest payoff (or expected payoff) that he can get, playing against an equally rational opponent. Let us now examine some nonconstant-sum games, where the sum of the two payoffs may vary with the outcome of the game. We shall also suppose at first that the rules preclude communication between the two players, which is the case in noncooperative games.

In this connection a word is in order about the meaning of "rules." In actual games, rules are agreements among the players on procedures to be adhered to in the course of the game. Such agreements are also sometimes observed in real life (although, of course, they are, generally speaking, neither as well defined nor as strictly adhered to as the rules of formalized games). We need not, however, identify rules with agreements. Sometimes the rules may be dictated by the constraints of the situation. In real life the set of available choices may be simply fixed by circumstances,.not necessarily by agreements. Choices are well defined by the situation, not how they were fixed; this is the important thing. The same remarks apply to the possibility or impossibility of communication. Communication may lead to a coordination of strategies of the two players and so to an outcome of the game agreed upon by the contracting parties. In the context of a parlor game the rules may or may not allow them to practice such coordination. For example, in bridge the coordination of moves made by the bid winner and his partner is facilitated by the rule that allows the partners to open their cards, but the coordination of the moves of the other two partners is not so facilitated. In real life there may or may not be opportunities for coordinating strategies among parties with totally or partially common interests. It may even happen that while opportunities for coordination exist in the sense of the absence of formal constraints against it, nevertheless coordination (or any kind of negotiation) cannot take place for psychological, political, or ethical reasons. It is usually extremely difficult to quantify the extent of negotiation or coordination possible in a given real life situation. Since game theory is a formal theory only, it bypasses this problem. In game theory only the extreme cases are recognized. Coordination of strategies is either possible or impossible among the players of a game. We shall first examine two examples of nonconstant-sum games in which negotiation of any kind is impossible.

As is usually the case in formal analysis, the best examples are those that are simplest and at the same time illustrate the principles to be brought out. A game must have at least two players. Consequently from the standpoint of the number of players, the simplest games are two-person games. Further, a player must have at least two alternatives from which to choose. Consequently, the simplest games are those in which each of two players must choose between two alternatives available to him. We shall consider these alternatives as strategies (not moves), which implies that they must be chosen by the players simultaneously. Thus, our games will have four possible outcomes corresponding to the four possible pairs of strategies chosen by the players. To each outcome corresponds a pair of payoffs, one to each player. The situation is conveniently represented by a *game matrix,* a rectangular array in which the horizontal rows represent the strategies available to player 1, the vertical columns the strategies available to player 2, and the entries are the payoffs, respectively, to player 1 and player 2. Two games are so represented in Fig. 1.

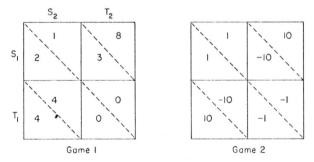

FIG. 1. The numbers to the left and below the diagonals are the payoffs to player 1, who chooses horizontal rows; those to the right and above the diagonals are the payoffs to player 2, who chooses the vertical columns.

Let us examine Game 1 first. Player 1 must choose between the rows labeled S_1 and T_1. If he knew player 2's choice, this decision would be easy. If player 2 were to choose S_2, player 1 would choose T_1 for a gain of 4. If player 2 were to chose T_2, he would choose S_1 for a gain of 3. But player 2 faces the same sort of decision problem. If he were sure that player 1 would try for his biggest gain (with T_1), then player 2 could do no better than choose S_2. But he cannot be sure that player 1 would not rather "play safe" and choose S_1 (in the expectation that player 2 will try for *his* biggest gain of 8). In that case, player 2 could get his largest gain.

We see that the game has no optimal pure strategies for either player. Let us see how it stands with mixed strategies. Ignoring for a moment the opponent's payoff, each player may select a strategy mixture which guarantees a minimum payoff *regardless* of the opponent's strategy. The actual mixture for player 1 in Game 1 is determined by obtaining the difference in payoff for each row (i.e., for row 1, $3 - 2 = 1$; for row 2, $4 - 0 = 4$) and then inverting the obtained values (i.e., 4 for row 1, 1 for row 2). These values indicate that player 1, to guarantee a maximum minimum payoff should, on a random basis, choose S_1 4 times for every single T_1 choice. By assigning a probability of 4/5 to S_1 and the complementary probability of 1/5 to T_1, player 1 can *guarantee* himself a gain of 12/5. This is so because if he uses this strategy mixture, he gets an expected gain of 12/5 regardless of the strategy chosen by player 2. (The reader can verify this by calculating player 1's expectation, assuming each of player 2's choices in turn.) Similarly, player 2 can guarantee himself a gain of 32/11 by a mixed strategy which assigns a probability of 8/11 to S_2 and 3/11 to T_2. We might consider this pair of mixed strategies (which guarantee a minimum "security level" to each player) as a "solution" of sorts of this game. However, this "solution" is less than satisfactory. Note than *both* players could get more than these guaranteed minima, if, for example, player 1 chose T_1 and player 2 S_2 or if player 1 chose S_1 and player 2 T_2. Had they been able to coordinate their strategies they could have gotten these larger gains. To be sure, they would still have had to face the problem of agreeing on one strategy pair or the other (or possibly on a mixture of the two), because the strategy pair (T_1, S_2) favors player 1, while (S_1, T_2) favors player 2. However, whatever strategy pair or whatever mixture of the two they would have agreed on, it would have given each of them more than the guaranteed levels of 12/5, and 32/11, respectively.

The inability to coordinate strategies for lack of an opportunity to communicate is not the only feature of a noncooperative game that may prevent the players from getting as much as they can. Consider now Game 2 in Fig. 1.[2] From the point of view of each of the players, it seems quite clear what he should choose. Clearly, player 1 should choose T_1, quite regardless of how player 2 chooses. For should player 2 choose S_2, player 1 is better off with T_1, which gives him 10, whereas S_1 gives him only 1. Should player 2 choose T_2,

[2]This game, called Prisoner's Dilemma, has attracted a great deal of attention in theoretical and experimental investigations of mixed-motive conflicts (Luce & Raiffa, 1957; Rapoport & Chammah, 1965).

player 1 is still better off choosing T_1 and accepting a loss of 1, whereas S_1 leads to a loss of 10. For exactly the same reasons it is "rational" for player 2 to choose T_2. The "rational" strategy pair (T_1, T_2) leads to a loss of 1 by both players. Had they chosen S_1 and S_2, respectively, they would have each *gained* 1. Note that in this game it is not the inability to coordinate strategies that prevents the players from getting as much as they could. There is only one strategy pair that leads to a gain for both, namely (S_1, S_2). Thus, there is no ambiguity about the choice that is in their *collective* interest (as there is in Game 1). What then prevents them from archieving it in the absence of communication? Evidently it is "acting in accordance with the *individual interest*" of each that leads them to the choice of strategy pair (T_1, T_2) rather than (S_1, S_2).

There is another way in which Game 1 and Game 2 are different. Suppose for a moment that the players somehow did agree on the strategy pair (T_1, S_2) in Game 1. Then there would be no motive for either player to break the agreement, because either would only impair his payoff if he chose the other strategy, while the other player stuck to the agreement. The same is true if they agreed on (S_1, T_2). Each of these outcomes is an *equilibrium*. Neither of the players can improve his payoff (and will generally impair it), if he moves away from an equilibrium while the other stays with the same strategy. In Game 2, the situation is different. Instead of two equilibria as in Game 1, there is only one, namely the outcome (T_1, T_2). But this would not be the outcome on which a pair of rational players would agree. If they agreed, they would rather agree on (S_1, S_2). This outcome, however, is not an equilibrium. Each player can get more by moving away from it alone (i.e., by breaking the agreement). But if they *both* do so, both lose.

We see, therefore, that there are powerful cross pressures on players in Game 2. There is a pressure for choosing T_1 (or T_2), because one does better with it regardless of the other's choice. And there is some pressure for choosing S_1 (or S_2), for both stand to gain if both choose it. The outcome (S_1, S_2) is in the players' *collective* interest, even though choosing the corresponding strategies is contrary to their *individual* interests. It is not hard to see that situations of this sort capture some essential features of human conflicts, which are quite frequently characterized by similar cross pressures.

V. BARGAINING

If the rules of the game (or the circumstances of the situation) permit communication and coordination of strategies, the situation is changed. For in that case the players may be able to agree on an outcome that benefits them both. Clearly they cannot do so in a constant-sum game, since in such a game whatever outcome is better for one of the players must be worse for the other. We have seen, however, that a nonconstant-sum game may have outcomes that are preferred by both players to other outcomes.

The simplest such situation obtains between a seller and a buyer. Assume that the highest price that the prospective buyer of a house is willing to pay is more than the lowest price that the seller is willing to accept. Then a transaction for any price between these two limits is preferred by *both* to "no sale." This situation, called the *elementary bargaining problem,* is represented in Fig. 2.

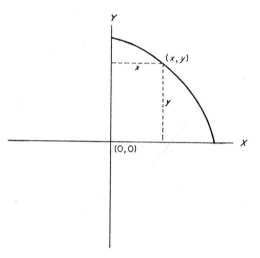

FIG. 2. The utility payoff space of the elementary bargaining problem. Curve: the negotiation set; origin: the status quo point; (x, y): a possible outcome, x: utility gain of player 1; y: utility gain of player 2.

The horizontal axis represents all possible payoffs to player 1, the vertical axis the corresponding payoffs to player 2. Thus, any point in the plane of the payoff space represents a pair of payoffs, by its two coordinates. In the case of buying or selling a house, the payoffs are to be interpreted as "gains in utility." Presumably, if the buyer agrees to pay a certain amount for the house, the house is worth to him at least that much (usually somewhat more). Likewise, if the seller agrees to sell for that amount, the money is worth to him at least as much as the house (usually somewhat more). Consequently each enjoys a gain of "utility" from the transaction. The points in our plane, then, represent payoffs not in money but in utility gains. There is a range of prices for which the house can be sold. Each price in this range represents a utility gain for *each* of the players. The totality of these points traces a curve in the plane. (We speak here of a generalized "curve" as the term is used in mathematics. It may be a broken line or even a straight line.) We can reasonably assume that the general direction of this curve will be from "northwest" to "southeast," because we assume that even though what the money is "worth" may not be proportional to the amount of money (if it were, the curve would be a straight line), still a larger amount of money is always worth more than a smaller amount, at least in a commercial transaction. Consequently, a gain of utility by the one player must mean a loss by the other. This is reflected in the direction of the curve. As it progresses to the right (a gain for player 1), it progresses also downward (a loss for player 2) and vice versa. The "no sale" outcome or the *status quo point* is at the origin of the coordinates, where both the seller and the buyer get zero.

The representation of our bargaining situation is now complete. The curve of possible outcomes of agreement is called the *negotiation set* (in diplomacy the "basis of negotiation"). The problem now is to find a *single* point on the curve which can be defended as a "rational solution" of the bargaining problem or, if one prefers, a rational conflict resolution.

The game theoretician begins to solve this problem by listing some "reasonable properties" of a solution. Recall that in the context of game theory, the players are not endowed with any psychological characteristics except those that may be reflected in the description of the game itself, for example, what each of the outcomes is worth to each of the players. Therefore, the desirable properties of the proposed solution cannot depend on any personal characteristics of the players beyond the utilities ascribed to the outcomes which are assumed to be known. For instance a solution cannot depend on the relative bargaining abilities of the players, the particular stances they may assume in bargaining (e.g., taking a tough or a conciliatory posture) or the like. From this it follows that if in a given bargaining game the roles of the players are interchanged, the solution should not be affected, except, of course, that the payoffs to the two players are also interchanged.

Next, it is assumed that the payoff pair offered as a solution should lie on the negotiation set. It should not be some point to the left and below the negotiation set, since if it were both players could do better by choosing some point on the negotiation set; and it cannot be to the right and above the negotiation set, because those payoffs are not attainable by the players.

Third, consider the points of the payoff space as alternatives of which one is to be chosen. If an alternative that has *not* been chosen is deleted from available alternatives, this should not change the preference among the remaining alternatives. If new alternatives are added but none of them is chosen in preference to one chosen earlier, then that choice should not be affected by the addition. Note that in elections this principle is sometimes violated. The withdrawal of a candidate who would not have won may shift the collective preference of the voters from one of the remaining candidates to another. This a consequence of decision rules governing elections and ought not to apply to decisions arrived at by concensus.

The fourth and last assumption concerns the question of comparing utilities of different persons. In general, it is very difficult to make such comparisons. It is assumed that the utilities of the various outcomes and of their mixtures can be established for each individual player but only on the so called *interval scale.* The zero point and the unit of such a scale remain arbitrary. This means that if all the utilities of a player are multiplied by a positive constant, or if a constant (positive or negative) is added to each of his utilities, or if both transformations are performed, the resulting scale will reflect the preferences of the player as well as the first one, and, therefore, one cannot decide between the two scales. (Similarly, both the Centigrade and the Fahrenheit scales measure temperature equally well, and it is impossible to say that one is in any sense "truer" than the other.) If utilities are given on interval scales only, it follows that any change of scale, in the sense just described, of one or both players should not affect the solution of the bargaining problem, except, of course, that the magnitudes of the payoffs to the respective players should undergo the same transformation as their utility scales.

These, then, are four assumptions or postulates to be satisfied by a solution to the elementary bargaining problem. The "desirable properties" are called *symmetry, Pareto optimality, independence from irrelevant alternatives,* and *invariance under positive linear transformations,* respectively. Nash (1950) has shown that only one point in the payoff space satisfies all four. Imagine all possible rectangles inscribed in the payoff space in such a way that the status quo point is one corner and the diagonally opposite corner is on the negotiation set. Of all such rectangles one will have a largest area. Then the point on the negotiation set which is a corner of this rectangle is the solution. Several of the rectangles and the one of maximum area determining a solution of a hypothetical bargaining problem are shown in Fig. 3.

In this elementary bargaining problem we took it for granted that the identity of the status quo point is known. For example it is clearly represented by the pair of utilities of "no sale" in the buyer–seller game. In general, the situation is not so clear. For example, it is not obvious what the status quo point of Game 1 should be. (The payoff space of that game is shown in Fig. 4.)

It might be argued, for example, that the status quo point should reflect what each player can guarantee for himself (regardless of what the other does). We have seen that in Game 1 the coordinates of this point are $(12/5, 32/11)$. If so, then it can be shown (by differential calculus) that the largest rectangle with corners at that point and on the negotiation set determines the point $(3.34, 6.65)$. The players can get these magnitudes as their respective (statistically expected) payoffs, if they adopt a mixed joint strategy which leads to (S_1, T_2) with probability of about 2/3 and to (T_1, S_2) with probability of about 1/3. In

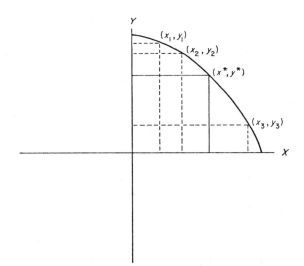

FIG. 3. Of all possible rectangles with one corner at the origin and another on the negotiation set, the solid rectangle has the largest area. Then (x^*, y^*) is the solution of the bargaining problem.

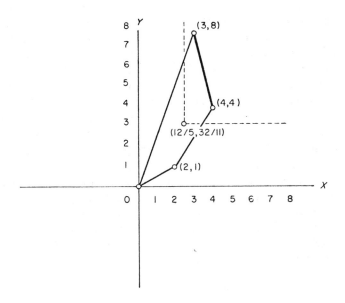

FIG. 4 The payoff space of Game 1. The corners of the quadrilateral are the outcomes resulting from choices of pure strategies by the two players. Any point on the boundary or inside the quadrilateral can be realized by an appropriate pair of coordinated mixed strategies. Thick line: the negotiation set; vertical dotted line: player 1's security level; horizontal dotted line: player 2's security level.

this way if they play Game 1 many times in succession, player 2 will "have his way" about twice as frequently as player 1. This advantage reflects the somewhat stronger bargaining position of player 2, *if the individual security levels of the players are taken as the status quo point.* While there is some merit in the argument for taking the security levels as the status quo point, there are arguments against this choice.

To guarantee himself the security level payoff, player 1 must play his two strategies with probabilities 4/5 and 1/5, respectively. If he does this, player 2 can get considerably more than his security level. Namely, by playing T_2 as a pure strategy, player 2 can get $8 \times 4/5 = 32/5$ (rather than his security level 32/11). Similarly, if player 2 plays his security level mixture (8/11, 3/11), player 1 can get 32/11 by playing T_1 as a pure strategy, that is, more than his security level, which is 12/5. It follows that each player would be tempted to depart from his security mixed strategy, if he knew that the other would stay with it. On the other hand, if *both* do so—for example, if each chooses his strategy that contains his largest payoff—both get zero. Consequently the outcome (T_1, T_2) with the payoffs (0, 0) could well be taken as the status quo point, since it is a result of a failure on the part of the players to agree (each insisting on the strategy most favorable to him). In general, it is assumed that to determine the status quo point, each player chooses a *threat strategy* (pure or mixed) independently; it is understood that if no agreement is reached, the pair of strategies so chosen shall determine the status quo point, and the associated payoffs will accrue to the players. If agreement is reached, that is, if a point on the negotiation set is to be determined, this determination shall be in accordance with the solution of the bargaining game described above with the pair of threat strategies constituting the status quo point.

Nash (1953) has shown that the choice of optimal threat strategies amounts to a choice of optimal strategies in a zero-sum game derived from the original game. The solution of this game is determined by the status quo point. Let us see how this comes about.

Suppose player 1 chooses for his threat strategy some mixed strategy x, according to which S_1 is chosen with probability x and accordingly, T_1 with probability $1 - x$. Similarly, player 2 chooses for his threat strategy a mixed strategy y, according to which S_2 is chosen with probability y and T_2 with probability $1 - y$. If these strategies go into effect (i.e., if agreement is not reached), the expected payoff to player 1 will be

$$x_0 = 2xy + 4(1 - x)y + 3x(1 - y). \tag{1}$$

The corresponding payoff to player 2 will be

$$y_0 = xy + 4(1 - x)y + 8x(1 - y). \tag{2}$$

Let us now examine the bargaining game in which the point (x_0, y_0) is the status quo point and whose negotiation set lies along the line connecting the points $(3,8)$ and $(4,4)$. The equation of this line is

$$Y = 20 - 4X. \tag{3}$$

(We designate the coordinate variables by capital letters to distinguish them from the threat strategies.) The solution of this bargaining game will be the point (X^*, Y^*) on the bargaining set, such that X^* maximizes the value of the expression

$$(X - x_0)(20 - 4X - y_0). \tag{4}$$

This maximizing value is found to be

$$X^* = \tfrac{1}{8}[20 - y_0 + 4x_0] \tag{5}$$

Now we substitute for x_0 and y_0 their expressions in terms of the threat strategies x and y and obtain

$$X^* = \tfrac{1}{8}[20 - xy - 4y + 4xy - 8x + 8xy + 8xy + 16y$$
$$- 16xy + 12x - 12xy]. \tag{6}$$

It is clearly in player 1's interest to choose a threat strategy x which will maximize his final payoff X^* or, equivalently, the expression in the brackets above.

Now let us transform Game 1 by multiplying player 1's payoffs by 4, as ' shown in Game 1'. The transformation amounts merely to choosing a different unit of utility for player 2, which does not change the strategic structure of the game.

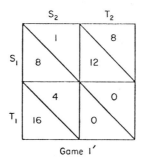

Game 1'

Next we form a *zero-sum* game, in which the payoffs to the two players are the algebraic differences of their payoffs in Game 1', as shown in Game 1".

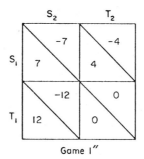

Game 1″

Let us calculate the payoff to player 1 in Game 1″, if he uses a mixed strategy x, while player 2 uses a mixed strategy y. The payoff to player 1 will be

$$7xy + 4x(1 - y) + 12y(1 - x) = (-9xy + 4x + 12y). \qquad (7)$$

which is the quantity he wishes to maximize. This is the same quantity that player 1 wishes to maximize in Game 1. Therefore, player 1's best strategy in Game 1″ must be the same as his best threat strategy in Game 1. However, Game 1″ is a zero-sum game with a saddle point at (S_1, T_2). Therefore, in this game a pure best strategy is available to player 1, namely S_1. Similarly it can be shown that also for player 2 Game 1 is strategically equivalent to Game 1″ and that his best strategy in the latter game (hence, his best threat strategy in the former) is the pure strategy T_2. These two threat strategies determine the status quo point (S_1, T_2). The payoffs associated with this point will accrue to the players, if they cannot agree. But the payoff to player 2 at (S_1, T_2) is in this particular case the *largest* payoff that he can get in this game under *any* circumstances (namely 8). Therefore, player 2 need not yield anything in bargaining with player 1. Player 2 has nothing to lose, if the threat strategies go into effect. He can "dictate" the outcome of the game.

As a check we can verify that player 1 has no better threat strategy than S_1. As an example, suppose player 1 chooses T_1 as his threat strategy. Coupled with T_2, this determines the point $(0, 0)$ as the status quo point. The formal solution of the resulting bargaining game leads to a payoff of 2.5 for player 1 and 10 to player 2. But the point $(2\frac{1}{2}, 10)$ is not in the payoff space of this game and so cannot be realized (see Fig. 4). The point *on the negotiation set* that maximizes the expression $(X - 0)(20 - 4X - 0)$ is again the point $(3, 8)$. In fact, even if $(2\frac{1}{2}, 10)$ were realizable, player 1 would be worse off than he is at the point $(3, 8)$.

Still other methods of solving the cooperative two-person game have been proposed. One of them, proposed by Raiffa (1953) depends on a "normalization" of the utility scales of the two players, that is, finding a common standard for the two scales. Specifically the lowest of the payoffs that can accrue in the game between the highest and the lowest payoffs becomes the unit of utility. The other payoffs are then determined on the interval between 0 and 1 so that the differences between pairs of payoffs remain proportional to the original differences. Game 1 so transformed is shown in Fig. 5A.

The game is now decomposed into two games, one of complete opposition and the other of complete cooperation. The game of complete opposition is obtained by transforming each player's payoff into the difference between his and the other player's payoffs. Since these differences are of opposite sign when referred to the two players, we obtain a zero-sum game (Fig. 5B). This game is then solved in the usual way. The solution determines a *difference* between the payoffs that shall accrue to the players which in this case is zero. Now the players play the completely cooperative game. They "move in the payoff space" along the straight line on which the payoff difference so determined remains constant (in this case zero) in a "northeasterly" direction until the negotiation set is reached (Fig. 5C). The point of intersection is the solution. When Game 1 is solved in this manner, player 2 "has his way" two-thirds of the time (Fig. 5D). The almost exact agreement with the solution referred to the security levels (see p. 14) is coincidental.

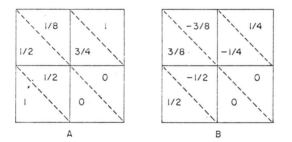

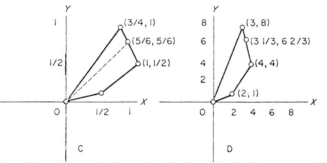

FIG. 5. Raiffa's solution of Game 1. (A) The normalized game matrix; (B) the competitive (zero-sum) game; (C) the cooperative game along the line of mutual benefit ($y = x$) leading to the point (5/6, 5/6) on the negotiation set; (D) the solution of the original game.

When applied to Game 2, every one of the solution methods described leads to a single result, namely, the strategy pair (S_1, S_2). This is not surprising in view of the complete symmetry of the game; it looks exactly the same from the point of view of each player. Hence no game-theoretical solution (assuming bargaining) should favor one player over another in this game (cf. Fig. 6).

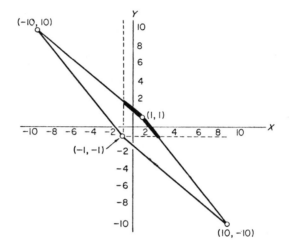

FIG. 6. Payoff space diagram of Game 2 (prisoner's Dilemma). Dotted lines: security levels. Thick lines: negotiation set. The symmetry of the game implies that all methods of cooperative solution lead to $(_1, S_2)$ with payoffs (1, 1).

The reader may have wondered why nothing was said about possible compensations that players might offer each other for agreeing to certain solutions. Note, for example, that in Game 1 the two players get *jointly* in (S_1, T_2) an amount larger than that in any other outcome, hence, larger than in any mixture of outcomes. Should not two rational players immediately agree on coordinating their strategies so as to obtain the outcome (S_1, T_2) and only then bargain about how the associated joint payoff is to be divided among them? The answer to this question depends on the assumptions we make about the nature of the payoffs. If we assume that the payoffs are in some commodity that is freely transferable from one player to another and worth the same per unit to each, then indeed it makes sense for the players to get as much of that commodity as they can first and worry about apportioning it later. So far, however, we have made no assumptions about the payoffs that would permit us to take this point of view. Some utilities are not transferable, for example, the amount of influence one exerts over others; some are not "conservative," for example, the sentimental value of objects. (Such objects can be transfered, but they lose their utility in the process.) If utilities are neither transferable nor conservative, then the utilities of two different players cannot be reapportioned, nor even meaningfully added. Thus, it makes no sense in this context to say that the outcome (S_1, T_2) awards the largest joint payoff to the two players. We have already stated this mathematically by pointing out that the zero point and the unit of a utility scale can be chosen arbitrarily and independently for each player. For example, if we make player 2's utility units eight times larger, we must divide each of his payoffs by eight. This gives player 2 a payoff of 1 in (S_1, T_2) and a payoff of ½ in (T_1, S_2). Then the joint payoff in (T_1, S_2) becomes 4½, larger than the joint payoff in (S_1, T_2), which is 4.

Note that our conflict resolution was accomplished not by prescribing an apportionment of the joint payoff between the players but rather by prescriptions of probabilities with which each will "have his own way," that is, the probabilities with which each player's most preferred outcome will obtain. In all cases these probabilities were so calculated as to be independent of the particular utility scales used (provided the ratios of the utility intervals on each player's scale remained the same).

Game theory treats also of situations where utilities are transferable and conservative and where, therefore, "side payments" can be brought to bear on the solution of the bargaining game. In fact, most of the theory of n-person games has been developed in that context. Let us, therefore, introduce the assumption of transferable and conservative utility and solve Game 1 accordingly.

It is now clear that in Game 1 a pair of rational players should coordinate their strategies so as to obtain the outcome (S_1, T_2), for that is the outcome that awards the largest *joint* payoff. The players face only the problem of dividing up this payoff of 11 units between them. In this context, we note that neither player needs to accept less than what his security level in this game guarantees him, for if the other player will not yield this amount, he can always get it by playing an appropriate mixed strategy. The bargaining problem then reduces to one with $(12/5, 32/11)$ as the status quo point and the straight line along which $X + Y = 11$ is the "northeast" boundary of the payoff space. The solution obtained by methods described above awards player 1 about 5.25 units and about 5.75 to player 2.

Note that in this conception, the strategic structure of the game that originally gave rise to the bargaining situation has completely disappeared. The only thing that has remained is a simple bargaining problem: Two parties are to decide how to divide 11 units among them; if no agreement is reached, one party is to get 12/5 and the other 32/11. This is the status quo outcome. Our principle of conflict resolution states that the product of the gains made by the players relative to their status quo positions will be the largest possible subject to the constraint that the sum of the final payoffs shall be 11. (Note that the area of the rectangle inscribed between the status quo point and the negotiation set equals the product of the gains.)

VI. SHAPLEY VALUE

The last mentioned solution of our Game 1 is called the Shapley value (Shapley, 1953).

There is another way of looking at its underlying principle which will help us understand its extension to the n-person game. We said that in the case of two players only one coalition is possible, namely the coalition between the two. (In fact, it is this coalition that allows the two players to coordinate their strategies and so to get the maximum joint payoff.) Mathematically speaking, however, not one but four coalitions can form, namely the coalition of the two, the "coalition" consisting of player 1 alone, the "coalition" consisting of player 2 alone, and the "coalition" of no players, the so-called "empty coalition." All but the first of these violate our intuitive notion of a coalition (especially the last one, which seems altogether absurd). However, for the mathematician a coalition is simply a subset of the set of players, and there is no logical difficulty of imagining subsets with only one element or the empty set. As we shall now see, this enlarged concept of a coalition facilitates analysis.

Imagine now that the coalition of the two players gets "built-up." That is, we start with the empty coalition. Then one of the two players "joins" it, thus forming a coalition consisting of himself alone; next, the other player joins this coalition, making the two-player coalition complete. Note that there are exactly two ways in which this process can take place, depending on which of the players joins the empty coalition first.

Now let the total payoff that the two-player coalition can obtain be apportioned according to the following principle. Each gets the amount that he brings to the coalition he joins by joining it. Suppose now the coalition builds up by player 1's joining the empty coalition first. The empty coalition, of course, gets no payoff. Player 1 in a coalition with himself can get his security level, which is 12/5. Consequently in this case he gets 12/5, namely, the amount he brought to the (empty) coalition which he joined. If, on the other hand, player 2 joins the empty coalition first, the one-man coalition can get 32/11 (player 2's security level). When player 1 joins, he enables the two-man coalition to get 11. Consequently he has brought in $11 - 32/11 = 89/11$ into the coalition he joined and is entitled to that amount. Finally we assume that the order in which the two-man coalition will be built up is a matter of pure chance. There being just two such orders, each is assumed to occur with probability of ½. Consequently the amount to be accorded to player 1 should be the even-weighted average of

12/5 and 32/11, namely, $\frac{1}{2}(12/5) + \frac{1}{2}(89/11) = 577/110$ or approximately 5.25, which is the result we obtained earlier. Player 2, of course, gets the remainder, namely $11 - 5.25 = 5.75$ (approximately).

It is easy to extend this method of solution to situations involving n players. The n-person game is now described as follows: Any subset of the n players can form a coalition. Suppose a coalition of this sort comprising, say, k players ($k \leqslant n$) forms, and suppose the remaining $n - k$ players form a countercoalition. Since the members of a coalition are able to coordinate their strategies, they play essentially as a single player. In other words, what results as a consequence of the organization of the players into two coalitions is a two-person game. This game may or may not be a constant-sum game. If it is, there exists an optimal strategy (pure or mixed) for each coalition, which guarantees to it a certain minimal payoff (positive or negative). If the game is not constant-sum, the strategy that guarantees a minimal payoff cannot now be called optimal (since both coalitions could get more by joining in a grand coalition); nevertheless, a certain minimal payoff is guaranteed to each of the $2^n - 1$ nonempty coalitions. (It is assumed that the payoff to the empty coalition is always zero.) These minimal guaranteed payoffs will be the basis of our further analysis. Each of these "security levels" will be called the *value* of the game to the coalition in question.

The rule that assigns to each coalition its value is called the *characteristic function* of the game and is denoted by $v(S)$. Here S denotes any of the subsets of the players and $v(S)$, the corresponding value, specifies how much this subset can get as a coalition. The characteristic function of our Game 1, for example, would be the following:

$$v(\emptyset) = 0; \quad v(1) = 12/5; \quad v(2) = 32/11; \quad v(1, 2) = 11. \qquad (8)$$

The symbol $\emptyset$ is the conventional designation of the empty set; 1 or 2 in parentheses alone designate players 1 and 2, respectively, in one-man coalitions; $(1, 2)$ designates the coalition of the two.

Next we note that two subsets of players joining in a single coalition can *jointly* get more than they can get (again jointly) if they remain in separate coalitions. This is because they can always get together what they can get separately (by choosing the same strategies), and they can possibly get more by further coordination of strategies. Expressed in symbols, this reads:

$$v(S \cup T) \geqslant v(S) + v(T), \qquad (9)$$

where $(S \cup T)$ stands for the union of the two subsets S and T. Note that this property of the characteristic function (called the *superadditive property*) does not mean that a larger coalition can always get a larger amount than a smaller one included in it. This is because the value of some coalitions may be negative; consequently, it is possible for $v(S \cup T)$ to be smaller than $v(S)$, or $v(T)$ even though $v(S \cup T) > v(S) + v(T)$. However, it is possible to relabel the values in such a way that the strategic structure of the game is not disturbed, and yet the value of the game to a coalition is never smaller than to any of its subcoalitions. This is done in the following manner: To each player whose value is negative we give a bonus ("just for playing the game") that compensates him for his loss. This bonus, being independent of the way he plays the game or what coalitions he joins, should make no difference in his choice of strategies or in his bargaining power. In fact if this bonus is taken away from him after the game, it should make no difference either, as long as these transactions are independent of what happens in the game. Therefore, we can substitute for our original game a *strategically equivalent* game in which the minimal guaranteed payoff to each coalition of one player is at least zero (is nonnegative). The characteristic function of this game will now be such that $v[S \cup (i)] \geqslant v(S)$, where (i) is a one-man coalition consisting of player i. This means also that $v(S \cup T) \geqslant v(S)$ for all subsets S and T. In other words, we can always convert our game into one in which the value to a coalition, in general, increases as the coalition grows. The foregoing analysis will determine the apportionment of payoffs in the transformed game. Then, we can establish the apportionment of the original game by taking away the bonuses from the players to whom we have given them. All this is done simply in the interest of simplifying the reasoning.

We have now a situation in which each player, by joining a coalition that has already formed, "brings in" some nonnegative amount into the coalition that includes him. Assume that he can claim this increment as his reward for joining the coalition. This assumption is, of course, open to the objection that if he gets the entire increment, there is no inducement for the members of the coalition to admit him. However, there is an inducement if he gets any amount *up to* what increment he brings. Since we cannot specify the cutoff point where the inducement is no longer an inducement, we shall suppose that he can get the entire increment.

Next, suppose that the order in which the players join the growing coalition (until all have joined) is determined by chance. If there are n players, there are $n! = n \times (n - 1) \times (n - 2) \dots \times 2 \times 1$ possible orders, and we assume them to be all equally probable. The amount to be given to player i is, therefore, an equally weighted average of all the increments he brings into the coalitions he joins, depending on his position in the order of coalition formation. The reader will recognize this solution as a generalization of the Shapley value to games with more than two players.

To illustrate an application of Shapley value let us solve a simple three-person game.

VII. THE LION'S SHARE

The Lion, the Tiger, and the Fox can by cooperating get a certain booty, say, a deer worth 60 units on their joint utility scale. The problem before them is how to divide the carcass. The Fox proposes a "democratic" procedure, namely, a decision by majority vote. The Lion and the Tiger reply that they have nothing against democracy, but that the relative power of the three hunters should be reflected in the voting rules. The Lion and the Tiger, being of almost equal strength, propose that they should have 50 and 49 votes each (the Lion getting the edge by virtue of his royal prerogative), while the Fox will be wise to accept the remaining vote of the total of 100 votes. They vote on this procedural matter, the Lion and the Tiger voting "Aye"; and since they are a majority, it is so ordained. They pass to the substantive matter.

The Lion and the Tiger have a majority. Therefore, they can, if they wish, take the whole deer. If they form a coalition (i.e., vote together), their minimal guaranteed payoff is 60. Also the Lion and the Fox have a majority. Consequently, the value of the game to that coalition is also 60. Of course, all three are also a majority, and, in fact, they already have the deer in their possession. The value of the game to the "grand coalition" is also 60. No other combination has a majority. The characteristic function of this game looks like this:

$$v(\emptyset) = 0; \quad v(L) = 0; \quad v(T) = 0; \quad v(F) = 0;$$
$$v(T, F) = 0; \quad v(L, T) = 60; v(L, F) = 60; \quad v(L, T, F) = 60. \tag{10}$$

Each of the beasts stands a chance of being the "pivot," that is, of supplying the deciding vote, in which case he changes a *losing* coalition (one that gets no payoff) to a *winning* one (one that gets a payoff of 60).[3] See Table I.

TABLE I
An Illustration of the Pivot in Each Order of Voting

Order of Voting:	LTF	TLF	FLT	FTL	TLF	LFT
Pivot:	Tiger	Lion	Lion	Lion	Lion	Fox

If the order of voting is decided by Chance and if the principal apportionment of payoffs is the Shapley value, we come to the following conclusion: The Lion's share is 2/3 of the carcass, while the Tiger and the Fox get 1/6 each.

The result is instructive in that it points out the limited relevance of the number of votes in the estimation of the relative "power" of the players. To see

---

[3] In the terminology of game theory, the winning coalition in a game with a single prize is the coalition which can get the prize. All other coalitions are losing coalitions including those that can prevent the countercoalitions from winning the prize, as long as they cannot win it themselves.

this clearly, had the Lion acquired 51 of the 100 votes, the number of votes commanded by each of his two partners would make no difference either to them or to him. He would always be in the majority and would need no partner in a coalition—a well-known circumstance in the control of stock companies. In the present case, the "largest stock holder" does need a partner to be in a winning coalition, but since either the Tiger or the Fox will do, while each of the latter must have the Lion as a partner in a winning coalition, the Lion has most of the power. He has, in fact, 2/3 of the power rather than ½, which is his share of the votes. Note that the Tiger with his 49 votes has no more "power" than the Fox with his one vote.

This method of apportioning payoffs among the players of an n-person game just described utilizes the notion of *pivotal power* of a player as the factor that determines his share. Pivotal power is defined as the probability that the player in question will be in a position of turning a losing coalition into a winning one. This was the case in the game just examined, where the coalition commanding a majority of the votes "takes all." In a more general context, the same principle awards to each player a share of the total (accruing to the grand coalition) that is proportional to his average contribution to the coalitions he joins, assuming that the orders in which the players join the growing coalition are all equiprobable.

How reasonable is this principle? The answer depends, of course, on what we mean by a reasonable principle of solution. We may interpret the principle as a *descriptive* model. In this sense it would be a good principle, if on the basis of it we could predict how the players of an n-person game presented in its characteristic function form (that is specified by the value of the game to each coalition) will actually apportion the total among them. To decide this question, we would, of course, need to make systematic observations, provided we can interpret the situations observed as well defined n-person games. Or we can interpret the principle as a *normative* one, that is, as one that prescribes how rational players ought to apportion the joint payoff. The justification for such a normative principle would have to come from certain notions of equity or fairness in a given population or culture. Finally we could raise the question of how the Shapley value of the game could be *enforced.*

The game with the Lion, the Tiger, and the Fox was a fairly simple one. Let us, however, simplify it still further by giving each of the three one vote. If we now calculate the Shapley value of this game, we see that each of the three has an equal chance of being the pivot; hence, the Shapley value awards to each an equal share of the prize. In view of the exact symmetry of the players, this seems eminently sensible and just, but can this decision be enforced if we adhere to the majority rule? Note that by the rules of the game any two can form a majority and so can decide to divide the 60 units of utility between them, leaving nothing to the third. The question is, which two will it be?

Communication and side payments being allowed, we can suppose that the three will bargain.

Imagine that the Lion and the Tiger have decided to form a coalition and to award themselves 30 units each. The Fox, unwilling to be left empty-bellied, could approach one of them, say the Tiger, with the following proposition:

"If you form a coalition with me instead of with the Lion, I will give you 40 units instead of 30 and will be content with the remaining 20 units."

Should the Tiger accept this proposition? He certainly gains if he accepts it. The Fox will gain too, and between them they can enforce the decision, being a majority. But if the Tiger accepts the proposition, he invites a rather unwelcome development. Namely, the Fox and the Lion will realize that between them they are to get only 20 units, whereas they could get all 60 if *they* formed a coalition against the Tiger. If the Tiger–Fox coalition has not yet been "finalized" (we assume an ongoing bargaining process), it appears that it is not stable, being subject to disruption by the hungry Lion who can offer the Fox a better deal. It turns out that *no matter how* the three apportion the prize among them, there will always be two of the three who *could do better* if they went off and formed a coalition by themselves. This raises an important question, namely, whether this is true of all games. The answer is no. But this sort of situation does obtain in all *n*-person, *constant-sum* games; that is, games in which the value to a coalition and the value to the corresponding countercoalition (of the remaining players) always add up to the same amount regardless of how the players split into the two coalitions.

VIII. THE VON NEUMANN-MORGENSTERN SOLUTION AND THE CORE

We next turn to other methods of solving *n*-person games. Actually, the different methods represent different conceptions of what should properly be called a "solution." Common to all the conceptions of a solution is some apportionment of payoffs to the several players. Since the game is presumably played for payoffs, one can expect that much from a "solution." In the case of the two-person constant-sum game, the solution was a definitive apportionment of the payoffs between the two players. Moreover, this apportionment was the result of each player's choice of a "best" strategy. No agreement between the players was needed in order to "enforce" the apportionment. In a way, therefore, the solution of the two-person constant-sum game represents a genuine "balance of power" outcome. Neither player can better his payoff as long as the other remains rational.

Some nonconstant-sum games also have this property. In Game 1, for example, if the two players agree on the outcome (S_1, T_2), neither can break the agreement (shift to the other strategy) without impairing his own payoff. The situation in Game 2, however, is different. Here if the two agree on (S_1, S_2), either can get more by shifting to the other strategy while his coalition partner keeps to the bargain.

In games with more than two players and on-going bargaining, the situation is again different. Consider an agreement between three players with equal pivot power to divide the prize equally (assuming that any two of them can take the whole prize). If any two decide to break the agreement by forming a coalition against the third to "freeze him out," the third player can do nothing to retaliate. The most he can do is *try* to entice one of the other two players away from the coalition by offering him a larger share of the prize. But the player receiving such an offer will do well to think twice before accepting, for we have seen that if he does, he opens up the possibility for his erstwhile partner to wean his new partner away by a similar stratagem. Nevertheless, because of the built-in temptation to shift partners, the egalitarian solution of the three-person constant-sum game, although it is attractively symmetric and apparently "just," is of questionable stability. And this instability of all definitive apportionment of payoffs characterizes at least all the *n*-person constant-sum games. This leads to another concept of a solution of an *n*-person game, namely, one that singles out not one but a whole set of payoff apportionments, which are somehow stable in their *totality*. That is to say, one looks for a *set* of apportionments with the property that there will be little or no temptation to choose an apportionment not in that set.

Apportionments of payoffs in which the *n* players receive jointly what they can get as a grand coalition and in which no player gets less than his value as a one-man coalition are called *imputations*. An imputation satisfies two criteria, namely, that of *individual rationality* and that of *collective rationality* of the entire set of *n*-players. This is so because in an imputation neither an individual player nor the whole set of players receive less than they could as coalitions. It is thus reasonable to look for sets of imputations that are in some sense stable.

One such set defines the so-called *Von Neumann-Morgenstern solution* of the *n*-person cooperative game with transferable conservative utilities. To describe this set we must first explain what it means for one imputation to *dominate* another. Recall that an imputation is an apportionment of payoffs among the *n* players. It can, therefore, be represented by an *n*-tuple of numbers $(x_1, x_2 \ldots x_n)$, where x_i is the payoff to player i. Moreover, by definition of an imputation, we must have

$$x_1 + \ldots x_n = v(N); \quad x_i \geqslant v(i) \tag{11}$$

where $v(N)$ is the value of the game to the grand coalition and $v(i)$ is the value of the game to player i.

Consider now two such imputations $(x_1, x_2 \ldots x_n)$ and $(y_1, y_2 \ldots y_n)$. Suppose there is some subset of players, each of whom gets more in the first imputation than in the second; moreover their joint payoff in the first imputation does not exceed the value of the game to them as a coalition. Then the first imputation is said to dominate the second. Roughly speaking one imputation dominates another, if some players would rather have the first apportionment than the second and have the power to back up their preference; that is, they can get at least what accrues to them in the first imputation by forming a coalition and playing against everyone else.

Now if the domination relation were an *asymmetric transitive relation,* that is, one which would allow an ordering of the imputations according to which dominate which, it would be easy to single out a stable set, namely, those imputations which dominate all others and are not dominated by any. Unfortunately, it may well happen that (a) two imputations dominate each other (naturally via different subsets of dissatisfied players), (b) neither dominates the other, or (c) imputation x dominates y, which dominates z, which dominates x. In the case of such cycles it is, of course, impossible to decide which imputation is the "most dominating."

Although the relation of domination does not permit an ordering of the imputations, it does enable us to define a set of imputations which is in a sense "stable." The set is defined as follows (Von Neumann & Morgenstern, 1947): No imputation in the set dominates any other imputation in the set, and for every imputation outside the set, there is one of the set that dominates it. The definition implies that no subset of players will "realistically" prefer any imputation in this set to any other in the set. It implies also that if a subset of players realistically prefers some imputation outside the set, there is always at least one other subset that will realistically prefer an imputation in the set to the latter; so that if a shift occurs to an imputation outside the set, another shift is likely to occur to an imputation within the set. This tendency of the imputations in the set to effect "returns" to them (in an ongoing bargaining process) is interpreted as a stability of sorts.

A more natural way of defining a stable set of imputations would be by way of singling out imputations which are not dominated by any others. This set is called the *core* of the game (Gillies, 1953). By definition no subset of players is motivated to shift away from the core to an imputation outside it. Unfortunately, many n-person games have no cores; the sets defined by the above property are empty. In particular no constant-sum n-person game has a core. It has been shown recently (Lucas, 1968) that some n-person games do not have any solutions in the sense of Von Neumann-Morgenstern. It is, however, easily seen that if a game has both a solution and a core, then the latter is a subset of the former.

By way of illustrating the idea of the Von Neumann-Morgenstern solution and the core, let us consider a three-person game in which the players are the seller of a house and two prospective buyers. Let the house be worth a units to the seller (player 1), b units to one of the buyers (player 2), and c units to the other (player 3). If both buyers are serious about wanting to buy the house, then each must be willing to pay at least as much as the house is worth to the seller. That is, both b and c must be at least as large as a and since it makes no difference how we label the players, we may write $a \leqslant b \leqslant c$.

A coalition of two players means the pooling of resources. Since the seller is in possession of the house and is not forced to sell, he is guaranteed a units of utility, i.e., what the house is worth to him. (He can get more if he sells it.) Since neither buyer is in possession of the house, they are not guaranteed anything in excess of zero. Nor are they guaranteed anything in excess of zero if they form a coalition, since the seller is not forced to sell. On the other hand, the coalition of the seller and the first buyer is guaranteed a payoff to b, since they have the house in their possession, and it is worth b to the first buyer. Similarly, the coalition of the seller with the second buyer is guaranteed a payoff of c. Of course, all three are guaranteed a payoff of c units. We can now write down the characteristic function of this game.

$$v(1) = a; \quad v(2) = 0; \quad v(3) = 0; \quad v(1,2) = b; \quad v(1,3) = c;$$
$$v(2,3) = 0; \quad v(1,2,3) = c. \tag{12}$$

The imputations of this game are all the payoff triples (x_1, x_2, x_3), where

$$x_1 \geqslant a; \quad x_2 \geqslant 0; \quad x_3 \geqslant 0; \quad x_1 + x_2 + x_3 = c \tag{13}$$

The core comprises all those imputations where

$$b \geqslant x_1 \geqslant c, \quad x_2 = 0, \quad x_3 = c - x_1. \tag{14}$$

The intepretation of this set of imputations is simple. The house goes to the higher bidder for some price between the low and the high bids. In game-theoretic terms, player 1 and player 3 in coalition divide their joint utility gain *in some way*. One would expect this to happen if the buyers bid against each other, since in that case, the low bidder would be eliminated. The identification of the solution with the core of the game gives us no further information on the final outcome.

Let us see what the Von Neumann-Morgenstern solution can tell us. It turns out that this game has an infinity of such solutions. Each solution, recall, is a set of imputations. Each such set turns out to be the totality of the imputations in the core *plus* all the triples (x_1, x_2, x_3) where

$$a \leqslant x_1 \leqslant b; \quad x_2 = f(x_1); \quad x_3 = g(x_1);$$
$$x_1 + x_2 + x_3 = c, \tag{15}$$

while $f(x_1)$ and $g(x_1)$ are fixed but arbitrary nonnegative monotonic decreasing functions of x_1.

Translated into English, this means the following: The house will go to the higher bidder for some price x_1 between a and c. If this price is more than b, the low bidder gets nothing. Consequently, the seller will emerge with the payoff x_1 and the higher bidder with the payoff $c - x_1$, i.e., the difference between what the house is worth to him and what he paid for it. If, however, the price is less than b, then the higher bidder must compensate the low bidder. The amount of this compensation is determined by the function $f(x_1)$, which specifies the amount to be paid by the higher bidder to the lower bidder corresponding to each sales price x_1. This function (or rule) is fixed but arbitrary, except that both bidders must benefit more the lower the sales price of the house. As a result, the seller emerges with the payoff x_1 (a number between a and b), the lower bidder with a payoff $f(x_1) \geqslant 0$, and the higher bidder with $g(x_1) = c - f(x_1) - x_1 \geqslant 0$.

Each function $f(x_1)$ determines a different solution. There is, therefore, an infinity of solutions of this game, and moreover each solution contains an infinity of imputations. Not only that but *every* imputation is contained in at least one solution. It seems, then, that the "solution" tells us nothing except that the apportionment of the payoffs will be an imputation. Of what use, then, is the solution concept in this case? Why not simply say that the "rational" outcome will be one of the possible imputations? To answer this question, let us pursue the interpretation further.

Let us interpret the compensation given by the high bidder to the low bidder if the house goes for less than b—the amount the low bidder would have been willing to pay. This compensation reflects the fact that in that case the two buyers must have formed a coalition. Specifically, the high bidder promised not to accept the house at a price between b and c (which he otherwise would have done), and the low bidder promised to retire from the market even if the price fell below b. Note that whatever price the house is sold for, it makes more sense (from the point of view of the coalition) for the high bidder to acquire it, since it is worth more to him than to the low bidder. (Recall that in this context we have assumed that the utilities of the players can be compared and side payments or compensations are possible.) The compensation paid to the low bidder is for having made it possible for the high bidder to acquire the house at a lower price.

As we have seen, the amount of the compensation is determined by some rule. The rule *itself* is assumed to be determined by considerations outside the scope of game theory. Von Neumann and Morgenstern call such considerations "social norms," or, if you will, the "going price" for the sort of agreement that the two buyers conclude.

Suppose now that the social norm prescribes the "going price" $f(x)$. This, in effect, singles out a *particular* solution of all possible solutions. To see whether the solution has any empirical content, we would have to observe several such transactions where the sales price varies to see whether the rule $f(x)$ is actually adhered to. To be sure, we could establish the nature of the function, $f(x)$, if such exists in a given milieu, directly, without recourse to game-theoretic concepts. We must, however, keep in mind that the apparent triviality of the results is partly accounted for by the extreme simplicity or the situation. Solutions of more complex n-person games are likely to be much more complex and to lead to insights considerably beyond "common sense." Such insights, one assumes, would come from the *interpretations* of the game-theoretic results. The example just cited is like an extremely elementary problem in arithmetic attacked by sophisticated mathematical methods. The solution so obtained must, of course, agree with the immediately perceived solution, but this does not necessarily indicate that the method is worthless. The value of the method is revealed in its power when applied to problems whose solutions are not immediate. Besides, it is important to remember that the "obviousness" of a solution often becomes apparent only after the solution has been obtained.

To complete the picture, we shall give also the Shapley value solution of the seller vs. two buyers game. This is the imputation:

$$\frac{2a + b + 3c}{6}, \quad \frac{b - a}{6}, \quad \frac{3c - a - 2b}{6}. \tag{16}$$

It gives the low bidder a compensation equal to $1/6$ of the excess of his bid over the seller's price. The interesting feature is that this compensation does not depend on how much the high bidder would bid.

To see the connection with the Lion–Tiger–Fox game, set $a = 0$, $b = c$. Then the seller gets $2/3$ of the prize (which is b), and the two buyers get $1/6$ each. The seller plays the Lion's role here. He can do business with either of the buyers, but each buyer can do business only with him.

IX. A QUESTION OF STABILITY

We have now described three types of solutions of an n-person cooperative game in characteristic function form, namely, the Shapley value, the Von Neumann-Morgenstern solution, and the core. Each reflects some "rational principle." The Shapley value reflects the *a priori* expectations of the players, assuming that these expectations are calculated as the average benefit of the respective players to the coalitions they could be asked to join. The Von Neumann-Morgenstern solution has a sort of dynamic stability, reflected in the tendency of the "state of the system" (designated by a proposed imputation) to return to the imputations in the solution. The imputations of the core have the appearance of being "self-enforcing" in the sense that they are not dominated by other imputations, which is generally not true of either the Shapley value or the imputations of the Von Neumann-Morgenstern solution. For this reason, it may appear that the imputations of the core (if such exist) are the most stable. This conclusion, however, is not always warranted. Let us see why.

If one of the core imputations is accepted by the players as a "resolution of their conflict of interest," no combination of players can do better if they break away from the grand coalition to form a coalition of their own (assuming that the remaining players form a countercoalition with the express aim of keeping the joint payoff of the defectors to its minimum). But there is no telling what the defectors will get if a countercoalition fails to form. It may even happen that a countercoalition does form; but if instead of "punishing" the defectors, it simply pursues its own interest, the defectors can gain by defecting.

Consider the following three-person game. Player 1 has a choice of saying "Yes" or "No." Player 2, being informed of what player 1 has said, has the same choice. Player 3, being informed of the two preceding choices, also has the same choice. This completes a play of the game. The payoffs are then awarded as follows: If all three have said "Yes," each gains one unit. If all three have said "No," each loses one unit. If two have said "Yes," and one "No," the yes-men get zero, and the no-man wins three units. If two have said "No," the lone yes-man loses two units, while each of the no-men wins two units. In short, it is best to be the only "No," next best one of two "Noes," next one of three "Yesses," next one of two "Yesses," and worst of all a lone "Yes."

Assume that the players can form coalitions. Then it can be shown (let the reader try his hand at showing) that a single player can guarantee himself -1; two players in a coalition can guarantee themselves 0; and the grand coalition can get a joint payoff of 3. We can, therefore, write the characteristic function of this game as follows.

$$v(\emptyset) = 0; \quad v(1) = -1; \quad v(2) = 0; \quad v(3) = 3, \qquad (17)$$

where the numbers in parentheses refer to the number of players in coalition.

This game has a core. If an imputation distributes the three units so that no player gets less than -1, nor any two jointly less than zero, no single player, nor any pair, can be sure of getting more in a coalition of his (or their) own. Yet any one of the players can very well risk breaking away from the grand coalition. For if player 1 says "No," and if players 2 and 3, instead of "punishing" him by saying "No" also, try to get as much as possible for themselves, which, under the circumstances is 0, at least one of them must say "Yes." In that case, player 1 will get either 3 (if both say "Yes") or 2 (if one says "Yes"); this is more than he gets in any imputation of the core that awards him less than 2. But an imputation in the core cannot award 2 to all three players. Therefore, a temptation to break the grand coalition always remains.

Note that "breaking a coalition" does not mean double-crossing one's partners. This would be the case if player 3, after having promised to say "Yes," said "No" after the others have said "Yes," and so got away with the largest payoff. Rather, "breaking away" means *announcing in advance* that one is no longer bound by the agreement of the coalition. Player 3 can make such an announcement *before* a play of the game begins and still get 2, if players 1 and 2 "make the best" of the situation and play to get the most they can instead of punishing player 3.

We see, therefore, that the existence of the core by no means guarantees the intactness of the grand coalition. It does so only if the potential defectors expect the worst.

The ambiguities and instabilities that seem to surround the concept of a solution of an *n*-person game stem, as has been said, from the blurring of the concept of rationality. In the context of the two-person constant-sum game, the meaning of rationality is quite clear. Rationality means the rationality of the individual decision-maker who pursues his own interest. In the context of the two-person nonconstant-sum game, the concept of rationality bifurcates into individual and collective rationality, the prescriptions of the two being often at variance. However, once this distinction is made, the meaning of each sort of rationality remains clear. Since there is only one "collective" (the two players in coalition), there is only one "collective interest." When the number of players exceeds two, there are several "collectives," and furthermore their *memberships may overlap.* The idea embodied in the core of a game is that of satisfying *all* of the possible collectives by giving each at least as much as they can guarantee for themselves by forming coalitions of their own. The fact that many games have no cores reflects the fact that in some situations no "compromise" can give every collective as much as they could actually get if they "stuck together" against every one else, that is, if their members resisted all temptations to be weaned away by better offers. Certainly common sense dictates as much. Conflicts that cannot be resolved by "pleasing everyone" are well known, and so are the advantages of group loyalty that overrides immediate individual interest. What game theory does, besides confirming this folk wisdom, is make the logical structure of the relevant conflict situations explicit and so suitable for rigorous analysis. It often happens that science confirms common sense. But science frequently exposes the fallacies of common sense also and, above all, points up distinctions between valid and invalid applications of common sense. Therein lies much of its cognitive value.

X. THE BARGAINING SET

We would expect that in multilateral conflicts with opportunities for forming coalitions, bargaining would take place among the conflicting parties, where side payments are offered to players for joining or staying in coalitions. To some extent the logical structure of such bargaining is captured by still another solution concept called the *bargaining set* (Aumann & Maschler, 1964). There are, in fact, bargaining sets of several levels of complexity. We shall examine only the simplest.

So far, the focus of attention has been on the imputations, that is, on how the value to the grand coalition shall be apportioned. The implication is that the grand coalition has formed, has obtained its value, and faces only the problem of distributing the joint gain among the members. But nothing guarantees that the grand coalition will actually form. To be sure, the formation of the grand coalition is demanded by the principle of collective rationality, since acting jointly, the players can get at least as much, often more (in toto) than acting in any other way. Nevertheless, the pressures and counterpressures on the several members of overlapping potential coalitions may prevent the grand coalition from forming. (In real life there are, of course, other obstacles to the formation of the grand coalition, for example, communication barriers, real and imagined.) For this reason, some game theoreticians turned their attention to situations where the players of an *n*-person game are split into several coalitions.

Suppose a situation of this sort obtains. Each coalition can be sure of getting its value, and its members face the problem of apportioning this value among themselves. The game theoretician, who looks at the whole situation from the outside, poses the following question: Suppose the prospective joint payoffs of all the coalitions are apportioned among the individual members in a certain way, will the resulting situation remain "stable?" Here "stability" has to do, as in previous analyses, with the satisfaction of the players. Now from the game-theoretic point of view, whether a player is satisfied or not matters only if a dissatisfied player can do something to better his payoff. What can he do? He can argue about his share with his coalition partners. But his arguments must be backed. In bargaining, arguments are backed by *quid-pro-quos*, that is, essentially by threats and promises. In the simplest case now under consideration, the arguments of a player are directed against just one other player in the same coalition. The arguments are of the following sort.

> I, player i, am offered the amount x_i as a member of a coalition, of which you, player j are also a member. I notice, however, that among all the *possible* coalitions there is one that includes me but excludes you, and it can afford to give all its members, including me, more than these players are presently offered. Consequently, unless I get more, I shall organize this other coalition without you.

If player i is in a position to say this to player j, he is said to have an *objection* against player j. Player j can defend himself against this objection, if he can counter it with an objection of his own. To do so, he must be able to point to another possible coalition which includes him, j, but not player i, and all of whose members could be better off than under the present arrangement. However, this is not enough. The potential coalitions alluded to by players i and j may have overlapping members. If the existing coalition structure is to be replaced by the one proposed by j, these overlapping members (who have a choice between player i's and player j's proposals) should prefer the arrangement proposed by player j. Only then can player j be said to have effectively countered player i's threat. If player j is not in a position to do so, player i is said to have a *justifiable* objection against player j.

We are now ready to define a stable situation. A situation involves both a coalition structure and a payoff apportionment in which the members of each coalition get jointly the value of the game to that coalition. It stands to reason that the situation is stable only if each player gets at least what he could get in a one-man coalition with himself. In addition, no player should have a justifiable objection against any of his coalition partners; otherwise he is in a position to demand more, threatening otherwise to change the coalition structure. The totality of stable situations constitutes a *bargaining set* of the game (Aumann & Maschler, 1964).

As an example, consider the following game. A prize worth 100 units is to be awarded jointly to three players if they can agree how to apportion it. Also, any two players can exclude the third, in which case, however, they get less than 100. Specifically, if players 1 and 2 exclude player 3, they get 60 to divide between them. If players 1 and 3 exclude player 2, they get 70. If players 2 and 3 exclude player 1, they get 90. A single player gets nothing. The characteristic function of this game is evidently the following.

$$v(1) = v(2) = v(3) = 0, \quad v(1,2) = 60, \quad v(1,3) = 70,$$
$$v(2,3) = 90, \quad v(1,2,3) = 100 \tag{18}$$

The theory of the bargaining set says nothing about which coalitions will form, or, in normative terms, which coalitions ought to be formed by "rational" players. If, however, a coalition structure does arise, bargaining set theory tells us which apportionments of payoffs are stable in the sense described above.

Clearly, if every man remains in a coalition only with himself, the only stable payoff apportionment in our game is (0, 0, 0), since no one can be forced to accept a negative payoff.

If players 1 and 2 form a coalition to exclude player 3, then the only stable division of their 60 units is 20 to player 1 and 40 to player 2. Let us see why this is so. If player 1 gets less than 20 (which implies that player 2 gets more than 40), player 1 has a justifiable objection against player 2, his partner. He states his objection by pointing out that he can offer player 3 up to 50 and still retain 20, since players 1 and 3 can get jointly 70. Player 2 cannot match this and still retain more than 40, since he and player 3 can get only 90. On the other hand, if player 2 gets less than 40 (therefore, player 1 more than 20), player 2 has a justifiable objection against player 1. In that case *he* can offer player 3 up to 50, since players 1 and 3 jointly can get 90 and player 2 cannot match this offer.

By similar reasoning, if players 1 and 3 form a coalition, the apportionment (20, 50) is the only stable one. If players 2 and 3 form a coalition, the apportionment (40, 50) is the stable one.

It remains to examine the case when the grand coalition forms. Then the only stable apportionment is (16 2/3, 36 2/3, 46 2/3), as the reader can verify by examining the feasible offers and counteroffers or threats and counterthreats.

It is interesting to compare this result with the Shapley value of this game, which prescribes the apportionment (25, 35, 40). This apportionment is based, as will be recalled, on what each player can contribute to each coalition that he can join. It turns out to be somewhat more egalitarian than the apportionments of the bargaining set. The reason for this is, roughly speaking, that the Shapley value solution is based more on "equity" than on the "bargaining power" that accrues to the players in virtue of what they can threaten or offer.

XI. THE RELEVANCE OF GAME THEORY TO THEORIES OF CONFLICT

We have touched only on a small sample of questions raised in the theory of games, but these topics ought to be sufficient for a general conception of the spirit and methods of game-theoretic investigations. It remains to evaluate the relevance of this approach to the construction of a substantive theory of conflict and of conflict resolution.

First it is instructive to trace the historical course of the development of game theory. The theory began with the analysis of games of strategy. The first general question put by the theory was, "What will happen if two perfectly rational players play a game of strategy, that is, a game in which the success of a player depends only on his skill in choosing among alternative courses of action?"

Practically all of the so-called parlor games (*Gesellschaftspiele*) are constant-sum games. As we have seen, the fundamental theorem of game theory asserts that in a two-person game of this sort there exists an optimal strategy (pure or mixed) for each player. However, the knowledge that an optimal strategy of a game exists is usually of no help in finding it, at least not in any parlor game worth playing. The number of strategies in such games is so formidably large that the algorithms for obtaining optimal ones are all but useless.

However, game theoreticians did not undertake this futile task. Instead they kept the game-theoretic investigations on high levels of generality, largely devoid of immediate "practical" utility. Nevertheless, the publication of the fundamental treatise on game theory (Von Neumann & Morgenstern, 1947) aroused considerable interest—at times, excitement—far beyond the circle of initiates. Was this interest justified? To answer this question, we must examine the sources of this interest.

One source stems from the preoccupations of men who are professionally engaged in the conduct of strategic conflict, for example, decision-makers in charge of military and diplomatic affairs and of competitive enterprises. The outcomes of such conflicts depend on two sets of factors, namely, on the one hand, resources (armed might, industrial potential, capital, credit, etc.) and, on the other hand, skill in the use of the resources (strategy and tactics in war, awareness of the strengths and weaknesses of others and a sense of timing in diplomacy, operational efficiency, and a sensitivity to opportunities in business). In military circles one speaks of these factors as "hardware" and "software," respectively. Hardware is a product of applied physical science. It is natural to expect that another product of applied science could produce a comparable harvest of software, to be used in the effective deployment of hardware. And just as physical science has evolved from a refinement, generalization, and logical organization of practical knowledge about the material world, so this new science could be expected to evolve from a refinement, generalization, and logical organization of the ideas immanent in military strategy and tactics, in diplomatic astuteness, and in business acumen. The appearance of game theory on the mathematical horizon was interpreted in some quarters as the birth of such a science. Demonstration of solutions of simple, highly idealized tactical problems, formulated as constant-sum games, were sometimes cited in support of this expectation, the implication being that just as theoretical physics grew out of solutions of simple idealized problems, so a mathematicized theory of military strategy could evolve from the solutions of elementary game models. Moreover, one rather sophisticated mathematical outgrowth of the theory of the two-person constant-sum game did find serious genuine military applications. This was the theory of so-called *differential games.* Best known examples of these applications are solutions of problems, formulated as games between, for example, two guided missiles, one pursuing, the other evading. Under given constraints (which in the case of guided missiles are physical, hence ascertainable parameters) both the optimal pursuit strategy and the optimal evading strategy can be calculated.

Given the limited but nonetheless fairly impressive successes of game-theoretic methods in the design of specific tactics, it is understandable that people concerned with such matters would look forward to widening the scope of application of game theory as a mathematicized strategic science or a science of "rationally conducted conflict."

Now from the standpoint of a party to a conflict, the practicality of a strategic science lies in its normative aspect, namely, the prescriptions one is able to make on the basis of rigorous findings on how one ought to act so as to win as much as possible or lose as little as necessary. We have already seen that such optimal strategies can be unambiguously prescribed in two-person constant-sum games. Pursuit games, for example, fulfill this requirement. The pursuer wins if he catches the evader; if not, the evader wins. Or, in a somewhat more general context, the pursuer attempts to maximize the probability of capture or to minimize the time to capture, while the evader attempts to do the opposite. When it comes to tactical problems on the battle field, the assignment of numerical utilities to outcomes is a more difficult matter. In formal examples, this is done mostly in terms of personnel and material losses or estimates of the relative values of different positions to be captured or defended. Questions may arise as to how realistic these estimates are and how realistic the assumption is that the enemy's utilities are always negatively related to one's own. Still the constant-sum paradigm can be defended in the situations depicted.

And that is just the trouble with the "practical applications" of elementary game theory to the conduct of conflict. Since the constant-sum game is, generally speaking, the only paradigm of conflict to which the concept of optimal strategy applies, there is a strong psychological pressure on those concerned with "winning" conflicts to see conflicts in the context of the constant-sum paradigm.

Let us assume for a moment that this *is* the most relevant conflict model, that is to say, that the most prevalent or important conflicts are bipolarized ones, involving two opponents with interests diametrically opposed. Assume further that game theory becomes a source of knowledge for discerning optimal strategies in such conflicts. Clearly, such knowledge, being of a purely logical nature, cannot be monopolized, at least not for long. In each conflict both parties will find optimal strategies, and in the last analysis no strategic advantage can accrue to either.

In the context of parlor games this development would only "kill" the fully investigated games. Short of that, the playing of the games would be progressively "refined"; that is, their levels of sophistication would rise. While human life can be said to be enriched by such refinements (providing a source of esthetic enjoyment for the connoisseurs), a similar evaluation will not be readily made in the context of real life conflicts, particularly of war, except possibly by the dedicated experts of the military profession.

In the context of business competition, the question of the social usefulness of competitive expertise is an open one. It may be that sometimes the population at large can profit by the "refinement" of competition among various business interests; but in some cases, at least, this is a doubtful prognosis. Moreover, quite aside from the direct social effects of increasing competitive expertise, one must also reckon with the fact that every developing field of expertise attracts increasing numbers of practitioners. The preoccupation of a whole society is reflected in its most valued fields of expertise. A successful development of a "science of rational competition" would be both a symptom and a determining factor of the nature of the society that has fostered it. It is doubtful whether a society that places great social value on competitive expertise can effectively attack vital problems whose solution depends on techniques, attitudes, and insights quite unrelated to success in competition or in power struggles.

XII. THE SOCIAL VALUE OF GAME THEORY

It seems to me that the real social value of game theory resides not in its earliest findings, related to bipolarized conflict, nor in the popularly imagined extrapolations from these findings, namely, a source of know-how for successful conduct of any kind of strategic conflict. Rather the value lies in the subsequent development of the theory beyond the context of the two-person constant-sum game. We have seen that in the course of this development, game theory turned completely away from the original problem posed by it—the problem of finding an "optimal strategy" in a conflict situation. It is noteworthy that this development stemmed not so much from a preoccupation with the nature or the social consequences of conflict as from the nature of mathematical investigations. The mathematician quickly loses interest in problems once solutions become routine, for instance, once the existence of a solution has been demonstrated and, perhaps, an algorithm for finding it has been indicated. Thereafter the mathematician turns his attention to a generalization of the problem. For example, once the existence of an optimal pure strategy in every game of perfect information has been demonstrated, the game theoretician naturally poses the question of how things stand with games that are *not* games of perfect information. The answer leads to a new concept (of mixed strategy) and to a justification of the importance of the distinction between the two classes of games. Once the optimality of certain strategies in two-person constant-sum games has been demonstrated, the game theoretician wants to know how matters stand in nonconstant-sum games. As a result, the ambivalence of "optimal strategy" in the more general context must be recognized. Thereafter attention is drawn away from the search for individually rational strategies and toward the problem of deciding the outcome of "rational bargaining." Game theory then ceases to be a theory of "rational conflict" and becomes a theory of "rational conflict resolution." With more than 2 players, problems of definition and classification rapidly multiply. The theory becomes an analysis of the purely logical problems that must be solved if a proposed resolution of a conflict (for example, the final apportionment of payoffs in an n-person game specified by a characteristic function) is to be defended as "equitable" or as "reflecting the bargaining positions of the players" or as "stable."[4]

The achievement of game theory, then, is that it relates logically precise concepts to conflict resolution that have hitherto had only an intuitive meaning or rather different meanings for different people in different contexts. Game theory can do this, because it is a purely mathematical (synonymously logical) theory. It must abstract entirely from all the psychological or sociological factors of conflicts, thus sacrificing immediate relevance for logical precision. This does not mean, however, that the relevance of the theory to the understanding of "real" conflicts is excluded. On the contrary, such understanding makes itself felt as the purely logical relations of conflict situations are uncovered and "factored out," as it were. For then what has been left out is revealed all the more clearly.

For example, the findings of game theory suggest a far-reaching experimental program. Conflicts of interest can be easily simulated in a laboratory where subjects are asked to choose among alternatives (strategies); it is understood that the outcomes (for instance, monetary payoffs) are determined by their and their coplayers' choices. The question to what extent these games simulate real life conflicts must be kept in abeyance. There is a great deal to investigate before this question is raised. The findings of game theory can be subjected to experimental test. The fact that in most situations game theory fails to prescribe uniquely rational choices creates no difficulty, since one can well ask which, if any, of the variously defined "solutions" of games are realized, and, if so, with what relative frequency. If systematic departures from these solutions are observed, one can look for psychological, sociological, or cultural factors influencing the direction and the magnitude of such departures. Can they be attributed to discrepancies between the numerical magnitudes and the utilities of the payoffs, to purely cognitive misconceptions, to ethical considerations intruding into strategic calculations or to the personalities of the players? How do people behave in response to specific strategies of their coplayers? Are there systematic differences between the outcomes of strategically equivalent

---

[4]We have seen what intricate considerations are involved, for example, depending on whether the utilities of players are comparable or not, on whether in the absence of agreement each player simply claims his "security level" or employs "threats" to get more. Clearly these questions touch on ethics; but the game-theoretic treatment of them never leaves the ground of strictly logicostructural analysis. For further discussion of these matters, see Braithwaite (1955).

games if their strategic equivalence is not apparent? If so, what is the source of the bias, etc?[5]

The results of such investigations could be organized into a behavioral theory. The theory would explain or predict the choices of people *in that laboratory situation* and, of course, would not warrant any extrapolation from it to real life. However, in view of the richness of the purely formal theory, on whose foundations the behavioral theory would be built, one could reasonably expect the latter to be of substantive psychological interest. Then this behavioral theory (treating so far only of the artificial laboratory "conflicts") could be made a point of departure of a "genuine" behavioral theory of conflict.

Presently the large gap between laboratory and life is viewed as a formidable obstacle in the task of developing a scientific approach to conflict resolution. It is indeed an insuperable gap, if one assumes that it must be crossed by an inductive leap from microcosm to macrocosm. Such a leap is possible only if the same "laws" govern both the events in the laboratory and those of the cosmos—as, for example, the physical laws. No such universal laws are discernible in human affairs. Therefore, there can be no question of an inductive leap but only of patient bridge building from the study of miniature conflicts under controllable conditions and with clearly defined issues to large conflicts among ambivalently identified actors for poorly defined "stakes," obscured by myriads of interlocking issues.

If it does nothing else, the combined game-theoretic analysis and laboratory method will reveal the emptiness of the unqualified phrase "rational decision making," which suggests to the uninitiated that the effective conduct of national or international affairs is a matter of strategic expertise. Such expertise implies the ability to find optimal strategies. Such ability, in turn, implies the existence of optimal strategies, which in turn implies decision situations on the lowest levels of complexity. If strategic expertise is to be utilized, the decision situations must be formulated on that level; and they usually are, frequently with disastrous results.

---

[5]We have seen how the analysis of a simple "weighted majority game" (Lion, Tiger, and Fox) reveals the irrelevance of the difference in the number of votes commanded by the Tiger and the Fox. In real life, this irrelevance may not be apparent. In choosing his coalition partner, the Lion may prefer the Tiger, "because he has more votes," or, on the contrary the Fox, "because having fewer votes, he will make smaller demands." The game-theoretic result (that the Tiger and Fox are "equally strong") does not warrant the conclusion that those other considerations are "irrational." It merely reveals them to be extraneous to the logic of the situation as *formulated*. In short, game-theoretic analysis separates the logical from the extralogical features of conflict, or, if you will, points to the necessity of reformulating the conflict situation, if the preferred solution appears to violate "common sense" or is at variance with experience. Gamson (1964) has reviewed some experimental work on coalition formation and has related the results to several hypotheses, including the Shapley value model.

Paradoxically, although game-theoretic analysis is pure strategic analysis, it may help to break the grip of "strategic thinking" on the conduct of public affairs. We have seen how the extension of game-theoretic analysis from two-person constant-sum to two-person nonconstant-sum games has necessitated a shift of emphasis from individually optimal strategies to jointly optimal strategies and to the paradoxical discrepancies between individual and collective rationality; how the introduction of a bargaining component pointed up differences between equitable, enforceable, and stable solutions; how the analysis of games with more than 2 players brought out the role of "social norms," i.e., extrarational considerations in the analysis of conflicts.

To be sure, there is nothing startlingly new in these ideas, which have been the stock-in-trade of social science for a long time. The important thing is that these concepts are introduced into the analysis of conflict *per force*, nor *a priori*, namely when a strategic analysis comes to an impasse or is faced with contradictions. This story has been told many times, especially in mathematics. The search for solutions of specific problems led to so-called "unsolved problems" (squaring the circle, solution by radicals of the general fifth degree equation, etc.) and through these to an enlargement of the repertoire of concepts and the formulation of entirely new classes of problems inconceivable in the old framework of thought.

In summary, the chief value of game-theoretic analysis is that it points to questions beyond its scope. In order to analyze a conflict situation as a game, certain questions must be answered without ambiguity. Who are the players? What choices of alternatives are available to them? What are the outcomes of these choices? How does *each* of the parties to the conflict (not just the party whose point of view has been assumed) value the outcomes? Is it a constant-sum game? Are coalitions feasible; if so, which? What is the value of the game (as formulated) to each of the feasible coalitions? Are any of the game-theoretic "solutions" of the conflict relevant to the situation as depicted? Are they enforceable, equitable, stable?

The so-called "science of strategy," developed first in the context of military confrontations and to some extent in diplomacy and in the management of competitive enterprises, was formulated by people entrusted with the *conduct* of conflict, hence by people committed to seeking strategies benefiting one side. To be sure, the principles of optimal strategy apply equally to either of the conflicting parties. However, to realize this does not yet mean to transcend the standpoint of individual rationality, but merely to assume the standpoint of an arbitrarily chosen player. Indeed, in the context of the two-person constant-sum game, no theoretical advantage derives from taking the standpoint of both players simultaneously.

The inadequacy of the constant-sum game paradigm as a model of international conflict was clearly noted in the recent writings of strategists

(Kahn, 1965; Schelling, 1958). However, the full implications of transcending the standpoint of individual rationality were not and could not be pursued as long as "strategic thinking" was identified with a search for optimal strategies to be prescribed to decision-makers in pursuit of the interests of their clients. Only when the tight coupling of the theory of conflict and the immediately perceived interests of individual participants is loosened can attention be redirected to the fundamental questions raised above. We have seen that this loosening is a consequence of the ambivalences in the analysis of conflicts revealed by so-called "higher" game theory. When "optimal strategy" can no longer be unambiguously defined, one is forced to seek points of departure other than the individual interests of players. In so doing, one is forced to reexamine the identities of the players, to question the relevance of "interests" hitherto taken for granted, to clarify the meaning of concepts like "stability" (hitherto used only metaphorically in theories of political systems or of international relations), "enforcement" (hitherto defined predominantly in terms of coercion), or "equity" (hitherto virtually excluded from "realistic" political theory). Although game theory cannot provide answers to any of those questions, it must be credited with having put them in an illuminating perspective.

REFERENCES

Aumann, R.T., & Maschler, M. The bargaining set for cooperative games. In M. Drescher, L.S. Shapley, & A.W. Tucker (Eds.), *Advances in game theory*. Princeton, N.J.: Princeton University Press, 1964, Pp. 443–476.

Braithwaite, R.B. *Theory of games as a tool for the moral philosopher*. London and New York: Cambridge University Press, 1955.

Gamson, W.A. Experimental studies in coalition forming. In I.L. Berkowitz (Ed.), *Advances in experimental social psychology*, Vol. 1. New York: Academic Press, 1964. Pp. 82-190.

Gillies, D.B. *Some theorems on n-person games*. Ph.D. thesis, Department of Mathematics, Princeton University, 1953.

Kahn, H. *On escalation: Metaphors and scenarios*. New York: Praeger, 1965.

Lucas, W.F. The proof that a game may not have a solution. *Memorandum* RM-5543-PR, January, 1968. Santa Monica, Calif.: The Rand Corporation.

Luce, R.D., & Raiffa, H. *Games and decisions*. New York: Wiley, 1957.

Nash, J.F. The bargaining problem. *Econometrica*, 1950, **18**, 155–162.

Nash, J.F. Two-person co-operative games. *Econometrica*, 1953, **21**, 128–140.

Raiffa, H. Arbitration schemes for generalized two-person games. In H.W. Kuhn & A.W. Tucker (Eds.), *Contributions to the theory of games II*. Princeton, N.J.: Princeton University Press, 1953, Pp. 361–387.

Rapoport, A., & Chammah, A.M. *Prisoner's dilemma*. Ann Arbor, Mich.: University of Michigan Press, 1965.

Richardson, L.F. Generalized foreign policy. *British Journal of Psychology,* 1939, No. 23 (Monograph Suppl.)

Richardson, L.F. War moods. *Psychometrika,* 1948, **13,** 147–174; 197–232.

Shapley, L.S. A value for an n-person game. In H.W. Kuhn, & A.W. Tucker (Eds.), *Contributions to the theory of games II.* Princeton, N.J.: Princeton University Press, 1953. Pp. 303–317.

Schelling, T.C. The strategy of conflict: Prospectus for a re-orientation of game theory. *Journal of Conflict Resolution,* 1958, **2,** 203–264.

Von Neumann,I.,& Morgenstern, O. *Theory of games and economic behavior.* Princeton N.J.: Princeton University Press, 1947.

Chapter 2

DETERMINANTS AND CONSEQUENCES OF TOUGHNESS

Otomar J. Bartos

Is it possible to predict whether a negotiator will be tough or soft from such background factors as his race, sex, age, and personality? Or must we forego such prediction because the determinants are to be found only within the context of the negotiation situation itself? Irrespective of what the determinants of toughness may be, what are its consequences? In particular, is toughness a good strategy in the sense that a tough negotiator is more likely to get a high payoff than is a soft negotiator? The present chapter is addressed to these questions.

I. PRELIMINARY CONSIDERATIONS

The main source from which we shall attempt to arrive at the answers to the above questions will be the data gathered in a large numbers of experiments.

However, before describing these experiments, we should provide some justification for their design.

A. The Essence of Negotiation

It goes without saying that, in order to be able to deal with negotiation either conceptually or experimentally, we must simplify it. More accurately, we must address ourselves to a relatively simple process that hopefully, resembles real life negotiations well enough to permit application of the conclusions to the real world. In other words, the simplified version must preserve the "essential" aspects of negotiation.

In a sense, to start a discussion of negotiation by defining its essential features is like putting the cart before the horse: Such a definition should be the result of the discussion, not its beginning. But then, a discussion of this nature cannot start without having such a definition, either. Hence, we will state what we view as essential and wait to see whether subsequent findings and deliberations will support this view.

Negotiation is basically a process whereby positions that are originally highly divergent become identical. Or, if you wish, it is a process whereby parties who disagree to start with reach an agreement.

This much will perhaps be accepted by most readers. But our view of what is essential to negotiation goes further that that: It is impossible to have what one usually calls "negotiation" without having a certain degree of ignorance. The give-and-take, whereby the originally divergent positions are brought closer, is possible only if each participant is *at least partially ignorant of his opponent's true interests.*

The argument is as follows: A typical negotiation process starts with demands that are unfairly high and then proceeds toward a settlement that is fair to everybody. But what exactly is the status of these "fair" demands? Why would one go through the lengthy haggling if, at the very beginning of the negotiation, (1) everybody agreed what it means to be fair, and (2) it were possible to apply this commonly accepted norm of equality to the dispute and determine a settlement?

In our view, it is possible to assume that everybody who participates in a negotiation is willing to accept the norm of equality. The settlement is fair, if it gives everybody *equal* payoff. What creates the problems and leads to lengthy bargaining is the fact that this norm cannot be applied at the beginning of the negotiation because, typically, the negotiators do not know their opponent's true interests. And, given this ignorance, they cannot determine the settlement which gives everybody an equal amount.

It may seem that insistence that equality is *the* norm of negotiation is culture-bound at best, quite wrong at worst. But some of these objections will disappear when we agree that the "interests" (payoffs) cover *all* aspects of the negotiation situation. Inversely, in a situation in which the payoffs are clearly defined, all considerations other than these payoffs must be viewed as irrelevant.

This point is of particular interest to anybody who wishes to design experiments that simulate the negotiation process. Suppose that subjects are told to consider an agenda on which each proposal has a definite payoff for each participant, and that the only things to be considered are these payoffs. Then all subjects are given the entire payoff matrix. What will happen?

If there is a proposal that gives equal payoff to everybody, what arguments can any participant advance against the acceptance of that proposal? How can he possibly argue that he should receive more than his opponent? He clearly cannot argue that he should receive more because he is poorer, stronger, or more "deserving," for such an argument draws upon considerations other than the payoffs themselves and is, therefore, (by definition) irrelevant. Thus, we should expect that, in such experiments, the equal payoff agreement will be arrived at whenever it is objectively possible. Furthermore, such a negotiation session would be very short, since there would be very little to discuss. The results of experiments by Siegel and Fouraker (1960) are quite instructive in this respect.

Contrast that situation with one which is identical in all respects except that each negotiator is ignorant of his opponent's payoffs. In this case, there is a lot to talk about, precisely because the norm of equality cannot be applied and hence it is not clear which settlement is fair. The negotiation may seem to be concerned only with the selection of the fairest settlement; in fact, however, it involves at least two considerations.

In the first place, we can expect that each participant will want to find out as much about his opponent's payoffs as he possibly can, because such knowledge will make it possible for him to judge what is fair and what is not. It should be recognized that the search for fairness is not idle curiosity: Without the "pressure" of such a supraindividual concept as "fairness," the negotiator would find it difficult to make the concessions that are needed if an agreement is to be reached.

Second, one can expect that a negotiator will take advantage of the fact that his opponent is ignorant of his payoffs. If he misrepresents his own interests by "understating" them, that is, if he claims that he is *less* interested in a proposal than he actually is, he can hope to secure for himself an agreement which is factually to his advantage, although it would appear to be fair to his opponent.

It is perhaps clear by now that the ignorance mentioned earlier is the very thing that gives negotiation its special character. It permits the participants to pursue and be influenced by two different and often conflicting considerations:

(1) Each negotiator can pursue his *individual* ("selfish") goal of defending

his own interests. He can do this by understating his interests.

(2) The two opponents together can pursue their common *group* interests by trying to apply the norm of equality. This they can do in spite of the fact that each of them may be misrepresenting their own interests, if they (a) apply the norm of equality to the declared interests as if these were true interests; if no solution exists for those interests, they can (b) apply the norm of equality to concession-making (redefinition of interests) by insisting on reciprocation.

B. Main Variables of Negotiation

Given the view of negotiation as a sequence of ever decreasing demands, it is possible to study such sequences empirically by distinguishing those that involve generally high demands from those involving generally low demands. In analyzing the experiments to be described shortly, the mean of all the individual demands made by a subject during the experiment (the mean demand) is used as the measure of "toughness." If this mean is high, he will be called a "tough" negotiator; if it is low, he will be called "soft." Hence, a "tough" negotiator will be the one who starts with a high demand and makes concessions only hesitantly, if at all. "Toughness," then, is a variable that describes the *process* of negotiation. Since one should, however, have a separate way of describing the manner in which this process *ends*, we shall use two related but conceptually distinct variables of "agreement" and "final payoff."

To start with, the most basic observation we can make about the outcome of a negotiation concerns its success or failure: Did the negotiators succeed in reaching an agreement? But we may wish to know more than whether the negotiation was successful. For the cases that did end in an agreement, one may wish to know how well each participant did. Since in all the experiments to be discussed every possible agreement had a unique payoff for each participant, we can use that payoff to evaluate the "goodness" of the agreement for each subject. We shall call this payoff the "final payoff" of the negotiator.

So far, we have discussed "agreement" and "final payoff" as two variables of the outcome. It will also be necessary to have a *single* measure that evaluates all the possible outcomes, including that of failure to reach an agreement to determine whether toughness was a good strategy in *all* cases, not only in those that ended in an agreement. For this reason, a zero payoff was assigned to the outcome "no agreement" (i.e., when the negotiators failed to reach an agreement, each of them received a zero payoff). Given this convention, the "final payoff" is a measure that includes all possible outcomes, not only those of successful negotiations. The question "Is toughness a good strategy?" becomes the empirically answerable question "Do the tough negotiators tend to make a higher final payoff than the soft ones?"

II. EXPERIMENTS

Our experiments in negotiation were first conducted in 1960 at the University of Hawaii. Since then, we have gathered a large amount of data in experiments that involved a great variation of design, each variation created to test a specific hypothesis. The most drastic variations, however, had to do with the amount and kind of communication that was permitted among the subjects.

A. Spoken Experiments

The design developed originally served as the basis for all subsequent experiments. The basic design will be referred to as the "spoken" design, since in it the subjects were permitted to say almost anything they wished. In one version of this design, five subjects were asked to play the roles of heads of state: Kennedy, Khrushchev, MacMillian, Mao Tse-Tung, and De Gaulle. Presumably, these five dignitaries were participating at a Summit Meeting to consider a five-point agenda: total disarmament, ban on nuclear testing, establishment of a United Nations police force, establishment of internationally located inspection stations, and destruction of nuclear stockpiles. Each of the five proposals had a definite payoff for each of the five participants. The payoff matrix used in one set of experiments is displayed in Table I.

TABLE I
*One of the Payoff Matrices Used in
Spoken Experiments*

	China	Soviet Union	Great Britain	United States	France[a]
1. Disarmament	−$ .50	$3.50	−$ .50	−$ .50	$ .50
2. Nuclear test ban	−$ .50	$2.50	$3.50	−$ .50	$ .50
3. UN police	−$1.50	−$1.50	$2.50	$3.50	$ .50
4. Inspection stations	−$3.00	−$ .50	$ .50	$2.50	$ .50
5. Destruction of nuclear stockpiles	$3.50	−$ .50	−$1.50	−$1.50	$ .50

[a]France was a "mediator"; hence her payoff depended on the time of agreement, not on the type of agreement.

Before coming to the actual experiment, each subject was given a dossier containing the agenda of the meeting, a list of his own payoffs, and a number of arguments which he could use to defend the interests of his nation (as represented by his payoffs). In some experiments the role was assigned so that a subject's private beliefs coincided with the interests (payoffs) of the nation he was asked to defend.

Several points about the design should be emphasized. In the first place the subject *never knew the payoffs of his opponents.* He was not shown their payoffs in his dossier nor could he learn them during the negotiation itself, since all participants were forbidden to reveal their own payoffs. Second, the subjects were required to reach a unanimous agreement. This agreement could encompass any one of the five proposals, or it could involve a "package deal" consisting of two or more of the five proposals. The payoff from a package deal was the *sum* of the payoffs from the individual proposals. As a result, the subjects using Table I could reach a total of 31 distinct agreements, as shown in Table II.

TABLE II
*All 31 Agreements That Can Be Reached from the
Payoff Matrix of Table I*

Package Deal[a]	China	USSR	G. Britain	USA	France
1	−$ .50	$3.50	−$ .50	−$ .50	$.50
2	− .50	2.50	3.50	− .50	.50
3	−1.50	−1.50	2.50	3.50	.50
4	−3.00	− .50	.50	2.50	.50
5	3.50	− .50	−1.50	−1.50	.50
1,2	−1.00	6.00	3.00	−1.00	.50
1,3	−2.00	2.00	2.00	3.00	.50
1,4	−3.50	3.00	.00	2.00	.50
1,5	3.00	3.00	−2.00	−2.00	.50
2,3	−2.00	1.00	6.00	3.50	.50
2,4	−3.50	2.00	4.00	2.00	.50
2,5	3.00	2.00	2.00	−2.00	.50
3,4	−4.50	2.00	3.00	6.00	.50
3,5	2.00	−2.00	1.00	2.00	.50
4,5	.50	−1.00	−1.00	1.00	.50
1,2,3	−2.50	4.50	5.50	2.50	.50
1,2,4	−4.00	5.50	3.50	1.50	.50
1,2,5	2.50	5.50	1.50	−2.50	.50
1,3,4	−5.00	1.50	2.50	5.50	.50
1,3,5	1.00	1.50	.50	1.50	.50
1,4,5	.00	2.50	−1.50	.50	.50
2,3,4	−5.00	.50	6.50	5.50	.50
2,3,5	1.00	.50	4.50	1.50	.50
2,4,5	0.00	1.50	2.50	.50	.50
3,4,5	−1.00	−2.50	1.50	4.50	.50
1,2,3,4	−5.50	4.00	6.00	5.00	.50
1,2,3,5	1.00	4.00	4.00	1.00	.50

TABLE II (Continued)

*All 31 Agreements That Can Be Reached from the
Payoff Matrix of Table I*

Package Deal[a]	China	USSR	G. Britain	USA	France
1,2,4,5	−1.50	5.00	2.00	.00	.50
1,3,4,5	−2.50	1.00	1.00	4.00	.50
2,3,4,5	−1.50	.00	5.00	4.00	.50
1,2,3,4,5	−2.00	3.50	4.50	6.50	.50

[a]The numbers in the column "Package Deal" indicate which proposals are included. For example, "2,4,5" indicate that proposals 2, 4, and 5 are included in that package deal.

The experiment ended if either a unanimous agreement was reached or a deadline arrived at. In the spoken experiments, the subjects had two hours to reach an agreement. If the deadline arrived and a unanimous agreement was not reached, everybody received a payoff of zero. If a unanimous agreement was reached, the subjects were paid, each payoff corresponding to that agreement (as given by a row of Table II).

The actual negotiation proceeded in a prearranged manner, the subjects speaking in the order in which they were seated. If a subject had nothing new to say, he reiterated briefly his last point. The speaker was required, however, to end his speech by stating clearly which proposal or proposals he advocated "now." The name "spoken" experiments was given to this design because the speaker was free to say whatever he wished, as long as he (1) ended by endorsing some proposals and (2) did not reveal what his payoffs were.

B. Abstract Experiments

The so-called "abstract" experiments were designed to overcome some of the problems encountered when using the spoken design. Foremost among these was the tendency on the part of the subjects to forego argument in favor of the proposals they were endorsing and simply stating what these proposals were. Their reason was the feeling that verbal arguments were a waste of time. What really mattered, they felt, was the payoff associated with a given proposal, not the lofty arguments used to defend it. The abstract experiments accommodated this tendency of the subjects by asking them to limit themselves to simple endorsement of a proposal. Consequently, the "speeches" in the abstract experiments were of the "I endorse proposal 5" variety. Since the speeches were so severely limited in content, it was unnecessary to give to the proposals any real life meaning, and hence they became identified merely through abstract numbers: proposal 1, proposal 2, and so on. For the same reasons, the subjects did not play any real life roles; instead they were identified by fictitious names such as "Algo" or "Erga." Finally, since the proposals had no real life content, it was unnecessary to distinguish between proposals and package deals consisting of several proposals. The subjects were negotiating on the basis of matrices such as given in Table II rather than Table I. Each of the 31 possible agreements of Table II was termed "a proposal." Consequently, the subjects were required to reach an agreement on one and only one of the 31 newly-defined proposals.

In all other respects, the abstract experiments were the same as the spoken experiments: The subject always knew only his own payoffs, the speeches were delivered in a fixed order, and a unanimous agreement was required and had to be reached before a definite (one hour) deadline. In spite of the similarities, the abstract design produced negotiations which appeared to be materially different from those in real life. In particular, we felt that the brevity of the "speeches" and the fact that negotiation went on to its conclusion without interruption meant that the subjects had very little time to reflect. In a sense, the abstract design tended to "devaluate" a speech: What could be accomplished by a single speech in real life had to be done through a series of speeches in the experiments—often through repeating the same endorsement. The so-called "team" experiments were designed to overcome these shortcomings.

C. Team Experiments

The basic design of the "team" experiments was the same as that of the spoken experiments—a number of negotiators played realistic roles, discussing a realistic agenda of five proposals. The fundamental difference, however, was that in the team experiments a negotiation was broken up into segments. After each negotiator delivered three speeches, the session was recessed and each negotiator was given a chance to reconsider his strategy in the privacy of a caucus room. To enhance the realism further, each party consisted of a two-man team. The members of a team took turns in representing their nation, and they discussed the matters of strategy together in their caucus room. Since this design had considerable space requirements, only two-team experiments have been conducted so far. The final important difference is that the deadline was defined with respect to the number of speeches delivered rather than with respect to time. After each team had met four times (each delivering three speeches during the meeting), the two teams met for the last time. Any order of speaking was permitted during this last meeting, but a three-minute deadline was imposed. If no agreement was reached within the three minutes, everybody received zero payoff.

The three basic designs—spoken, abstract, and team—were utilized with a number of variations. In some experiments, the number of negotiators was varied; in others, some of the negotiators were "confederates" who were instructed how to negotiate. And, of course, many different payoff matrices were used in the experiments. Thus, the data to be reported came from a great variety of experimental conditions. We shall refer to these variations whenever appropriate.

III. FINDINGS

The experiments just described were conducted over a period of about seven years, and hence a considerable amount and variety of data have been gathered. This chapter will be limited to the determinants and consequences of "toughness." (A more detailed account of this research is found in Bartos, 1970.)

A. Size of the Correlations

Table III shows the influence upon toughness of various social factors, ranging from the "distant" social factors such as age and sex to such "close" factors as performance in the previous experiment. It should be explained that, since a large number of different payoff matrices was used, each variable was "standardized" into z-scores. In this way, the variation due to different payoff structure was minimized and all data could be pooled to obtain correlations based on a large number of cases.

TABLE III

Correlates of Toughness: Zero-Order Correlations

Independent variables	Toughness in:			
	Abstract experiment	Spoken experiment	Team experiment	All experiments
1. Own age	−.03	−.10	−.12	−.06
2. Own sex (male)	−.05	.04	.13	.06
3. Own race (Caucasian)	−.05	−.09	−.37[a]	−.09[a]
4. Own personality (adjusted)	−.05	−.08	−.22	−.08[a]
5. Opponent's age	−.02	−.09	−.01	−.04
6. Opponent's sex (male)	−.06	−.07	−.19	−.08[a]
7. Opponent's race (Caucasian)	−.07	−.10	.12	−.06
8. Opponent's personality (adjusted)	−.06	−.18[a]	.05	−.09[a]
9. Opponent's toughness	−.04	−.11	−.32[a]	−.09[a]
10. Own toughness at $t-1$[b]	.20[a]	.19[a]	.47[a]	.22[a]

TABLE III (Continued)
Correlates of Toughness: Zero-Order Correlations

Independent variables	Toughness In:			
	Abstract experiment	Spoken experiment	Team experiment	All experiments
11. Own payoff at $t-1$	.04	$.12^a$	.37	.09
12. Duration at $t-1$	.04	.08	.17	.07
13. Agreement at $t-1$	.03	−.04	e	.01
14. Own toughness at $t-2^c$	.20	−.28	−	.11
15. Own payoff at $t-2$	.10	−.30	−	.02
16. Duration at $t-2$	.06	.06	−	.06
17. Agreement at $t-2$	.07	−.11	−	.03
Number of cases^d	465	239	80	784

[a]Significant beyond the .05 level.

[b]Variables 10−13 are defined one experiment after the experiment in which toughness is defined. Abstract experiments for these variables involve 272 cases, spoken 156, and team 40.

[c]Variables 14 to 17 are defined two experiments after the experiment in which toughness is defined. Abstract experiments for these variables involve 122 cases, spoken 31 cases.

[d]Number of cases is the number of subjects (or teams) multiplied by the number of times each subject (team) participated in an experiment.

[e]All team experiments ended in an agreement.

For all experiments combined (784 cases), most correlations are below .10, whereas many of the coefficients for the team experiments (80 cases) were .20 and above. But, of course, we must not be misled by the low size of the correlations into dismissing the findings altogether. Even though the relationships shown in Table III are quite weak, as long as they are significant beyond the .05 level (shown by a in the table), we may be reasonably confident that they exist.

But there is another factor to consider than the size of the correlation and its statistical significance. Many of the relationships in the table have the same sign for all three types of experiments. This is just as important as the mere size of the coefficient, because the three types of experiments differ quite profoundly in the type of experience they offer to the subject. In an abstract experiment, the subject behaves not unlike a machine that plays the odds. He does not really communicate with his opponents; he merely hurls at them repetitious demands at a fast rate, trying to wear them down by sheer repetition. In a spoken experiment, he can reason with them, trying to change their minds as he goes along. In a team experiment, he is bound by the strategic decisions which he and his teammate made in their last caucus. If a relationship between a background factor and toughness survives that wide variation in experimental conditions, there must be something rather basic about it.

Finally, it should be remembered that, within each of the three major experimental categories (abstract, spoken, and team) there was considerable variation as well. Some experiments involved only two subjects, others as many as five. In some experiments there were "stooges" who were instructed how to behave. In some experiments, the subjects were given information about the background of their opponents; in others they were exposed to pressures to change their beliefs about the nature of negotiation. In still others, the subjects were asked to estimate the payoffs of their opponents, and thus were distracted from their main job of bargaining. Each experimental variation had a specific research objective of its own, although for the purposes of the present chapter all the data have been combined.

B. Influences Shaping Toughness

Having said all that, let us look at the data of Table III. The most important finding has to do with the impact of own previous toughness: *The subject who was tough in the last experiment tended to be also tough in the next.* This is indicated by the coefficients of .20, .19, and .47 for the abstract, spoken, and team experiments in the tenth row of the table. All of these correlations are significant well beyond the .05 level.

Let us use this finding as a basic fact, and try to interpret the rest in its light. In the first place, the correlation between the amount of experience and toughness is not significant. In other words, as a subject participated in more and more experiments (3 experiments per subject being the average), he grew neither tougher nor softer. Passage of time in bargaining situations per se thus does not seem to alter his negotiation style. (Graphic representations of the relationship between experience and toughness do not suggest any simple curvilinear relationship either.) What does make a difference is not the amount of experience, but the *type* of experience, e.g., having been tough earlier and—as is suggested in row 11—having received a high payoff. Those who were tough and those who received high payoff tended to continue being tough.

This being the case, we must ask the following question: If those who start tough continue being tough, what determines that original level of toughness? Conceptually, there can be four categories of factors:

(1) Conditions that shaped the negotiator's behavior *before* he started negotiating. These are the factors that are revealed by variables such as his age, sex, racial background, and personality.

(2) The impression the negotiator gains of his opponents at the beginning of a session, and, hence, the expectations he has concerning their toughness. Such impressions could be conveyed by such more or less visible features of the

opponent as his age, sex, rate, and perhaps even less visible characteristics such as his personality.

(3) The impression the negotiator gains of his opponent *during* the session. This impression may be formed by opponent's willingness to compromise or by his refusal to do so. In other words, the degree to which the opponent is actually tough may further modify or stabilize the expectations he has about his opponent.

(4) Pure chance. It is conceivable that, whether or not the negotiator becomes tough depends on whimsical factors that cannot be captured by our systematic analysis. For example, a subject might have misunderstood our instructions and thought that we wanted him to be tough, i.e., wanted him not to make any concessions. By the time he found out his mistake, he also found that toughness is rewarding [leads to high payoff (see Table IV)] and hence stuck with that particular style.

Let us consider the first three of these four categories. To start with, *a priori* factors seem to play a very modest role, but for some of them this role is the same in all three types of experiments. The correlations in Table III indicate that the *tough* subjects tended to be

   (a) Male
   (b) Young
   (c) Noncaucasian (students of Oriental ancestry)
   (d) "Poorly adjusted"[1]

It is difficult to go much beyond the mere fact of recording these slight but consistent tendencies among the subjects, although one interpretation does seem to fit the findings reasonably well.

This interpretation has as its point of departure the assumption that the "adjustment" tapped by our measure of personality is the adjustment to the *cooperative aspects of American culture.* This interpretation is supported by the additional analysis of the data which shows that American Caucasians and older subjects tend to be better "adjusted" than their opposites ($r = .19$ and $.11$, respectively, $N = 223$). It certainly seems reasonable to assume that Caucasian Americans have internalized the cooperativeness of American culture better than

---

[1]The personality measure was the California Personality Inventory (CPI), our scoring of which was somewhat unorthodox. Although normally the questionnaire yields 18 separate scales, we averaged all these scales into a single score. The justification for doing so was the statement by the author of the CPI: "If nearly all scores are above the mean standard score line, the probabilities are that the person is one who is *functioning effectively* both socially and intellectually. Conversely, if most scores are below the mean, the chances are good that the individual is experiencing significant *difficulties in his interpersonal adjustment* (Gough, 1960, p. 15)." (Italics added.) The assumption, therefore, that those whose mean score on the CPI is high tend to be better adjusted than those whose mean score is low, seemed justified.

Americans of Oriental background, and that the older subjects had more time to be acculturized than the young. [For further discussion of this point see Bartos (1967b).] One can thus account for the slight tendency of the Caucasians, older subjects, and those who are "adjusted" to be soft negotiators in the experiments on purely cultural grounds.

To summarize what Table III suggests about the influence of the first impressions, a negotiator tends to be tough *against women*. This correlation is the only one that is both sufficiently high and consistent for all three types of experiments. And its meaning seems to be rather clear. In American society, woman is expected to play a submissive role.

Turning to the manner in which the *a priori* influences are modified by the negotiation process itself, the data indicate that *toughness tends to generate softness, softness to generate toughness*. This is indicated by the fact that the correlations between a negotiator's toughness and that of his opponent is negative: $-.04$ for the abstract experiments; $-.11$ for the spoken; and $-.32$ for the teams. This tends to suggest that the norm of equality (reciprocity) was relatively weak. By and large, the subjects tended to be soft as a result of pressure (when the opponent was tough), not as a result of the opponent's conciliatory attitude (his softness).[2]

There is, however, a tendency for *subjects to reciprocate concessions* (see Table IV). As is suggested by the captions of the table, these data were gathered by counting the number of times a negotiator made a concession (lowered his demand) immediately after his opponent(s) made one. It can be seen that the data are based on a very large number of "rounds" (a round being a set of *n* consecutive speeches of which "our" negotiator's is the last, *n* being the number of participants), a total of over 100,000. In the abstract and spoken experiments, a subject was more likely to make a concession after his opponent(s) made one than when he (they) failed to make one.

There is, of course, one exception to this tendency to reciprocate: the team experiments. There is practically no difference between the proportion of those who responded to a concession by making a concession (.51) and those who responded by not making one (.52). It should be recalled that the subject participating in a team experiment was not free to respond as he wished, that he had to say for three consecutive speeches what he and his colleague agreed upon in their last caucus. (Recall that all team experiments alternated between a caucus in which each team separately decided on their strategy and an actual

---

[2]Data not published here suggest that the correlation for the abstract experiments is a a low $-.04$ mainly because most of the abstract experiments involved 5 participants. This large number of opponents seemed to make it difficult for a participant to react to their toughness as a whole. For the 46 cases that involved two-man abstract experiments, the correlation between own and opponent's toughness is a significant $-.71$.

joint session which involved three speeches from each team representative. After the third speeches, a new caucus was called to set new strategy.) Hence a subject typically could not reciprocate even if he had wanted to. But, while reciprocation was difficult—perhaps impossible—as an "immediate" reaction to a speech, it was still possible as a "delayed" reaction to a block of three speeches. After listening to the speeches delivered during the opening part of the negotiation, a team could not decide, during its private caucus, to reciprocate. Unfortunately, our data do not show this "delayed" caucus-to-caucus relationship; they show only the "immediate" speech-to-speech relationship.

TABLE IV

Impact of Opponent's Concession-Making

| Type of experiment | Behavior in round r-1 | Behavior in round r | | N^a |
		Negotiator concedes	Negotiator does not concede	
Abstract experiments	Opponents concede[b]	.28	.72	65,214
	Opponents · do not concede[c]	.22	.78	38,150
Spoken experiments	Opponents concede[b]	.30	.70	4688
	Opponents do not concede[c]	.24	.76	3702
Team experiments	Opponents concede[b]	.51	.49	842
	Opponents do not concede[c]	.52	.48	796
All experiments	Opponents concede[b]	.28	.72	70,744
	Opponents do not concede[c]	.22	.78	42,646

[a] N stands for the number of rounds.
[b] At least one opponent concedes.
[c] None of the opponents concedes.

How does this tendency for subjects in the abstract and spoken experiments to reciprocate concessions square with the earlier finding that toughness produces softness? *That* finding shows the exact opposite (i.e., lack of reciprocation). There seems to be only one logical explanation of this seeming paradox: While the fact of a concession was reciprocated, the *size* of a concession was not. To put it differently, the data suggest that, by and large, subjects tended to make a concession when the opponent made one. But there was a difference between those who ended up being tough (with a high mean demand) and those who ended up being soft (with a low mean demand) in that *the tough negotiators tended to make smaller concessions,* trading a chicken for a cow, so to speak.

This, of course, is perfectly consistent with the view that the negotiation process has a dual nature. It seems that the negotiators were fair where unfairness would have been obvious, were aggressively pursuing their own (unfair) advantage where this fact was hidden from their opponents. The point is that, even in these experiments, it was difficult for a subject to pretend that he was making a concession when, in fact, he was not. Certainly, the very least he had to do was change his stand in order to be believed at all. It is true that he could change his position by actually upping his demands while claiming that he was lowering them; this was hard to put over on his opponents, since they usually knew approximately his preference ranking. In the spoken and the team experiments, ranking was known because the proposals were realistic items such as nuclear disarmaments, and the payoffs assigned to, say, China were again a realistic representation of China's position. In the abstract experiments, the negotiations were sufficiently long to permit each player to get an idea (from previous patterns of endorsement) what the opponent's preference ranking was like. On the other hand, the subjects had no way of knowing the *intervals* of this preference ranking, since nobody was allowed to give out the exact amount of payoff associated for him with a proposal. Thus, it was quite easy to pretend that the concession a negotiator made was larger than it actually was.

C. Influences Shaping Final Payoff

Figure 1 gives the relationship between toughness and (1) the probability that no agreement will be reached; (2) the probability that a subject will receive high payoff *if the group reaches an agreement;* and (3) the probability that a subject will receive a high payoff (whether or not an agreement was reached).

The third relationship (indicated by a solid line in Fig. 1) is the relationship that determines whether toughness was a good strategy. The first two relationships (indicated by broken lines in the figure) help us to understand why toughness is or is not a good strategy.

Referring to Fig. 1, note that there is a general tendency for high payoff to be associated with toughness. The tougher a subject was,[3] the more likely he was to receive high payoff.[4] This visual conclusion can be verified from the correlation between toughness and final payoff (see Table V) which is, for all experiments, a significant .20. But Fig. 1 suggests what is not obvious from the coefficient of correlation. As we move from average toughness to moderate and then to extreme toughness, the probability of high payoff does *not* change. In fact, Fig. 1 suggests that it is not so much that toughness was a good strategy, rather, it seems that *softness was a bad strategy!*

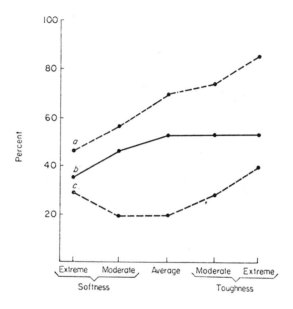

FIG. 1. Relationship between toughness and final outcome, all experiments. Curve *a*: percent with high final payoff (groups reaching an agreement); curve *b*: percent with high final payoff (all groups); curve *c*: percent not reaching an agreement.

The relationship between toughness and final payoff in experiments that reached an agreement (the top broken curve) does not help to explain this finding. But the relationship between toughness and probability of agreement does. The graph (from average toughness to extreme softness) indicates that *softness actually hindered the progress toward an agreement.* A negotiator who

---

[3]A subject was classified as "extremely tough" if his mean demand was more than one standard deviation above the grand mean. He was classified as "moderately tough" if his mean demand was more than .3 but less than 1 standard deviation above the grand mean and so forth.

[4]A subject was said to receive "high payoff" if his payoff was higher than the mean payoff received by those playing his role.

was extremely soft was actually more likely to end without an agreement than a negotiator who was moderately soft or "average."

Returning to the simpler linear relationship of the positive correlation between toughness and final payoff, recall that the data shown in Table III indicated that the characteristics predisposing toward toughness were being male, young, of Oriental ancestry, poorly adjusted, and having a female for an opponent. Since toughness is positively correlated with final payoff, we would expect these very same characteristics to predispose one to make high final payoff.

Inspection of Table V shows that only two of these five predictions are supported and even then only weakly. Men and subjects of Oriental ancestry tend to make a higher payoff than women and Caucasians, respectively, but no clear tendency is found for the young, the poorly adjusted, and those with female opponents to make high payoff.

TABLE V

Correlates of Final Payoff: Zero-Order Correlations

Independent variables	Final payoff in:			
	Abstract experiment	Spoken experiment	Team experiment	All experiments
1. Own age	.05	−.01	−.02	.03
2. Own sex (male)	.03	.09	.14	.06
3. Own race (Caucasian)	−.04	−.01	−.15	−.05
4. Own personality (adjusted)	−.04	.12^a	.08	.00
5. Opponent's age	.11^a	.09	.02	.10^a
6. Opponent's sex (male)	−.08	.03	−.24^a	−.06
7. Opponent's race (Caucasian)	−.03	.07	.24^a	.01
8. Opponent's personality (adjusted)	.08	.21^a	.23^a	.13^a
9. Opponent's toughness	−.28^a	−.26^a	−.52^a	−.30^a
10. Own toughness at t	.20^a	.07	.58^a	.20^a
11. Own toughness at $t-1$^{b}	−.01	−.03	.53^a	.03
12. Own toughness at $t-2$	−.02	−.12	−	−.04
13. Own payoff at $t-1$	.01	−.09	.52^a	.01
14. Own payoff at $t-2$	.00	−.23^a	−	−.01
15. Agreement at $t-1$	.00	−.01	−	−.00
16. Agreement at $t-2$	.10	−.07	−	.07
17. Duration at $t-1$	.04	−.06	−.08	−.00
18. Duration at $t-2$	−.08	−.05	−	−.07
Number of Cases	465	239	80	784

^{a}Significant beyond the .05 level.

^{b}Variables 11–18 are defined prior to the dependent variables. They involve fewer cases than indicated in the last row of the table.

What is the reason for this failure to predict? To some extent, undoubtedly, it is due to the weakness of the relationships between background and toughness. On the other hand, however, it should be noted that final payoff is influenced by different aspects of the negotiation situation than is toughness. The final payoff depends on the *opponent* and his behavior. Notice that the correlations between opponent's age, personality, and his actual toughness, on the one hand, and final payoff, on the other (Table V), is much stronger than the correlation between these variables and toughness (Table III). In other words, a negotiator was likely to receive a high payoff if he had (a) an older opponent, (b) a well-adjusted opponent, and (c) a soft opponent.

However, in general, toughness leads to the failure of the negotiation (see Table VI). Subjects who were poorly adjusted and were tough as well as those who had poorly adjusted and/or tough opponents were likely to fail in their search for agreement. Thus, the very factors that make for high final payoff also mitigate against it, lending support to the conclusions based on Fig. 1. Toughness plays a dual role and has contradictory consequences. On one hand, toughness *decreases* the likelihood of an agreement, while on the other hand, it *increases* the payoff of those who survive this possibility of a failure.

TABLE VI

Correlates of Agreement: Zero-Order Correlations

Independent variables	Percent reaching agreement in:			
	Abstract experiment	Spoken experiment	Team experiment	All experiments
1. Own age	.05	−.01	b	.03
2. Own sex (male)	.00	.05	−	.02
3. Own race (Caucasian)	.00	.01	−	.01
4. Own personality (adjusted)	.06	.13[a]	−	.09[a]
5. Opponent's age	.07	.04	−	.06
6. Opponent's sex (male)	−.04	.06	−	−.01
7. Opponent's race (Caucasian)	.00	−.06	−	−.02
8. Opponent's personality (adjusted)	.10[a]	.13[a]	−	.11[a]
9. Opponent's toughness	−.22[a]	−.20[a]	−	−.21[a]
10. Own toughness at t^c	−.18[a]	−.11	−	−.16[a]
Number of cases	465	239	0	704

[a] Significant beyond the .05 level.

[b] All team experiments reached an agreement.

[c] Meaning: toughness in the same session in which probability of agreement is assessed.

The final question has to do with spuriousness: How many of the relationships discussed in the present chapter are spurious in the sense of being a result of some other factors? In order to answer this question, *partial* coefficients of correlation were computed between each of the background variables and final payoff. More specifically, each one of the 12 independent variables was correlated with final payoff, controlling statistically for all remaining 11 variables. The results are given in Table VII.

TABLE VII

Correlates of Final Payoff: Partial Correlations; All Groups

Independent variables	Abstract experiment	Spoken experiment	Team experiment	All experiments
	Final payoff in:			
1. Own age	.06	.04	.06	.05
2. Own sex (male)	.01	.09	−.01	.02
3. Own race (Caucasian)	−.06	−.04	.13	−.03
4. Own personality (adjusted)	−.02	.00	.01	−.01
5. Opponent's age	.07	.09	−.10	.06
6. Opponent's sex (male)	−.07	.02	−.07	−.04
7. Opponent's race (Caucasian)	−.06	.01	−.04	−.03
8. Opponent's personality (adjusted)	.10^a	.09	.22^a	.11^a
9. Opponent's toughness	−.27^a	−.15^a	−.49^a	−.26^a
10. Own toughness at t	.22^a	.14^a	.51^a	.22^a
11. Own toughness at $t-1$[b]	−.03	−.07	.36^a	−.01
12. Own toughness at $t-2$	−.04	−.09	−	−.02
Multiple correlation R	.45^a	.49^a	.78^a	.50^a
Number of cases	465	239	80	784

[a]Significant beyond the .05 level.

[b]Variables 11 and 12 are defined prior to the dependent variable. They involve fewer cases than indicated in the last row of the table.

Comparison of these results with those of Table V discloses relatively few differences. The correlations that are low in Table V remain low in Table VII (or, on occasion, change their sign); the high correlations remain essentially unchanged. But since the partial correlations of Table VII are generally even lower than the total correlations of Table V, we see even more clearly the general conclusions that emerge from our analysis:

(1) The whole set of twelve independent variables is only a fair predictor of final payoff. As the multiple correlation of .50 shows, only about 25% of variation in final payoff is explained by the set.

(2) Of the variables that characterize the negotiator, the variable of "previous" toughness is by far the best predictor. The more "remote" social-background variables are relatively unimportant.

(3) The *opponent* plays an important role in determining a negotiator's

final payoff. Both his personality and his behavior count. If the opponent is well-adjusted and soft, the payoff of the negotiator tends to be high.

IV. DISCUSSION

Negotiations have a peculiarly dual nature and this duality presents considerable problems not only to the negotiator himself, but also to those who study his behavior; this is the main notion that runs throughout the discussion.

A. Dual Nature of Negotiation

Perhaps the most basic fact about negotiation is the tension between the individual and the group. In a typical negotiation, the two are juxtaposed with greater urgency than in most social situations. To negotiate *means* to pursue the twin (and usually contradictory) goals of maximizing one's own (individual) payoff and reaching an (group) agreement.

In order to build a foundation for a theory of negotiation, one should assume that a negotiator begins with a very tentative knowledge of his opponent's interests. To put it somewhat differently, negotiation should be viewed as a process through which *the various individual interests* (maximization of own payoff) *are gradually transformed into one group interest* (the agreement).

The beginning of a negotiation session is dominated by the individual interests in two respects: First, each negotiator typically starts by making "outrageous" demands (misrepresents his true interests most blatantly). Second, he does not know what a fair agreement would look like. In other words, at the beginning, the individual attempts to maximize own payoff are virtually unhampered by any norm of fairness.

While the typical opening speeches are expressions of unrestrained individualism, the closing sessions tend to be an exact opposite. They tend to emphasize the need to subordinate individual interests to the broader need for a fair agreement. That this shift occurs as a result of increase in information is the point to be emphasized. The longer the session lasts, the more definite do the beliefs about opponent's payoffs become. Whether or not these beliefs are factually correct is, in one sense, irrelevant. Once they exist, it becomes possible for the negotiators to start to apply the (group) concept of fairness; this is what matters.

B. Role of Beliefs

Although the above may describe a typical progress toward an agreement, we are not suggesting that all negotiations are exactly alike. They differ in at least two important respects: the extent to which the participants start with having *fixed* beliefs about their opponents; and the extent to which these beliefs are *correct*. Some negotiations—for example, some of the experiments described above—start without any beliefs whatsoever. Others, such as labor—management negotiations, start with a rather firm and accurate set of beliefs. Still others, such as international negotiations involving two nations meeting for the first time, fall somewhere in between.

This point is of both theoretical and practical importance. It is important theoretically because it enables us to predict whether a negotiation will be short or long, or whether it will occur at all. In general, we hypothesize that *the more fixed are the beliefs about the opponent's interests, the shorter will be the negotiation session.* This follows from the general supposition that (1) true bargaining is possible only when the participants have no firm beliefs about their opponent's interests, and (2) as soon as such beliefs are fixed, some norm of fairness can and will be applied to yield an agreement, thus terminating the bargaining.

We saw that toughness was a good strategy in our experiments, that those who were tough tended to receive a higher payoff than those who were soft (Table V). Furthermore, the main reason for this was the fact that toughness in the bargaining situation did *not* impede progress toward an agreement too seriously (Fig. 1).

A general hypothesis can be offered to account for this finding: *The more accurate are the negotiators' beliefs about their opponent's interests, the more likely is toughness to prevent an agreement.* Again this hypothesis follows from the general argument that if a negotiator has reasonably accurate beliefs about his opponent's payoffs, he is in a position to demand a fair agreement that gives everybody the same payoff. But a tough person is, by definition, one who demands more than is fair. And demanding more than is fair will be rejected by most men as soon as the unfairness of the demand is obvious.

Given this hypothesis, the finding that toughness is a good strategy can be placed in proper perspective. This generalization holds for negotiations that start without realistic beliefs about the opponent's payoffs. For negotiations which start with realistic beliefs, toughness is less advisable and may be even a definitively bad strategy.

It so happens that the findings lend some support to the above argument. In the abstract experiments, each subject started in a state of complete ignorance. In the spoken (and team) experiments he could guess at the general nature of his opponent's interests because the experiments involved realistic situations, such as given in Table I. When a small subset of the experiments is compared, one which involved 46 abstract experiments and 22 spoken experiments that were similar in several respects (notably in that they all involved only two participants), one finds that (1) all abstract experiments ended in an agreement while only 82% of the spoken did, and (2) the correlation between own toughness (mean demand) and own final payoff was .87 for the abstract experiments but only .05 for the spoken experiments. In other words, having some initial idea about the opponent's payoffs makes toughness less rewarding, since toughness (under these conditions) increases the probability that the negotiation will fail.

C. Consequences and Causes of Toughness

The preceding discussion regarding the consequences of toughness may be summarized as follows:

(1) An equal payoff agreement will be reached (a) if all the participants view equal payoff as fair; (b) if there exists an agreement that gives everybody equal payoff; (c) if everybody knows everybody's payoffs accurately and reliably, so that everybody can verify which agreement is fair.

(2) The more nearly conditions 1a–c are met, the more likely it becomes that insistence on an *unfair* agreement will lead to the failure to reach any agreement.

(3) Condition 1c is never met fully in real life. However, negotiations do differ with respect to the extent to which the participants have fixed beliefs about their opponent's payoffs and the extent to which such beliefs are accurate. It is not difficult to see that these assumptions suggest that toughness is a better strategy when the participants have only vague beliefs about their opponent's interests,[5] than when their beliefs are fixed and reasonably accurate.

When we review out findings concerning the causes of toughness such as sex, race, and age, we cannot help feeling somewhat dissatisfied. To be sure, the findings are fairly consistent in that they suggest that men, students of Oriental ancestry, the young, and the "poorly adjusted" tend to be tough. It is also true that a possible explanation for these findings is that the underlying factor may be conformity to American culture, and that women, older people, those of American ancestry, and the "well adjusted" simply are more likely to have internalized the fundamental cooperativeness of American culture than did their opposites. But why are these correlations between background and toughness so weak? How does one explain the fact that once a subject was tough, he was

---

[5]For a more detailed discussion of the reasons why this is so, see Bartos (1967a, pp. 261–265).

quite likely to be tough again in the subsequent experiments, when one is seemingly unable to account convincingly for the factors that started him on the road to toughness in the first place?

One could argue that the measures of background were inadequate. Perhaps a different measure of personality should have been used or different variables of background altogether. Perhaps, had more adequate measures been used, the correlations between background and toughness would have been larger. But we do not believe that this is the reason. For one thing, the results indicate that a rather simple instruction to the subjects is capable of completely reversing the relationship between background and toughness. When some of the subjects were told that their opponents were tough and others that they were soft, we found that the young people, the Orientals, the men, and the poorly adjusted tended to be *softer* than their opposites (see Bartos, 1967b). It seems, then, that the relationship between background and toughness is intrinsically a weak one, that this weakness is not a mere artifact due to a faulty design.

A different explanation seems preferable. A typical negotiator—and, in particular, an inexperienced negotiator such as the one who participated in our experiments—is caught between the "push" of his background and the "pull" of the strategic aspects of the negotiation situation itself. When nothing is said to emphasize the strategic dependence upon one's opponent, the "normal" push of the American culture is in the direction of cooperativeness. When this strategic aspect is made salient to the participants, this cultural influence may be destroyed.

Although we do not understand exactly how this happens, it seems that the net result of the push and pull of the various, and often contradictory, forces is more or less random. Some negotiators end up being tough, others soft. The ambiguity of the negotiation situation may be so great that the only thing that makes sense is personal consistency. And thus those who happened to be tough to start with, continue being tough thereafter.

D. Future Research

It is perhaps obvious that our understanding of the consequences of toughness is better than that of its causes. It might seem that this gap in our knowledge is none too disturbing, since quite often negotiations are studied because of a desire to know how one *should* behave, whether to be tough or soft. Once the consequences of toughness are known, this basic curiosity is satisfied, and we can afford not to know what causes toughness in the first place.

But, unfortunately, this optimism is ill-founded. It turns out that our knowledge of the consequences of toughness is much too general to give us guidance in any specific instance. While our discussion suggests that toughness is a better strategy when information about opponent's payoffs is lacking than when it is available, it does not specify just how tough one should be in any particular instance. And it turns out that the determination of the exact degree of toughness is predicated upon some idea about the opponent's toughness. In short, in order to decide how tough one should be, we must be able to predict how tough the opponent is going to be. And it is this type of know-how that we do not have.

Thus, although we seem to have no choice but to continue empirically examining the question of what causes toughness, we must also continue to make some theoretical sense out of the findings. In particular, it seems that we ought to continue providing explanations that use rationality as a crucial concept. Should we find that reciprocation yields the best results [there are some indications that this may indeed be the most effective strategy; see, for example, Solomon's discussion (1960) of the tit-for-tat strategy], we should be able to supply a theory that implies that softness is a better response to the strategy of reciprocation than is toughness. Only after we have been able to reconcile the empirical findings with a broader theory of human behavior can we claim to have made significant progress in the search to understand negotiation and make it an efficient means for solving social conflicts.

ACKNOWLEDGMENTS

Much of the work reported here was conducted under a grant from the Air Force Office of Scientific Research, AFOSR-62-314.

Most of the experimental work was conducted while the author was affiliated with the University of Hawaii. The cooperation of that University's Social Science Research Institute is gratefully acknowledged.

REFERENCES

Bartos, O.J. *Simple models of group behavior.* New York: Columbia University Press, 1967. (a)

Bartos, O.J. How predictable are negotiations? *Journal of Conflict Resolution,* 1967, **11,** 481–496. (b)

Bartos, O.J. *Negotiation under experimental conditions.* New York: Columbia University Press, 1970. (In press)

Gough, H.G. *California personality inventory.* Palo Alto, Calif.: Consulting Psychologists Press, 1960.

Siegel, S., & Fouraker, L.E. *Bargaining and group decision making.* New York: McGraw-Hill, 1960.

Solomon, L. The influence of some types of power relationships and game strategies upon the development of interpersonal trust. *Journal of Abnormal and Social Psychology,* 1960, **61,** 223–230.

Chapter 3

CONFLICT AND POWER

Bertram H. Raven and Arie W. Kruglanski

I. INTRODUCTION

It is our purpose in this chapter to examine the interrelationship between social power and social conflict, particularly in terms of the type and degree of power attempted or utilized. It will be our thesis that the intensification and resolution of conflict will be determined not only by the amount of power at the disposal of the antagonists, but also by the qualitative nature of power which is brought to bear on the situation. It will also follow that the amount and type of power utilized will vary with the intensity of the conflict and with interpersonal attributions.

Social conflict is defined as tension between two or more social entities (individuals, groups, or larger organizations) which arises from incompatibility of actual or desired responses. Thus, we can most readily see social conflict stemming from incompatibility in goals. Two persons who desire a common object which cannot be shared will be in conflict so long as either one or both do not redefine their goals. Competition is, then, one form of conflict. Such competitive conflict may be in respect to scarce resources, the friendship or love of a third person, status, power, or any of a number of other objectives, provided that sharing is not seen as possible.

Conflict can also arise from incompatibility with respect to means or subgoals (see Raven & Eachus, 1963; Thomas, 1957). It is not uncommon for persons in workgroups who are directed toward a common goal to have conflicts in coordinating their activities toward those goals. Two boys working together to build a radio receiver may have conflict if both need their one Phillips-head screwdriver at the same time. Or there may be disagreement as to the paths toward a goal—teachers in a school may all desire to improve education, but may disagree as to how this should be accomplished. Most research and discussions under the heading "conflict" have centered on incompatibility with respect to goals or competition for scarce resources. The greater part of this chapter also centers on goal conflict. Disagreement with respect to means, as we shall see, is ordinarily more readily resolved and leads to a lesser degree of continued tension (Rappoport, 1965). Indeed, we shall note that one strategy for the reduction of goal conflict is through the two parties' redefining the situation as one of means conflict with common ultimate goals.

A. Personal and Impersonal Bases of Conflict

The discussion of incompatibility of goals and responses thus far has centered on *impersonal* bases, that is, conflict which is not specific to the mutual evaluation of the two or more antagonists. We must not overlook, however, the *personal* bases of compatibility and incompatibility. Discussions of group cohesiveness and interpersonal attraction (e.g., Cartwright & Zander, 1968; Raven & Rietsema, 1957) point out that attraction of one person toward a social entity may arise from an interest in common goals or from desirable personal characteristics of that entity. Negative cohesiveness or repulsion may result from incompatibility in goals or from a dislike of the characteristics of the person involved. Similarly, conflict can arise from personal dislike, coupled with a conscious or unconscious desire on the part of one party to injure the other, which may in turn be countered by person-oriented retaliatory acts from the other party. Such *personal* social conflict can be seen as following logically from the general conceptualization in terms of incompatability of responses or goals; obviously, the subject of personal attack will attempt to defend himself if not to counterattack. Such a distinction between person-oriented and non-person-oriented conflict was presented in Simmel's early statement (1908) and further elaborated by Coser (1956) (cf. Fink's distinction between "object-centered" and "opponent-centered" conflict, 1968). Simmel also indicated that each of the two bases of conflict may affect the other. "It is *expedient* to hate the adversary with whom one fights, just as it is expedient to love a person whom one is tied to (Simmel, 1908, P. 34)." It is also true that development and emphasis of incompatible goals is more likely between two persons who have personal dislike or distrust for one another (Rapoport, 1965).

The reciprocal relationship between affective relationships and interdependence has also been observed by Heider (1958) in terms of his balance analysis. This is clearly illustrated in the classic field experiment by Sherif and Sherif (1953) in which initially friendly boys, separated into groups such that they were in competition with one another, developed high levels of hostility. The study further indicates that having developed hostility, objectively neutral bases of interdependence were interpreted in terms of competition and conflict, and potentially cooperative relationships were avoided. Only through persistent introduction of high degrees of mutual threat and clearly defined necessity of mutual cooperation could positive affective relationships be restored—and then with considerable resistance from the conflicting groups.

B. Manifest and Underlying Conflict

Deutsch (1969) makes an important distinction between "manifest" and "underlying" conflict. What we have described above as "impersonal" conflict closely parallels Deutsch's manifest conflict—it is the more obvious conflict, such as two children fighting to obtain possession of a favorite toy, or management and labor representatives quarreling over what is the appropriate wage scale. "Underlying" conflict includes the personally based conflict described above, but is actually much broader. The two children may actually be fighting because they do not like each other and the toy gives them a rational excuse for fighting, or the general desire for dominance over the other may be independent of the specific object. Other underlying bases for conflict may include general distrust of the motives of the other, a masochistic desire for punishment, a desire for the favors of a third party who dislikes the opponent, and a desire to overcome feelings of inferiority. Deutsch correctly points out that "manifest conflict often cannot be resolved more than temporarily unless the underlying conflict is dealt with or unless it can be disconnected and separated from the underlying conflict so that it can be treated in isolation (Deutsch, 1969, p. 10)."

It again follows that the manifest conflict in one situation can lead to underlying bases for conflict in another situation. After years of painful conflict for equal rights in employment, the black student brings to the school situation underlying bases for conflict stemming both from hostility toward the white power structure and from a desire to overcome feelings of powerlessness. Manifest bases for conflict may be there in actual inequities in education, but the possibilities for conflict are further increased as the result of underlying factors transferred from other situations.

II. POWER, INFLUENCE, AND CONFLICT

The simplest instance of conflict is the unidirectional influence situation as commonly described in the social psychological literature. One social entity, A, attempts to get another, B, to do something which is contrary to B's desires or tendencies. B's responses are contrary to A's desires and conflict exists either until B complies with A's requests or until A alters his desires. That is, *impersonal* conflict ceases with successful influence, though underlying bases of conflict may continue, or, indeed, even increase after B's compliance. It is, thus, of particular importance to understand the form of influence which is likely to reduce conflict, through compliance of B, but it also is of importance to consider the manner in which conflict is reduced, including the factors which are likely to lead to increased hostility, personal rejection of A by B, mutual distrust, and underlying bases for future conflict. A brief review of the bases of social power and influence, as proposed by French and Raven, 1959; French, 1956) and further discussed elsewhere (Collins & Raven, 1969; Raven, 1965), would thus be useful at this point. Social influence is defined as a change in one person which has its origin in another person or group. Power is then defined as potential influence. Six bases of social influence are discussed in French and Raven and the papers which followed: information, reference, expertise, legitimacy, reward, and coercion. We will define each of these, in turn, illustrating with a common example. Our initial influence–conflict example is a rather mundane one, quite familiar to current city dwellers.

Mr. Baker has the habit of parking his large station wagon on the street in front of Mr. Able's home. Mr. Able finds that the narrowness of the street and the location of his driveway make it difficult for him to back his car out each morning and wishes that Baker would park his car elsewhere. However, Baker prefers his usual street parking place, given its convenience to his home, parking restrictions elsewhere, and the possibility of being sideswiped in an alternative parking place which fronts on a busy thoroughfare. How then might Able influence Baker to cease parking his station wagon at that particular spot?

III. THE BASES OF UNILATERAL POWER IN CONFLICT

A. Informational Influence

Able might first try *informational influence*, or persuasion. By providing information not previously available to Baker, or by pointing out contingencies of which Baker had not been aware, Able might show how parking elsewhere would be in Baker's best personal interest—aside from any consideration for Able or possible rewards or punishments which Able might mete out. Does Baker not know that parking on any street always carries with it the danger of being sideswiped? Is he aware of the effects of the elements on the car's finish which would diminish its resale value? Is he aware of the increase of vandalism reported in the neighborhood? Certainly these factors should outweigh the inconvenience and loss of storage space which it would cost for Baker to park in his garage. Or alternatively, he might at least park a block down the street where the streetlighting would deter vandalism. There would be many advantages to Able's using informational influence, if it were indeed successful. He is tying the changed behavior into Baker's system of values and needs; Able would not be beholden to Baker for the changed behavior. Indeed, Baker might be grateful for the information. If the information were convincing, the change would be internalized, such that constant reminders or surveillance by Able would not be necessary. However, it is not unlikely that Baker will *not* be convinced. He would likely have considered these factors previously and found them wanting. If there are underlying bases for conflict, e.g., if Baker is actually getting back at Able for certain indiscretions committed by Able's dog on Baker's lawn, then the information would simply not be relevant to Baker.

Informational influence is then an effective means of achieving change and reducing conflict, since it rapidly becomes independent of the influencing agent, and thus does not require reinstatement or surveillance for its effectiveness. However, for informational influence to be effective, the content communicated must indeed tie the changed pattern of behavior into an existing cognitive structure and value system. Failure of informational influence often stems from the failure to appreciate the value system of the person upon whom influence is attempted, including the large number of values which tend to support the original behavior. Thus, informational campaigns aimed at showing that discrimination in employment is counter to basic democratic values have often proven unsuccessful. Those attempting informational influence also generally overlook underlying bases for noncompliance, such as need for independence, hostility toward the source, and desire for acceptance from other influencing agents.

B. Referent Influence

Able might also attempt to influence Baker through referent influence. Referent influence stems from B's identification with A, or from a desire for such identification—a desire for "oneness." Similarity of belief, attitude, or behavior becomes an end in itself. Able then might emphasize his similarity to Baker. They are, after all, neighbors, with similar occupations, similar political viewpoints, similar concerns about their possessions. Given these similarities, would it not seem appropriate that they treat their automobiles similarly? Mutual feelings of identification can indeed forestall disagreement and conflict. However, it does not seem likely that referent influence would be a factor here. As with all bases of power, referent power has a limited domain, and this would not likely include choice of parking area. It also assumes a positive identification or desire for identification. A desire for similarity will be greater if there is a mutual attraction. Negative reference may operate as well, and, as described above, an underlying basis of conflict—dislike or hostility of Baker toward Able—might indeed lead Baker to want to distinguish himself from Able, to be different rather than similar. The effects of positive referent influence might also operate such that Baker would try to convince Able that *he* should park *his* car on the street, or, indeed, the disagreement might lead to reduction of referent influence, through personal rejection.

Thus, an appeal to similarity and an emphasis on mutual attraction may lead to referent influence as a basis for resolving disagreements and conflicts, but a careful consideration of domain of referent influence and the actual degree of reference is required before one can be assured of the effectiveness of referent power. A prior history of continued conflict or disagreement would make referent influence particularly unlikely.

C. Legitimate Influence

Legitimate influence of A over B stems from internalized values of B which dictate that A, by virtue of his role or position, has the right to prescribe behavior for B in a given domain, and B is obliged to comply (French & Raven, 1959). Though legitimate power is normally discussed in terms of a formal organization, such that the supervisor is seen as having the right to prescribe work behavior for a subordinate, we would consider it to be a much more pervasive phenomenon. Any compliance which has an "ought to" quality about it would fall into this category. Able can impress upon Baker that neighbors have a legitimate right to make requests of one another where one's action impinges on the convenience or freedom of the other's everyday living conditions. Thus, obviously, his request that Baker not park his car in front of Able's house is a legitimate request, to which Baker is obliged to comply. Able could also appeal to what he considers the legitimate right of a property owner to have something to say about what goes on in front of his own house, even though there may not necessarily be a law formally regulating such behavior.

An interesting basis for social power, which we would consider as an instance of legitimacy, is "the power of the powerless" as presented in experiments by Berkowitz and his co-workers (Berkowitz & Daniels, 1963, 1964; Berkowitz, Klanderman, & Harris, 1964; Daniels & Berkowitz, 1963; Goranson & Berkowitz, 1966). According to their conception, one person can be legitimately expected to comply to the requests of another person who depends upon him. The helpless female, her car immobilized on the freeway by a flat tire, can legitimately request the assistance of the capable male driver. Able could conceivably use such a means of influence, if he were old, helpless, and lacking in coordination in his driving. Baker might then consider Able's request as legitimate influence. The power of the poor, disadvantaged segments of our society in the past has been of this sort. They could legitimately request food and lodging for their families, since they were helpless and could not provide it for themselves. The more fortunate members of society, if they accepted the legitimacy of the demand, would then be obliged to assist with "charity." The problem, of course, is that the use of such a means of influence can be degrading to the self-esteem of the less powerful and tend to maintain their inferior role.

Legitimate influence can be an effective means of forestalling conflict through achieving influence of one person over another. It has the advantage of externalizing the basis for the influence and thus sometimes can avoid any further obligation by the person who attempts influence. Indeed, legitimacy can be considered as a functionally developed societal mechanism to regulate potential conflict. It is limited to situations in which the person upon whom influence is attempted, both accepts the basis for legitimacy, and recognizes that the influencer occupies the position which specifically vests such legitimate power in him. Legitimate influence will not ordinarily lead to negative personal feelings toward the source of influence and also has the advantage of not requiring surveillance.

D. Expert Influence

The expert power of A over B increases to the extent to which B attributes superior knowledge or ability to A within the domain within which influence is attempted. It decreases to the extent to which B distrusts A, and B attributes personal motives such that A would attempt to mislead B. Indeed, if B suspects that A is using his superior knowledge to convince B to do something which would benefit A, but might harm B, then *negative* expert influence would occur (e.g., B is a customer and suspects that A, the salesman, is using his knowledge of the products to get B to buy an article which is inferior but which would likely give A an added commission).

When Able tells Baker that he has seen a number of prowlers and vandals at night and advises Baker to park off the street, or if Able says that, as a former automobile salesman, he knows that the moist evening air will soon damage the finish on Baker's car, then his effectiveness for Baker will depend upon Baker's trust. Is it possible that Able is just saying these things because he does not like to have Baker's car in front of his house?

Expert influence can thus be an effective means of reducing conflict through influence, provided there is a high degree of trust. However, most conflict situations, by their very nature tend to reduce trust and with it the possibility of expert influence. Of course, this is particularly true where there is incompatibility in goals. Where the conflict is with respect to *means* and the goal is held in common, then trust is more likely and expert influence more feasible. Obviously B would not suspect that A was misleading him, if A would also be hurt thereby.

E. Coercive and Reward Influence

If A can mediate punishments or rewards for B, then he can have coercive or reward power over B. It should be emphasized that it is A's *mediation* of punishments or rewards which distinguishes these two bases of power from those discussed earlier. A's expert power can contribute toward B's reaching some positive goals or avoiding punishment. Similarly, B may experience some inner satisfaction from increasing his similarity to A or by following the legitimate request issued by A. The satisfactions or punishments in these latter cases are not mediated by A, however. French and Raven (1959) considered it important to differentiate these two sources of power from the others because coercive power and reward power require surveillance by A. B would not comply with A's requests *in order to receive A's reward* if A would not be aware of the compliance. Similarly, B would not fear punishment for noncompliance if surveillance by A were not possible.

Ordinarily, reward power and coercive power are dealt with in terms of concrete and physical rewards and punishments—bonuses, candy, monetary rewards; fines, physical injury, or dismissal as punishments. However, approval, love, and affection can serve as effective rewards under some circumstances, just as disapproval, hate, and dislike can be highly effective punishments.

In our continuing example, Baker's desire for the approval of Able and his wish to avoid Able's hatred might be the most important source of reward and coercive power of Able over Baker. This would be true to the extent to which Baker values Able's friendship. The continual use of this personal reward and coercion by Able, however, might ultimately lead to Baker's rejecting Able personally, such that he would no longer be concerned about Able's approval or disapproval. He might still be able to use nonpersonal means of coercion, by threatening to turn on his lawn sprinklers and wetting Able's automobile, for example. He might also offer to curb his dog as an inducement to Able's moving his automobile. In this example, surveillance is generally possible by Able, since he can obviously see whether Baker has responded to his request.

French and Raven (1959) and Thibaut and Kelley (1959) suggest several reasons for distinguishing between coercion and reward as bases of power: (1) There is good reason to believe that reward is more likely to lead to a more positive attitude of B toward A, and increase the possibility of later use of personal reward and referent power. (2) Coercive power will likely lead to the influencee's abandoning the social relationship entirely, if there are no barriers against it, where reward power would more likely increase the possibility of the influencee's remaining in the influence situation. (3) Surveillance, and ultimate effectiveness of influence, is not as difficult with reward power, since the influencee will not only desire to comply but also to bring his compliance to the attention of the influencing agent. He would attempt to hide his degree of compliance when coercion is involved. Thus, coercive power, in order to be effective, may involve threats of punishment for noncompliance, but also punishment for concealment (Kelley & Ring, 1961; Ring & Kelley, 1963). It is of particular importance to note that when coercive power is brought into the manifest conflict situation, it is particularly likely to increase the *underlying* basis of conflict. With a personal rejection of the source of power, the influencee also increases his desire to retaliate and to avoid influence wherever possible. Thus, as we shall see, the initial introduction of coercion will tend to necessitate continuing coercion, unless the agent can somehow contribute toward an acceptance of the *fait accompli,* a change in attitude or belief through locomotion or dissonance reduction.

F. Differing Responses to Unilateral Power

For an analysis of responses to unilateral power, we will utilize a distinction proposed by Horney (1945). Horney suggested that an individual in relating to others might follow a strategy of "moving toward," "moving away," or "moving against." Pettigrew (1967, p. 27ff) used similar categories in examining reactions of Negroes toward white oppressors. Although Horney presented these as unitary overall response tendencies, characterizing personality types, we would prefer to consider them as being in part a function of the influence situation. Furthermore, it seems useful to differentiate between movement in behavior which can be readily observed by the influence agent, movement in private opinion or belief, movement in manner of interaction with the influencing agent, and movement in evaluation of the influencing agent.

When A attempts to influence B, B can "move toward" A by changing his behavior in the manner which A suggests, by changing his belief so as to accept the behavioral change privately, by involving himself in more intense but positive interaction with A, or by increasing his identification and affection toward A. He can "move away" from A by simply disregarding A's influence attempt on his behavior and his underlying belief, by maintaining his original private opinion, by withdrawing from interaction with A, or by increasing his perception that he is different from A. B can "move against" A by actively changing his overt behavior in a manner opposed to that advoctated by A or publicly indicating active opposition, by privately changing his underlying opinion or belief so as to be actively opposed to the position advocated, by interacting negatively with A or opposing A personally, or by actively disidentifying with A and rejecting A personally. These reactions to A's influence attempt—toward, away, against— may vary independently within the four dimensions we have described.

In various papers, the distinction between public and private change has been discussed (e.g., Cartwright 1965; Collins & Raven, 1969; Festinger, 1953; French & Raven, 1959; Kelman, 1958, 1961; Raven, 1965). Similar distinctions have been presented by Willis and Hollander (1964; Willis, 1965). Raven and French (1958) pointed out that coercion by a supervisor will lead to "movement toward" in public behavior (change in behavior), "movement against" in private opinion and in identification (personal rejection of the supervisor). Legitimate power will lead to "movement toward" in behavior, private belief, and in evaluation of the supervisor. Ordinarily we might expect that "movement toward" in private belief would be accompanied by positive change in public behavior. However, some examples of "reactance" presented by Brehm (1966) suggest that when a person feels that his independence is being infringed upon inappropriately, he may indicate negativism in his behavior even while he accepts change privately. "He is probably right, but I'll be damned if I will give him the satisfaction of admitting it." A supervisor who feels that it is inappropriate for him to be influenced by his subordinate may refuse to admit he is wrong and continue his previous pattern or behavior, while privately he is considering the logic of his subordinate's request; he may interact negatively with his subordinate, criticizing his disrespect, while he privately increases his admiration for him.

The interrelationships between social power and reactions to the influencing agent are not yet entirely clear. However, we will attempt here to suggest some tentative assumptions. We will again begin with the six bases of social power, in their simplest form, and attempt to deduce the influencee's reactions; as indicated in Table I. First we look at situations where A's power is sufficient to change B's behavior so as to "move toward" A. This is indicated by a "+" in the table. "Movement away" is indicated with a "0" and "movement against" with a "−." Where there is no clear effect in the manner of our analysis, the space will be left blank.

TABLE I

Effects of the Utilization of Social Power in Terms of Moving Toward (+), Moving Away (0), and Moving Against (−) the Agent

Source of A's power	Effects on B's			
	Overt behavior	Private beliefs	Interaction with agent	Identification with agent
Reward	+	0	+	0
Coercion	+	−	−	−
Legitimacy	+	+	0	0
Expert	+	+	0	0
Information	+	+	0 ?	
Referent	+	+	+	+
Illegitimate reward	+	−	+	−
Information coupled with need for independence	−	+	0	−
Unsuccessful attempt to use reward	0	−	−	−

1. Reward Power

Where A has sufficient reward to influence B, the change will ordinarily be moving toward or compliance in overt behavior, which ordinarily will be further supported by moving toward in favorable interaction. B will tend to behave in accordance with A's requests and also to behave in a friendly fashion. Reward will not immediately lead to positive identification with A, however. The fact that A has greater resources than B may lead B to differentiate himself more clearly from A. If the reward basis of power is salient, furthermore, B will not initially change his private beliefs toward A. Thus, compliance will not necessarily be accompanied by private acceptance. French and Raven (1959) suggest that positive attitudes resulting from receiving rewards will lead to a halo effect, which in turn might lead to positive identification and attraction toward B, along with private acceptance of the changed behavior. The conditions under which this will occur are not entirely clear. Indeed, where B perceives that reward is being used inappropriately, as a bribe, then he may disidentify with A, and reject the changed behavior privately.

2. Coercive Power

Here, as we see in Table I, overt behavior will show compliance or "moving toward," while identification with the agent becomes more negative. There is active "moving against" the influencing agent in identification, in private beliefs, and, unless coercive power can subdue negative communications, in interaction with the agent as well.

3. Legitimate Power

Where A utilizes legitimate power effectively, there is moving toward both in overt behavior and in private beliefs. However, we might expect moving away in identification. Differentiation in social structure which allows for legitimate power will become salient, reducing perceived similarity of B with respect to A. In many circumstances, we might also expect that there would be moving away in interaction, since B would wish to avoid a situation in which he might be legitimately requested to do something which he would prefer not to do.

4. Expert Power

Ordinarily, one should expect that expertise would result in positive change both in overt behavior and in private beliefs. However, expertise would also emphasize the difference between B and A. It is A's superior knowledge which makes him capable of influencing B, so that there would be "moving away" in identification. As with legitimacy, it may also be true that where expertise is used to get B to do something which he would prefer not to do, then B would avoid further interaction with A.

Robert F. Goheen, President of Princeton University, in his 1969 commencement address stated that "If you would persuade someone to your view, you can't afford to be more than 85% right." Goheen's statement may be considered in terms of the interrelationship between expert and referent power. He is suggesting that the infallible expert is rejected as a basis for self-evaluation, that increased expert power may lead to a process of moving away in identification and interaction.

5. Informational Power

Information would, by its definition, provide for positive change in both private beliefs and behavior. However, what about interaction and identification? We cannot make clear predictions here, although again, the possibility that A will provide information which would suggest that B should change his behavior might lead to avoidance of further interaction. If the providing of information indicates some superiority on the part of A, there might also be moving away in identification.

6. Referent Power

When A influences B through the use of referent power, there will be moving toward both in overt behavior and in private beliefs. The resulting change, which was determined by B's positive identification with A, will in turn lead to still greater perception of similarity and thus additional positive identification. Furthermore, the perception of similarity and identification will lead to *moving toward,* positive interaction with A. In earlier discussions (e.g., Collins & Raven, 1969; French & Raven, 1959; Raven, 1965), it was suggested that where informational power is available, it has definite advantages over other bases of power. The change becomes independent of the influencing agent and thus appears to be more permanent. However, where one is concerned about continued positive interpersonal relationships, there seem to be clear advantages for referent influence. The independence or moving away from the influencing agent which may result from the use of information may lead to a less stable interpersonal relationship. Thus, the parent who emphasizes informational power in the family ("Do those things I ask you to do only if you can understand the reason for doing so.") is later shocked to find that his children do indeed become independent of him. The parent who encourages compliance on the basis of familial identification may find that his positive relationship with his children continues for a longer period, though this may occur at the expense of seeing his children being more interpersonally oriented and less independent in their thinking.

7. Compounded Power

Ordinarily, a power relationship includes several bases of power, and it would be of some importance to explore how these interact with one another. We will not explore all of these combinations here, particularly since such an analysis would have to examine the even greater complexity which is involved when there are differing degrees of each power base operating in a given influence situation. The one point which should be emphasized is that when power bases are combined, the result is often nonadditive. If expert power reduces identification and referent power reduces perception of difference, then the two power bases used together might cancel each other out. To further complicate the analysis, individual interpersonal needs may operate to counteract the effects of power. For example, if B has a great need for independence, then we might find that A's informational power would be sufficient to bring about private changes in beliefs while B *moves against* or *moves away* in his public behavior. We can see this in the example of the child whose parent may convince him that he will catch a cold if he goes out of doors in his bare feet (see Table I). The child accepts the logic of the argument, but yet insists on disobeying the parent in order to demonstrate his own independence.

G. Bases of Social Power and the Attribution of Causality for Change

It is well to keep in mind that each of the parties in the power—conflict relationship enters the conflict situation with prior perceptions and evaluations both of himself and of the other. Prior cognitions about self and other determine the choice of power base which each attempts to use, the extent of compliance of the recipient of influence, the degree of acceptance of change, and subsequent patterns of interaction. These consequences in turn, interacting with the prior conceptions, produce changes in each actor's cognition of self and other, which in turn determine subsequent power exchanges.

An important tool for understanding these patterns of power and cognition is provided in developments in "attribution theory," as originally suggested by Michotte (1963) and Heider (1958), and more recently developed further by Jones and Davis (1965), Kelley (1967), and their co-workers. The attributional analysis focuses on the manner in which the individual attempts to determine the locus of causality in his environment. A person's behavior may be seen as being caused by factors outside himself. He is "forced" to commit an act, or the behavior may be interpreted as being initiated by the person himself. Influence may then be interpreted, in Michotte's terms, as a "launching effect," or a "releasing effect." In the latter instance, the influencing agent is seen as providing the opportunity for the influencee to change under his *own* power. When a college student agrees to a request that he give blood to the Red Cross, his behavior is seen as "launched," or attributed to the influencing agent, if the agent is a professor; it is seen as "released," or attributed to the student himself, if the agent is a college freshman (Thibaut & Riecken, 1955). Similarly, Jones, Gergen, and Jones (1963) found that when high status ROTC personnel influenced low status members to change their opinions, the change was interpreted as "ingratiation" or, in our terms, personal reward power. When low status persons influenced high status, the change was interpreted as a sincere representation of his opinion. Both participants and nonparticipating observers then evaluated the high status "sincere" conformer more positively than the "ingratiating" low status conformer.

It is thus reasonable to assume that influence which results from informational power would be interpreted as a "releasing effect," with the influencee changing voluntarily. It is the *information* which is seen as bringing about the change. Bem, using Skinner's terminology (Skinner, 1957), interprets such influence as stemming from a *tact*—a response to a specific nonvarying stimulus from the environment (Bem, 1965, 1967). Change following high reward or coercive power is interpreted as a "launching effect" or as resulting from Skinner's "mand" the reinforcing nature of the social demands. What, then, about attributions resulting from other sources of power? Presumably these would provide less clear attributional interpretations than reward, coercion, and information. We might speculate that legitimacy has a "mand" quality, with less volition attributed to the person who has been influenced. Jones et al. (1963) do indicate that conformity to a high status person is more likely to be seen as nonvoluntary, if the status relationship is relevant (legitimate) to the opinion which has been influenced. Expert power, we expect, is more similar to informational power in this respect and, therefore, more likely to be interpreted as stemming from the decision of the influencee. Referent is still less clear, but it might also prove to operate like a "tact." More careful empirical evidence is required to explore these relationships.

H. The Choice of Power Base by the Influencing Agent

The relative effectiveness of various bases of power in inducing change has been explored in innumerable studies. Ordinarily, as we have indicated, the influencing agent has a choice of a number of different bases of social power which he can use in differing degrees. What then determines which of these he selects? Such an analysis of social power preference has not been examined thoroughly, though the problem has been presented (Gamson, 1968). Let us then list some of the factors which would determine the agent's choice of social power. We shall see that the personal–impersonal and underlying–manifest dimensions of conflict can also be applied to the choice of power base.

1. Likelihood of Long Lasting Change

The rational agent should evaluate his bases of power and select that base combination which is most likely to produce change. He should also consider the permanance of the change which he might produce. Information, as we have indicated, might ordinarily produce the most long lasting effect.

2. Costs of Power

Sometimes the most "effective" basis of power also involves the most effort or cost for the agent. Coercion or reward can involve considerable expenditure of effort or resources, not only in the influence act but in the need for continued surveillance. Harsanyi places particular emphasis on "the opportunity costs of power (1962)." Information can also be costly, if it requires lengthy explanation at a time when there is considerable time pressure.

3. Desire for Continued Dependence

The agent who wishes to continue to have the influence dependent upon him would not likely use informational influence. Expert influence would lead to greater dependence. Unless the expert influencing agent communicated the basis for his expert advice, the influencee would still be dependent upon the agent for advice as to what he should do in the future. Referent influence would also tend to continue the dependent relationship as would personal reward power.

4. Distrust of Other

When the agent is distrustful of the other, he tends to be especially concerned about whether the other is continuing to comply. He will, therefore, attempt to use force or coercion to maximize the likelihood of continued compliance. Coercive power will then necessitate continued surveillance. While it is obvious that distrust of another will lead to a greater tendency to maintain surveillance, Kruglanski (1970) has also shown that surveillance is likely to increase distrust—"If I am watching him, he cannot be that trustworthy."

5. Frustration, Hostility, and Displacement of Aggression

Hostility and a desire to punish another may manifest itself in the use of coercive power where other bases of power might produce change even more effectively. Punishing another, through forcing him to engage in an undesirable act, then may become the predominant basis for action. The amount of threatened or utilized punishment may be quite out of proportion to that required to bring about conformity. In a training situation in which one S was given the opportunity of using shock to bring about correct responses in another, the amount of shock actually used was related to the extent to which hostility was made salient through prior experience with aggressive words (Loew, 1967).

6. Legitimacy and the Evaluation by Third Parties

A's decision to use coercion may be determined in part by the extent to which he considers it appropriate or legitimate to use threats of punishment. Indeed, the possibility of the use of threat to obtain one's ends is actually quite great for most individuals, provided they are willing to pay the costs of the use of such power, both in the discomfort in going against their own consciences or value systems and in terms of the disapproval or threats which third parties may provide to counter the use of coercion. Wheeler and Smith (1966) demonstrated that verbal aggression against another with a deviant opinion was increased when the subject heard another coparticipant using such coercion; aggression was reduced when the coercive coparticipant was censured by the experimenter. Milgram's experiment, in which an experimenter encouraged a subject to use extreme electric shocks to modify the behavior of a coparticipant has been interpreted as an instance in which the experimenter provided legitimacy for the use of coercion. Milgram (1964) and Brock and Buss (1964), in a somewhat similar situation, found that providing justification for the use of shock increased the amount of shock administered and reduced the guilt of the person administering the shock. When B has used punishment against A in the past, it follows that this in itself provides some justification for A's responding similarly. When B has aggressed against others, some justification is also provided. The extent to which such a process of justification may extend is indicated in a study by Berkowitz and Geen (1966). After seeing a film ("The Champion") in which actor Kirk Douglas played the role of a vicious boxer, Ss were more likely to use shock to influence a coparticipant if his name happened to be "Kirk," as compared to a coparticipant named "Bob." Similar effects of legitimacy and concern about evaluation of others likely apply to the use of reward and other power bases, though perhaps the effects are not as dramatic.

7. Self-Esteem and Need for Power

Frantz Fanon in his "Handbook for the Black Revolution" advocated that "the wretched of the earth" utilize violence. He recommends threats and violence by the "natives" to gain concessions from the "colonialists" even when the latter may be persuaded to grant concessions. His reasoning follows: "... violence is a cleansing force. It frees the native from his inferiority complex and from his despair and inaction; it makes him fearless and restores his self-respect (Fanon, 1963, p. 94)." Thus, we see that coercive power may be used to increase self-esteem, to give one person a feeling of superiority over the other. Viewed in attribution theory terms, we have noted that the agent who successfully influences another through informational power or persuasion might still interpret that change as originating in the influencee. Change accomplished through coercion may be attributed to the action and the power of the influencing agent. If the agent is successful in his use of coercive power, he has also communicated his superior power position to the influencee, who will also interpret his change as being caused by the agent, rather than as a voluntary act on his part. The status gain may thus be more important to the influencing agent than the change in behavior which has resulted. The tendency to use coercion, even when it involves considerable cost to the agent, will become particularly pronounced when the agent has been humiliated before a third party (Brown, 1968). In Fanon's discussion, the use of violence was also to provide a means for the black militant to gain the admiration and support of noninvolved blacks. The demonstration of power through the use of coercion serves to raise the self-esteem of others who identify with the influencing agent. The agent's referent power for his group members is increased even as his use of violence leads the "colonialist" to "move against," both in interaction and identification. Thus, as Coser has pointed out, conflict, and particularly the use of coercive power in conflict, can have the effect of strengthening intragroup identity even as it increases intergroup hostility (Coser, 1956, 1967). Leaders who decide to use coercion rather than reference or legitimacy in influencing an outgroup will often have such strategy in mind.

IV. DYADIC CONFLICT WITH RECIPROCATED POWER BASES

We began our analysis with the simplest conflict situation in which one party attempted to influence the other with a single basis of power, that is, the typical social influence situation. We now examine the conflict situation in which the two parties each have power with respect to the other. For simplicity of presentation, we will further limit ourselves initially to that situation in which they may utilize the same power basis with respect to one another.

A. Reciprocated Reward and Coercive Power

The typical conflict experiment in the social psychological literature involves mutual use of coercive and/or reward power on the part of two participants or antagonists. The analysis, as usually presented, utilizes the game matrix as suggested by Luce and Raiffa (1957), Thibaut and Kelley (1959), Deutsch (1958), and others. (See Chapter 3.) The costs and rewards of each of the members is represented in the matrix and it is specified that the outcomes for each person are determined both by his behavior and by the behavior of his coparticipant; or rephrased in social power terms, each can exert varying degrees of reward power or coercive power over the other since he controls to some extent the costs and rewards which the other will receive. Applying the concepts of reward–reward and coercion–coercion conflict to on-going social situations, we can see, for example, that two nations with incompatibility in a given sphere may have the military potentials to inflict damage on one another (coercive power) or the economic potential to improve each other's lot, as when each nation controls resources which can contribute to the welfare of the other (reward power). Of course, the pure cases of reward or coercive potentials may be rare, the majority of relationships being characterized by some combination of these two, with other power bases operating as well. Our purpose in this section is to consider some ways in which different aspects of reward and coercive power may affect personal and impersonal, manifest and underlying conflict.

A convenient departure point for our discussion is research by Deutsch and Krauss (1960, 1962) on the effects of threats on interpersonal negotiations. These investigators used a two-person game in which the players acted as the operators of trucking firms interacting on a one-way road en route to opposite destinations. An alternative, longer way to reach the goal was available but its use involved inevitable loss to the player who chose to take it. Each person's profits in the game depended on the amount of time he took to reach the goal. The conflict of interests between the players stemmed from the fact that each wanted to be first through the one-way road. Coercive capacities were introduced into this situation in the form of unilaterally controlled gates. These could be used to stop the other player from going through the one-lane road, i.e., to force him to either wait in front of the gate or take the long alternative route (and the attendant loss). Three experimental conditions were compared: "unilateral threat" in which only one of the two players had the coercive capacity, "bilateral threat" in which both players had it, and "no threat" in which none had it.

With the players' joint profits as the dependent variable, Deutsch and Krauss report that introduction of threats considerably reduced the participants' success in resolving the existing conflict of interests. Players in the "no threat" condition attained highest joint profits, those in the "bilateral threat" condition, the lowest profits, while Ss in the "unilateral threat" condition fell in between the above two. These findings led the authors to suggest that the ready availability of weapons tempts bargainers to threaten their use. Such threats in turn elicit counterthreats and aggression, thus destroying any possibility of agreement (Deutsch & Krauss, 1962).

While objections have been raised (Kelley, 1965; Gallo, 1966) regarding the degree to which the above findings fit the theoretical interpretation advanced by the authors, this will not be our present concern. Rather, we propose to use the analysis and the experimental paradigm developed by Deutsch and Krauss as a reference point for further speculation regarding the effects of punishments and rewards as modes of conflict resolution.

To begin with, we should differentiate the effects of (1) possessing coercive (or reward) capability; (2) communicating the intention to employ it to the detriment (or benefit) of the other side; and (3) its actual utilization. While it may be true that these aspects of a given type of power tend to be associated (as implied in the Deutsch and Krauss analysis), we submit that they affect distinct aspects of behavior in conflict and thus warrant conceptual separation.

1. Effects of Possessing Reward vs. Coercive Capabilities on Individuals' Initial Attitudes toward Each Other

The mere possession by a side in conflict of a capacity to reward or punish the other may have important consequences for the individuals' subjectively perceived incompatibility.

Thus, the image reflected by a side endowed with harmful potential is likely to differ markedly from that conveyed by one lacking such capacity or endowed with a reward capability. Specifically, we suggest that in case of coercive potential there will be the inference of negative or harmful intent, whereas in case of reward potential the inference of benign intent will be more likely. Such "inference of intent from capability (Pruitt, 1965)" is consistent with a model of "cognitive balance (Heider, 1958)." Specifically, the cognition "X has the means to harm me" may, in the interest of cognitive consistency, lead to the suspicion "X may choose to harm me," and the imperative "I'd better watch out or defend myself against X." Similarly, none of the above may fit well with the cognition "X is my friend who wishes me well." The latter thought is more likely to occur following the realization "X has the means to reward me."

The tendency to respond aggressively to a person who possesses aggressive capabilities is illustrated in an experiment by Berkowitz and LePage. In that study, subjects who had received either one or seven shocks, supposedly from a peer, were then given an opportunity to shock that person. In some cases, a rifle and revolver were on the table near the shock key, which weapons were said to belong, or not belong, to the other participant. The greatest number of shocks were given by subjects who had themselves received the greater number of shocks and who saw the weapons on the table. Weapons aroused strong aggressive responses, particularly with men who had just received punishment themselves (Berkowitz & LePage, 1967).

So far we have discussed the way in which possession of reward or coercive capability may affect the individual's image as perceived by the other side to the conflict. Let us outline now the possible impact of reward vs. coercive power on *underlying* bases of conflict, e.g., the effects of possessing destructive vs. constructive capabilities on the individual's *own* attitudes and impressions *vis à vis* the opposite side. We propose that having coercive power is likely to give rise to the belief that one's counterpart in the relation harbors hostile intentions. In contrast, having control over rewards may lead to the belief that the other is benevolently disposed toward oneself. This assertion can be supported by two separate arguments. First, it is possible for one to infer one's own intentions from his capabilities, especially (as will frequently happen in real life) if these were acquired through the exercise of conscious effort and/or free choice. In turn, intentions thus inferred may instigate attitudes toward the other side consistent with the former.

For example, a side endowed with destructive capacity may come to believe that he will actually employ it against the other party. In the interest of cognitive consistency these beliefs may lead him to attribute negative intentions and characteristics to the other party. The above "psychologic" may be represented by the cognitions: "I have (acquired) the capacity to inflict damage on X . . . (therefore) I shall probably use it against X . . . because this is the only way it is possible to deal with a person like X, an obstinate, unreasonable, hostile individual . . . "

Similarly, having the capacity to reward the other side may lead to the self-attributions of benevolent intentions *vis à vis* that party which may then engender positive evaluations of the latter question.

A second avenue whereby the capacity to bestow benefits or impose punishments may affect one's orientation toward the other side is by the mechanism of "anticipated reactions." Specifically, someone who controls coercive power may anticipate that the opponent will become aware of this fact, presume that the destructive potential is intended to be used against him and respond in kind, i.e., by attempting in devious and/or aggressive ways to undo him. Such expectations would tend to give rise to a perception of the other as hostile and unfriendly and further strengthen the determination to use one's destructive potential for defense against possible counterattack.

In a similar vein, possessing the capacity for reward could induce expectations of grateful and friendly reactions from the other side which, in turn, would lead to positive evaluations of that person and enhance the tendency to treat him well.

In brief, then, we have suggested that possessing coercive capabilities may lead the sides in conflict to perceive each other as hostile and thus unlikely to resolve the incompatibilities involved in reasonable, unaggressive ways. In contrast, reward capabilities are likely to engender optimism about the chances of reaching a satisfactory resolution by way of peaceful negotiations. In other words, superimposing coercive potentials on the structure of conflict is likely to enhance "subjective" conflict whereas introducing reward capabilities is likely to reduce "subjective" conflict.

2. Effects of Possessing Reward vs. Coercive Capabilities on the Patterns of Interpersonal Communication in Conflict

The attitudes of mutual benevolence or hostility fostered by the possession by one or both antagonists of reward or coercive power could importantly determine the nature of communications between them. Here we shall dwell on two aspects of communications: volume and content.

There is evidence that a suspicious, hostile atmosphere will act to depress the tendency to communicate while a friendly, benevolent climate will tend to enhance it (Sherif & Sherif, 1953). Considering the above assertion in conjunction with our earlier analysis it follows that coercive power should restrict the volume of communications while reward power should expand it. Deutsch and Krauss (1962) furnish experimental evidence consistent with the first part of this proposition. In one variant of the trucking game the *S*s were allowed to communicate verbally. As it turned out, the amount of actual communication was least in the Bilateral Threat condition, somewhat greater in Unilateral Threat and greatest in No Threat.

Whether the parties in conflict control reward or coercive capacity could importantly affect the content of messages exchanged. Specifically, it is not unlikely that in the former case communications would convey information about the benefits at the communicator's disposal as well as *promises* stating the conditions of their dispensation. In the case of coercive power, communications are likely to announce the interactants' coercive capabilities and state threats of their use.

Furthermore, initial promises of benefits to be bestowed are likely to create an atmosphere conducive to *free* and *open* interchange on a variety of topics, thus promoting the exploration of the outcomes available in the relationship (Thibaut & Kelley, 1959) including mutually satisfactory ways of resolving the existing conflict. In contrast, initial threats might tend to underscore the incompatibilities involved and limit communications to further exchange of threats, finally resulting in a hostile atmosphere inimical to parley of any kind (Newcomb, 1947; Thibaut & Kelley, 1959).

To conclude, through its restrictive effects on the volume and content of communications, coercive capability is likely to heighten subjective conflict. Similarly, by instigating open and voluminous communication, reward capability is hypothesized to suppress subjective conflict.

3. Communicating Threats and Promises

In their initial experimentation, Deutsch and Krauss (1962) made no attempt to differentiate operationally between threats, i.e., expressed intentions to inflict harm, and the actual use of force. This distinction appeared later in a doctoral dissertation by Hornstein (1965). This investigator found that those trials on which the players initiated their interaction with a threat were *less* likely to end in a mutually acceptable agreement than those in which the interaction was initiated without a threat. Also, actual administration of punishments was negatively correlated with the likelihood of reaching an agreement.

In a more recent study, Gumpert (1967) has argued that at a high level of coercive potential, the capacity to communicate threats may have a deleterious effect on conflict resolution. Specifically, in the absence of the possibility of sending threatening messages one might be wary of employing his force against the other side for fear of retaliation and mutual destruction. Though the capability of threatening the other side might be viewed as a potentially useful bargaining tool, such strategy ignores the negative psychological effect of threats on the threatened party—specifically humiliation and hurt feeling which are likely to instigate a resentful counterthreat. Consistent with Deutsch's analysis (1966; 1969), the ensuing sequence of threats and counterthreats will then result in a spiral of mounting aggressiveness and hostility markedly increasing the probability of actual force being unleashed. Communication of threats, then, increases underlying and personal bases of conflict. In an experimental study aimed at examining the above notions, Gumpert obtained some support for the idea that at a high level of punitive potential, allowing the players to send threatening messages decreases their chances of reaching mutually beneficial agreements.

While Gumpert's concern is with the effect of *threatening messages,* his general argument has interesting implications for the role of the communication variable in conflict with reward as opposed to coercive power. The general notion that ability to communicate is an important precondition for satisfactory resolutions of conflict (e.g., Douglas, 1957; Rapoport, 1960) must thus be reconsidered. While the opportunity to communicate might have beneficial effects when the sides control reward potentials, it may have detrimental effects when a coercive base of power prevails. As we have proposed earlier, in the coercive case the communication channel will be used primarily to convey threats and counterthreats. According to Gumpert's analysis this would ultimately enhance the probability of actual force being used. In contrast, under reward power, communications are likely to consist of promises and exchanges of information regarding the positive outcomes each side has in store for the other, thus increasing the likelihood of a mutually satisfactory agreement. In terms of our earlier discussion, equipped with punitive capacities, the sides are likely to communicate threats which (by virtue of their offensive nature) might intensify *underlying interpersonal* conflict. A liking relationship, reducing *interpersonal conflict,* is hypothesized to result when communications between the parties convey possible rewards. Walton and McKersie (1965) provide evidence for such a process in their discussion of labor–management negotiations.

In this context, it might be considered that the communication aspects of the use of reward and coercion also carry over to concern about appearances before third parties. It is undoubtedly true that the use of coercion may be restricted when it is likely to lead to disapproval, censure, or punishment by a third party. However, it is also likely that the recipient of coercion may feel more of a need to retaliate when he believes that this places him in a bad light in the presence of an admired observer. Thus, coercive power may add an additional underlying and personal basis for conflict. Such was, in fact, observed in an experiment by Brown (1968) in which the Deutsch and Krauss experiment (1962) was repeated essentially in front of an observer. When the observer gave a participant programmed feedback which suggested that he looked foolish and weak, retaliation was more likely and with greater severity, even though it ultimately involved sacrificing available outcomes. When the observer indicated that he felt that the participant "looked good" because he "played fair," then retaliation was much less likely.

4. Effects of Implementing Rewards or Punishments

Here, we wish to consider the effects of the *actual utilization* of "reward" or "coercive" influence as distinct from merely possessing the capacity to use it or expressing the intention of doing so. On the coercive side, an important contemporary distinction is between limited vs. massive employment of force. Presumably, the function of massive force is to pressure the opponent into submission by materially destroying his capacity to resist. In a situation where both sides to a conflict possess "massive" potential there exists the imminent danger of mutual destruction.

One rationale for employing limited warfare under these conditions is to relate to the other side one's tenacity and force without at the same time running the risk of inviting doom implicit in massive confrontation. But the hidden danger in limited warfare lies in the possibility of gradual escalation of hostilities as each side attempts to gain the upper hand in the struggle. The escalation process is likely to be paralleled by the attribution of increasing importance to the issues at stake (perhaps as a way of rationalizing the constantly growing investment), or by the intensification of "perceived incompatibility." Furthermore, continued combat is likely to enhance the competitive motivations of the opponents (e.g., to attain a victory or retaliate for a defeat)—in other words, escalate what we have called underlying and interpersonal conflict. Gumpert (1967) presents data that lend some support for such expectations.

Carrying the "limited" vs. "massive" distinction to the reward side it may be argued that controlling limited as well as massive (as opposed to massive only rewards) could have a facilitating effect on conflict resolution. For one thing, it may seem inappropriate to dispense considerable rewards to the other side in the absence of the assurance of reciprocation. Thus, the interacting parties may hesitate a long while before communicating their intention to bestow "massive" favors on one another. Also, communicated promises of rewards are less likely to appear credible to the recipient to the extent that the rewards appear excessively large. Furthermore, sudden reception of considerable benefits might arouse suspicion and resentment, as when the rewards are interpreted as "bribes" or attempts at trickery. On the assumption that one is never given something for nothing, the individual's perceived salience of the outcomes at stake (i.e., one determinant of subjective conflict) is likely to increase. In addition, the feeling that the other side is being untruthful may instigate a strong feeling of resentment and lead to a resolution to resist the influencer on *interpersonal* grounds.

In contrast, the capability to dispense limited rewards may serve as a means of establishing a friendly parley in which a gradual exploration of the possibilities of agreement on contested issues is facilitated.

5. The Parlance of Threats and Promises

It has been argued (Kelley, 1965) that threats of intended punishments convey a message offensive to the threatened individual as they implicitly relegate him to an inferior position *vis à vis* the threatener. We have suggested that promised rewards convey the message of friendliness and positive evaluation. Our preceding analysis implies that the above generalizations are subject to limitation as a function of the size of the rewards and/or punishments involved.

Earlier we suggested that beyond a certain point increasing rewards begin to have the ring of untruthful, dishonest attitudes. It is also possible to argue that beyond a certain point increasing threats begin to lose their offensive character. Specifically, to threaten someone with a very small punishment (e.g., a small fraction of one's punitive might) is to convey the obviously offensive notion that the individual under threat does not require much to be forced into submission. In a similar vein, throwing a considerable amount of threat (e.g., one's entire destructive arsenal) behind a demand may in some sense be taken as a sign of respect for the opposite side as it implies that nothing less (than the punishment stated) is likely to affect the opponent's decision.

The generality of our former assertion concerning the offensive nature of threats is subject to further limitations. For example, Kelley (1965) suggests that when threats are perceived as caused by a strong need or desire, they convey the message of weakness and dependency. In such cases, threats may reduce interpersonal conflict as they imply the inferior status of the threatening party relative to the threatened one.

Threats may also faciliate conflict resolution when issued under the aegis of a cause accepted as legitimate by the opposite side. The usefulness of threats (vs. other modes of influence) in these circumstances is due to their dramatic value. By force of its rhetoric, coercion, and the threats thereof, may highlight a situation which (at least in theory) is unacceptable to the opposite side. For example, a majority may uphold values strongly opposed to suppression of, or discrimination against, minorities, yet continue such practices while remaining unaware of the inconsistency. This state of affairs is particularly likely to prevail when the majority (as often happens) finds the situation convenient and/or profitable. Under these conditions mild protests by the minority are likely to go unnoticed and only strong dramatic effects (such as may be achieved by the use of coercive, violent means) are likely to jolt the majority out of its apathy and force it into making the choice between actively defending the status quo, thereby taking a counter valuative stand, and supporting the moral values involved, which implies change in the direction demanded by the threatening group. In the above sense, then, threats may enhance manifest conflict by forcing into the foreground an incompatibility hitherto ignored.

The effects of combining legitimacy and threats becomes complicated further by the fact that, in our culture, coercion has an almost inherent aura of illegitimacy. Thus, it is likely that when faced with incongruency involved in a "legitimate threat," the individual's reaction to threats will become polarized. Some persons may react to the legitimacy of the demands and comply with the requests advanced by the threatening group, while others may respond to the illegitimacy of coercion and counter it in kind.

B. Reciprocated Legitimate Power

Social theorists as early as Hobbes (1651) have emphasized the functional value of the social contract or norm as a basis for reducing or minimizing interpersonal and intergroup conflict. Without such mutual agreement by man to accept influence in given domains from his fellow man, Hobbes said, his life would be "nasty, brutish, and short." The functional value of legitimate power in preventing conflict becomes quite evident in military situations, where the superior officer in combat cannot always rely on either coercion or reward, or upon expertise, reference, or persuasion in ordering his subordinates into battle to fend off attack. The legitimate right of women and children on a sinking ship to request men to surrender their place on the first lifeboats may fit into our general cultural values, but it also diminishes conflict and provides a basis for queuing when conflict would lead to jamming and mutual loss as demonstrated experimentally by Mintz (1951), Schultz (1965), Kelley, Condry, Dahlke, and Hill (1965), Kruglanski (1969), and others. In the unilateral power condition, where both A and B accept A's legitimate power to prescribe a given behavior for B, then conflict is practically eliminated.

Several recent experiments and discussions (e.g., Pruitt, 1967; Thibaut, 1968; Thibaut & Faucheux, 1965) have stressed the conflict limiting function of legitimate norms. The basic assumption underlying such emphasis rests in interpersonal and intergroup conflict (characterized by spying, distrust, overt hostilities, etc.) which is disruptive of the normal functions of society.

Thus, when the two potentially conflicting parties have a mutually understood and accepted legitimate basis for determining the influence patterns of one over the other, conflict may be limited or eliminated. In comparison with reciprocated reward and coercive power, the reduction of conflict through mutually accepted legitimate power not only minimizes manifest conflict, but is also unlikely to increase latent conflict as would be the case with coercive power. Mutual surveillance would not be necessary and mutual trust would continue. Impersonal conflict would be resolved without subsequent increase in person-oriented conflict and hostility.

Legitimate power, of course, will not reduce conflict unless there is mutual acceptance of the basis of legitimacy and of the legitimate domain of power for each party. A husband and wife may each have clear conceptions as to the legitimate domain of authority of the other. However, these will frequently not coincide, particularly if the two partners come from differing cultural backgrounds. If conflict is to be diminished through legitimate power, there must be a new mutual agreement, which would likely involve the use of informational influence or persuasion with respect to what should be the legitimate power of husband and wife. Conflict may arise through differential conceptions of legitimacy when more than one legitimate basis of power might arise. Legitimate power based on property rights would allow the rancher who owns the water hole to deny access to anyone; legitimate rights based on some broader conception might allow the itinerant shepherd to assume that he has the right of access, if the water hole is the only one in the area and his sheep are thirsty. The conflict which results is then likely to revert again to coercive power, unless some other means is determined, such as the development of a new social contract which would involve turning to a third party to adjudicate the conflict.

When there is potential loss through mutual threat or possibility of greater gain through accommodations, legitimate bases of power may be developed; in other words, in a group or interpersonal interaction situation, the development of social contracts may proceed in the same way that Locke observed for their development in society. A point of particular interest is the determination of the conditions under which such contractual limitations, and establishment of mutual legitimacy, would develop, and when, instead, the possibility of threats would lead to actualization of mutual punishment and a further increase in manifest and personal conflict. Pertinent to this question is work by Thibaut and Faucheux in which they focused on structural features of the conflict situation which might be conducive to the acceptance of conflict limiting rules (Faucheux and Thibaut, 1964; Thibaut, 1968; Thibaut and Faucheux, 1965).

These investigators used an experimental paradigm in which inter-dependent pairs of Ss (A and B) negotiated the distribution of points between them. A was the more powerful member as he was authorized to decide how to split the points. His degree of "usable power" vis à vis B increased with the number of points to be divided. The authors refer to this kind of power as internal threat. B's power vis à vis A was of a different kind; B had the choice of leaving A for an alternative situation, which would thus be rather punishing for A, since he could not now receive some rewards which might be available to him through interaction with B. The attractiveness of the alternative situation for B was thus varied. The investigators defined this possible "coercive power" of B as the "external threat."

Following an initial play, the two participants were given an opportunity to form contracts between them and determine the degree of their enforcement. The available contracts were of three kinds: (1) the EA rule limiting the use of external threat; (2) the D rule restricting the use of internal threat; and (3) the RC rule irrelevant to the experimental manipulations.

The central finding replicated several times in the course of this research is that only when both the external and internal threats are high (as opposed to conditions where only one was high or both were low) was there a significant increase in the players' tendency to form enforceable contracts of the EA and the D kinds limiting the use of threats.

From these findings it is possible to draw the following generalizations concerning the structural features of conflict relevant to the development of contractual norms. Contracts are likely to be formed (1) when they provide a solution acceptable to both parties, and (2) when the threat they guard against would otherwise have a high probability of being used. It is important to note that the above conditions are probably insufficient for the formation of contracts. The contracts were presented by a neutral and authoritative third party (a critical aspect of the research just considered), namely, the experimenter, Thibaut (1968) cites the work by Wells which suggests that the presence of such a third party is at least highly facilitative if not indispensable to the formation of formal norms.

Apart from the structural features of conflict which may be relevant to the invocation of legitimacy, certain other aspects of the situation may strongly indicate, "demand," or legitimize a given behavior. Thus, in research by Deutsch (1960), "cooperative" instructions by the experimenter explicitly stated for the subjects that cooperation was indicated under the circumstances. Similarly, "competitive" instructions established the legitimacy of competition. It is not surprising to find that the Ss cooperated in the former case and competed in the latter.

In a study by Wilson, Chun, and Kayatani (1965) the subjects played the same Prisoner's Dilemma game within and between teams. It was found that the preponderance of cooperation occurred in the former case while in the latter the interaction was mainly competitive. It appears that defining the relationship as "in group" indicated the appropriateness of cooperation while defining it as "out group" legitimized competition.

C. Reciprocated Referent Power

Competitive conflict is less likely to occur if both parties have a high degree of identification with one another, or a mutual desire for such identification. Indeed such mutual referent power might be an underlying basis for avoidance of conflict or aggression even when there is incompatibility of needs and goals such that conflict might ordinarily be expected (Wheeler & Levine, 1967). During the "honeymoon period" of marriage, a desire for mutual identification may be particularly great such as to overcome the particularly great discrepancies in needs and behaviors between the newly-wed couple. Appeals to national unity in times of stress may also be sufficient to bring about reduction in conflict between groups with discrepant needs. In the Sherif and Sherif study (1953) of the development of conflict in a boys camp, increased referent power between two boys' groups was accomplished through introduction of superordinate goals (e.g., arranging a jointly organized social event or creating a situation in which both groups had to work together to unplug a stopped up water reservoir) or by providing a common threat or enemy. Presenting a common enemy has been used effectively by many political figures in bringing about national unity. The enemy serves as a common *negative* referent, and through what is essentially a process of cognitive balance, the two conflicting groups may then focus on their mutual similarities and on diminishing their mutual differences. The negative reference of the outgroup then further provides for a contrast effect, minimizing perceived differences within the groups. Thus, in effect, conflict within groups is reduced by increasing conflict between groups. The superordinate goal approach to conflict reduction is applied to larger groups and international relations by Sherif (1966). It is also true that as conflict increases, and particularly as certain bases of power are resorted to, such as coercive power, then reference decreases and discrepancies between subgroups may be emphasized.

D. Reciprocated Expert Power

When two parties are in competitive conflict, it is difficult to conceive of either utilizing expert power with respect to the other. Expert power of A over B stems not only from B's attributing superior knowledge to A, but also from B's trusting A. If there are incompatible goals, then B can reasonably assume that A is using his superior knowledge to influence B in a direction which would favor A and not B. Obviously, if two countries were involved in a border dispute, country B would not be influenced by an expert from country A who ventured the opinion that a particular allocation of land would be in B's best interests. Only if A can supplement his expertise with well-developed informational influence could he anticipate that this influence would be accepted. When the two parties are interdependent with respect to goals, and when the conflict is with respect to means, then expertise can become a prominent basis for influence. However, expert power of A over B within a given domain depends upon the degree of superiority in knowledge of A *relative* to B. Thus, if they both have an equally high degree of expertise in a given domain, the degree of expert power of each over the other will be slight. Two physicians, both of equal competence, who are in conflict as to the best means for treating a given patient cannot rely on their expertise, even though they both trust one another: both have the patient's therapy as a common goal. They must then each rely on informational power, on persuasion, each marshalling the evidence to support his position.

Equivalent expert power may become more important when the expertise of the two parties, though equal, is in different domains. Such expert conflict is evident in current international policy in which experts in military matters argue for one pattern of national policy, but experts in diplomacy argue for different action on the international level. Each has a high and possibly equal degree of expertise in his own domain, and there may well be a recognition of common ultimate goals and common mutual trust, yet there is conflict. The resolution of such conflict becomes particularly difficult without the intercession of third parties. Though we have suggested that means conflict is generally more readily resolved than goals conflict, failure at resolution may lead to increased underlying personal conflict. The military expert may attribute to the diplomat an undue concern with personal goals over group goals or even national disloyalty; the diplomatic expert may come to believe that the military expert is more concerned with maintaining his position in the military organization than he is concerned with the establishment. Either or both may be correct in whole or in part. Conflicts will often involve mixed motive relationships and concern about group means may also be intertwined with concern about individual goals. However, conflict with respect to means may lead to further emphasis and exaggeration of such tendencies, to increased underlying conflict and distrust, or to subsequent reduction of each party's expert power with respect to the other. Where expert and referent power of each over the other is high, distrust may lead to reduced expert power and diminished referent power as well.

There is also reason to speculate that an increase in expert power will also reduce referent power. Expert power stems from attributed superiority; referent power increases with perceived similarity. This is exacerbated when the expert is self-conscious about his expertise and superiority and manages to communicate this to the person who is influenced. The result may be the development of negative referent influence. Such is obvious in the example of the "ugly American" technical expert who manages to alienate the very people whom he is trying to influence (Lederer & Burdick, 1958). Expert power may then become a basis for underlying personal conflict.

E. Reciprocated Informational Power

Just as informational influence is often considered the ideal means for changing attitudes, opinions, or behavior, it is similarly seen as the preferred means for reducing or forestalling conflict. Two well-intentioned parties, it is felt, should be able to get together to discuss their differences, to understand one another's needs and limitations, and to make appropriate concessions and compromises. If conflict is resolved in this way, then each party will likely accept the changes privately as well as publicly, and, it is hoped, the resolution will remain permanent. The limitations of informational power, however desirable, have been spelled out elsewhere (Collins & Raven, 1969; Raven, 1965; Sherif, 1966). Informational influence, while *socially* independent, is nonetheless dependent on other elements in the influencee's cognitive structure. One cannot influence a person to change his attitudes or behaviors with respect to some object through changing his perception of the relationship between previous attitudes and his more basic values (Carlson, 1956; Rosenberg, 1960). However, such change is dependent both on the influencee's holding the assumed basic values, on his not holding stronger values which are counter to the change, and on the effectiveness of the informational message. In competitive conflict situations, the problem is made more difficult, since the distrust which results from discrepant goals will lead to further distrust, with even greater tendencies to avoid the communication entirely, to question its veracity, and to reinterpret it in terms of one's own initial needs. Reciprocal informational power is more likely to be effective in resolving means conflict than in reducing goal or competitive conflict. The distrust and mutual dislike which occurs in competitive conflict, particularly after some instances of coercion by one party or the other, are such that the two parties are likely not even to make use of the communication channels which are available to them (Deutsch & Krauss, 1962). Even when communication occurs, it is likely to be selectively listened to by both parties. Stagner has characterized such communication as a "dialogue of the deaf" (Stagner, 1967). Thus, though it would be satisfying to believe that conflicts could be resolved if adequate means for conflicting parties to discuss their differences were provided, there is considerable evidence to the contrary. Indeed, there are many instances in which the opportunity for communication of differences has been used for expression of mutual hostility, with subsequent escalation of conflict.

F. Reciprocated Power and Response

Much of what we have said above can be summarized and extended through the application of the "moving toward, against, away" indicated in Table I. If we now consider the table as duplicated, so as to indicate the effects of B's power on A's behavior, beliefs, interaction, and identification, we can then examine the possible combinations. We can reasonably consider the conditions under which the two tables are indeed additive. Unfortunately, we would find that very often they are not since the same power which A could use to get B to surrender some commodity might also be utilized to deter B from using an aversive pattern of power against A. Thus, the combination coercion–coercion, with A and B having an equal amount of coercive power, would likely lead to "moving against" in identification, interaction, and private beliefs, but the combination would not likely lead to mutual "moving toward" in behavior. The stalemate with respect to influence on overt behavior would further increase hostility, leading to further "moving against" in the other dimensions. With respect to reward-reward, we might anticipate mutual "moving toward" in overt behavior and interaction. Might we not also find that the possibility for mutual exchange and the demonstration of mutual ability to reward the other would also lead to increased perception of similarity and identification? With respect to legitimacy–legitimacy, perhaps we would find that the feelings of mutual obligation, providing adequate rationale for reciprocated compliance, might continue to allow for "moving away" in identification. Expert–expert might produce uncertainty in identification. On the one hand, the mutual exchange of expertise would emphasize interdependence and possible identification; yet since expertise emphasizes discrepancy, it could also emphasize difference. Furthermore, as indicated previously, where the two parties lay claim to some degree of expertise, each would reject the expert power of the other. With informational power, a similar distrust could operate. Each party attempts to persuade the other but rejects the information of the other as merely being an attempt at manipulation. It is only with reciprocated referent power that we can have some confidence that there would be mutual moving toward in all dimensions, provided, of course, that mutual referent power could be established. The two parties with a common basis for identification, a common goal, a common threat, or a common enemy can then mutually exert referent power over each other leading to mutual moving toward in behavior, belief, interaction, and further identification. This is, indeed, what was demonstrated in the Sherif and Sherif camp studies. As mentioned earlier, the only devices which they could use in getting conflicting groups of boys to reestablish friendly cooperative relationships were common threats and mutual superordinate goals (Sherif, 1966; Sherif & Sherif, 1953).

V. DYADIC CONFLICT WITH NONRECIPROCATED POWER BASES

We began with a discussion of the effects of unilateral power, considering each basis of power separately and then in combination. We next considered reciprocated power bases in dyadic conflict in which both parties utilized the same basis of power with respect to the other. As a next logical step in our analysis, we might not consider the possible combinations of power in dyadic conflict in which each party had available, or was inclined to utilize, one basis of power and where these two bases did not correspond. There are fifteen such possible combinations. At this point we will not attempt to review all relevant studies in the literature but merely present a few examples—the reader will undoubtedly be able to think of others.

(1) *Coercion vs. reward.* A Prisoner's Dilemma game in which the cell entries are appropriately determined.

(2) *Coercion vs. legitimate* and (3) *reward vs. legitimate.* Power of the powerless, e.g., employer has the power to fire the worker or to increase his wages, while worker may appeal to his right to request a living wage.

(4) *Coercion vs. expert* and (5) *reward vs. expert.* Employer has power to fire worker, worker may emphasize his direct knowledge of the job and the extent to which he is indispensable to the employer.

(6) *Coercion vs. informational* and (7) *reward vs. informational.* Appeals of discriminated minority to the immorality of the actions of the powerful majority, or to their moral rights to certain rewards or benefits.

(8) *Coercion vs. referent* and (9) *reward vs. referent.* Black demonstrator appealing to black policemen *not* to arrest him since they are both black. Wife requesting funds to purchase a new dress on grounds that "it is all in the family."

(10) *Legitimate vs. expert.* Supervisor insisting that subordinate is obliged to perform his task as requested; subordinate arguing that his direct experience with the task leads him to believe that such a procedure would prove inefficient.

(11) *Legitimate vs. informational.* Same example as above except that subordinate attempts to prove to the supervisor that the recommended procedure would prove inefficient.

(12) *Legitimate vs. referent.* Subordinate attempting to overcome "legitimate" demands that he perform an unpleasant task (e.g., officer's request that soldier storm a dangerous hill) on grounds that "we are all part of the same team."

(13) *Expert vs. referent.* Similar to legitimate–referent, except that here supervisor relies on his expertise as a basis for requesting the subordinate to perform the unpleasant act.

(14) *Expert vs. informational.* Doctor relying on his expertise in prescribing specific form of physical therapy to the patient while patient attempts, through logic, to convince physician that a program would be impossible to carry out.

(15) *Referent vs. informational.* Parent trying to persuade his young child that he should get to bed early and get some rest. Child arguing that since parents are staying up, he wants to stay up.

We will not further elaborate our discussion of this section except to point out the potential analyses of conflict in such terms. What would be the relative effectiveness of one type of power when juxtaposed against another? Obviously, the answer to this question could not be complete until we had determined the degree of each type of power which each party could mobilize in the given situation. Further examination would also involve a consideration of the effects of these types of power in terms of "moving toward," "moving against," and "moving away" in behavior, belief, identification, interaction.

VI. DYADIC CONFLICT WITH MULTIPLE POWER BASES

Continuing our examination of conflict from the more simple to its more complex and more general forms, we must now take cognizance of the fact that both parties to dyadic conflict often have more than one basis of power available to them. Each then must determine the basis of power, or the combinations of power, which he will utilize with respect to his adversary. In our parallel discussion of unilateral power, we indicated that both personal and impersonal underlying and manifest factors will determine the basis of power which would be utilized. The factors related to choice of power base in that section—likelihood of longlasting change, costs of power, desire for continued dependence, distrust, frustration and displacement of aggression, legitimacy of power choice, evaluation by third parties, and self-esteem and power needs—would also be present in dyadic power relationships. The further complexity is added by the interaction between use of power by one party and the choice of power options by the other. Each party's choice of power base is determined in part by his perceptions of the other person and his expectations regarding what type of power the other will use on him, and these perceptions will both contribute toward the choice of power which each utilizes and, with the use of power, affect future changes in perception of each party both of himself and of the other.

A complete analysis of the power-conflict situation might well take the following form:

(1) Consideration of the characteristics and self-perception of each of the antagonists. What are his individual and interpersonal needs, what are his values, what expectations does he have both of himself and of others?

(2) What bases of power are available to each antagonist? What restrictions or costs are related to the use of each of these bases of power?

(3) What are the important manifest and latent, personal and impersonal, factors which lead him to use one type of power rather than another?

(4) What is his perception of the antagonist? What expectations does he have of his opponent and the type of power which he might utilize?

(5) On the bases of such an analysis of each of the antagonists, one might then attempt to predict what basis of power each would in fact use.

(6) What then would be the effects of the mutual use of power on each of the antagonists? Would each "move toward," "move away," or "move against" in his interaction, identification, behavior, and beliefs?

(7) How does the use of power change each person's perception of himself, the other, and objects of controversy?

(8) Then repeat the steps in the analysis 1–7, following each successive use of power by each of the parties.

A Social Power Analysis of the Process of Escalation

There have now been a number of social psychological analyses of the process of escalation in conflict (e.g., Deutsch, 1962, 1969; Etzioni, 1962; Newcomb, 1947; Osgood, 1962; Pruitt, 1965, 1967; Sherif & Sherif, 1953; Stagner, 1967). These studies of escalation have many common elements. Following from our preceding theses, we would argue that a study of the process of escalation can become even more meaningful if we consider the power relationships involved in the conflict situation. We will not carry out a complete examination in these terms but will merely suggest the manner in which social power analysis could be utilized.

In the typical analysis of escalation, it is pointed out that conflict with respect to goals is likely to lead to mutual distrust. Communication by the other is likely to be distorted and rejected as manipulative. Thus, informational influence is rejected. Expertise will be similarly rejected since even if B attributes superior knowledge to A, he is likely to reject A's recommendations as being merely a use of A's superior knowledge to manipulate or exploit B. The hostility and distrust which accompany competition will undermine legitimate power. Distrust and negative interdependence will further destroy the possibility of referent power. Differences will be emphasized and similarities will be minimized. Reward power may prove effective temporarily but always under suspicion. Reward will be considered as a bribe or as stemming from a desire to maintain dependence and superiority. Thus, when reward is effective, it would nonetheless lead to moving against in belief, interaction, and identification. A anticipates the ineffectiveness of each of the above bases of power and, thus, may avoid using them—or if he does attempt to use them, he will soon find that they are indeed not effective. B will go through a similar process in attempting to influence A. Each side thus comes to the realization that only coercive power is effective. A further attributes to B the desire to use coercion, both because he assumes a reasoning process on the part of B which is very similar to his own and because such an attribution provides justification for A's use of coercion. B goes through a similar process of attribution with respect to A. The use of coercion is then seen as justified by the circumstances; the attribution of coercive power to the other becomes a self-fulfilling prophecy (Merton, 1957). Legitimate restraints against the use of coercion are thus removed so that the use of coercion is interpreted as countercoercion, preretaliation, or a justified first strike.

Frustration and hostility resulting from being the recipient of coercive power then leads both parties to "move against" in behavior, belief, interaction, and identification. Concern about appearance before third parties and lowered self-esteem increase further the desire to influence the other by means of coercion even where other bases might conceivably prove effective. Thus, the underlying and personal bases of conflict become even greater. The power preferences of the two antagonists then further increase the possibility of further use of coercion by each.

The various analyses of escalation mentioned above also point to the difficulty of reducing conflict when escalation has begun. Once coercion has begun, "moving against" in communication or interaction and behavior and belief further diminish the possibility of other means of influence other than coercion. As discussed previously, Deutsch and Krauss found that once coercion had been used, available communication channels were not utilized even when each party was being seriously injured by continued use of coercion (Deutsch & Krauss, 1962). They found, indeed, that the third party had to force the use of communication in order to reduce escalation. In international affairs, the United Nations sometimes serves this function in interpersonal matters; the legal system often plays such a role. In the Sherif and Sherif camp studies (1953), the experimenter manipulated mutual threats and goals to increase mutual referent power. Osgood (1962), Deutsch (1969), Sherif (1966), Pruitt (1965), and others have offered suggestions as to how to undo the effects of escalation. However, it seems that we have learned more about how escalation develops than we know about how to reverse the process.

VII. SUMMARY AND SOME LOOSE ENDS

This chapter has attempted to illustrate the manner in which theories and findings regarding social power and social influence in interpersonal relations can be applied to the understanding of social conflict. We began by defining the typical unilateral social influence situation as a social conflict situation in that it involved a discrepancy between what one party wished the other to do and what the other was inclined to do. The unilateral power situation was then examined in terms of how the use of reward, coercive, legitimate, expert, referent, and informational bases of power affected the simple conflict situation. Horney's conceptions of "moving toward," "moving against," and "moving away" seemed particularly applicable in this regard. Both underlying and manifest, personal and impersonal conflict determined the choice of power by an influencing agent.

Having examined the unilateral power-conflict situation, we extended our analyses to dyadic conflict and power. The power analysis provided a richer basis for the analysis of dyadic conflict, but the interaction of the various power bases and various reactions to the use of power made the analysis particularly complex. The full analysis of dyadic conflict would require a consideration of the characteristics of the two parties, their self-perceptions and perceptions of others, and the sources of power available to them; from these we might predict what basis of power would in fact be utilized by each of the parties. The utilization of a particular constellation of power sources would, in turn, alter the perceptions which each has with respect to himself and with respect to the other. This, in turn, will again lead to changes in power preference on the part of each of the parties, and the analysis would then continue. The application of social power analyses to the escalation process was provided as an example.

For the student of social conflict, our analysis may point toward some critical directions for research and study. Yet it is also likely that we have raised more questions than we have answered. The process of analysis becomes increasingly complex as we apply it to interpersonal, intergroup, and international conflict. The introduction of third and fourth parties to the conflict, and the processes of coalition formation add complexity. Yet we are convinced that if we are to understand the processes of conflict, and look toward means of reducing conflict, the social power analyses described above will provide directions for exploration.

REFERENCES

Bem, D.J. An experimental analysis of self-persuasion. *Journal of Experimental Social Psychology,* 1965, **1**, 199–218.

Bem, D.J. Self-perception: An alternative interpretation of cognitive dissonance phenomena. *Psychological Review,* 1967, **74**, 183–200.

Berkowitz, L., & Daniels, L.R. Responsibility and dependency. *Journal of Abnormal and Social Psychology,* 1963, **66**, 429–436.

Berkowitz, L., & Daniels, L.R. Affecting the salience of the social responsibility norm: Effects of past help on the response to dependency relationships. *Journal of Abnormal and Social Psychology,* 1964, **68**, 275–281.

Berkowitz, L., & Geen, R.G. Film violence and the cue properties of available targets. *Journal of Personality and Social Psychology,* 1966, **3**, 525–530.

Berkowitz, L., Klanderman, S.B., & Harris, R. Effects of experimenter awareness and sex of subject and experimenter on reactions to dependency relationship. *Sociometry,* 1964, **27**, 327–337.

Berkowitz, L., & LePage, A. Weapons as aggression-eliciting stimuli. *Journal of Personality and Social Psychology*, 1967, 7, 202–207.

Brehm, J.W. *A theory of psychological reactance*, New York: Academic Press, 1966.

Brock, T.C., & Buss, A.H. Effects of justification for aggression and communication with the victim on post-aggression dissonance. *Journal of Abnormal and Social Psychology*, 1964, 68, 403–412.

Brown, B.R. The effects of need to maintain face on interpersonal bargaining. *Journal of Experimental Social Psychology*, 1968, 4, 107–122.

Carlson, E.R. Attitude change through modification of attitude structure. *Journal of Abnormal and Social Psychology*, 1956, 52, 256–261.

Cartwright, D. Influence, leadership, and control. In J.G. March (Ed.), *Handbook of organizations*. Chicago: Rand McNally, 1965, Pp. 1–47.

Cartwright, D., & Zander, A.F. (Eds.) *Group dynamics*, (3rd ed.), New York: Harper, 1968. Pp. 99–100.

Collins, B.E., & Raven, B.H. Group structure: Attraction,coalitions, communication, and power. In G. Lindzey & E. Aronson (Eds.), *Handbook of social psychology*. Vol. 4 (2nd ed.) Reading, Mass.: Addison-Wesley, 1969, Pp. 102–204.

Coser, L.A. *The functions of social conflict*. New York: Free Press, 1956.

Coser, L.A. *Continuities in the study of social conflict*. New York: Free Press, 1967.

Daniels, L.R., & Berkowitz, L. Liking and response to dependency relationships. *Human Relations*, 1963, 16, 141–148.

Deutsch, M. Trust and suspicion. *Journal of Conflict Resolution*, 1958, 2, 265–279.

Deutsch, M. The effect of motivational orientation upon trust and suspicion. *Human Relations*, 1960, 13, 123–139.

Deutsch, M. Cooperation and trust: Some theoretical notes. In M.R. Jones (Ed.), *Nebraska symposium on motivation*, Lincoln, Neb.: University of Nebraska Press, 1962. Pp. 275–319.

Deutsch, M. Bargaining, threat and communication: Some experimental studies. In Kathleen Archibald (Ed.), *Strategic interaction and conflict. Original papers and discussion*. Berkeley, Calif.: University of California Press, 1966, Pp. 19–41.

Deutsch, M. Conflicts: Productive and destructive. *Journal of Social Issues*, 1969, 25, 7–42.

Deutsch, M., & Krauss, R.M. The effect of threat upon interpersonal bargaining. *Journal of Abnormal and Social Psychology*, 1960, 61, 181–189.

Deutsch, M., & Krauss, R.M. Studies of interpersonal bargaining. *Journal of Conflict Resolution*, 1962, 4, 52–76.

Douglas, A. Peaceful settlements of industrial and intergroup disputes. *Journal of Conflict Resolution*, 1957, 1, 69–81.

Etzioni, A. *The hard way to peace*. New York: Collier Books, 1962.

Fanon, F. *The wretched of the earth*. New York: Grove Press, 1963. (Translated by Constance Farrington.)

Faucheux, C., & Thibaut, J. L'approche clinique et expérimentale de la genèse des normes contractuelles dans différentes conditions de conflit et de menace. *Bulletin, du Centre d' Etudes et Recherches Psychologie*, 1964, 13, 225–243.

Festinger, L. An analysis of compliant behavior. In M. Sherif & M.O. Wilson (Eds.), *Group relations at the crossroads*. New York: Harper, 1953. Pp. 232–256.

Fink, C.F. Some conceptual difficulties in the theory of social conflict. *Journal of Conflict Resolution*, 1968, 12, 412–461.

French, J.R.P., Jr. A formal theory of social power. *Psychological Review*, 1956, 63, 181–194.

French, J.R.P., Jr. & Raven, B.H. The bases of social power. In D. Cartwright (Ed.), *Studies in social power*. Ann Arbor: University of Michigan, 1959. Pp. 150–167.

Gallo, P.S., Jr. Effects of increased incentives upon the use of threat in bargaining. *Journal of Personality and Social Psychology*, 1966, 4, 14–20.

Gamson, W.A. *Power and discontent*. Homewood, Ill.: Dorsey Press, 1968.

Goranson, R.E., & Berkowitz, L. Reciprocity and responsibility reactions to prior help. *Journal of Personality and Social Psychology*, 1966, 3, 227–232.

Gumpert, P. Some antecedents and consequences of the use of punitive power by bargainers. Ph.D. Dissertation, Teachers College, Columbia, 1967.

Harsanyi, J.C. Measurement of social power, opportunity costs, and the theory of two-person bargaining games. *Behavioral Science*, 1962, 7, 67–79.

Heider, F. *The psychology of interpersonal relations*. New York: Wiley, 1958.

Hobbes, T. *Leviathan,* 1651. (Reprint of 1st ed. London and New York: Cambridge University Press, 1904.)

Horney, K. *Our inner conflicts*. New York: Norton, 1945.

Hornstein, H.A. The effects of differential magnitudes of threat upon interpersonal bargaining. *Journal of Experimental Social Psychology*, 1965, 1, 282–293.

Jones, E.E., & Davis, K.E. From acts to dispositions. In L. Berkowitz (Ed.), *Advances in Experimental Social Psychology*, Vol. 2. New York: Academic Press, 1965. Pp. 219–266.

Jones, E.E., Gergen, K.J., & Jones, R.G. Tactics of ingratiation among leaders and subordinates in a status hierarchy. *Psychological Monographs* 1963, 77, (3, Whole No. 566).

Kelley, H.H. Experimental studies of threats in interpersonal negotiations. *Conflict Resolution,* 1965, 9, 79–105.

Kelley, H.H. Attribution theory in social psychology. In D. Levine (Ed.), *Nebraska symposium on motivation*. Lincoln, Neb.: University of Nebraska Press, 1967. Pp. 192–238.

Kelley, H.H., Condry, J.C., Jr., Dahlke, A.E., & Hill, A.H. Collective behavior in a simulated panic situation. *Journal of Experimental Social Psychology,* 1965, 1, 20–54.

Kelley, H.H., & Ring, K. Some effects of "suspicious" versus "trusting" training schedules. *Journal of Abnormal and Social Psychology,* 1961, 63, 294–301.

Kelman, H.C. Compliance, identification, and internalization: Three processes of attitude change. *Journal of Conflict Resolution,* 1958, 2, 51–60.

Kelman, H.C. Processes of opinion change. *Public Opinion Quarterly,* 1961, 25, 57–78.

Kruglanski, A.W. Incentives in interdependent escape as affecting the degree of group incoordination. *Journal of Experimental Social Psychology,* 1969, 5, 454–467.

Kruglanski, A.W. Some mechanisms of attributing trustworthiness in supervisor-worker relations. *Journal of Experimental Social Psychology,* 1970, in press.

Lederer, W.J., & Burdick, E. *The ugly american*. New York Norton, 1958.

Loew, C.A. Acquisition of a hostile attitude and its relationship to aggressive behavior. *Journal of Personality and Social Psychology.* 1967, 5, 335–341.

Luce, R.D., & Raiffa, M. *Games and decisions: Introduction and critical survey*. New York: Wiley, 1957.

Merton, R.K. *Social theory and social structure*. (Rev. ed.) Glencoe, Ill.: Free Press, 1957.

Michotte, A. The perception of causality. London: Methuen, 1963.

Milgram, S. Group pressure and action against a person. *Journal of Abnormal and Social Psychology,* 1964, 69, 137–143.

Mintz, A. Non-adaptive group behavior. *Journal of Abnormal and Social Psychology,* 1951, **46**, 150–159.

Newcomb, T.M. Autistic hostility and social reality. *Human Relations,* 1947, **1**, 3–20.

Osgood, C.E. *An alternative to war or surrender.* Urbana, Ill.: University of Illinois Press, 1962.

Pettigrew, T.F. Social evaluation theory: Convergences and applications. In D. Levine (Ed.), *Nebraska symposium on motivation.* Lincoln, Neb.: University of Nebraska Press, 1967. Pp. 241–315.

Pruitt, D.G. Definition of the situation as a determinant of international action. In H. Kelman (Ed.), *International behavior: A social psychological analysis.* New York: Holt, 1965. Pp. 391–433.

Pruitt, D.G. Reaction systems and instability in interpersonal and international affairs. Technical Report No. 2, 1967 Contract N00014-67-C-0190, State University of New York at Buffalo.

Rapoport, A. *Fights, games and debates.* Ann Arbor, Mich.: University of Michigan Press, 1960.

Rapoport, A. Game theory and intergroup hostility. In M. Berkowitz & P.G. Bock (Eds.), *American national security: A reader in theory and policy.* New York: Free Press, 1965. Pp. 368-375.

Rappoport, L.H. Interpersonal conflict in cooperative and uncertain situations. *Journal of Experimental Social Psychology,* 1965, **1**, 323-333.

Raven, B.H. Social influence and power. In I.D. Steiner & M. Fishbein (Eds.), *Current Studies in Social Psychology.* New York: Holt, 1965. Pp. 371–382.

Raven, B.H., & Eachus, H.T. Cooperation and competition in means-interdependent triads. *Journal of Abnormal and Social Psychology,* 1963, **67**, 307–316.

Raven, B.H., & French, J.R.P., Jr. Legitimate power, coercive power, and observability in social influence. *Sociometry,* 1958, **21**, 83–97.

Raven, B.H., & Rietsema, J. The effects of varied clarity of group goal and group path upon the individual and his relation to his group. *Human Relations,* 1957, **10**, 29–47.

Ring, K., & Kelley, H.H. A comparison of augmentation and reduction as modes of influence. *Journal of Abnormal and Social Psychology,* 1963, **66**, 95–102.

Rosenberg, M.J. A structural theory of attitude dynamics. *Public Opinion Quarterly,* 1960, **24**, 319–340.

Schultz, D.P. Theories of panic behavior: A review. *Journal of Social Psychology,* 1965, **66**, 31–40.

Sherif, M. *In common predicament: Social psychology of intergroup conflict and cooperation.* Boston: Houghton-Mifflin, 1966.

Sherif, M., & Sherif, C.W. *Groups in harmony and tension.* New York: Harper, 1953.

Simmel, G. *Conflict: The web of group affiliations.* Glencoe, Ill.: Free Press, 1908. (Translated by K.H Wolff, 1955.)

Skinner, B.F. *Verbal behavior.* New York: Appleton, 1957.

Stagner, R. *Psychological aspects of international conflict.* Belmont, Calif.: Brooks-Cole, 1967.

Thibaut, J.W. The development of contractual norms in bargaining: Replication and variation. *Journal of Conflict Resolution,* 1968, **12**, 102–112.

Thibaut, J.W., & Faucheux, C. The development of contractual norms in a bargaining situation under two types of stress. *Journal of Experimental Social Psychology,* 1965, **1**, 89–102.

Thibaut, J.W., & Kelley, H.H. *The social psychology of groups.* New York: Wiley, 1959.

Thibaut, J.W., & Riecken, H.W. Some determinants and consequences of the perception of social causality. *Journal of Personality,* 1955, **24**, 113–133.

Thomas, E.J. Effects of facilitative role interdependence on group functioning. *Human Relations,* 1957, 10, 347–366.

Walton, R.E., & McKersie, R.B. *Interpersonal interdependency. A behavioral theory of labor negotiations: An analysis of social interaction system.* New York: McGraw-Hill, 1965.

Wheeler, L., & Levine, L. Observer-model similarity in the contagion of aggression. *Sociometry,* 1967, 30, 41–49.

Wheeler, L., & Smith, S. Censure of the model in the contagion of aggression. *Journal of Experimental Social Psychology,* 1966, 2, 1–10.

Willis, R.H. Conformity, independence, and anticonformity. *Human Relations,* 1965, 18, 373–388.

Willis, R.H., & Hollander, E.P. An experimental study of three response modes in social influence situations. *Journal of Abnormal and Social Psychology,* 1964, 69, 150–156.

Wilson, W., Chun, Natalie, & Kayatani, M. Projection, attraction, and strategy choices in intergroup competition. *Journal of Personality and Social Psychology,* 1965, 2, 432–435.

Chapter 4

SOCIAL POWER IN INTERPERSONAL NEGOTIATION

Charles L. Gruder

I. INTRODUCTION

The goal of the participants in a mixed-motive or bargaining situation is to reach some agreement as to how to divide between themselves the total outcome available from their relationship. They are interdependent inasmuch as each participant's share of the outcome is determined, in part, by the other's decision and, in part, by his own. The bargaining revolves around the attempts by each to influence the other to make a decision which would yield one a relatively greater share of the total at the other's expense. Concomitantly, each does his best to resist the influence attempts of the other. In most "real world" settings each is aware that the other has an alternative to negotiations in this interpersonal relationship, even if that alternative is only to "leave the field" and receive nothing. It is, therefore, assumed that negotiations will not occur unless each party believes that he can gain more from the relationship than by withdrawing from it—that the relationship is better than the alternative to it. Each bargainer must beware that he does not demand too great a share of the outcomes; if the other perceives this as a threat to his profits, he may be forced to opt for his alternative, thus destroying the potentially profitable relationship. However, the relatively attractive outcomes available within the relationship serve as an incentive for both to continue negotiations in order to work out a mutually acceptable agreement.

Kelley (1966) has characterized this situation by a set of dilemmas bargainers face in the course of negotiations to an agreement. These dilemmas arise from the conflicting motives guiding each bargainer's behavior. By cooperating with his fellow player, through compromise and concession, he stands a relatively good chance of reaching agreement. By competing with his opponent for a greater share of the total, he runs the risk of driving him from the relationship.

Certainly one factor which determines the style and strategies a bargainer employs is his *power* over his opponent in the relationship. It seems self-evident that the more power he has, the better is his chance of success in any competition. This is all said very easily, but the meaning of power remains unclear. Hence, the first part of this chapter is addressed to the conceptualization of power. Although the concept of power is basic to discussion of any social influence process, nowhere is it more applicable than in research on interpersonal and intergroup negotiations. In no other situation has it more face validity. In the world of formal negotiations, big business, big labor, blacks and whites, public service employees, and aspirants to public office all extol the necessity (if not the "virtues") of power.

There have been a number of attempts in social science to deal with the concept of social power theoretically (Schopler, 1965); the present discussion will employ the orientation and terminology presented by Thibaut and Kelley (1959). A brief résumé of their approach is appropriate before launching into a discussion of power in interpersonal negotiation. Their initial focus on the dyad as a social exchange facilitates identification of sources of power in mixed-motive relationships. Once these sources are identified, attention is turned directly to interpersonal conflict and its resolution. It is generally assumed that the conflict between parties is a function of the *structure* of their relationship—the pattern of outcomes available as a joint consequence of decisions made by them. Behavior in the conflict situation is discussed first in terms of strategies and styles employed by bargainers. It is clear that behavior in a conflict does not necessarily lead to resolution of that conflict. The goal of such behaviors is often short-term dominance and gain, with little concern for subsequent interaction or extended resolution of the conflict. With the latter goals in mind, research is reviewed on the resolution of conflict through the distinctively social psychological process of norm adoption. Finally, the related issues of intergroup negotiation and power within a bargaining party are discussed.

II. THIBAUT AND KELLEY'S CONCEPTUALIZATION OF SOCIAL POWER

Power, in their terminology, is the capability one person has of affecting another's outcomes in an interpersonal relationship. These investigators consider an interpersonal relationship to be a social exchange in which the parties' behaviors yield them *rewards* at the expense of *costs* involved in maintaining the relationship. The *outcomes,* then, are the balance of the rewards and costs involved in interpersonal behavior. The assumption is made that outcomes can be ordered according to their utility for an individual, outcomes with a greater reward-to-cost ratio having a higher scale value of "goodness" than those with a lower ratio. To limit the discussion to a dyad, as Thibaut and Kelley do, the extent of one individual's power over the other is defined by the potential range of outcomes which the individual can determine for the other.

It is necessary to introduce two closely related concepts for further discussion of social power. The *comparison level (CL)* is "the standard against which the member evaluates the 'attractiveness' of the relationship or how satisfactory it is . . . . It may be taken to be some modal or average value of all known outcomes, each outcome weighted by its 'salience,' or strength of instigation . . . (Thibaut & Kelley, 1959, p. 21)." Given this definition, it becomes clear that a relationship in which outcomes are evaluated as falling above CL on some continuum of "goodness" are experienced as satisfying to the individual. Where the outcomes received fall below the established CL, the relationship is an unattractive one.

Even if outcomes are below CL, however, the individual may remain in the relationship. Whether he dissolves the relationship by leaving it, is determined by the relation of his experienced outcomes to a second construct—his *comparison level for alternatives (CLalt)*. Thibaut and Kelley define CLalt as "the lowest level of outcomes a member will accept in the light of available alternative opportunities . . . .The height of the CLalt will depend mainly on the quality of the best of the member's available alternatives . . . (pp. 21–22)." The CLalt may be the option of leaving the relationship for no other interpersonal relationship, i.e., being alone. While the outcomes an individual receives in an interpersonal relationship may be compared to his CL to assess his *attraction* to the relationship, his outcomes may be compared to his CLalt to yield an indication of his *dependence* on the relationship for outcomes. Both CL and CLalt are dynamic concepts inasmuch as the former is assumed to change with the quality of the outcomes experienced, and the latter with the quality of the outcomes anticipated in the best alternative relationship.

Thibaut and Kelley employ a matrix to exhibit the outcomes to the two parties in an interdependent relationship. This matrix is formed by one member's set of available responses being arrayed along one axis and the other's possible behaviors appearing along the perpendicular axis. Interaction in the relationship is depicted as joint enactment from each member's available responses, and the outcomes to each member are shown in the cells defined by the row and column intersections of those behaviors. Of course, any discussion of a dyadic relationship usually focuses only on a particular, limited number of responses from the entire behavioral repertoire of each participant. In other words, practical use of such matrices is limited to investigation of the course of interaction where each participant has available only a few restricted and well-defined responses. This is easily recognizable as similar to the use of matrices by decision and game theorists. And as these theorists do, Thibaut and Kelley assume that individuals will respond to maximize their outcomes.

Thibaut and Kelley discuss two ways in which members of a dyad may control one another's behavior. *Control* means that power is activated to affect the other's outcomes, causing him to alter his behavior. These two kinds of control are defined by the structure of the interaction matrix. Figure 1 depicts a situation in which each respondent has available two responses: A has a_1 and a_2, and B has b_1 and b_2. Any combination of responses by A and B yields each an outcome; A's outcomes are located above the diagonal, and B's below the diagonal in each cell. It is obvious that regardless of what B does, if A does a_1, B will receive 1, and if A does a_2, B will receive 4. A is said to have *fate control* over B. At the same time, B has *behavior control* over A. That is, by changing his behavior from b_2 to b_1, B can influence A to change his behavior from a_1 to a_2. (It is appropriate to reiterate the assumption that both parties choose options which they feel will maximize their outcomes.) B should have no preference between b_1 and b_2. His outcomes are not directly affected by his own responses; whether he gets 1 or 4 is entirely a function of whether A chooses a_1 or a_2. At first glance, it would appear that when A has fate control over B, he cannot actually influence B's responses in the way that B can influence his responses. However, through a process Thibaut and Kelley call *conversion of fate control to behavior control*, A can exercise this influence. A must monitor B's responses and make his responses contingent upon B's. That is, when B chooses b_2, A should choose a_1, and when B chooses b_1, A should choose a_2. In this way, A can guide B's behavior so that B always responds with b_1, resulting in a mutually satisfactory outcome, given that A continues to choose a_2.

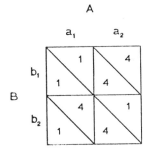

FIG. 1. Fate control and behavior control.

Power was defined earlier as the *capability* or *potential* one member has to affect the other's outcomes. Although the greater power a party possesses to control another's outcomes might seem to imply easier and more effective control of another's behavior, given Thibaut and Kelley's definition, this is not always the case. As we shall see, attempting to implement power to affect another's responses is the basis for much of the intricate and subtle behavior that constitutes "bargaining" in a mixed-motive situation. There are a number of restrictions on the realization of the potential for changing another's behavior. Thibaut and Kelley introduced the notion of *usable power* to make allowance for these restrictions. Very simply, a person's usable power is "the power that it is convenient and practicable for him to use (p. 107)."

For example, when the use of power to affect another's outcomes adversely affects the user's outcomes adversely at the same time, he should be less likely to resort to it. Figure 2 shows such a situation. It seems reasonable that A would be quite unlikely to exercise his fate control over B, given the effect of such a move on his own outcomes.

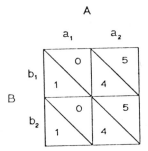

FIG. 2. Adverse effects of power use. Taken from Table 7.4, Thibaut and Kelley (1959, p. 107).

Usable power is also delimited by the *relative power* of the two members of the dyad. Relative power is determined by comparing the range of the other party's outcomes each party can control, whether through fate control or behavior control; it identifies power advantage. In Fig. 3, a situation of *mutual fate control,* B has greater relative power than A because he can move A through a greater range of outcomes than A can move him through. It is sometimes convenient to consider a dyadic power relationship from the point of view of one party. When we talk of A's potential response to B's exercise of power over him, we talk of A's *counterpower* over B; this really refers, more simply, to A's power over B. In the relationship described in Fig. 4, while B still has greater relative power than A, A's counterpower is greater than it is in the relationship of Fig. 3. The less the difference in relative power between the two parties (i.e., the greater the counterpower of the less powerful party), the less usable power the more powerful party is thought to have. So, B's usable power is less in the relationship of Fig. 4 than that of Fig. 3 because A has more counterpower over B in the relationship of Fig. 4. B's use of his relative advantage is restricted by the implicit threat of A's retaliation; this threat is greater where A has more counterpower. The concepts apply to relationships where the nature of the power each party possesses over the other differs; for example, in the relationship of Fig. 1, A has fate control over B and B has behavior control over A. There may be any number of unique patterns of interdependence between A and B, but these different patterns may all be interpreted in terms of the power relationship. There may be a dominant cell in the matrix, in which case usable power might be used only sparingly, or eschewed altogether, in the attempt to coordinate joint responses to share in the mutually satisfactory outcomes. Or there may be a conflict of interest between A and B, resulting in competitive behavior—use of power to control the other's responses by altering his outcomes.

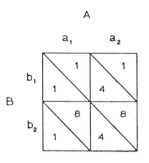

FIG. 3. Mutual fate control.

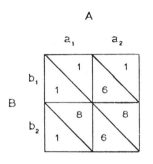

FIG. 4. Mutual fate control.

Another limitation on use of power is a somewhat indirect one. The less attractive A's CLalt, the worse the outcomes he will tolerate in his relationship with B. That is, the lower A's CLalt, the greater the range of his outcomes under B's control (the greater B's power). So if A has only a poor alternative to the outcomes he can obtain in his relationship with B, *and particularly if he knows that B knows this,* A would be unlikely to exercise his power. He is *dependent* on the relationship for outcomes, and would be unlikely to endanger its continued existence by exercising his power and forcing B to abandon their relationship for *his* CLalt. So greater dependence implies less usable power, as well as less relative power within the relationship.

III. SOURCES OF POWER IN MIXED-MOTIVE BARGAINING

Where there is a conflict of interest in an interpersonal relationship, the potential outcomes to the two parties are noncorrespondent. In other words, there is a negative correlation between the two players' outcomes over all possible joint decisions they can make. In the usual laboratory relationship they make one, or a series, of these joint decisions. In essence, this procedure amounts to the two parties deciding how to divide the total available between themselves. Relative to their next best alternatives, they both stand to gain from interacting, but each is motivated to compete for a greater share of the total outcome available. Each party employs his power to implement strategies to gain at the other's expense.

Power has five sources in the mixed-motive situation. The first three are related in that they can be used to alter the other's share of those outcomes about which there is a conflict of interest; they are the incentive and reason for the existence of the particular relationship being considered. In other words, these behaviors enable one member to affect the outcomes the other can receive from the "game" itself. The other two sources of power reside in the bargainer's ability to alter outcomes available to his opponent from other relationships, either with the bargainer or with third parties.

A. Alteration of Outcomes the Other Receives in the Relationship under Study

1. Choose Alternatives to Interaction with Other

One source of interpersonal power is the availability of alternative outcomes to those gained through interaction with the other party. There are two senses in which a member can exercise this power.

a. Leave the Relationship for CLalt. First of all, the bargainer may choose to leave the relationship, and to obtain his own outcomes from his next best alternative, his CLalt. Opting for his CLalt simultaneously forces the other party to his CLalt; potential outcomes through interaction are foregone. Choosing the CLalt, then, constitutes a source of power in that it is possible by choosing it to reduce the other's outcomes, although at some cost to oneself. A strike by labor against management is a common example of using this source of power. Workers decide to leave their jobs in order to force management to concede to demands for higher wages, better working conditions, a greater role in the organization's decision-making, etc. By stopping work, labor reduces production and profits of the organization, publicizes its own plight, presents management and the organization in an unfavorable light in the public eye, etc. Labor reduces management's outcomes by striking, but only at some cost to itself. After all, compared to continuing to work, striking has unfavorable consequences to labor, as well as to management; labor is also identified with the organization, and unfavorable publicity labor causes may also reflect on it. Labor foregoes wages during the strike period, with no guarantee that settlement of the dispute will include reimbursement.

b. Provide Additional Options within the Relationship. A second sense in which a party may use alternatives as a source of power is when he provides response options for himself which are not formally defined as part of the relationship's structure. Where bargaining decisions are ad lib, he may refuse to make offers or to acknowledge offers made by the other. Refusal to negotiate can, in some relationships, result in time running out and both parties gaining nothing. However, where the rules require that he make decisions in a regulated series, he may exercise power by persevering with one choice. This may have the same effect as refusing to respond altogether—drastically reducing both parties' outcomes. The option chosen for perseverance would ordinarily be the one most favorable to himself and least favorable to the other. This would motivate the other to retaliate in kind, resulting in a mutually unprofitable stalemate. Depending on the relative reductions in outcomes, however, this may provide one party with more power than the other, perhaps resulting in a break of the stalemate.

In a sense this is analogous to choosing an alternative to interaction. In both instances, in order to induce the other to make decisions more favorable to himself, the party threatens to, or actually sabotages the relationship. Where there are a number of iterations or plays of the game, he may actually choose his CLalt or refuse to negotiate one or more times to convince the other of the seriousness of his demands.

2. Control of Outcome Allocation

The second source of power to affect the other party's game outcomes coincides with what is perhaps an intuitive definition of power. One party may alter outcomes the other receives by the nature of his choices from the legitimate set available to him.

a. Direct Control. The extreme case of this source of power is where outcome allocation is left totally to one party. For example, in the experimental game devised by Thibaut and Faucheux (1965) for their research on norm adoption, one S in the dyad was given the task of deciding the final outcome allocation after he and the other party reached a tentative agreement regarding it. Or, for an example from an everyday situation, the instructor makes the final decision as to whether he will give a student a requested change of grade after negotiations between the two are terminated.

Where one party ultimately has complete control over outcome allocation, the other party's counterpower is restricted, by definition, to attempts at extending his power to outcomes his superior may receive from outside the game itself. The subordinate may threaten blackmail, or more subtly point out to his superior that decisions which are unprofitable to him (the subordinate) will create a bad image in the eyes of some relevant third party. In other words, the subordinate's goal is to change his superior's perception of the utility of his own (the superior's) outcomes. The subordinate wants the superior to see those behaviors which are more attractive to the subordinate as, in fact, more attractive to the superior as well. Such strategies sound like those which young, weakly organized labor groups purportedly used in their sometimes hostile negotiations over wage and benefit increases with the decision makers of management. It is possible that unilateral capability of altering within-game outcomes leads to attempts by the weaker party to establish counterpower by altering exogenous outcomes. Such "illegitimate" attempts may be the reason why there is often resort to impartial arbitration to resolve the dispute.

b. Control through the Nature and Pattern of Own Decisions. In a typical experimental game used in laboratory research, each player must make a decision by choosing one of the options available to him. The players are dependent on one another for outcomes: What each receives is determined, in part, by his own choice and, in part, by the other's choice. So, one party, by the nature of his decisions, may alter the other's outcomes. What is of greatest interest, however, is his pattern of choices over a series of decisions. Does he attempt to influence the other to change his behavior by making his own choices contingent on the other's choices? If so, how does he implement his power? Does he reduce the other's outcomes when the other selects an option unfavorable to him; does he increase the other's outcomes when the other has decided favorably for him; or does he use some combination of these contingent responses? On occasion he will have the opportunity to communicate his intentions to the other party; in this case, does he threaten or promise to make his responses contingent on the other's?

Kelley and Ring (1961) and Ring and Kelley (1963) report research on the use of reward ("augmentation") and punishment ("reduction") as means of behavior control. Kelley, Thibaut, Radloff, and Mundy (1962) investigated behavior in a relationship of mutual fate control (Fig. 5). Kelley *et al.* (1962) concluded that while there was some development of cooperation in the dyad, the parties' awareness of the contingencies of their interdependence fostered even greater resolution of conflict. Perhaps S was more likely to attempt to convert his fate control to influence the other person's responding when he knew his behavior would have some effect on the other's outcomes—when he perceived that he had power over the other. Sidowski (1957) demonstrated that awareness of reinforcement contingencies did not affect the incidence of mutually reinforcing responses. However, as Kelley *et al.* argued, Sidowski may not have explained the nature of the interpersonal contingencies in sufficient detail to obtain an effect. In the Prisoner's Dilemma, too, a *change* in choice of

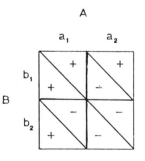

FIG. 5. Mutual fate control.

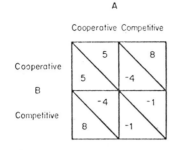

FIG. 6. Prisoner's Dilemma.

rows or columns can be interpreted as an attempt to use power. By playing the "cooperative" choice, one sets the conditions for the other to receive more favorable outcomes, regardless of the other's choice (Fig. 6). In the sense that this response alters the other's outcomes it is an exercise of power. It may result in control over the other's behavior. The other may interpret this cooperative choice as a signal that the chooser is willing to be trusting and cooperative, and consequently opt for his own cooperative choice.

c. *Influence Other's Decisions.* The intricate communication which takes place through the pattern of game decisions admits a great deal of "noise" into the channel. This means that signaling and the exercise ,of power are often ambiguous and inefficient in accomplishing their purpose—resolving the conflict of interest. Where verbal communication is permitted, on the other hand, the parties can attempt to influence the option the other chooses much more directly. However, this directness may be offset by the subtleties involved in the employment of strategies. Certainly, the possibility exists with verbal communication that the negotiators will say one thing and do another. The bargaining at the verbal level may not foster resolution, so they will conduct all "real" bargaining through their decisions (as just discussed in Section III, A, 2, b). An example of verbal negotiations which seemed to have worked counter to the goal of conflict resolution occurred between US and North Vietnamese diplomats during their preliminary peace talks in Paris in 1968. Each side's prepared statements read at negotiation sessions and public comments which followed were propagandistic in tone. If anything, these statements seemed to drive the two parties further apart rather than to draw them closer together. Any progress toward termination of the war could only be identified by an observer of the actual decisions about the conduct of the war which each government made. A bombing halt by the US or a cessation of guerrilla attacks on South Vietnamese cities by the Viet Cong and North Vietnamese would be such decisions. But the negotiation statements, while having face validity for a negotiated resolution of the war, seemed, in fact, to be unrelated to behavior that constituted steps in that direction.

3. Implement Power Available in Further Interaction

The two parties may engage in further interaction in this same relationship; we may distinguish two cases.

a. Iterations of the Game. A number of plays of the game may occur within one session, as in much laboratory research. For example, in research on Prisoner's Dilemma (Rapoport & Chammah, 1965) or Deutsch and Krauss' trucking game (1960, 1962), Ss knew that they would engage in a series of joint decisions. Concessions during play could sometimes be traded off for the other's promise of concessions during the next play. It is also possible that each iteration may occur during a different session, sessions being separated by days, months, or even years. Annual labor–management contract negotiations exemplify this situation.

b. Negotiation of More Than One Issue. There may be more than one source of outcomes available in the experimental game. As an example of this case, consider the experimental situations employed by Bass (1966) and Kelley (1966). In both studies, bargaining parties were required to reach agreement on a number of issues. Bass' situation was more of a simulation (of labor–management negotiations) than Kelley's; the issues Bass' subjects negotiated were named and described in detail: wages, union checkoff of dues, etc. The students in Kelley's classroom negotiations, on the other hand, bargained about five content-free issues. There was a moderate noncorrespondence of their outcomes over these five issues. The importance of an issue for a party was defined by the range and magnitude of the outcomes available from settlement of that issue; the most important issue was the one with the widest range and/or the highest value. The importance of issues did not necessarily correspond for the two parties. Each party knew only his own range of outcomes for each issue, so it was possible for an astute bargainer to make concessions on what was for him a relatively unimportant issue in return for concessions from the other on a more important and valuable issue.

Kelley's game serves to emphasize the point being made here—relative power advantages in one aspect of the relationship (viz., on one issue) may be used to yield gains in others. This tendency was so prevalent in the experimental situations employed by Kelley and Bass that with some experience, bargainers learned not to commit themselves to agreements on one issue prematurely; instead, they made tentative agreements on all issues. This enabled them to avoid a dilemma involved in unalterable commitment to an agreement on an issue: Once a concession is final, it cannot be used as effectively in strategy as when it is only promised. If a concession is just tentatively agreed upon, a threat to recall this promised concession may be used as a means of forcing the other to concede on issues of greater importance to the promiser. Once the concession is final, on the other hand, it is a much less potent source of power; the conceder can only appeal to a norm of reciprocity for good deeds in order to influence his opponent to decide in his favor.

B. Alteration of Other's Outcomes from Exogenous Sources

The remaining two sources of power in a mixed-motive situation are related to the capability one party has of altering outcomes his opponent may receive, but which are not those Ss negotiate directly. These were alluded to in the discussion of a "one-sided" power relationship (Section III, A, 2, a). These sources of power must be distinguished from those outlined in Section III, A, 3; the outcomes under consideration in that section were the basis of negotiation—typically, the values entered in the game matrix. The first part of this section centers on sources of outcomes for which the parties are interdependent, but which are independent of the game matrix. These may be available in other aspects of the same relationship, or in other relationships to which they may both be committed. The second part of this section concerns power one party may have to alter outcomes the other may receive from relationships with third parties. As R. Wyer (personal communication) has suggested, exercise of these sources may have the effect of raising the other's utility for responses in the game which result in favorable outcomes to the power user. The power user may gain control over outcomes outside the game, and make presentation of them contingent upon the other's responses within the game.

1. Future Interaction with the Other

Power available from future interaction with the other may be implemented as follows: Once aware of their future interdependence, parties may take advantage of this commitment to express intentions as to how they will behave during this interaction. Although it is not usually possible, a party might be able to alter the other's *future* outcomes *in advance*, i.e., during the present negotiations.

a. Exogenous Outcomes within One Relationship. Anticipation of inter-dependence for additional sources of outcomes in the same relationship has been operationalized in two studies—Marlowe, Gergen, and Doob (1966) and Gruder (1968). Ss were told that following play of the game or negotiations they would discuss with the opposing party what transpired. The outcome which Ss anticipated they would be able to alter during subsequent interaction were of an entirely different nature than those which were the subject of negotiations. For example, the bargainer who felt that unfair advantage might be taken of him during negotiations could anticipate charging the potential offender with violation of norms of equity and fair play. An offended party could hope to force the other to admit its guilt publicly, following negotiations. Transgressions of norms during negotiations could result in "loss of face" in the eyes of any observers as well as opponents, following negotiations. The effects of anticipation of future interaction on bargaining style and on the outcome of negotiations were interpreted in accord with the present argument.

In the study by Gruder, half of the bargainers faced a programmed opponent, whom they saw as attempting to exploit them. Half of these threatened parties anticipated future interaction with their uncooperative opponent and half of them did not. Anticipation seems to have served as counterpower for the threatened parties, who assumed a more unyielding stance against the aggressor than the bargainers who did not expect to meet their opponent following negotiations. According to Gruder, bargainers who did *not* have recourse to future discussion as a source of counterpower gave in to the demands of their opponent, perhaps in an attempt to reach *some* agreement on this one and only bargaining trial. On the other hand, threatened negotiators who anticipated mutual "accounting" with their opponent did not experience the urgency of reaching agreement during the game itself. They could forego the outcomes available through negotiation, because they would have the opportunity to recoup their loss by publicly accusing their opponent of unfairness during the subsequent accounting session. Refusal of their opponent to concede a reasonable distance toward their relatively fair offer could be used as evidence against him.

Marlowe *et al.* obtained similar results in an experiment in which Ss played Prisoner's Dilemma. The investigators manipulated the perceived personality of the opponent ("self-effacing" vs. "egotistical") rather than the cooperative or competitive nature of his play as Gruder did. Ss either anticipated discussion of the play following the game or not. Marlowe *et al.* found that anticipation of interacting with an egotistical opponent resulted in more competitive play than no anticipation.

Where an opponent appears to be cooperative, one has the option of reciprocating his cooperation or taking advantage of him. Knowing that the other will have the opportunity to exercise sanctions for inequitable play should curtail exploitation. Evidence seems to support this analysis. In Gruder's study, Ss were more compromising (less competitive) with an opponent whom they saw as fair, when they were accountable to him than when they were not. Marlowe *et al.* obtained a similar finding for anticipated interaction with a self-effacing opponent.

b. Exogenous Outcomes in Another Relationship. There is the possibility that the parties may meet again in another, entirely different relationship. The best example of this case is negotiations between friends. They tend to share the same reference groups, and future interaction is likely to occur over a wide range of situations. Behavior during the negotiations under investigation are certain to be affected by the bargainers' awareness of this state of affairs.

Research by Morgan and Sawyer (1967) bears out this expectation. They found that when negotiating against a friend, a bargainer with lower potential outcomes was more likely to behave as he thought the other expected him to behave—even where that meant foregoing relatively greater outcomes. This self-sacrificing behavior did not appear among nonfriends, those who had expressed negative affect for one another. Furthermore, this sacrifice only occurred when the friends were not aware of each other's expectations. When they were allowed to communicate, they agreed that each should get an equal amount, thus actually favoring the party with the lower potential outcomes. It seems that with no communication, the weaker party made an unnecessary sacrifice; this only became apparent when agreements were compared with those reached under conditions of communication between the parties. Implicit in this sacrifice is the proposition that a friend would not want to endanger the outcomes available in their relationship outside the laboratory by exercising the power he possesses in the experiment. As Morgan and Sawyer put it, "this implies that the asymmetry of the experimental situation is less important than the symmetry of the larger situation (1967, p. 145)."

Swingle (1966) and Swingle and Gillis (1968) found that in Prisoner's Dilemma players responded *in kind* to friends; that is, they responded cooperatively to cooperative friends, and uncooperatively to uncooperative friends. Nonfriends did not show this contingency phenomenon in their play. That friends behaved cooperatively in response to cooperative play complements Morgan and Sawyer's finding that friends anticipated and accommodated one another's preferences where preferences were not communicated.

It still remains to explain the uncooperative behavior Swingle (1966) observed between friends. Uncooperative behavior constitutes an attempt to use power available within the game. A player may realize that allowing a friend to take advantage of him by exercising power available in the game endangers the viability of their extralaboratory relationship. His friend's use of power *without his own retaliation* could upset the balance of outcome sharing they had achieved in their friendship. If the threatened partner did not at least attempt to thwart the other from exploiting him in the game, it might be expected that he would demand retribution in their extralaboratory relationship. Because retaliation is probably expected to occur anyway in subsequent interaction, it is not inconsistent (as Swingle elucidates) for liked partners to have uncooperative exchanges within the game. As Swingle and Gillis (1968) point out, friends tend to match their partner's behavior. This leads to a pattern of interaction in which power is employed sensitively, contingent upon the other's responses.

2. Information Available to Additional Persons

Even though a negotiator may not be able to alter his opponent's outcomes directly, he may be able to do so through other parties—parties which do have the power to alter his opponent's outcomes. By providing them with information or by exercising power he has over them, the negotiator will have indirect control over his opponent. Thibaut and Kelley (1959, p. 191ff.) considered this possibility in their discussion of interpersonal relationships in the triad. They analyzed the simplified case in which each of three parties in a triadic relationship can exercise power (as either behavior control or fate control) over *one* of the other parties. If party A wants party C to behave in a manner favorable to A, A must deal with party B, over whom he does have power. A arranges to be magnanimous to B, if B uses his power over C to influence C to provide A with favorable outcomes.

a. Observers. Brown (1968) demonstrated the effects on a negotiator's bargaining of providing him with knowledge of observers' reactions to his style and strategy. In other words, the observers' reactions constituted an additional source of outcomes to the negotiator. The quality of these outcomes was ostensibly contingent upon the negotiator's performance. When he was led to believe that the observers thought him an ineffective bargainer early in the session, he was more likely to employ aggressive, competitive responses later, even at a cost to himself, than where he did not see the observers as critical of his bargaining.

In Brown's study the observers' responses were controlled by E so that this factor could serve as an independent variable. But it appears reasonable that this source of power exists in naturalistic settings, as well. It is necessary that observers' reactions be a source of outcomes for one negotiator. His opponent can then exercise power over him simply by publicizing the observers' reactions. Or his opponent might have to use his influence over the observers to have them announce their reactions publicly.

b. Other Parties to the Conflict. The existence of more than two parties to the conflict brings the study of coalition formation into the discussion (Caplow, 1956; Chertkoff, 1967; Gamson, 1964). In situations in which coalitions are likely to form, two or more parties agree to combine their power because their *joint* power is sufficient to resolve the multiple conflicts of interest. Rather than each of the several parties applying its individual powers directly against all opponents, some reach agreement with one another to unify their powers. The parties to this coalition then jointly direct their greater power against those parties outside the coalition. This provides a resolution of the complex pattern of interdependencies among parties. Where coalition research has been concerned with the determinants of unification, other research (to be discussed in Section VI) has investigated the effects of various intraparty power relationships on interparty negotiations.

Gamson (1964) has systematically reviewed the theories proposed to account for when a coalition will be formed, and to predict which of the possible coalitions will be formed. Predictions from two of these theories are based on the power relationships which will exist *within* the potential coalitions. *Minimum resource theory* considers each party's initial resources to be its base of power; the joint initial resources of prospective coalition partners determine whether they will be strong enough to control the parties outside the coalition. This theory maintains that the coalition most likely to be formed is the one in which the parties' combined initial resources are just large enough to control the remaining parties.

Minimum power theory also bases its prediction of which coalition will be formed on the minimum joint power necessary to control the parties outside the coalition. However, in this theory, power is not equated with initial resources— that is, a party with higher initial resources does not necessarily have greater power. Power is defined by the proportion of coalitions in which the party can be involved in which its resources would make that coalition a winning one. This is known as the party's *pivotal power.*

Once a coalition is formed, interparty conflict is reduced: The coalition is now dominant in the competition involved in the relationship. However, there is the added dimension of conflict within the coalition. The issue is how the parties to the coalition will divide the spoils of their joint action. Minimum resource theory is based on the *parity norm,* which implies that the parties should receive shares proportional to their initial resources. Minimum power theory, on the other hand, seems to recognize that as long as neither party is powerful enough to win alone, both parties are equally important to the coalition, and each should receive an equal share of the winnings.

The two theories reviewed by Gamson (1964) do not make use of the concept of social power. *Anticompetitive theory* was the result of a generalization of findings from research in which the Ss were primarily females (Bond & Vinacke, 1961; Uesugi & Vinacke, 1963; Vinacke, 1959). These Ss behaved as if they were interested in keeping disruption in the relationship at a minimum. Coalitions were predicted among parties of equal power—they would have the least difficulty in dividing the winning share. These Ss seemed less concerned than Ss in the studies supporting minimum resource and minimum power theories with the formation of a coalition as a means of reducing the total conflict. The explanatory principle in *utter confusion theory* is random choice; coalitions are thought to be simply the result of nonsystematic factors such as physical proximity among parties and noise in the communication channels. Although the value of these last two theories may seem dubious, it is possible that they will help to explain certain inconsistencies between the "power" theories and observed data (as pointed out by Chertkoff, 1967).

Gamson reviews evidence which supports each of these four theories, and concludes that features of the experimental situations may be identified which, when manipulated, should increase the likelihood of support for each. To obtain results supportive of minimum resource theory (Gamson, 1961; Vinacke & Arkoff, 1957), competitively oriented subjects should be allowed sequential communication among themselves to bargain for moderately high stakes. In addition, the parity norm should be made salient by means of prior experimental tasks. Results favoring minimum power theory (Kelley & Arrowood, 1960; Willis, 1962) should occur where Ss are strangers who are allowed controlled, free communication in bargaining for the highest possible stakes. In addition, the individuals should be rotated in different triads to prevent stable interpersonal relationships from forming. Anticompetitive theory should be supported by results of an experiment using as Ss acquaintances who anticipate future inter-action with one another. (Bond & Vinacke, 1961; Uesugi & Vinacke, 1963; Vinacke, 1959). Females would be the best Ss, and they should bargain for minimal stakes. Results favoring utter confusion theory (Kalisch, Milnor, Nash, & Nering, 1954; Willis, 1962) should obtain with unacquainted, unsophisticated Ss who are prevented from forming stable relationships over trials. Rules should be complicated, communications difficult, and time pressure great. Outcomes available from alternative coalitions would be similar and much greater than out-comes available from exclusion from any coalition.

Although conflict may begin among interdependent parties whose out-comes are not correspondent, other parties may become a part of the relationship. Schelling (1963, p. 24ff.) describes how one party may bring another party into the relationship, essentially to form a coalition against an opponent. Schelling gives an example of the way in which such a move may be used to demonstrate one's commitment to a bargaining offer. If a potential buyer says that he will pay no more than $16,000 for a house for which the seller is asking $20,000, the buyer's statement is no more than a bid or an offer—he has not used power over the seller in order to force a concession from him. It is one's offer against the other's. In order for the buyer to gain power over the seller, he must find some way of restricting the seller's potential range of outcomes; lowering the maximum price he can pay for the house is one possibility for restricting the range. But the buyer must be able to implement this power, to demonstrate that the restricted range of outcomes is beyond his control to alter. If the buyer can make a bet with a neutral and reputable third party to the effect that if he buys the house for more than $16,000, he forfeits $5000 to the third party, he has a demonstrable commitment to his position. He has gained power over the seller in the sense that he has reduced the seller's maximum obtainable outcome in the relationship from $20,000 to $16,000. Before placing his bet, the buyer had no way of affecting the seller's outcome. Where, prior to the bet, the seller might have hoped to get his asking price from this buyer, subsequent to the bet, he knows that the buyer has restricted his own concession possibilities by his commitment. If anyone is to concede, the seller knows it will have to be he; without increasing the seller's profit, the buyer has raised the cost of the house to himself by $5000 if he pays more than $16,000. This means that the buyer could not reasonably buy the house for more than his final offer of $16,000.

Schelling also raises the intriguing possibility that the seller could find the third party, offer him a sum to release the buyer from the bet, and threaten to sell the house to the buyer for $16,000, if the third party refuses to accept the seller's proposition. (If the seller carried out his last threat and sold the house to the buyer for $16,000, the third party would lose his bet with the buyer.) For example, if the third party accepts the seller's offer of $1000, and the seller sells the house to the now powerless, uncommitted buyer for $18,000, he would end up with a $1000 profit over what he would have earned had the bet remained in force and had he sold for $16,000.

Schelling also takes care to note that a bargainer does not always have a convincing way of demonstrating his commitment to an offer. Perhaps the highly unlikely nature of his example is evidence for the difficulty of providing such a demonstration. This problem will arise again in the discussion of strategies which follows.

The above discussion has considered the dyadic and triadic relationships as social exchanges which provide the parties with power, with the ability to alter outcomes of others. But this discussion did not answer the important questions of how, when, and why such power is used. In the next section, the specific ways in which different sources of power may be implemented in mixed-motive situations will be delineated. In addition, commonalities in power use over situations will be identified.

IV. STRATEGY

A. Definition and Purpose in Mixed-Motive Bargaining

Although every person who finds himself in a conflict of interest with another will handle the situation differently, it is possible to identify regularities in bargaining behavior over individual bargainers. There may be *solutions* to conflicts; solutions can be carefully specified prior to negotiations. They identify how both negotiators should respond in order to guarantee themselves mutually satisfactory outcomes. The solution for a mixed-motive game in which the negotiators' goal is to maximize their own outcomes would be different from the solution where this goal is to maximize the difference between their outcomes. Information each may have about his opponent's utility for outcomes and how the other plans to negotiate would be taken into account in determination of the correct solution. As the negotiations proceed, these factors are likely to change, thus dictating changes in the solution. It seems that any prescribed solution would either have to be very complex or very general to take account of all these contingencies. Solutions which are too complex would probably not be very useful to a negotiator because it would be too difficult to monitor all the contingencies necessary to guide behavior. Solutions which are too general would not provide enough information as to how they might be implemented.

Although there may not be many useful solutions to mixed-motive negotiations, there are certainly *resolutions*. The conflict is resolved, but not necessarily to the parties' mutual satisfaction. The outcome of a solution is specifiable prior to negotiations; the outcome of a particular resolution may take many forms. We can identify commonalities in the ways in which conflicts are handled by different negotiators. These commonalities may be called strategies. The term is often used in two senses. The first refers to a plan for behavior which takes account of a party's goals in negotiations. If a negotiator wants to reach an agreement in which he receives a larger share of the outcomes than his opponent, he would be likely to adopt what might be called a "competitive strategy." More accurately, this first sense refers to a general orientation toward the bargaining, which will be referred to here as *style* rather than as strategy. *Strategy* will be reserved for the other sense in which the term is often used—to refer to specific behaviors, the intention of which is some relatively immediate effect on the other's behavior, the attainment of a subgoal. Strategies are techniques used to increase usable power in bargaining. While the sources of power described in Section III are often present, their implementation is not guaranteed. A negotiator must use his power cleverly or his opponent will be able to mobilize counterpower to prevent the move from having its intended effect. This is where strategies are valuable. The strategies employed make up the negotiator's style. He can be characterized as a "competitive," "fair," or "ineffective" bargainer by the way he uses the power available to him.

B. Examples

The problems of communication, trust, suspicion, and temptation ordinarily built into mixed-motive situations provide vast opportunities for the imaginative and effective use of strategies. Strategies are often attempts to convince the other that one should receive a greater share of the total outcomes than the other offers or is willing to agree to. To do this a negotiator can implement power he possesses, or he can attempt to distort his opponent's perception of the power relationship.

1. Commitment and Refusal to Compromise

One of the simplest strategies is to maintain one's bargaining demands— that is, not to concede. Because this violates negotiation mores (Iklè & Leites, 1962) it may be more difficult to do when there is full communication between the parties. With communication, the stubborn negotiator would be expected to defend his position. Without communication, it is impossible for the stubborn negotiator to explain or justify his bargaining stance, and this is to his advantage. As described earlier (Section III, B, 1, a), Gruder (1968) found that a negotiator who faced a fair and compromising other was *less* compromising when the bargaining was anonymous and there would be no subsequent confrontation than when the negotiator felt he would have to justify his style and strategies to his opponent following negotiations.

Thibaut (1968) reports a study (the dependency variation, Section V, F) in which bargainers had the option of "stalling," of wasting the limited time allowed for each negotiation trial. Negotiators were charged for the time taken to reach agreement; these costs were subtracted from their gross outcomes. If no agreement was reached, each side received its alternative source of outcomes. A strategy to force the other party to compromise, then, was to refuse to compromise with him; this forced the opponent to make the decision to accept less in the interest of reaching agreement. The strategy is based on the assumption that the other will accept a smaller share in order to avoid the time costs.

Deutsch and Krauss' studies (1960, 1962) also employed a cost for time used to reach agreement. In the conditions in which the parties did not have weapons or threats (i.e., gates), their only defense was an offense. In order to prevent an opponent from achieving his goal, a negotiator merely had to attempt to achieve his own goal. This resulted in a mutual standoff, and a waste of valuable time. Borah (1963), using a modification of Deutsch and Krauss' game, measured the time subjects stood head-to-head in a standoff on the one-lane path. He found no difference on this measure between the gate and no-gate conditions. The availability of electric shocks as another means of threatening the other did not seem to affect use of this strategy either.

The problem facing the bargainer choosing to employ the strategy of commitment and refusal to compromise is how to convince his opponent that he will not, under any circumstances, compromise further. Ostensibly, in the time-wasting strategy, the longer a bargainer holds out, the more convinced his opponent will become that the bargainer is committed to his standing offer. Particularly when there is communication between the bargainers, this "stand pat" strategy is enhanced by the availability of a response indicating that the negotiator is committed to his position. Schelling (1963) provides an insightful discussion of the role commitment plays in negotiation. By commitment he means that the bargainer conveys to his opponent that he has taken a position from which he is incapable of moving. The oft cited example attributed to Schelling is when one of the contestants in a game of "chicken" locks the front wheels of his car in place, and within the other driver's view discards his steering wheel, so as to force the other to "chicken out." Schelling's emphasis on commitment in bargaining was also commented on in another context (Section III, B, 2, b).

Even where there is no communication between the parties, commitment is possible in the nature of the offers made; Schelling calls this phenomenon *tacit bargaining*. He provides an example drawn from military operations. One infantry unit (A) is likely to withdraw to a river or a road, and to take a stand there. As soon as unit A retreats even slightly behind such a natural dividing line, its enemy (B) is convinced that A is not committed to that point, and it is B's to take without a costly struggle. A river provides a prominent or obvious boundary at which the retreating army should make a stand. Their pursuers would recognize their commitment to this position and weigh carefully their decision to attack.

Such a coordination of independent expectations also occurs in *explicit bargaining*, according to Schelling. Despite the fact that you have told an automobile salesman that you want to pay a maximum of $3000 for a new automobile, he may attempt to sell you a more expensive car. As soon as you indicate an attraction for a particular optional feature which would bring the price even slightly above $3000, the salesman has the upper hand. He senses that your commitment is not as strong as you would have him believe, and should you make a minimal concession, say to $3025, he will try to take advantage of it by trying to sell you other "extras." You have abandoned the original bargaining position to which you were ostensibly committed, indicating an openness to further exploitation.

2. Threats and Promises

A negotiator may convince his opponent to change his behavior without actually altering the opponent's outcomes. If the opponent knows that the negotiator possesses the power to affect his outcomes, he is going to be responsive to suggestions from the negotiator. The negotiator can offer to use his power magnanimously, or not to use it detrimentally, if the opponent yields to the negotiator's demands. Or the negotiator can explain that he will reduce the opponent's outcomes, if the latter does not comply with the negotiator's requests. Promises and threats involve placing contingencies on an opponent's compliance or noncomplaince with bargaining demands. They may be used singly or in combination. Schelling (1963) points out that a threat takes on less credibility without an accompanying promise. A judge who threatens to "throw the book" at the confessed offender unless he reveals the names of his accomplices is unlikely to elicit cooperation without an associated promise of leniency.

While threat has perhaps been the most studied strategy in mixed-motive relationships (Borah, 1963; Deutsch & Krauss, 1960, 1962; Gallo, 1966; Gruder, 1968; Kelley, 1965; Shomer, Davis, & Kelley, 1966), it has also been defined differently by these many investigators. Deutsch and Krauss equated it with use of a weapon. Shomer *et al.* (1966) provided *S*s with separate responses for threatening to use, and actually using, their weapons. By far the most restrictive definition is Schelling's (1963, p. 123ff). He classifies threat as a special instance of commitment, in which the threatener conveys that he has no alternative but to carry out the threat, if the other does not comply. Without demonstrating commitment to carrying out this action contingent on the other's non-compliance, the threat becomes simply a *warning*. A warning is what has been commonly referred to as a threat by many other investigators. Schelling also looks upon promise as a special, contingent case of commitment. The objective of these commitments is to throw the initiative for action to one's opponent—he must either accept or reject agreement on the commited party's terms.

Deutsch and Krauss (1960, 1962) showed that the availability of weapons led to their use. Where both parties had this weapon, use of it by one stimulated the other to use it in retaliation; a spiraling and escalation of competition resulted. Kelley and his colleagues (Borah, 1963; Kelley, 1965; Shomer *et al.,* 1966) took issue with Deutsch and Krauss' interpretation of how their *S*s understood the trucking game. For one thing, Kelley (1965) points out that *S*s may have seen and used the gates either as a means for signaling, or as a weapon, rather than only as a threat. Also, *S*s' interpretations of the use of the gates by their opponent could have varied. Kelley shows how the results Deutsch and Krauss observed could be explained without appealing to spiraling of threat, aggression, and competitiveness.

Borah (1963) provided *S*s with an alternative means of threat in a modification of the trucking game: *S*s could deliver unpleasant electrical shocks to their opponents. In another experiment *S*s had the option of using a mild shock or a stronger shock. None of these means of exerting influence had a systematic effect on Borah's measures of the outcome of negotiations, or on competitiveness as he attempted to measure it. Borah argued that " . . . subjects can communicate just as much about their intentions and desires (and hence, develop a competitive interaction) by their moves in the game as they can by means of the 'threats' provided by Deutsch & Krauss' barriers or by shocks . . . (Borah, 1963, p. 44)."

An experiment by Davis (reported in Kelley, 1965, and in Shomer *et al.*, 1966) demonstrated the marked effect of the availability of the alternate route on the joint outcome of the two parties. The presence of gates led to no gain in joint outcome only when an alternate route was present. Without the long path, gates did not prevent a gain in mean joint profit over a series of fifteen trials.

Eliminating the alternative paths, Shomer (Kelley, 1965; Shomer *et al.*, 1966) provided Ss with one response which threatened the infliction of a fine and another which carried out the fine. These two responses could be used independently of one another, in any order. Joint profit was not affected by the availability of these responses. Shomer also reports evidence that some Ss perceived and used the threat response as a signal that the user wanted to use the common path first, rather than as an intention to fine.

The role of threat as a strategy in interpersonal negotiations, while it has perhaps been more extensively investigated than other strategies, remains ambiguous.

Gruder (1968) arranged for Ss to bargain against a standard program of offers and arguments which they thought came from another naive S. All Ss received the same offers and arguments from the stooge, regardless of their experimental condition; independent variables were manipulated by means of other information provided S about the stooge's ostensible bargaining position. Ss could send any number of prepared arguments (up to a maximum of twelve) with their bargaining offers. These arguments were catagorized and the categories clearly labeled for Ss as threat arguments, attempts to deceive the other about one's own true situation, personal appeals, and arguments emphasizing mutual gain from agreement and mutual loss from failure to agree (i.e., compromise and cooperation). Ss who were led to see the stooge as competitive and exploitative used more threatening messages in communicating with the stooge than Ss who saw him as fair and compromising. The latter Ss, on the other hand, used more personal appeals and offers of willingness to cooperate.

3. Lies and Distortions of Opponent's Perception of Negotiator's Bargaining Position

Where communication and information about the other's outcomes are restricted in mixed-motive bargaining, it is possible to present one's own position in a distorted manner. For example, by presenting his alternative source of outcomes (CLalt) as more attractive than it actually is, a negotiator can lead his opponent to believe that he must obtain a relatively large share of the total in order to remain in the relationship. He wants to appear less dependent on the relationship for outcomes, forcing the other to yield if they are to continue sharing the relatively profitable outcomes. It would be worthwhile for a negotiator to misrepresent his alternative, only if the opposition believes that he would actually choose it when they called his bluff. That an attractive alternative source of outcomes is truly a viable alternative is well-documented. In studies reported by Schellenberg (1965), Thibaut (1968), and Thibaut and Faucheux (1965) an alternative to a mixed-motive relationship was chosen more often when it was more valuable than when it was less valuable relative to the outcomes available in the relationship.

Miller (1966) showed that allowing each negotiator to keep the value of his alternative source of outcomes private from his opponent led, as expected, to a greater incidence of threat actualization than the presence of a public alternative did.

A negotiator may convince his opponent that the latter is taking advantage of him. This is possible where each negotiator only knows his own outcomes for each possible agreement they can reach. The negotiator may argue that the agreement suggested by his opponent is just not profitable enough for himself. This was possible in some conditions of the mixed-motive relationships constructed by Fouraker and Siegel (1963), Kelley (1966), Kelley, Beckman and Fischer (1967), and Siegel and Fouraker (1960). Kelley et al. (1967) tabulated the incidence of lies by the negotiator about the profit an offer would yield him if he accepted it. These investigators observed that the incidence of lies was at a maximum when the offer would yield the negotiator a small profit (about one-third as much as the maximum possible profit). When the offer would yield him less than this small profit, he was no longer lying when he said that the offer did not provide him with a reasonable profit. So the incidence of lies was less when the offer was unprofitable; what had been a lie (e.g., "You are not giving me enough") became the truth. The incidence of lies also decreased with more favorable offers. Kelley et al. reason that perhaps a negotiator is unwilling to lie too early in the proceedings when his own demands are extreme. He is likely to concede from this extreme position, disconfirming the untruthful statement he presented as the truth about his minimum necessary share. Or perhaps he does not lie early in the negotiations because he has not yet conceded to a point at which he feels it would be inequitable for him to concede further—perhaps he must be motivated to lie by his opponent's continued pressure for concessions from him.

Even if accurate information about each other's outcomes is available, it is sometimes possible for negotiators to "chisel." Shubik (1968) has described this as when a negotiator either claims there is "noise" in the communication with his opponent or injects noise. In this way he may make decisions favorable to himself and unfavorable to his opponent while denying knowledge of the latter consequence. For example, the noise can be a claimed misunderstanding of the opponent's preferences, or a claimed misunderstanding of the consequences of the decision for the opponent.

While it is advantageous for the negotiator to *claim* ignorance of his opponent's preferences, it is also advantageous for him to know his opponent's true preferences, without letting his opponent know that he knows. In this way he can prevent his opponent from deceiving him in a like manner. A corresponding defensive maneuver is for the negotiator to make sure his opponent is aware of his (the negotiator's) ostensible preferences, while, of course, publicizing false preferences and concealing true ones. These offensive and defensive moves often require the use of espionage. This has not been systematically investigated to the author's knowledge, but certainly ought to be, important as it is as a strategic maneuver. There is sufficient anecdotal and documented evidence of its use, between governments, and between and within private industrial organizations, to provide a starting point for empirical research. Information regarding an opponent's CLalt and preference ordering for possible agreements can place the negotiator in a distinctly advantageous position. If he can withhold the same information about his own position from his opponent, he is more likely to effect unilaterally profitable concessions.

C. Conclusion

Strategies are used to resolve conflicts of interest; successful use leads to concessions by the opponent of the user. Competent use of strategies results in the most effective employment of available power. Power deficiencies may even be overcome by intelligent use of strategies. But over repeated interactions, strategies may be learned by the opposition, and effective defenses and counterstrategies may be developed. The level of competition in an ongoing relationship which involves a negative correspondence of outcomes will not necessarily be reduced by the use of strategies. On the contrary, the deceptive nature of many strategies may lead to an enhancement of the conflict when their use has been discovered.

We often observe long-standing resolutions of interpersonal and intergroup conflicts. The differences of opinion which arise and are resolved in the course of a business partnership are of this nature, as are the relations among siblings. How do these parties manage the problems which arise in sharing outcomes available to all the members of the group? How do they avoid the costs involved in repeated applications of personal power? Following Thibaut and Kelley's analysis (1959), Faucheux and Thibaut (1964) and Thibaut and Faucheux (1965) proposed that norms are adopted by the parties in conflict to replace direct use of interpersonal power. The research stemming from this proposition will be discussed in the next section.

V. RESEARCH PROGRAM INVESTIGATING RESOLUTION OF CONFLICT BY THE ADOPTION OF NORMS

There are many types of norms which may serve to replace the direct use of power interpersonally. Wells (1967) has considered norms to be ordered along a dimension of "formality." The most informal norms are implicit agreements between the parties to behave in accord with understood rules. There need not be a statement of the rules; rather, the parties may simply follow them to maintain a mutually satisfying pattern of interaction. Such norms truly emerge from the context of the relationship to regulate behavior within it.

At a somewhat more formal level are explicit agreements about prescriptions and proscriptions for behavior within the relationship. A "gentleman's agreement" falls into this category. The parties agree to limit their freedom for their mutual benefit. Ordinarily, we do not think of such informal agreements as containing provisions for sanctions in case of violation by one or both parties. There are two related consequences to a violator. One is a loss of face for having gone back on his word. Furthermore, it would be less likely that the violator would be trusted in a similar agreement in the future by anyone aware of his disregard for the honor of his word in the earlier relationship.

Parties to an agreement may include in the agreement specific sanctions for its violation. It is then necessary for each to maintain surveillance over the other so as to be able to administer the sanctions contingent upon a violation, or the sanctions will have no value in maintaining conformity with the rules. There may be further problems in demonstrating unequivocally that the violation actually occurred. It is for these reasons that the addition of a sanction for violation often leads to the employment of a disinterested third party to maintain surveillance of both parties, identify violations, and administer sanctions. We have here, of course, the essential components of a legal system. Legislation, enforcement, and justice constitute the most formal type of norm we adopt to govern our behavior.

The research to be discussed has investigated norms which fall at various points along the formality dimension. Sometimes norms emerge from the relationship, and at other times they are imported from other relationships where they have served a regulatory function.

A. Paris Study

While it is reasonable to suppose that appeals to norms may be useful in resolving conflicts in any situation of noncorrespondence of outcomes, there may be circumstances in which agreements are more likely than in others to be successful. Thibaut and Faucheux (1965; see also Faucheux & Thibaut, 1964; Thibaut, 1968) reasoned as follows. Agreements must be entered into by *both* parties. Behavioral rules which will be adopted are those which eliminate potentially disruptive behaviors. If both parties can engage in behaviors which prevent them from receiving mutually satisfactory outcomes, norms are most likely to provide a viable resolution of the conflict.

To demonstrate just this, Thibaut and Faucheux constructed an experimental, dyadic relationship in which there were two sources of stress on the continuation of interaction. These two sources were based on the fact that each party in the dyad was able to behave disruptively, preventing either from receiving the higher outcomes available when there was no disruption. Each was given a different disruptive response; the probability of whether they would enact these responses was manipulated by varying the attractiveness of the outcomes available from doing so. There were two levels of attractiveness for each of the two disruptive responses, yielding a 2 × 2 factorial design.

One party, A, was either strongly or mildly tempted to exploit the other, B. After tentatively agreeing on a particular division of the total outcome between himself and B, A could go back on his word and take more than he agreed to take for himself. He was strongly tempted, his power was greater, when the range of outcomes he could change independently was wider. B was either strongly or mildly tempted to disloyalty—he had either a relatively attractive or a relatively unattractive alternative source of outcomes to those available in the relationship. In other words, B could guarantee himself a certain outcome independently of A. While A also had this same alternative, it was of less consequence to him than his ability to divide the larger total outcome available within the relationship between himself and B.

Thibaut and Faucheux predicted that only where both sources of stress were high, where both parties were strongly tempted to disrupt the relationship, would norms be adopted to control disruption and lead to reduction of the conflict. In this condition each party was expected to succumb to temptation—A for the purpose of self-aggrandizement and B for defense or in retaliation for past exploitation by A. The parties would experience the negative consequences of disruption. Each would want the other to eschew its disruptive response. Because each could offer to give up its own source of power over the other, norms would be likely. These norms would include a pledge of equity and fair-sharing (to limit exploitation by A) and an agreement to be loyal to the dyad (to prevent B from opting for his independent source of outcomes).

Where only one party was strongly tempted to be disruptive, his opponent would have little power to persuade him to forego his disruptive behavior. Hence, few normative agreements would be adopted. Where neither party was tempted to disruption, there would be no need for proscriptive norms such as those under discussion. These dyads were expected to divide the profits equally, with little difficulty in arriving at this arrangement.

The results of their study confirm Thibaut and Faucheux's hypothesis. As expected, on early trials dyads with two strongly tempted parties experienced disruption of the smooth working of their relationship by both parties. When given structured norms which they could adopt or reject at will, these same dyads adopted them more readily than dyads in any of the other three conditions. The norms which were adopted were formal ones presented to the dyads after a series of preliminary trials. They could include anywhere from one to all three rules offered, and they could include a fine (paid by the violator to E) or an indemnity (paid by the violator to his opponent). Two of the rules specifically prohibited the disruptive behaviors available to the two parties. The third rule was a "dummy," included to determine whether norms were being adopted simply because they were being offered—if their adoption were a function of some demand characteristics, rather than the independent variables.

In the condition in which there was virtually no temptation to either party to be disruptive, relatively few formal norms were adopted. These dyads seemed able to arrive at informal agreements as to how the total outcome ought to be divided. Predominantly, such agreements involved an equal division to the two parties. Neither party having much power to demand otherwise, this was a mutually acceptable resolution.

B. Double Dyads Variation

Ss in Thibaut and Faucheux's study were French schoolboys. In order to provide evidence for the generality of the observed phenomenon, a replication was attempted in the United States with male college sophomores as Ss (reported in Thibaut, 1968). Although the independent variables were the same, there were two variations in the procedure of the replication. In pretesting this experiment it was noticed that bargaining parties which were dyads became more involved in the negotiations, bargaining more imaginatively and actively than individual undergraduates. For this reason, bargaining was between dyads rather than individuals in this study.

In addition to this change, a cost for adopting norms ("forming contracts") was added in the replication. This was done to help avoid a possible ceiling effect in the number of contracts formed in the conditions in which both sources of stress were high. All dyads in the condition in the Paris study formed at least one contract.

The results are similar to those obtained in the Paris study: The number of contracts formed and the number of quartets forming at least one contract were significantly larger in the condition in which both stresses were high (High–High) than in the other three conditions combined. However, there was a higher incidence in both measures in the condition in which A could severely exploit B, while B had only an unattractive alternative, providing him with weak counterpower (High–Low). It seems clear that B would have preferred to have a normative agreement protecting him from A's exploitation; but how could B persuade A to agree to such a curtailment of the latter's power?

Subsequent research (Thibaut & Gruder, 1969) has identified the cause of this inflated incidence of norm adoption. It was thought that perhaps the presence of a partner provided B with a source of power not available to a lone bargainer. The two players in the B role could support one another's suggestions for strategies and bargaining demands; they might be less likely to yield to the demands of their opponent than either one alone might be. Therefore, one independent variable in the follow-up experiment was whether the bargaining parties were individuals or dyads. All negotiations were conducted under conditions of strong temptation for A to be exploitative. Half the Bs had a relatively attractive alternative (High–High) and half had a relatively unattractive alternative (High–Low). This manipulation, then, reconstructed the High–Low condition of the Paris and double dyads studies, the condition in which the results of the two studies differed.

Thibaut and Gruder found no significant differences due either to the value of the alternative or the size of the bargaining party in the number of groups adopting norms, or in the number of norms adopted. In other words, all conditions of this experiment replicated the results of the High–High and High–Low conditions of the double dyads study. The number of contracts and the number of groups forming contracts were greater in the High–Low condition of both the double dyads and the present study than they were in the Paris study. It will be remembered that in all three studies, where Bs had an attractive alternative (i.e., in the High–High condition), their threat to choose it and disrupt their relationship with A was enough to convince A of the need for a contract. What could Bs who had an unattractive alternative (i.e., in the High–Low condition) muster in place of a higher alternative as a source of power? Analysis of the tape recorded bargaining discussions revealed the mechanism by which Bs with a low alternative were able to convince As to form contracts. In order to induce As to restrict their exploitative behavior, Bs with a low alternative offered As a much greater share of the total outcome than Bs with a high alternative did. And, low power Bs made this generous offer concomitant with mention, either by themselves or by As, of the possibility of adopting a restrictive norm. In Fisher's terminology (1964), Bs were *coupling* a contract which would protect their outcomes from A's exploitation, and a resource they could provide As for eschewing use of their power.

Thibaut and Gruder suggest that the reason coupling occurred in this experiment was due to a difference between the procedures used in this and earlier studies of introducing and familiarizing negotiators with contracts. Specifically, in Thibaut and Gruder's study Ss were required to consider carefully the minimum share of the total outcome they would demand in order to agree to contracts with all possible combinations of rules. This was done in an attempt to identify the *bargaining range* (Iklè & Leites, 1962). Perhaps this extensive consideration of outcome division in conjunction with contracts stimulated coupling by Bs.

Generally, it would be expected that any factors which force negotiators to consider carefully all sources of power available to them (in the sense of altering the other's outcomes favorably and unfavorably) would have the same result which the attempt to determine the bargaining range had in Thibaut and Gruder's study. One such factor might be the presence of a partner. The double dyads replication of the dyads study (Paris study) provides *post hoc* evidence for this hypothesis. As many double dyads formed contracts, and formed about the same number of contracts, in the High–Low condition as in the High–High condition. Perhaps a partner stimulated Bs to consider more carefully and in new ways the dilemma facing them—how to persuade As to agree to a regulatory agreement. Perhaps in this setting, two heads were, in fact, better than one, in the two Bs were able to hit upon the coupling resolution of their dilemma more frequently than a lone B was. This would account for the lack of a difference in contract formation observed in the High–Low and High–High conditions of the double dyads replication. But this interpretation is only speculative; unfortunately, the appropriate data to assess this hypothesis are not available from the dyads and double dyads studies. In addition, data which seem to contradict this hypothesis come from Thibaut and Gruder's study, in which there was no difference in contract formation between the dyads and double dyads treatments. However, *S*s in both of these treatments completed the extensive, bargaining range questionnaire. The effect of this feature of the procedure may have overwhelmed any effect due to the size of the bargaining party. That is, any increase in B's understanding of his own sources of power which a partner may have provided was undetectable. The increase in understanding caused by the questionnaire may have served to reduce any existing dyads–double dyads difference.

C. Perceptual Variation

Another variation of the Paris study was done by Murdoch (1967). This increased the generality of the findings of earlier studies in the following way: The sources of stress in the Paris study and the double dyads variation were based on the "structure" of the relationship. Each party's threat of disruption was a function of the likelihood that he would make the disruptive response. With narrow limits on the range of the outcome division subject to A's unilateral control and with a relatively unattractive alternative available to B, each would see the other as unlikely to use his disruptive response—the gains would not outweigh the costs involved in the direct use of personal power. On the other hand, where A and B each had relatively great usable power, each would be seen by the other as likely to disrupt their relationship. And, in fact, As and Bs behaved according to each other's expectations.

Analyzing the earlier studies in this way, Murdoch concluded that the manipulations of mutual threat could be accomplished by providing Ss with information about their opponent's behavioral tendencies. There was no need to vary the game structure directly, if all it did was affect Ss' perceptions of how their opponents would react. To test this notion, Murdoch had all Ss bargain under the one condition of earlier studies in which both structural sources of stress were high (High–High). What he varied was the nature of the information he gave Ss about how their opponent was likely to play, cooperatively or competitively. Half the As were led to believe that previous Bs had been predominantly loyal, only rarely opting for their alternative, and half were told that previous Bs had been disloyal. Half the Bs were told that As in past dyads had been magnanimous, and half that As had been exploitative, taking more than they had tentatively agreed to take. Murdoch provided Ss with evidence that these generalizations were accurate for their particular opponent by feeding them bogus information about how their own opponent played on a series of practice trials before actual negotiations got underway.

In this experiment, as in its predecessors, it was expected and found that formal norms would be most likely to be adopted where there were perceptions of mutual distrust. Murdoch demonstrated, then, that the appeal to norms can be independent of variations in game structure. If the relationship is one in which duplicity is possible, formal norms are most likely to be adopted where the parties see each other as prone to be untrustworthy.

D. Formality and E Legitimization of Norms

Wells' classification (1967) of the formality of norms which may be adopted to resolve interpersonal conflict has been described (Section V). This classification was used as a dependent variable in a study of the effects of legitimization by E of normative agreements in a bargaining game. One independent variable was in all essential respects equivalent to Murdoch's perceptual manipulations of stress in the relationship (1967). Wells compared dyads in which the parties were led to be suspicious of each other's intentions with those in which one or both parties were not suspicious. A second independent variable was whether or not E told Ss that regulatory agreements were appropriate and acceptable to him if they found they wanted to form them: E either legitimized norm adoption or not. A final factor in Wells' design involved the presence of a third party (actually a paid accomplice of E) who assumed a role neutral to the mixed-motive relationship existing between A and B. This third party existed for half the dyads, and sat in on their negotiations.

Wells hypothesized that although the jointly stressful relationship would result in more disruptive behavior than where only one or neither source of stress was high, only when normative agreements were legitimized by E would they be adopted as a means of conflict reduction. Further, he anticipated that the presence of the third party, potentially to serve as a witness and/or enforcer of norms, would lead to more formal or legal agreements than his absence.

As predicted, there was greater disruption of the relationship in the form of exploitation and disloyalty where both sources of stress were high than otherwise. Wells found a significant interaction between the stress and legitimization factors on agreements formed, indicating that the condition of mutual distrust led to more formal and explicit informal agreements (see categorization at beginning of Section V) only where regulatory agreements had been legitimized by E. The presence of the third party led to significantly more of the most informal, tacit agreements in the dyad than where the neutral party was absent. While this latter finding seems not to be in accord with the expected effects of the third party, Wells had qualified this prediction: The third party would be needed to enforce legal agreements only if such strong agreements were necessary to control disruption. The nature of the actual finding suggests that, paradoxically, such stringent measures were not necessary when a neutral observer sat in on dyadic negotiations. With a third party present, one consequence of behaving disruptively was that a person outside the relationship would be aware that S had violated the norm of fair sharing or the norm of loyalty. That is, the third party may have acted as an external conscience to the dyad, present to witness acts of duplicity by both parties. This function may have been sufficiently effective to enable potential disruption to be precluded by only minimally formal agreements. Such weak agreements were not sufficient to control dusruption in dyads without a neutral observer.

More research is indicated on the role of a neutral third party in bargaining. Judges, mediators, and arbitrators are playing an increasingly widespread and influential role in the settlement of real world disputes. Perhaps study of nonlaboratory conflicts will yield valuable ideas about the functions and functioning of the neutral third party. Related to this role is the role of the audience in Brown's study (1968) (Section III, B, 2, a), and Schelling's discussion (1963) of forming a coalition with a third party (Section III, B, 2, b).

E. Joint Work Task Paradigm

In another attempt to increase the generality of the findings of previous research, Murdoch and Rosen (1968) changed the nature of the experimental task. A mixed-motive relationship is by no means restricted to a setting which has face validity as a bargaining situation. What is necessary is that there be a negative correlation between the outcomes of two parties who are interdependent on one another. The investigators devised a task which met these requirements. Each member of the dyad was randomly assigned a role; one was the searcher and one the timer. The timer assisted the searcher on a number of identification tasks. Both parties' outcomes were dependent on the searcher's performance: The more accurate he was, the more points he received; the faster he completed the task, the more points the timer received. False information and feedback were provided for the searcher and timer indicating that there was a negative correlation between the searcher's speed and accuracy. Motivation to earn points was stimulated by offering $10 prizes to the searcher and the timer who earned the most points of all searchers and timers, respectively. This procedure maintained all the characteristics of the mixed-motive situations previously employed, without the obvious identification of the relationship as a bargaining one.

The searcher's source of power resided in his ability to control his speed of working on the task. He could work slowly and accurately, earning more of the fixed total number of points available, while the timer earned less; or the searcher could work quickly, resulting in inaccurate work and a loss of points to the timer. The extent of the negative correlation which the dyad believed existed between the searcher's speed and accuracy constituted the manipulation of an internal stress on the relationship. When the correlation was a large negative one, this sources of stress (i.e., the temptation of the searcher to exploit the timer) was high. When the correlation was presented to the dyad as a low one, this stress was relatively insignificant.

The timer's power resided in his option of choosing a guaranteed alternative source of points; for half the timers this was a relatively attractive CLalt, while for the other half it was relatively unattractive. In other words, this external source of stress was either strongly or mildly tempting to the timer, making it either important or unimportant to his relationship with the searcher.

The manipulations of the two sources of stress, then, may be seen as structural ones—as in the earlier study by Thibaut and Faucheux (1965) and the double dyad variation reported in Thibaut (1968). As in these experiments, the appeal to norms was expected to be greatest where both parties exercised disruptive behavior during the course of their relationship. The use of interpersonal power, in Murdoch and Rosen's work task paradigm, however, was expected to lead to a different kind of norm than it led to in the earlier studies.

Analyzing previous mixed-motive situations, Murdoch and Rosen hypothesized that formal contracts had been adopted because of particular features of the experimental settings—specifically, limited communication between parties, the opportunity for duplicity, and the presence of a third party to enforce contracts. Two or all three had been present in preceding research. Without these features, the investigators argued, there would be less likelihood of formal norms being adopted. Conflict would be more amenable to resolution by the invocation of informal agreements. Their experimental situation was designed to provide full communication, no opportunity for duplicity, and no third party to sanction and/or enforce formal agreements. The dyads were offered the opportunity to adopt formal contracts, at a slight cost for each.

The results of Murdoch and Rosen's study confirmed their expectation regarding formal norms: None was adopted. There were many informal agreements, however. These were identified by means of a content analysis of the tape recorded discussions between the searcher and the timer. There was an interaction between the exploitation-by-searcher and disloyalty-by-timer independent variables, such that where both of these sources of stress were high, agreements were more likely than in any of the other three conditions. So it is apparent that the resolution of interpersonal conflict is not restricted to "bargaining" settings, and formal, contractual norms are not the only manifestation of this mode of conflict resolution.

F. Dependency Variation

Each of the studies in the research program under discussion provided the two parties with different sources of power. That is, A's ability to disrupt the relationship by affecting B's outcomes adversely was A's direct, unilateral control of all outcomes available within their relationship. B's disruptive capability lay in his independent, guaranteed alternative. In an attempt to give the two parties an equivalent base of power (but not equivalent power), the value of each party's alternative was varied in the present experiment (reported in Thibaut, 1968). A always had a more valuable (higher) alternative than B. A's ability to determine the division of the total outcome, a prominent feature of earlier experiments in the series, was eliminated.

Thibaut and Kelley's analysis (1959) of the correlation between power and dependence provides a framework for understanding the intent of the manipulation of relative alternative values. Since B's CLalt was lower than A's, B was more constrained than A to remain in the relationship in order to obtain the best possible outcomes. If either party chose his alternative, the other also received his alternative; in other words, by choosing his alternative, A could reduce B's outcomes more than B, by choosing his alternative, could reduce A's outcomes. So, B's greater dependence on his relationship with A meant that B had less power in it. A was, therefore, in a position to demand a greater share of the total available to both.

In the present experiment there were still two levels of alternatives, High and Low; however, A's alternative was greater than B's within each level. And there was either a wide range of possible divisions of the total outcome, constituting a High conflict of interest between A and B, or a narrow range, constituting a Low conflict. As in Thibaut and Faucheux's study (1965), formal contracts were expected to be most likely where the level of alternatives and the conflict of interest between A and B were both high. This is what was found.

It ought to be mentioned that the potentially disruptive responses of each party were different in this variation from those in the earlier studies. A was tempted to choose his more attractive alternative. B was tempted to stall the negotiations, resulting in an increased cost to both parties for time used in reaching agreement. This was a procedural feature of this experiment not present in Thibaut and Faucheux's study, or in the double dyads or perceptual variations.

To sum up the dependency variation, there was either a High or a Low conflict of interest between the bargainers. Their alternatives were either relatively attractive (High) or unattractive (Low). A's usable power stemmed from his alternative, which was always higher than B's. B's usable power resided in his ability to stall negotiations, resulting in mutual loss to A and B. The attempt to equate the source of power for A and B was not really successful. Nevertheless, where the conflict and level of alternatives were High, formal norms were more frequently adopted. The parallel to the other studies in the series holds.

G. Conclusion

The program of research which began with the study by Thibaut and Faucheux (1965) has been carried forward, with the generalizability of the underlying principles simultaneously increasing. It has been possible to specify some of the conditions under which a mixed-motive conflict of interest is likely to be reduced by the adoption of norms prohibiting disruptive behavior. It is reasonable at this point to propose a general statement regarding the nature of the disruptions by each party which will lead to norm adoption. The only requirement seems to be that the disruptions cause a stress on the continued receipt of both parties of mutually satisfying outcomes. The following strategies have been demonstrated to lead to attempts at control of disruption via norm formation: (1) unilateral control of outcomes (Murdoch & Rosen, 1968; double dyads variation reported in Thibaut, 1968; Thibaut & Faucheux, 1965; Thibaut & Gruder, 1969; Wells, 1967), even with varying degrees of precision of control (Murdoch, 1967); (2) refusal to negotiate (dependency variation reported in Thibaut, 1968); and (3) withdrawl from the relationship to a CLalt (Murdoch, 1967; Murdoch & Rosen, 1968; double dyads and dependency variations reported in Thibaut, 1968; Thibaut & Faucheux, 1965; Thibaut & Gruder, 1969; Wells, 1967).

Furthermore, disruption may be fostered by manipulation of either the outcome structure of the relationship (Murdoch & Rosen, 1968; double dyads variation reported in Thibaut, 1968; Thibaut & Faucheux, 1965; Thibaut & Gruder, 1969), or the negotiator's perception of his opponent's bargaining style and strategy intentions (Murdoch, 1967; Wells, 1967). Kahan (1968) showed that a manipulation of the two negotiators' levels of aspiration can also exert a disruptive stress on the relationship; however, no conclusions could be drawn from this study regarding the nature of the control of disruption.

There is also evidence to warrant a generalization regarding the nature of the norms which control disruption and help to resolve the conflict of interest. Norms can range from the most tacit, informal agreements which arise in the relationship to maintain a satisfactory resolution, to the most explicit, legal contracts. The nature of the norms adopted is known to be a function of legitimization by E and presence of a neutral third party (Wells, 1967). In Murdoch and Rosen's analysis (1968), limited communication between A and B, the opportunity for duplicity by A and B, and enforcement of agreements by E were proposed as necessary conditions for the adoption of formal norms. This proposition was based on the following facts. Previous research which included these conditions demonstrated that Ss adopted formal agreements. Murdoch and Rosen's study and, in part, Wells' study (1967), which did *not* include these conditions, demonstrated that Ss did *not* adopt formal agreements, but adopted informal ones instead. Finally, Murdoch and Rosen (1968) found that informal agreements can serve to reduce a conflict of interest in a mixed-motive relationship that was not an obvious bargaining situation.

It seems that future research should have the joint goals of continuing to increase the generality of the principles discovered, while simultaneously attempting to establish specific empirical relationships among the relevant variables which have already been revealed.

VI. POWER WITHIN THE BARGAINING PARTY

With a few exceptions (Gruder, 1968; double dyads variation reported in Thibaut, 1968; Thibaut & Gruder, 1969), the discussion to now has primarily considered *interpersonal* negotiation. Quite pertinent for generalizability to formal negotiations in the real world is research on *intergroup* negotiation. Negotiators for labor, management, congressional lobbies, or nations are ordinarily representatives of a larger group.

Three studies will now be considered which have been directed at the effects of the power relationships among the members of a party on bargaining between parties (Druckman, 1967; Gruder, 1968; Hermann & Kogan, 1968).

The negotiator can be the leader or decision maker of the group. Or he may be a spokesman for the group, responding to offers and demands of the opposition as he is instructed by his constituency. There can be any number of possible relationships between these extremes. That is, the constituency may give their representative any one of various degrees of independence to negotiate without its surveillance.

Although naturalistic instances of intergroup negotiation often involve quite large parties, the studies cited above have focused on bargaining parties which were dyads. In the study by Gruder (1968), one person ostensibly represented his dyad in negotiations with the (programmed) representative of the other dyad. Negotiators were told that their (programmed) constituent was engaged in a problem-solving task while negotiations were under way. The problem the constituents were ostensibly to solve was related to the issue being negotiated by the spokesmen—a trade agreement between companies, with the spokesmen playing the roles of bargaining representatives for the companies. The independent variable of this study which is relevant to intraparty power is the nature of the spokesman's relationship with his constituent. Spokesmen either felt accountable to their constituent or not. Accountability was manipulated by identifying another S to a spokesman as his constituent and leading the spokesman to believe that he would have to defend his bargaining to his constituent following negotiations; where the spokesman was not to be accountable to his constituent, these procedures were omitted. It was thought that accountable spokesmen would perceive their constituent as capable of altering their exogenous outcomes (i.e., other than money earned in negotiations)—as possessing power over them. It was expected that accountable spokesmen would further perceive their constituent as desiring a very profitable agreement with the other spokesman. This reasoning led to the prediction that accountable spokesmen would take a firmer, less yielding bargaining stand than nonaccountable spokesmen: They would compromise less and would use more arguments indicating unwillingness to cooperate. In the main, the data did not bear out this hypothesis. There were no differences on all but one of the many measures of bargaining style between spokesmen who were accountable to their constituents and those who were not. The lone difference came on the size of the first concession: As predicted from the above analysis, accountable spokesmen made significantly smaller first concessions than those who were not accountable. The first concession tended to be the largest one made, and therefore, was considered an important indicator of overall bargaining style. Spokesmen who were accountable to their constituents were less willing to begin negotiating by making a large concession than spokesmen who were not accountable. Yet, the fact that there was no corroborating support from other data leaves the status of the effects of this variable in doubt.

Data collected by Druckman (1967) also indicate no systematic effects on a bargainer's behavior of representing a group or bargaining for himself. Groups were triads; each member negotiated with a member of another triad. Each member understood that to determine a team score, the share of the total outcome he earned through bargaining would be added to the shares his two partners earned through their individual bargaining efforts. Each anticipated comparison of his performance on the group's behalf with the other members' performances. While bargainers who were not group representatives were also initially grouped in triads, each understood that the outcome of his bargaining pertained only to himself, and not to any other bargainer's outcomes. The average distance separating two bargainers' offers, and the average distance a bargainer yielded were not affected by the group–individual variable. However, Druckman pointed out that the nature of his manipulation may not have been an appropriate one to cause effects on the measures he used.

Hermann and Kogan (1968) also investigated the effects of intraparty relationships on interparty negotiations. Bargaining parties were dyads composed of a "leader" and a "delegate." There were three differences between these roles. The leader was an upperclassman and the delegate an underclassman at the same university; they were unacquainted, however. While both leaders and delegates were told they would meet with their partner following separate negotiations between the leaders and between their delegates, only delegates were told they would have to defend their bargaining and its outcome to their partner. In addition, after reaching agreement on each issue, delegates were required to rate how satisfied they thought their leaders would be with the outcome of their bargaining.

Leaders and delegates first arrived at a dyadic consensus on Kogan and Wallach's choice-dilemmas task (1964) before they engaged in interparty negotiations, each with his counterpart from another dyad. It was expected that in these interparty negotiations leaders would be more independent than delegates, as a joint function of the leaders' greater extrarelationship status and their relative lack of accountability to their delegates. There were two measures of bargaining behavior which supported Hermann and Kogan's hypothesis. First, leaders were more likely than delegates to agree on one party's position; one conceded all the way to the other's initial position. This tendency was interpreted as reflecting the leader's feeling of freedom to decide as he wished, even radically changing his position. Second, delegates were more likely to compromise than leaders. Hermann and Kogan interpreted this to be a function of a delegate's motivation to present a respectable record to his leader. When both delegates conceded approximately equally, they minimized their maximum loss. Furthermore, significant correlations showed that delegates were *less* satisfied the more they deadlocked (i.e., could not reach agreement on an item) while this correlation was not significant for leaders. Given the assumption that delegates wanted to present a creditable conclusion of their bargaining to their leader, delegates' dissatisfaction with deadlocks might imply that delegates were concerned that their leaders would look unfavorably upon deadlocks. However, delegates did not perceive their leaders as being as dissatisfied with deadlocks as delegates themselves were, or as the leaders actually were. So this additional interpretation of Hermann and Kogan's data, while it is suggestive, failed to receive convincing support.

As further evidence that leaders felt less responsible to their delegates than the latter were to them, Hermann and Kogan looked at the shift to riskier decisions made by Ss in the two roles. As the investigators expected, leaders changed their initial positions (as expressed in consensus with their delegate before interparty negotiations) significantly more in the direction of greater risk than delegates did. Leaders were free to be influenced in discussions with another leader; they were not as committed to their dyad's consensus as were the delegates, who anticipated reporting back to their superior on their defense of this consensus.

The negotiator's interpersonal quandary in dealing simultaneously with partners and opponents in a mixed-motive situation is central to a truly general account of bargaining in a mixed-motive situation, and is, therefore, deserving of more concerted research efforts. To this end the Transnational Working Group on the Dynamics of Conflict[1] has begun a program of research which attempts to identify important social psychological variables and their effects on intergroup negotiations. One variable is the correspondence of outcomes of members of the same party: whether there is a positive or negative correlation among the group members' outcomes from attainment of a particular group goal. Another is the composition of group members with regard to their positions on the issues in question: Some groups are homogeneous and some heterogeneous in the positions they represent. Allied to this variable are two others. One is the position assumed by the other group: whether the two groups are generally in accord or opposed. A second related variable is the private position of the group's representative *vis à vis* his group's consensus and other other group's consensus: He may deviate from his own group's position and agree with the opposition, or he may be a loyal representative.

[1] This is a group of social psychologists from the US and western European nations who have formally organized to conduct research on interpersonal and intergroup conflict. The members of this group are: Morton Deutsch, Columbia University; Claude Faucheux, Sorbonne, Paris; Claude Flament, University of Aix-Marseilles; Harold H. Kelley, University of California, Los Angeles; John T. Lanzetta, Dartmouth College; Serge Moscovici, Sorbonne, Paris; Mauk Mulder, University of Utrecht, The Netherlands; Jozef Nuttin, Jr., University of Louvain, Belgium; Dean G. Pruitt, State University of New York at Buffalo; Jaap Rabbie, University of Utrecht, The Netherlands; Gerald Shure, Systems Development Corporation, Santa Monica; Henri Tajfel, University of Bristol, England; and John Thibaut, University of North Carolina, Chapel Hill.

There are a number of examples of situations in which the interplay of these variables may be readily imagined. One is the joint efforts of legislators of the Democratic and Republican political parties in the United States to reach agreement on the provisions of a bill which needs the support of members of both parties in order to be passed by a majority of the legislature. Another instance is the negotiations among the various factions of one political party in the preparation of a platform on which their candidate can run. Research on these interparty variables is only just getting under way.

VII. SUMMARY AND CONCLUSIONS

It was an implicit contention of this chapter that it would be fruitful to survey experimental social psychological research on the resolution of inter-personal conflict using an interpretive framework by the construct *social power*. The benefit of such an approach would be in the organization of known data which it provides and the extent to which forthcoming data and both assimilated and generated by it. At this very early stage of research on interpersonal conflict resolution in experimental social psychology, there have been few extensive theoretical accounts of empirical findings (see Kelley & Thibaut, 1969). Perhaps a preliminary attempt, such as the present one, to consider existing data in terms of an existing framework will serve as a constructive move in the direction of attempting to link many disparate research programs.

This chapter has considered variables which affect the course of conflict in a mixed-motive interpersonal relationship. Social power, in the way it is defined by Thibaut and Kelley (1959), was used as an analytical construct which enables the identification of aspects of the interpersonal relationship which seem to affect the course of bargaining. Sources of power in the mixed-motive setting were identified; a negotiator may use his power to alter the various outcomes available to his opponent—both outcomes available only within the relationship under study, and those which come from other, overlapping interactions between the two parties. A discussion of strategy outlined the means by which usable power over the opponent could be increased in order to influence the proceedings to a resolution more favorable to the strategist. A program of research on the adoption of norms as a means of conflict resolution was reviewed. Finally, the problems raised by bargaining parties composed of more than one person were considered; the recent, but limited research on this issue was reviewed.

ACKNOWLEDGMENTS

The author would like to express his gratitude to Peter Murdoch, John Thibaut, and Robert S. Wyer, Jr., for their critical readings of an earlier version of this chapter.

REFERENCES

Bass, B.M. Effects on the subsequent performance of negotiators of studying issues or planning strategy alone or in groups. *Psychological Monographs,* 1966, 80, (6, Whole No. 614).

Bond, J.R., & Vinacke, W.E. Coalitions in mixed-sex triads. *Sociometry,* 1961, **24,** 61–75.

Borah, L.A., Jr. The effects of threat in bargaining: Critical and experimental analysis. *Journal of Abnormal and Social Psychology,* 1963, **66,** 37–44.

Brown, B. The effects of need to maintain face on interpersonal bargaining. *Journal of Experimental Social Psychology,* 1968, 4, 107–122.

Caplow, T.A. A theory of coalitions in the triad. *American Sociological Review,* 1956, **21,** 489–493.

Chertkoff, J.M. A revision of Caplow's coalition theory. *Journal of Experimental Social Psychology,* 1967, **3,** 172–177.

Deutsch, M., & Krauss, R.M. The effect of threat on interpersonal bargaining. *Journal of Abnormal and Social Psychology,* 1960, **61,** 181–189.

Deutsch, M., & Krauss, R.M. Studies of interpersonal bargaining. *Journal of Conflict Resolution,* 1962, **6,** 52–76.

Druckman, D. Dogmatism, prenegotiation experience, and simulated group representation as determinants of dyadic behavior in a bargaining situation. *Journal of Personality and Social Psychology,* 1967, **6,** 279–290.

Faucheux, C., & Thibaut, L. L'approche clinique et expérimentale de la genèse des normes contractuelles dans differentes conditions de conflit et de menace. *Bulletin du Centre d'Etudes et Recherches Psychotechniques, Paris.* 1964, **13,** 225–243.

Fisher, R. Fractionating conflict. In R. Fisher (Ed.). *International conflict and behavioral science: The Craigville papers.* New York: Basic Books, 1964. Pp. 91–109.

Fouraker, L.E., & Siegel, S. *Bargaining behavior.* New York: McGraw-Hill, 1963.

Gallo, P.S., Jr. Effects of increased incentives upon the use of threat in bargaining. *Journal of Personality and Social Psychology,* 1966, 4, 14–20.

Gamson, W.A. An experimental test of a theory of coalition formation. *American Sociological Review,* 1961, **26,** 565–573.

Gamson, W.A. Experimental studies of coalition formation. In L. Berkowitz (Ed.), *Advances in experimental social psychology* Vol. 1. New York: Academic Press, 1964. Pp. 81–110.

Gruder, C.L. Effects of perception of opponent's bargaining style and accountability to opponent and partner on interpersonal mixed-motive bargaining. Unpublished doctoral dissertation, University of North Carolina at Chapel Hill, 1968.

Hermann, Margaret C., & Kogan, N. Negotiation in leader and delegate groups. *Journal of Conflict Resolution,* 1968, **12**, 332–344.

Iklè, F.C., & Leites, N. Political negotiation as a process of modifying utilities. *Journal of Conflict Resolution,* 1962, **6**, 12–28.

Kahan, J.P. Effects of level of aspiration in an experimental bargaining situation. *Journal of Personality and Social Psychology,* 1968, **8**, 154–159.

Kalisch, G.K., Milnor, J.W., Nash, J.F., & Nering, E.D. Some experimental *n*-person games. In R.M. Thrall, C.H. Coombs, & R.L. Davis (Eds.). *Decision processes.* New York: Wiley, 1954. Pp. 301–327.

Kelley, H.H. Experimental studies of threats in interpersonal negotiations. *Journal of Conflict Resolution,* 1965, **9**, 79–105.

Kelley, H.H. A classroom study of the dilemmas in interpersonal negotiations. In Kathleen Archibald (Ed.). *Strategic interaction and conflict.* Berkeley: Institute of International Studies, University of California, 1966. Pp. 49–73.

Kelley, H.H., & Arrowood, A.J. Coalitions in the triad: Critique and experiment. *Sociometry,* 1960, **23**, 231–244.

Kelley, H.H., Beckman, Linda L., & Fischer, C.S. Negotiating the division of a reward under incomplete information. *Journal of Experimental Social Psychology,* 1967, **3**, 361–398.

Kelley, H.H., & Ring, K. Some effects of "suspicious" versus "trusting" training schedules. *Journal of Abnormal and Social Psychology,* 1961, **63**, 294–301.

Kelley, H.H., & Thibaut, J. Group problem solving. In G. Lindzey & E. Aronson (Eds.). *The handbook of social psychology.* Vol. 4 *Group psychology and phenomena of interaction.* (Rev. ed.). New York: Academic Press, 1969. Pp. 1–101.

Kelley, H.H., Thibaut, J., Radloff, R., & Mundy, D. The development of cooperation in the "minimal social situation." *Psychological Monographs,* 1962, **76**, (19, Whole No. 538).

Kogan, N., & Wallach, M.A. *Risk taking: A study in cognition and personality.* New York: Holt, 1964.

Marlowe, D., Gergen, K.J., & Doob, A.N. Opponent's personality, expectation of social interaction, and interpersonal bargaining. *Journal of Personality and Social Psychology,* 1966, **3**, 206–213.

Miller, M.D. The effects of privacy or publicity and symmetry or asymmetry of alternative on bargaining in the interdependent dyad. Unpublished Master's thesis, University of North Carolina at Chapel Hill, 1966.

Morgan, W.R., & Sawyer, J. Bargaining, expectations, and the preference for equality over equity. *Journal of Personality and Social Psychology,* 1967, **6**, 139–149.

Murdoch, P. The development of contractual norms in a dyad. *Journal of Personality and Social Psychology,* 1967, **6**, 206–211.

Murdoch, P., & Rosen, D. Norm formation in an interdependent group through the use of threat. Unpublished manuscript, University of Iowa, 1968.

Rapoport, A., & Chammah, A.M. *Prisoner's dilemma.* Ann Arbor, Mich.: University of Michigan Press, 1965.

Ring, K., & Kelley, H.H. A comparison of augmentation and reduction as modes of influence. *Journal of Abnormal and Social Psychology,* 1963, **66**, 95–103.

Schellenberg, J.A. Dependence and cooperation. *Sociometry,* 1965, **28**, 158–172.

Schelling, T.C. *The strategy of conflict.* London and New York: Oxford University Press (A Galaxy Book), 1963.

Schopler, J. Social power. In L. Berkowitz (Ed.). *Advances in experimental social psychology.* Vol. 2. New York: Academic Press, 1965. Pp. 177–218.

Shomer, R.W., Davis, Alice H., & Kelley, H.H. Threats and the development of coordination: Further studies of the Deutsch and Krauss trucking game. *Journal of Personality and Social Psychology,* 1966, **4**, 119–126.

Shubik, M. On the study of disarmament and escalation. *Journal of Conflict Resolution,* 1968, **12**, 83–101.

Sidowski, J.B. Reward and punishment in a minimal social situation. *Journal of Experimental Psychology,* 1957, **54**, 318–326.

Siegel, S., & Fouraker, L.E. *Bargaining and group decision making.* New York: McGraw-Hill, 1960.

Swingle, P.G. Effects of the emotional relationship between protagonists in a two-person game. *Journal of Personality and Social Psychology,* 1966, **4**, 270–279.

Swingle, P.G., & Gillis, J.S. Effects of the emotional relationship between protagonists in the Prisoner's Dilemma. *Journal of Personality and Social Psychology,* 1968, **8**, 160–165.

Thibaut, J. The development of contractual norms in bargaining: Replication and variation. *Journal of Conflict Resolution,* 1968, **12**, 102–112.

Thibaut, J., & Faucheux, C. The development of contractual norms in a bargaining situation under two types of stress. *Journal of Experimental Social Psychology,* 1965, **1**, 89–102.

Thibaut, J., & Gruder, C.L. The formation of contractual agreements between parties of unequal power. *Journal of Personality and Social Psychology,* 1969, **11**, 59–65.

Thibaut, J., & Kelley, H.H. *The social psychology of groups.* New York: Wiley, 1959.

Uesugi, T.K., & Vinacke, W.E. Strategy in a feminine game. *Sociometry,* 1963, **26**, 75–88.

Vinacke, W.E. Sex roles in a three-person game. *Sociometry,* 1959, **22**, 343–360.

Vinacke, W.E., & Arkoff, A. An experimental study of coalitions in the triad. *American Sociological Review,* 1957, **22**, 406–414.

Wells, R.B. The control of disruptive behavior in a bargaining game. Unpublished doctoral dissertation, University of North Carolina at Chapel Hill, 1967.

Willis, R.H. Coalitions in the tetrad. *Sociometry,* 1962, **25**, 358–376.

Chapter 5

THREATS AND PROMISES

James T. Tedeschi

I. INTRODUCTION

The interaction of two or more entities, be they individuals, groups, institutions, or nations, is likely to produce, and in fact be characterized by, a certain degree of conflict. Yet, the case of an interaction of pure conflict, that is, where there is no degree of tacit understanding of ground rules or shared norms as to how the conflict should be conducted, is a rare one in the world of affairs and is perhaps found only in artificially contrived situations (Schelling, 1960). Most conflicts are nonzero sum in character, where there is something to be gained by both parties by some degree of cooperation. Thus, most conflicts can be viewed as bargaining situations in which there is opportunity for one party to influence the other.

The study of social influence may actually be coextensive with most of the study of social science. K.W. Deutsch (1966) has indicated his belief that political science is definable as the study of how compliance is obtained. Bazelon (1965) suggests that economics can be conceived as a system of threats and promises. Homans (1958), drawing from elementary economics, makes social exchange the basis of all sociology. Boulding (1964) defines a social system as "the relevant history of two or more persons in contact (p. 70)." He breaks the social system down into three major subsystems: the exchange system, the threat system, and the integrative system. Promises of favorable acts between persons characterize the exchange system, while the creation of expectations of unfavorable consequences resulting from failure to do as demanded, characterizes the threat system. In the integrative system is found a convergence of value systems resulting in one person gladly agreeing to the other's wants as an expression of mutual empathy. Although frequent conflict is expected in the exchange system, it is most conspicuous in the threat system. Conflict for the affection of another or from misplaced trust may arise in the integrative system.

Parsons (1963) specifically focused his attention upon different forms of influence. He conceptualized influence processes as ways of getting results in interaction. The first type, deterrence, relies on threats, coercion, or punishment for effectiveness. A second negative type is the activation of commitments, an appeal to norms causing a reassessment of what would be appropriate behavior for the situation. Deterrence is related to Boulding's threat system, while the activation of commitments is related to Boulding's integrative system by virtue of its value appeal. Boulding's exchange system is characterized by promises of rewards and, therefore, is related to Parsons' third mode, inducement. Parsons adds a fourth type of social influence, persuasion, which he classifies as positive along with inducement. Persuasion is an attempt to restructure the goals or attitudes of the target through the employment of propaganda, argument, or special or technical knowledge.

Social psychologists are more prone than other social scientists to develop problems that fit into the laboratory, and are, therefore, busily investigating leadership, social power, propaganda and attitude change, group problem solving, bargaining, decision-making, and many other manageable phenomena included in the study of social influence. Lack of broad integrating theories and concentration on single processes (e.g., cognitive dissonance) prevent social scientists from developing shared definitions. As a consequence, scientists studying similar processes in different problem areas are not cognizant of each other's work or fail to understand that they are studying the "same thing." Even more common is the degree to which people who use different definitions and operations believe they are studying the same phenomena when they are not. The organizing role of theory which explains the data and facilitates communication between scientists is only now beginning to develop in social psychology.

The present chapter will focus upon deterrence and inducement. An attempt will be made to examine the definitions of threats and promises. A review of the research literature, particularly as it reflects upon contingent threats and promises, will be presented. Finally, some of the factors involved in the influence process will be examined.

A. Definition of Threats and Promises

There is a lack of consensus among social scientists with regard to the genus and differentia of threats and promises. Failure to be precise in defining conceptual elements surely has stunted the growth of a theory of influence and prevented interdisciplinary communications. Cohen and Nagel (1934) state that the logical function and purpose of a definition is to "lay bare the principal features of the structure of a concept, partly in order to make it definite, to delimit it from other concepts, and partly in order to make possible a systematic exploration of the subject matter with which it deals (pp. 231–232)." Particularly important for development of a theory of influence is conceptual clarity concerning the nature of threats and promises.

Much confusion has been generated by the fact that some theorists prefer to think of threats as hypothetical constructs rather than as measurable cues in the environment. The bifurcation between internal and external definitions of threat seems on the whole not to be recognized either in the theoretical or empirical literature (e.g., Singer, 1963). Explicit recognition of the problem might help to facilitate a connection between the events referred to by both classes of definitions. A cognitive theory could accept a cue–perception–action orientation. At any rate, to sort out and relate the variables is a task for theory construction.

Brody, Benham, and Milstein (1966) defined threat perception as anxiety over probable damage to oneself precipitated by environmental cues. Singer (1958) and Pruitt (1965) have similarly defined threat perception as based on perceived intent and perceived capability of an opponent who deliberately plans to block goal attainment. Threat is conceived as an act or behavior by one person that has the intent to produce threat perception in another person. Whether a particular act is identifiable as a threat requires that questions about the motivation generating the act be answered. This empirical problem is similar to that in a court of law which requires that intent to commit a criminal action be demonstrated. That this is so can be extracted from Pruitt's statement that "the more benefit another person can derive from harming our interests, the more threatened we are likely to feel (1965, p. 400)." This generalization rests on the connection between a source's intentions and the target's perceptions.

Although it is true that one has considerable discretion in defining concepts, one cannot ignore the consequences of the definitions once formed. Unfortunately, the anchors on either side of Pruitt's generalization are subjective in nature. There are no independent, nonsubjective criteria or anchors proffered for identifying the existence of a threat. Nor is it clear that a threat perception could ever be determined to be nonveridical in nature. Intentions can always be found by those who feel threatened, while intentions can almost always be disguised by those who are clever. (It is probably the case that intentions cannot be totally concealed unless the source actually gives up his attempt to influence the target.)

Problems also arise for the harm-intention, threat-perception theorists in relating capabilities to intentions. Someone may have an intent to harm another but lack the capability of carrying out the intent. The question arises as to whether actions can be called threatening, if the target knows the source lacks capability of inflicting harm. The lack of objective criteria for determining whether intent actually exists and (if so) to what extent leaves the hypothetical conception of threat immune from test by empirical research. This may be the reason that Pruitt's theory focuses upon how predispositions and other internal states of the perceiver affect threat perception rather than on the environmental stimuli that trip off responses, which in turn are mediated by internal states of the organism. At the present time, the Brody, Singer, and Pruitt type of definition lacks objective criteria for establishing intent, for identifying veridicality of threat perception, or for deciding how believable a target finds a threat or what the target believes the magnitude of the harmful consequences are likely to be.

The above definitions of threat, then, are revealed as emphasizing organismic processes. The lack of connections between objective and independent environmental stimuli and cognitive factors is probably related to the paucity of research using this definition of threat. On the other hand, a psychology of intentions and perceptions cannot be avoided when studying threats. It will be necessary to reconceptualize these events so that they are more amenable to empirical investigation.

Schelling (1966) has focused his considerable theoretical talent on how a threatener converts his intentions into communications that the target both understands and believes. According to Schelling, a threat does not merely convey an intent to do harm, but rather is focused on the use of punishments to coerce another to further the threatener's goals. In fact the threatener should make clear that he does not wish to harm the other but may be forced to do so if the target forces the issue. Deterrence threats are communications, tacit or explicit, ordering another not to do something that the threatener considers harmful to himself. Compellence threats are communications which seek to gain behaviors from another which confer benefits upon oneself.

Schelling outlines the bargaining features related to threat systems and indicates some of the factors that affect believability by the target in the source's communications. He has also managed to place the entire study of threats within a game theoretical framework. Notwithstanding that the strategic analyses offered in his books and a multitude of journal articles are extremely insightful and heuristic, the concepts are not developed in a formal manner. No hypotheses are drawn which are clearly testable; nor are functional relationships specified. Yet, no theory of influence could ignore the factors that Schelling has pointed out.

Sawyer and Guetzkow (1965) define a threat as a representation that if another party acts in a way one disfavors, one will take an action detrimental to him. They indicate that promises have a logical structure essentially similar to that of threats. Promises are characterized as representations that if another behaves in a way one favors, one will then take an action beneficial to him, even though one might prefer not to do so. Both of these definitions are contingent in character and take a logical if–then implicative form.

Regardless of the theoretical position taken, there are three basic components to a theory of influence which involves threats and promises: a source, a signal system, and a target. The view to be taken by this author is that the signal system consists of messages, which take the form of threats and promises, and that the believability by target in the messages and consequent compliance to them will depend not only on experiences with other stimuli of similar kinds, but on characteristics of the source. One might question whether a message is a threat simply because it takes a particular logical form, since a message by a servant to a king that takes such a form hardly affects the king's behavior or perception (except perhaps to make him angry). Similarly, a courteous invitation from the king to the servant may be perceived as a command, no matter how nice the phrasing of the message. These reactions by targets, however, can be explained as related to source and target characteristics rather than to the messages involved. Thus, the implicative if–then form tied to messages requesting specific behaviors from the targets of the influence attempts constitute an objective criterion for identifying threats and promises, while the belief in such messages will involve other factors, including source and target characteristics.

Promises could be defined in a manner corresponding with the internal or organismic definitions of threats (e.g., a promise could be defined as hope of probable gain for oneself). Promise perception, like threat perception, could be defined as perceived facilitation of own goals by another person who has the intention of producing hope (promise perception) in another person. Then, to paraphrase Pruitt's threat generalization, the following hypothesis could be offered: The more benefit another person can derive from furthering our interests, the more hope we are likely to feel. Presumably, we could go about operationalizing concepts in order to partially evaluate such a theoretical position. However, the approach proffered here attempts to avoid the pitfalls associated with such organismic definitions by accepting the stimulus definition of both threats and promises. By starting with such empirical anchors, the study of threats and promises and compliance is provided with a firm basis so that inferences to organismic processes such as threat perception can be made with more assurance than has been the case heretofore.

B. Conceptual Distinctions between Message Forms

There are many indicators for determining the intentions of an actor. Facial expressions, connotations of communications, and many other behaviors (Goffman, 1959; Hall, 1959) yield subtle cues for an experienced and mature adult observer. Such cues are frequently used for tacit communications which imply the same content and form as do more explicit verbal communications. One research strategy (to be adopted herein) would be to develop theory and evidence in regard to explicit threats and promises, and later attempt to include other more ambiguous tacit communications.

A promise message can be either noncontingent or contingent. If the promise is noncontingent, it constitutes a self-prediction by the source purposefully communicated to target that source will do something at a specifiable future time that target prefers be done. A noncontingent promise takes the form: "I will do X," where X is an action, the withholding of an action, the production of a commodity, or the removal of noxious stimuli, any of which can be considered beneficial by the target. If the promise is contingent, the source expresses an intention to reward particular target behaviors and implies thereby that other target behaviors not included in the promise message will not be rewarded, at least not by source. The contingent promise takes the form: "If you do X (or not X), then I will do Y," where Y is an action by source beneficial to the target.

Threats may also be noncontingent or contingent. A noncontingent threat takes the form: "I will do Z," where Z is an action, the withholding of an action, the production of a noxious stimulus, or the removal of a positive reinforcement, any of which can be perceived by target as detrimental or punishing. Threats *formally* differ from promises in that, though both may call for some target response, the former predicts punishments and the latter predicts rewards. Source's perceptions of target's utility functions are important if intentions of source and perceptions of target are to correspond. If source intends as rewarding what target perceives as punishing, then an intended promise is perceived as a threat. If source intends as punishing what target perceives as rewarding, then an intended threat ends up being interpreted as a promise. Given the same cultural milieu, the sign of the reinforcer or utility as negative or positive, if not the degree associated with the sign, is clear enough so that intentions and perceptions usually grossly correspond with each other.

Demos (1957) indicated that a threat is not merely disjunctive. When a government threatens its citizens that if they do not pay their taxes, they will be thrown into jail, the government is not bargaining. It is not merely saying, "You can either pay your taxes or go to jail; it is all the same to us which you prefer." The government *wants* its taxes paid and does not particularly want to incarcerate its citizens. The threat is a force exerted upon the person to coerce him to do as the source wishes. The construction of a threat as merely the statement of a disjunction misses the essential element of coercion.

The social nature of promises and threats needs to be emphasized. Social attribution theory (Kelley, 1967) alerts us to distinguish between those conditions within which source controls the rewards and punishments and those in which source does not control the contingencies. In the former, the source carries out or causes to be carried out both the communication of contingencies and the administrations of rewards or punishments. When source merely describes to target contingencies which are beyond source's control or influence and where the outcomes would be punishing to target, the message constitutes a contingent warning to target. A positive prediction of a contingency between a target's behavior and a favorable outcome, not controlled by source, may be called a mendation.[1] Presumably, attitudinal changes and long-term behavioral modifications by a target in reaction to a source who issues warnings and mendations would be different than would be the consequences involved when the source originated threats or promises.

Warnings and mendations are psychologically more complicated for a target than are threats and promises. The target must take into account not only the intentions and capabilities of the source, but also whether, in fact, source has any influence over the contingency he points out, whether in fact the contingency is probable, and if the contingency is probable, the magnitude of the consequences. In addition, a target may have to consider the intentions, capability and influenceability of a possible third party who does control the contingency. Thus, all of the factors involved in the perception of threats and promises plus other factors are involved in perceptions of warnings and mendations. On the other hand, from source's point of view, warnings and mendations may be simpler than threats and promises since no obligation or responsibility rests with him, except perhaps for the responsibility associated with him as a monitor of events. Deterrence theorists often advocate that a volitional deterrent force be converted into an automatic trip-wire retaliatory device, that is, that a threat be converted into a warning (Kahn, 1962; Schelling, 1960). The point of view taken by such theorists is invariably that of the source.

In summary, there are a number of practical and theoretical difficulties associated with a definition of threat which stipulates only organismic or hypothetical processes as the identifying criteria. Yet the intentions of the

---

[1] The only dictionary terms that relate to what is called mendations are slang terms such as giving tips or touting. The word "mendations" was drawn from "recommendations."

source and the perceptions of target are important mediating factors associated with threats and promises. The definition of threats and promises as measurable environmental stimuli serves to provide a firm anchor to which cognitive processes can be tied. Explicit and contingent threats and promises are most easily identified as messages of the form "if–then" sent by a source to a target. A threat makes punishment contingent upon noncompliance and a promise makes reward contingent upon compliance. A threat or promise implies that the source of the message is also the controller of the punishments or rewards. Warnings and mendations refer to messages which convey punishment and reward contingencies for target over which source has no control. Although implicit, tacit, and sometimes symbolic threats and promises are frequent in social interactions, the research strategy herein is to develop the study of more explicit messages.

II. EMPIRICAL STUDIES

The two dependent variables of interest when studying the target of social influence are cognitive change and behavioral compliance. A review of all of the literature which might fit these categories is far beyond the scope of this chapter. Rather, to be included, the dependent variable must be behavioral compliance and the message used must be explicitly (not tacitly) a promise or threat, a warning or a mendation. Many studies have been carried out with tacit threats and the primary focus for research on social influence has been cognitive change. The latter will for the most part be excluded from the following review.

A. Warnings and Mendations

In a study which included a measure of behavioral compliance, Janis and Feshback (1953) used high and medium levels of possible damage included in the warning of communications in regard to consequences of tooth decay. A message (not a warning) described to a control group the nature of tooth growth and structure. With all groups the same series of recommendations concerning oral hygiene were presented. One week before and one week after these recommendations, Ss were administered questionnaires concerning oral hygiene practices. Warnings produced less conformity and less stability in face of counterpropaganda, and resulted in fewer verbal reports of compliance with the recommendations than did the control condition. Other studies have confirmed this finding and established a curvilinear relationship between magnitude of "threat" and attitude change (Krech, Crutchfield, & Ballachey, 1962). However, the control group message appears to have been a noncontingent one, whereas the high level warning appears to have been a contingent message. This distinction may help to account for the fact that others have found that the more fear-arousing the communication, the greater its persuasive impact (Berkowitz & Cottingham, 1960; DeWolfe & Governale, 1964; Leventhal, Singer, & Jones, 1965).

Dabbs and Leventhal (1966) also focused upon behavior change rather than attitude change. Level of fear was indirectly manipulated by presenting different discussions concerning the danger of tetanus to experimental groups. Innoculations were described as more or less effective in preventing tetanus and more or less painful to take. These communications can be considered to have varied the perception of how efficacious compliance would be and the costs associated with compliance. Compliance with the recommendations was measured by Ss' stated intention to take shots and by their actual shot-taking behavior. Compliance was not affected by either the degree of probability of success associated with the message or the degree of cost. However, manipulation of fear influenced both intentions to take shots and actual shot-taking behavior. The effect was linear with compliance being greatest under high fear.

In an experiment using fifth and sixth grade Taiwan students, Chu (1966) used communications about the danger of roundworms to health as warnings. Efficacy was defined as the amount of loss that could be averted minus the cost of taking compliant actions. Ss in the high fear condition were told that roundworms would make them vulnerable to encephalitis. In the low fear condition, encephalitis was not mentioned. Since there was an epidemic of encephalitis at the time of the study, the addition of that disease to the warning may have affected the subjective probability assigned to the harmful consequences as well as the magnitude of the harm involved. Efficacy was manipulated by telling Ss that a drug cured 80, 60, or below 30% of the roundworm cases. The dependent variable was neither attitude change nor compliance but rather a measure of anxiety. Threat perception or anxiety varied directly with the efficacy associated with the message. Ss also expressed more willingness to take the drug under the high fear condition.

Leventhal and Niles (1965) found an increased concern related to driving an automobile and an increased desire to take preventive action, the longer the duration of exposure to a movie depicting the consequences of serious accidents. The longer the interval between exposure to the movie and the administration of the attitude questionnaire, the less effective the communication, which lends some credence to the Freudian defense mechanism of "denial."

Feshback and Singer (1957) differentiated between a personal "threat" and one which is perceived as affecting a group. In their experiment, communications to individuals were either personal warnings, shared warnings, or neutral messages. The dependent measure following the communications was a test of social prejudice. Personal warning Ss were more prejudiced than control Ss who, in turn, were more prejudiced than shared warning Ss. This study provides indirect evidence that personal warnings are more frustrating than are shared ones, and that increases in aggressive or hostile attitudes are associated with the former.

In all of the above studies, if the Ss did not do what the message said to do, the source of the communication would not administer the aversive consequences indicated in the communication. Often the contingency between responses and harm or prevention of harm is vague, and the degree of probability (credibility of the warning) is either unmeasurable or unmeasured. The experimental manipulations seem to focus more often on induced fear than on warning–attitude change or warning–compliance relationships. The stimulus factors remain subjectively determined by the experimenter on the basis of whether they will elicit fear rather than on strict operational criteria. The Ss usually are not placed in any real conflict situation with another person who is either the source of the warning or one designated as the probable administrator of punishment by the source. Until more systematic research is done on warnings, few, if any, generalizations can be made. Similarly, not only is there no word to describe the event named "mendations" herein, but also little or no research has been done on the events referred to by that word.

B. Threats

Although the author prefers the definition of threat as an environmental stimulus, the organismic definitions of threat have led to important experimental results which need to be integrated within a theory of social influence. Threat stimuli should lead to threat perceptions which then could arouse fear or anxiety and eventually produce attitude changes or affect performance factors. Distinctly different emotional responses and persuasion possibilities are associated with contingent and noncontingent threat stimuli.

1. Noncontingent Threats

One strategy followed in the study of threats is to focus upon what happens to a group member who is perceived as a source of threat to other group members. Schachter, Nutton, de Monchaux, Maucorps, Osmer, Duyker, Rommetreit, and Israel (1954) directed their cross-cultural study at precisely this question. They assumed that the magnitude of threat was a function of the valence of a goal and the probability of goal attainment. Ss chose to build one of five possible model airplanes, one of which was a nondescript glider. The best model was to be chosen for a high valence prize, or, in another condition, the low valence prize. A probability of winning was given by instructions. Sociometric measures showed that the most general reaction to a confederate who always chose to build the glider was rejection. The high valence, low probability of winning condition (high threat) produced the most rejection of the stooge. Thus, appearing to be instrumental in improving the group's success, enhances the particular group member's attractiveness, whereas advocating actions which would appear to deter the group's success subtract from a member's attractiveness. It would be of interest to determine if rejection of a group member increases the cohesiveness of the other group members. The more general question would be: Does a purge or "cultural revolution" increase the legitimacy of an existing government?

Mulder and Stemerding (1963), using a highly realistic threat to Dutch shopkeepers reputed for their stubborn independence, found that the highly threatened people became more strongly attracted to the group they were forming than did less threatened people. The threatened shopkeepers were especially attracted to the leader of the group. These results, at least, suggest that when individuals are threatened they do tend to seek the support of the group and particularly the group's leader to help them cope with external danger.

Threats may be tacit or explicit in nature (Schelling, '1966). Responses other than those involving explicit communications may be interpreted by the perceiver as revealing the source's intention and/or capability to do him harm. For example, Robinson and Snyder (1965) define a crisis as an unplanned decision situation in which there is a short time available for response, and where high value consequences are involved. Since harm can occur, but the response necessary is unspecified, a crisis can be considered a noncontingent tacit threat. However, some crisis like that during which President Kennedy specifically stated that if the missiles were not removed, Cuba would subsequently be bombed, may be specific contingent threat situations. North, Brody, and Holsti (1964) and Holsti and North (1963), using the internation simulation (INS) as the experimental environment, found that in crisis situations, the probability is high that those who perceive themselves as threatened will respond with threats of their own. A consequent spiral of threat perception, threat, response by threat, confirmation, and further threat results. Also, decision-makers during crisis tend to perceive their own range of alternatives to be more restricted than those of their adversaries; that is, they will perceive their own decision-making as characterized by necessity and closed options, whereas those of the adversary are characterized by open choices. Robinson (1962), also using the INS game, found that perceived time available to decision-makers decreased as threat increased, even when objective time was held constant.

An experiment by Deutch and Krauss (1960) produced a research paradigm which has frequently been used to study threat within a two-person nonzero sum game. S's are asked to imagine that they are operating trucking companies carrying merchandise over a road to a destination. Each of two S's starting from different points and going to different destinations must take a path at one point which is large enough for only one truck. Although alternate routes are available, they are longer, and since "time is money" in terms of costs and gains, each operator would like to take the mutually shared path. Gates are sometimes given to one or both operators to prevent the other's truck from passing through the "one-lane road." Sometimes, a red light is used as a signal that the gate will be lowered.

Any stimulus which signals punishment, but which does not indicate any specific avoidant responses, can be considered a noncontingent threat. In the trucking game, the experimenters assume that the light will be used and interpreted as meaning that the recipient should allow the source to use the one-lane road first. Thus, the threat mechanism is intended as a contingent one, but the contingency is tacit rather than explicit.

Given the basic paradigm, the three conditions of threat were employed by means of providing gates to one, both, or neither of the subjects (Deutsch & Krauss, 1960). Thus, the three conditions of no threat, unilateral threat, and bilateral threat were established. The ability of subjects to reach agreements, as reflected by the magnitude of their joint payoffs, was inversely related to the amount of threat present. The gates were used more frequently in the bilateral than in the unilateral threat condition.

Kelley (1962, 1965) has directed his criticisms of the trucking game experiments (Borah, 1963; Deutsch & Krauss, 1960, 1962; Gallo, 1966; Krauss & Deutsch, 1966; Shure, Meeker, & Moore, 1963) at the assumption that the threat mechanism is a contingent one. Gates, Kelley claims, can be used to punish the other person, to trick him, to administer revenge, to signal whose turn it is to use the shorter route, and so on. There is also the problem of how the target perceives its use. The assumption that the operators use and perceive the gates as contingent threats intended to modify specific behavior is questionable. The added inference on the dependent variable side that the lower the joint payoff resulting from a play of the trucking game, the more competitive the pair, is also unsupportable, e.g., Ss may think that the gates have been introduced into the experiment for some reason, so they use them to enliven the proceedings, as a matter of curiosity, or for some other reason.

Tedeschi, Bonoma, and Novinson (1969a) have attempted to check some of the assumptions uncovered by Kelley's criticisms of the trucking game paradigm for studying threats. The Prisoner's Dilemma game (PDG) was modified so that each subject was given fixed options to send explicit contingent threats to a simulated target. The simulated target was either capable of retaliating on those trials on which he was punished by the subject for noncompliance or the simulated target was unarmed. To equate the costs to the subjects for using their power across the unilateral and bilateral threat conditions, the subject was charged a fixed cost for penalizing the target on noncompliance trials in the unilateral threat condition and the fixed cost was equivalent to the retaliatory power of the target in the bilateral condition. Although there were no differences in the number of threats sent by subjects in the two conditions, subjects in the bilateral threat condition were more likely to punish noncompliance than those in the unilateral threat condition. Degree of cooperativeness and winnings were not affected by the degree of threat present. These results indicate that the assumption made by Deutsch and Krauss that gates are perceived as threats is justified, since the bilateral threat condition, as in their experiment, apparently did increase the degree of conflict in the situation. However, the lack of supportive findings in the PDG paradigm in relation to the threat condition and winnings or degree of cooperation indicates that the introduction of gates in the trucking game produces artifactual results in regard to these dependent variables. The use of gates takes time and time itself affects winning. Thus, mutual use of gates in the bilateral threat condition produces less winnings in the Deutsch and Krauss study because the gates were used by both players.

Shomer, Davis, and Kelley (1966), on the basis of criticisms similar to those of Kelley, designed a study of noncontingent threats within a two-person game. One player could press a threat button (signal) indicating to the other player an intention to deliver a fine ("harm"). Another button could be employed to actually impose the fine. It was not necessary for the S to precede a fine with a threat, nor follow a threat with a fine. The possession of threat and fine options did not significantly affect the joint profits of Ss as compared with Ss who did not have such options. Many Ss, in fact, interpreted the threat as a signal for turn-taking rather than as a threat. Such Ss tended to be members of dyads with high joint payoffs.

The above review of studies of noncontingent threats indicates that there are difficulties associated with unambiguously differentiating between noncontingent threats and tacit contingent threats. The difference is often in the eye of the beholder. This ambiguity suggests that perception of tacit threats is more a function of the predispositions of the target than the intentions of the source. Further studies might attempt to probe more deeply into the personality factors affecting threat perception than has so far been done (see Chapter 6).

2. Contingent Threats

The group of experiments reviewed in this section differ from those discussed previously in that "threat" is a clear verbal if–then communication which promises administration of punishment for noncompliance. However, instead of focusing upon compliance, some of these experiments use as a dependent variable some measure of cognitive change. An example of the latter was a study by Aronson and Carlsmith (1963) in which children were led into a strange room and asked to rank a group of toys as to their preferences. The second ranked toy was a forbidden object. In the mild threat condition *S*s were told not to play with the forbidden toy or *E* would be annoyed. In the strong threat condition, *S*s were told not to play with it or *E* would be angry, would take all the toys, go home, never to come back, and would think of the *S* as just a baby. *E* then left the room for a while and upon returning asked the *S*s to rank the toys again. It was found that mild threat led to more derogation·of the forbidden toy than the severe threat.

Using a similar design, Turner and Wright (1965) found that in a mild threat condition (you should not play with it) *S*s tended to decrease their liking for the critical toy, while in the strong threat condition (if you play with it you cannot play with any of the other toys), *S*s appeared to increase their evaluation of the critical toy. Freedman (1965) looked at the long-range effect of such threats. *S*s who did not play with the toy under either threat condition were given a second opportunity to play with the toy several weeks later with the original threat removed. *S*s who resisted temptation under mild threat were less likely to play with the critical toy in the second session than those who resisted under severe threat. Recently, in a study in which boys were threatened with the loss of a valuable (severe threat) or a less valuable (mild threat) gift if they played with a second ranked of five attractive toys, Pepitone, McCauley, and Hammond (1967) reported that rankings of the toys before and after a temptation period showed that mild threat lowered the forbidden toy's attractiveness, and severe threat raised its attractiveness. Measures of latency and duration of play with the critical toys after removal of the prohibition revealed that *S*s in the mild threat condition had longer latencies, whereas *S*s in the severe threat condition, played longer with the forbidden object.

In a study by Hermann (1966), internation simulation served as the research environment. *S*s were given three goals for their nations. Then potential threats to national goals were induced by members of the simulation staff posing as *S*s. The experimental situations were designed to warn a nation that one of its goals would be blocked unless some remedial action was forthcoming (e.g., renounce nuclear development or face military steps or a trade boycott). The results demonstrated that *S*s tended to perceive their more important goals as threatened. The number of *S*s perceiving a more generalized threat increased as negative affect increased. The greater the negative affect the *S* experienced, the more important he considered his threatened goals after encountering the experimental situation. Thus, emphasis was on the *S*'s subjective experience of stress. Credibility of the threat or how the *S* dealt with the threat, important factors in "real world" situations, were not examined.

In one of the first studies which investigated unambiguous contingent threats as they affect behavior, Hornstein (1965) tested the hypothesis that if threat potential, i.e., the degree to which one can harm another, was differentially distributed between pairs of bargainers, the use of threat would itself be encouraged or discouraged by the relative threat potential of the bargainers. *S*s were instructed to imagine that they were realtor owners who were trying to come to agreement with other realtors regarding the number of acres and cost per acre in sale of land. *S*s sent two kinds of offer slips. The first communicated terms of a particular offer to the other. The second was a notice slip, but in this case the offer was made as part of a threat. With a threat, *S*s could reduce the other's profit by a certain percent. To do this *S*s had to send the "if" type notice slip. After a notice slip was sent, a realtor was allowed to send a "stock sale" slip on his following turn, i.e., he could aggress. Threat potential was the percent by which a realtor could reduce the other's profit. There were six pairs of conditions: 90–90%, 50–50%, 10–10% (equal conditions); 90–10%, 50–10%, 20–10% (unequal conditions). It was found that if one or both *S*s issued a threat at the start of negotiations, or if threat or aggression occurred during negotiations, the likelihood that agreement would be reached was reduced. The data failed to support the notion that a bargainer's use of threat was a negative function of the magnitude of his opponent's deterrent force. Bargainers with weaker threat potential did not yield to threat more often than stronger ones. While stronger bargainers initiated more threat under conditions of high disparity in threat potential, weaker bargainers initiated more threat under conditions of low disparity in threat potential. Bargainers with equal threat potentials were no more likely to aggress than bargainers in the unequal threat potential conditions. Under conditions of low disparity in threat potential, the weaker bargainers aggress less, whereas under conditions of high disparity in threat potential, the stronger bargainers aggress least. Hornstein concluded that the reason his results do not support deterrence theory is that *S*s saw themselves and their partners as students (peers or equals), and that these perceptions overrode the experimental manipulations which were intended to produce differences in power between them.

Hornstein measured compliance to threats by dividing the number of times *S* marked compliance slips "O.K." by the number of times he could have done so. In other words, compliance ratio is obtained by dividing the number of times *S* complied into the number of times a threat was sent. An aggression ratio was calculated as the ratio of number of stock sale slips sent to the total number of times they could have been sent. Although Hornstein did not conceive of his measure as such, the aggression ratio actually is a measure of credibility of the threat. No objective credibility can be established for successful threats, since, when the target complies, there is no occasion presented for punishing him. Only when threats are unsuccessful can credibility levels be established for them. Thus, credibility would be the ratio of times *S* was punished to the number of times he could have been punished. Unfortunately, Hornstein's experiment failed to control for threat credibility and his results may be somewhat confounded as a consequence.

In a more recent experiment, Hornstein, Deutsch, and Benedict (1966) compared compliance to two types of threats: (1) source threatened to harm target if target did not comply with source's wishes; and (2) source threatened to harm a third party if target did not comply with source's demands. Ss played a Market Board game for money. A three-person situation included a Producer (the naive S), a Buyer, and an Observer (both stooges). In a two-person version,, the Observer was eliminated and his payoffs were removed from the Market Board. Ss were led to believe roles were assigned according to a lottery. After giving Ss a fifty-cent stake, it was explained that their job was to decide whether to produce wheat or rice. Profits depended upon the product chosen and how many kilos the Buyer purchased. The Buyer always chose after the S announced his choice. Prior to the game, Buyer communicated to the S that unless he always selected his less desirable alternative (rice), the Buyer would select a number of kilos, depending on the experimental condition, which would result in the S losing or receiving no profit and/or the Observer losing or receiving no profit (depending on the condition). The results indicated that Ss were as unwilling to comply to threat when compliance caused harm to another as when it caused harm to themselves. Increasing the magnitude of threat or absence or presence of an Observer under conditions of threat to self had no effect. The authors suggested that the second type of threat did not produce relatively more compliance as hypothesized, because the lottery assignment of roles led Ss to believe that they initially shared the same risk of becoming an Observer and, therefore, being selected for that role created no special claims on any of the others.

Robinson and Snyder (1965) have stated that if the direct connection between the credibility of a deterrent threat and its effectiveness in deterring certain actions holds (empirically), then a theory specifying antecedent and consequent conditions of credible messages could be developed. Horai and Tedeschi (1969) modified the Prisoner's Dilemma game (PDG) so that threats of varying credibilities could be communicated from a confederate source to a target S. Several conceptual distinctions led to their study. Credibility was equated with veracity of the message and was operationally defined as the relationship between deeds and words. If a target complies with a threat, no opportunity is presented to the source for punishment. Thus, successful threats were assumed to have no credibility even though an increment in believability by target in the threat could occur simply because he had complied with it. Credibility was defined as the probability that a target would suffer a loss in points when he did *not* comply with the threat, "If you don't make choice 1, I will take n points away from you." By interspersing threat messages throughout iterations of the PDG, Horai and Tedeschi established a criterion number of 10 unsuccessful threats for each of their Ss, punishing compliance one, five, or nine times (credibility levels of 10, 50, or 90%) by taking away 5, 10, or 20 points. The number of successful threats was allowed to vary. All data except for the measure of compliance were analyzed by covariance in order to statistically remove the effects produced by varying numbers of successful threats across experimental conditions. The simulated source always defected as a game strategy on the iteration following an exchange of messages. Hence, given the matrix values used for the PDG, the S was faced with a least-of-evils choice; he either lost 5 points for complying (cooperating or making choise 1) or he lost 4 points for noncomplying (competing or making choice 2). In the latter case, there was also a probability of a loss of 5, 10, or 20 points as punishment for noncompliance. The results showed that both credibility and magnitude of punishment were positively and linearly related to behavioral compliance. These results were replicated when only 10 and 90% credibilities and 5 and 20 point punishments were employed (Lindskold, Bonoma, & Tedeschi, 1969a). These empirical results support assumptions made by deterrence theorists, but leave open the possibility that higher levels of punishment (other than loss of points) would yield decreasing increments in compliance (overkill).

Tedeschi, Horai, Lindskold, and Gahagan (1968b) studied the effects of conflict intensity, threat credibility, punishment magnitude, and sex upon behavioral compliance to contingent threats and the message-sending behavior of the target Ss. The manipulation of conflict intensity involved changes in the matrix values of the modified PDG (Jones, Steele, Gahagan, & Tedeschi, 1968; Rapoport, 1967; Steele & Tedeschi, 1967). The failure to replicate the linear effects of credibility and magnitude of punishment to compliance found by Horai and Tedeschi (1969), and by Lindskold, Bonoma, and Tedeschi (1969b), was attributed to the different payoff matrices used in the studies. In the Tedeschi et al. study (1968b), if the S complied with the threat he lost 10 points, while the confederate won 10 points. The competitive advantage to the confederate was thus 20 points. On the other hand, the S lost only one point for noncomplying. Even if he was punished, he lost only an additional 10 or 20 points. Apparently, Ss prefer the probability of losing some amount than a certainty of losing the same amount, especially when they can retaliate by imposing a loss of one point on the threatener as well. If the S is indifferent to the magnitude of the punishment and thus resists a threat, the credibility of that threat no longer affects compliance. The intensity of conflict manipulation was accomplished by varying the two payoffs which could not occur on the threat-related trials, given that the simulated source always defected as a game strategy following the exchange of messages. And, for the very reason that the differences in intensity of conflict were not relevant to the threat trials, no effects of conflict level upon behavioral compliance of target Ss were found. The study also found that males lie more often than females when the former say they will comply as a response to the threat message. This sex difference replicated the findings of Horai, Tedeschi, Gahagan, and Lesnick (1969).

A model for studying contingent threats was developed by Tedeschi and Horai (1968). The model assumes that the confederate always defects as a game strategy on a threat trial, that the target has perfect information, and the target is rational. The equation is

$$C = S_{\mathrm{p}} - \left\{ [(Z_{\mathrm{pr}})(P_{\mathrm{p}} + z)] + [(1 - Z_{\mathrm{pr}})(P_{\mathrm{p}})] \right\}$$

where C is the predictor of compliance, S_{p} is the S-payoff in the PDG matrix,[2] Z_{pr} is the probability with which the target is punished for noncompliance (credibility level), P_{p} is the P-payoff in the matrix, and z is the magnitude of punishment for noncompliance. Thus, S_{p} in the equation indicates what happens when the target complies, and the rest of the equation indicates what happens when the target noncomplies. If $C = 0$, to comply or noncomply leads to the same long-term results and a rational S will be indifferent in his choices. If $C > 0$, the target will gain more (lose less) by complying. And if $C < 0$, then target will gain more by noncomplying.

The contingent threat model predicted the rank order of 7 of 9 means in the study by Horai and Tedeschi, all 4 means in the Lindskold et al. study (1969a), and 10 out of 12 means (with the other 2 tied in rank) in the Tedeschi et al. study (1968b).

Gahagan, Tedeschi, Horai, Long. and Lindskold (1969b) attempted to replicate the Horai and Tedeschi results with a population of preadolescent black children. Fifth and sixth grade children played 100 iterations of the PDG, modified for the introduction of threats from a confederate to the target Ss. The threats were 10, 50, or 90% credible and promised 5, 10, or 20 points punishment for noncompliance. Overall preplanned strategies of either 10 or 50% cooperations were played by the confederate. Black and white Es were used in a deliberately confounded design. More compliance was obtained with the threats of 90 and 50% credibility than with threats of 10% credibility. However, the degree of compliance did not differ between the 50 and 90% credibility conditions. Since credibility refers to the probability of punishment for noncompliance and the magnitude of punishment is explicitly stated in the threat message, the concept of negative utility may be appropriately affixed to their interaction. Given that punishment magnitude did not produce a main effect on degree of compliance, it may be inferred that children have more difficulty than adults in discriminating utilities (Tedeschi, Hiester, & Gahagan, 1969d). In addition, the children were more compliant when E was black than when he was white.

---

[2] The use of R, T, S, and P refer to values in a 2×2 matrix in a PDG follows the convention of game theorists (Rapoport & Chammah, 1965).

Analyses of the overall strategy selections by Ss over both message and nonmessage trials indicated credibility, confederate strategy, and sex main effects. Children playing against a 90% credible threatener were more co-operative than those playing either a 10 or 50% credible threatener. However, no difference in overall cooperations occurred as a function of the change from 10 to 50% credibility. The children playing against the confederate who cooperated only 10% of the time were less cooperative themselves than they were against a more cooperative (50%) threatener. This result was interesting because strategy manipulations of these magnitudes do not ordinarily affect Ss' strategy selections in an unmodified PDG (Bixenstine, Potash, & Wilson, 1963; McClintock, Harrison, Strand, & Gallo, 1963; Tedeschi, Aranoff, & Gahagan, 1968a). Apparently, the introduction of threat messages sharpens the target's discrimination of differences in source's overall strategies. In addition, females cooperated more than males. This finding is contrary to the usual sex differences found in the unmodified PDG, if, in fact, sex differences are found at all (Rapoport & Chammah, 1965). However, females have consistently been found to be more influenceable and conforming than males (McGuire, 1969; Marlowe & Gergen, 1969).

Tedeschi (1968) has presented a theory of influence within dyads which borrows from the literature on persuasion, attitude change, and conformity and applies empirical generalizations to the responses of targets to threats and promises. Aside from message utility, other source and target characteristics are assumed to affect the degree of believability a target assigns explicit threats and promises. Among these factors are the degree of attraction or liking that target has for source, the status of source, and the self-esteem of target.

Tedeschi, Bonoma, Schlenker, and Lindskold (1969b) induced high and low attraction in Ss by using a technique devised by Byrne (1961). For the high attraction Ss, a simulated attitude scale was falsified which showed the "other" player's attitudes as similar to S's; for the low attraction Ss, the scale depicted "other's" attitudes as radically opposed to those held by the Ss. The Ss perused the false scales after filling out their own, and were told that each person was evaluating the other when the only information they had about each other consisted of the responses each had made on the attitude scale before the exchange took place. Two levels of threat credibility (10 and 90%) made up the second factor of the 2×2 experimental design. The results of the pretest and posttest attraction measures showed that the inducement procedure did affect attraction in the desired manner and that the effect persisted throughout the experimental session. However, high attraction Ss liked "other" less at the end of the experiment than at the beginning and low attraction Ss liked "other" more at the end than at the beginning. An attraction by credibility interaction was obtained on the compliance of Ss to the threat messages; low credibility, high attraction Ss complied least, while high credibility, high attraction Ss complied most to threats. Low attraction Ss were intermediate with respect to the former two groups, and the credibility manipulation did not significantly affect their compliance to threats. In addition, low attraction Ss rated source as more potent on the Semantic Differential than did high attraction Ss. This last finding is analogous to several previous potency findings which showed that low threat credibility yielded higher ratings of source's potency (Gahagan, Lindskold, Faley, & Tedeschi, 1969a; Lindskold, Bonoma, & Tedeschi, 1969b). These potency results may indicate that a source is perceived as potent to the degree that he does *not* use his power. Apparently, low attraction Ss expect source to use his power and respond according to that expectation rather than to the negative utilities actually assigned to the threats; their rating of source as potent may result from the fact that source was not 100% credible and violated their expectations by not always using his power. High attraction Ss apparently did not expect source to use his power by punishing noncompliance and thus did not comply with the 10% credible threats; they did, however, respond quickly once they learned that the threatener intended to punish them and consequently complied more with the 90% credible threats than did the low attraction Ss. This implies that a threatener who knows he is disliked by the target may expect compliance without necessarily establishing high credibility for his threats. However, if source knows that the target likes him and still attempts to coerce target into compliance, high credibility should be used in order to gain such compliance.

In a study which operationalized status in terms of rank within the ROTC program, Faley and Tedeschi (1969) had low rank cadets and high rank cadets play against a simulated source. Low–Low, Low–High, High–Low, and High–High status conditions were established. The low status target complied more often to threats from a high status source than did Ss in the Low–Low or High–Low conditions. However, the high status target complied frequently to threats from a source who was equally high in status. A strictly hierarchical theory of status cannot explain these results. Apparently, equals of high status bestow respect upon each other by displaying deference patterns that are similar to those displayed by low status individuals toward high status individuals. Potency ratings of the simulated source obtained following the experimental interaction indicated that potency was directly related to threat credibility, a finding which is inconsistent with the studies reported above and with other as yet unreported results. Since the same apparatus, experimenters, and procedures were utilized in the Faley and Tedeschi study as in the others, the potency finding was attributed to the population involved. It was suggested that the attribution process is affected by the institutional affiliations of the person making the attribution and that in the military program it is the use of power and not the withholding of it that is considered to be a sign of potency.

Fifth, and sixth grade children were divided by Lindskold and

Tedeschi (1969b) into high and low self-esteem groups based upon their scores on the Coopersmith scale (1967) and then exposed to either contingent threats or contingent promises issued by a simulated peer whose messages possessed 100% credibility. High self-esteem target Ss were more compliant to both threats and promises—a finding which is consistent with the tendency observed by Faucheux and Moscovici (1968) in a chronic, contrasted with induced, self-esteem condition. High self-esteem individuals should expect approval and rewards from others, while low self-esteem individuals should expect disapproval and punishment from others. The fact that the simulated source was 50% exploitative and 50% accommodative on message trials may have led the high self-esteem children to expect that threats were being used as signals to bring about coordination of cooperative outcomes and thus led them to cooperate more often than low self-esteem Ss, who may have focused upon the exploitative intentions of the inconsistent source.

Empirical research has established that behavioral compliance to threats is a function of the credibility of threats and the magnitude of punishment associated with threats. However, when the target is caught in an avoidance–avoidance conflict in which he will be harmed if he complies or noncomplies, and where the magnitude of harm is about equal in either case, then the target will noncomply with the threats and will be indifferent to the credibility associated with such threats. A model of negative message utility which predicts the degree of compliance to be expected from a target given a two choice situation has received empirical support. In addition, the higher the status of the source, the more compliant the target is to threats. If target likes source, he will not comply if the threats from source are of low credibility but will comply, even more than will low attraction Ss, if the threats from the liked source are highly credible. If the target does not like source, then a moderate amount of compliance to threats will be displayed but threat credibility will not affect the degree of compliance. Finally, the self-esteem of target is related to his perceptions of source's intentions and the degree of compliance given to the latter's influence attempts. High self-esteem individuals are likely to perceive source's intentions as accommodative and respond positively to source's influence attempts. Low self-esteem individuals are likely to perceive source's intentions as exploitative and respond negatively to source's influence attempts.

C. Promises

Very little research has been carried out to investigate the effects of promises upon attitude change or behavior. Some conceptual confusion in designing the studies which allege to focus upon promises makes it difficult to draw conclusions from results and makes assignment to either contingent or noncontingent categories arbitrary.

1. Noncontingent Promises

A stimulus which signals a reward in a situation in which the reward is not contingent upon any particular response is a noncontingent promise. So far as can be determined, no experiment has been done relating noncontingent promises to the attitudes of target Ss.

Loomis (1959) used the PDG as a research tool in his study of the effects communications have upon social conflicts within dyads. Half of his Ss sent, and half received standardized notes expressing intention (noncontingent promise), expectation, retaliation (contingent threat), absolution, and various mixtures of these messages. The Ss were not bound by the choices indicated in their notes. Loomis defined perceived trust as existing when an S expected that the other person intended to cooperate, and mutual trust as displayed when perceived trust induced cooperation by the perceiver. The number of Ss who perceived trust increased with each level of communication from intention up to the combination messages. Ss who did not perceive trust cooperated less than those who did.

In a study carried out by Evans (1964), a confederate source made a promise to the target S that source would cooperate as long as the target did. There was an "enforceable promise" condition which consisted of levying a fine against source when he failed to respond according to his promise. On a rating scale completed following the six iterations of the modified PDG, S rated the opposing player as to his trustworthiness. The simulated player was rated as more trustworthy in the two-promise conditions than he was in a no-promise condition, but there was no difference between the enforceable and unenforceable conditions. Cooperative responding was greater in the enforceable-promise condition than in the no-promise condition, but neither differed from the unenforceable-promise condition. It is difficult to draw any conclusions from these results.

Radlow and Weidner (1966) found that unenforced commitments provided almost as much security as enforced commitments did. The communications Ss consisted of a series of five messages which could be sent by each S. The messages were sent until the same message was used three successive times or until 15 exchanges took place. The content of all of the messages expressed an intention for the particular trial following the message as well as making statements about subsequent responses which would be contingent upon the other's responses. All commitments were exchanged before play began. It was found that commitments which, if honored, would lead to cooperative play, did so, while those which would lead to competitive behavior led to competitive strategy selections. The high amount of cooperative behavior exhibited by the Ss differed from all previous studies based on 100 trials or more, and could be accounted for by the way in which the final monetary payoffs were determined. Ss received the payoff from a trial randomly chosen from the experimental trials. At any rate, the messages referred not to a specific occasion for cooperation, but rather to a sequence of occasions and carried an implied threat to compete if cooperation from target was not forthcoming. The results may indicate that messages carrying *both* promise and threat options are more effective in eliciting cooperation than either promises or threats alone.

Gahagan and Tedeschi (1968a) specifically studied the factor of credibility as applied to noncontingent promises in the modified PDG. A confederate source sent ten noncontingent promises, one after each ten iterations of a 110 trial game, but honored the promises, 3, 6, or 9 times to establish 30, 60, or 90% credibility conditions. They found that the highest credibility level did induce more instances of cooperation on the trial following the message exchange than did the other two conditions, but that credibility differences had no spread of effect to nonmessage trials. They concluded that promises do resolve conflicts but that even highly credible promises may lead to only limited conflict resolutions.

If a promisor's messages carry only moderate credibility, the source could develop a strategy designed to deceive the target. The source could honor his initial promises to "sucker" the target into becoming vulnerable to exploitation on later occasions. A sort of halo effect may carry over from initial contacts so that a perfidious person could take advantage of a conciliatory target. Tedeschi, Powell, Lindskold, and Gahagan (1970b) investigated the effects of different patterns of implementing noncontingent promises of 50% credibility. They honored the first five of ten promises, the second five, every other promise or the middle five of ten promises. A control condition in which no messages were exchanged was also included in the design. The data clearly indicated that the patterning of credibility makes little difference in the way people respond to moderately credible noncontingent promises. The fact that Ss who did not exchange messages responded no differently than Ss who received 50% credible promises, indicates some modifications in the conclusions reached by Gahagan and Tedeschi (1968a) and Loomis (1959). Although Gahagan and Tedeschi found that highly credible promises led to more cooperative behavior on the trial following message exchanges, they could say nothing about the absolute level of cooperation induced by sending promises to Ss since they included no control condition in their experiment. Loomis, on the other hand, concluded that messages with varying content led to more cooperative play than no communications at all. But Loomis did not study credibility levels and used only five trials in his study. It seems apparent that noncontingent promises of 50% credibility, regardless of how the credibility is patterned, are no better (and no worse) at reconciling parties to conflict than no communications at all. Finally, it was clear that females were more likely than males to reciprocate promises and to honor them. This sex difference has been consistently found (Gahagan & Tedeschi, 1968b; Lindskold & Tedeschi, 1969a; Tedeschi, Feuer, & Bonoma, (1969c).

Tedeschi, Lindskold, Horai, and Gahagan (1969e) found that targets who were equal in power to the source were more cooperative than either weak or strong targets on the trials following receipt of a noncontingent promise from a simulated source. The more credible the noncontingent promise, the more likely equal power targets were to cooperate on the critical message trials. Weak targets were more cooperative when the strong simulated source sent messages of low credibility, and most exploitative on message trials when the source's promises were highly credible. Strong targets were quite competitive in all cases, impervious to the credibility of promises and, indeed, to whether promises were received or not. The fact that weak targets took advantage of the unilateral initiatives of a highly credible but powerful source, and the fact that powerful targets are impervious to the promises of a weak source, indicate that Osgood's proposal (1962) related to unilateral initiatives as a tactic for resolving conflicts must be restricted to adversaries who are equals in power. Over all trials, weak players were as cooperative as equal power players and both of these groups were more cooperative than the highly competitive strong players. The presence or absence of promises in the situation had no affect on overall strategy selections by players, and thereby, provides further support for the findings of Gahagan and Tedeschi (1968a), and Tedeschi et al. (1969f) that credibility levels associated with promises of a noncontingent nature affect only message trial responses in the modified and enriched PDG environment.

Weak players lied more often when using a noncontingent promise as a reply message to the strong source. The frequency with which weak targets lied increased as the credibility of the powerful source's noncontingent promises increased. Equal and strong targets were similar to each other and were as truthful in one credibility condition as another. However, strong targets did lie more often than equal power targets when they chose to send a reply message that they intended to compete. Finally, females, proportionately more often than males, did what they said they would do when they sent the reply message indicating intent to cooperate.

Tedeschi et al. (1969c) used 5th grade children as targets of noncontingent promises in a version of the PDG especially modified for use with children (Tedeschi, Hiester, and Gahagan, 1969d). The children were separated into high and low scorer's on Cruse's test (1963) of social desirability (SD). The confederate source's promises were 10, 50, or 90% credible and he played an overall proportion of cooperative strategy selections of either 25 or 75%. Credibility was linearly related to winnings with 50% credible promises yielding the same results as a control condition. Females were more cooperative when faced with a conciliatory source, while males were more cooperative when faced with a low credibility, less cooperative adversary. Ss high in SD responded in an approval oriented way to socially desirable responses by the source, while Ss low in SD responded in an approval oriented way to a source not concerned about performing socially desirable responses. These results reflect the complexity of interactions between structural, role and personality factors in social conflicts.

From the above studies it may be concluded that noncontingent promises do have ameliorative effects on conflict, but that effects of message credibilities apply only to the specific circumstances referred to by the promise. Noncontingent promises must have a rather high credibility before a target will reciprocate by cooperating with the source on message occasions. Moderate level credibilities (50%) are no better or worse in solving conflicts or inducing reciprocation than having no communications at all. It is still to be determined whether very low credibility noncontingent promises actually exacerbate conflicts. Sex differences across experiments consistently indicate that females are more responsive to cues to cooperate than are males. It seems clear that the ameliorative effects of highly credible noncontingent promises only occur when the target is equal in power with the source. In fact, weak targets attempt to exploit a strong and credible source, while a strong target ignores the message received from a weak source.

2. Contingent Promises

The definition of a contingent promise contains three elements: (a) a statement from source of the behavior desired from target, (b) a description of the reward for behaving appropriately; and (c) an indication that the promisor will, himself, provide the reward contingent upon target's performance of the desired behavior.

Lindskold and Tedeschi (1969a) modified the PDG to permit sending a promise from a simulated source to S, stating that he would be given additional points if he made the cooperative choice on the next trial. The credibility of the promise was manipulated by giving the promised reward of 5, 10, or 20 points, 10, 50, or 90% of the time S complied over a criterion number of 10 successful promise occasions. The number of unsuccessful promises was permitted to vary in the experiment. An important part of the procedure was that the source always cooperated and thus was totally accommodative on message trials. His overall strategy was either 50 or 90% cooperative.

Different levels of credibility of contingent promises had no differential effect on the behavior of Ss. Evidence regarding impression formation (Semantic Differential) showed that a 10% credible source was perceived as less impotent than a 90% credible source for the reason that he withheld granting the excessive, unnecessary rewards. Varying the magnitude of reward also had no differential effect on the behavior of Ss. Impressions of the source who used a 90% cooperative strategy were that he was more impotent and less active than the 50% cooperative simulated players. Females rated the benign and rewarding source more positively on the evaluative dimension, cooperated more, lied less, and won less than did males; Lindskold and Tedeschi interpreted their failure to find effects of credibility and reward magnitude as due to two factors. Ss could gain by complying, whether or not the promisor delivered the additional promised reward, because the source was unconditionally cooperative on promise trials. Although the Ss could gain a little more by exploiting the source on promise trials, the norm of reciprocity (Gouldner, 1960) was apparently operative and caused Ss to reciprocate the accomodative strategy of the source. The overall level of cooperation by subjects was much higher than has been obtained over 12 studies and a thousand subjects when threats were used or when the PDG was unmodified for the introduction of messages. Lindskold and Tedeschi suggested that the message utility of promises might be related to compliance in a situation in which the promisor is more exploitative and deceitful. This hypothesis is currently being tested.

The finding that the "good" impression of the source by female targets was related to their cooperative play is a relatively rare one in social psychological research and demonstrates a positive relationship between attitudes and behavior.

The research program dealing with contingent promises has not progressed as far as the study of threats. However, the relationship between attraction and compliance to contingent promises has been investigated by Tedeschi, Schlenker, Lindskold, and Bonoma (1969g). Using Byrne's procedure for inducing attraction, high and low attraction conditions were created and contingent promises of 10 and 90% credibilities were sent to Ss by a simulated source. The results of the pretest and posttest measures of attraction indicated that the procedure did induce the desired effects and that the effect persisted throughout the experimental session. Pre-post test differences indicated that high attraction target Ss liked source less at the end of the experiment than at the beginning, if promise credibility was high and only slightly more if promise credibility was low. Low attraction Ss liked source better as a function of the dyadic interaction experience and as a direct function of the source's credibility. No differences in compliance to promises were obtained either as a function of credibility or attraction. High attraction Ss were more cooperative than low attraction Ss and the latter won more points than the former. However, high attraction dyads (S and simulated player) won more than did low attraction dyads, indicating the individual, more competitive orientation of the latter and the more cooperative and perhaps more norm (reciprocity) inspired behavior of the former. It may be the case that the felt necessity of responding according to normative demands, particularly in the 90% credibility condition in which the promisor was exceedingly rewarding to them, caused the high attraction Ss to decrease their liking for source.

III. PARAMETERS AFFECTING SOCIAL INFLUENCE

Science often progresses when a new paradigm or model is developed. Such models often deliberately simplify reality, and thus are limited in scope. Experimental games have provided a research paradigm for the study of threats and promises. There is a need to develop a theory of social influence so that the paradigm can be systematically applied to testing specific predictions. Much of the literature dealing with threats and promises has tested single hypotheses, or more often, merely tested to ascertain whether influence attempts of one sort or another really modify attitudes and/or behavior.

The first task of theory construction is to identify those parameters which the theorist believes to be operating on the phenomena in which he is interested. Then the relations between parameters must be stated and tied to empirical indicators which confirm or disconfirm the theory. The remainder of this chapter will explore some of the factors involved in the simplest form of the influence process—dyadic interaction—with the specific intention of developing some hypotheses for future study. The factors to be considered are characteristics of source and target, media of communication, message content variables, and the types of rewards and punishments associated with threats and promises.

A. Source and Target

Source characteristics which lend believability (or credulity) to communications have often been referred to as source credibility (Cohen, 1964; Kelman and Hovland, 1953). Aside from the fact that no clearly objective measurement of source credibility has been offered, it is important that source characteristics be specified rather than lumped together. It is the contention here that the concept of source credibility is confusing and should be abandoned. The target either believes or disbelieves source's messages, and he may do either because of source characteristics which lead target to distort the objective probabilities involved in content credibility. Also, source characteristics are related to the type of influence attempt that will be made, how often, and with what degree of credibility. Source characteristics which affect the influence process might include power, role, legitimacy, or group affiliation of source as well as his personality make-up. Similar characteristics related to target may affect his general persuasability.

The personality dispositions of both source and target will affect the influence process. For example, if a target has a high variance preference for risk, he may more often comply with contingent promises or noncomply with contingent threats. A high risk-taker should be more likely to take a chance on receiving rewards or avoiding punishment, if he is the target of an influence attempt. On the other hand, it might be expected that a high risk-taking source will send more incredible threats and promises than would a source that did not like to take risks. A high risk-taking source might risk having influence attempts fail when in fact he is not willing to enforce noncompliance to threats, or to pay off for compliance to promises. Obviously, many other personality dispositions may be involved in the willingness to incur costs, send threats, break promises, or any of the other behaviors involved in the influence process.

It should be kept in mind that Tedeschi, Lesnick, and Gahagan (1968c) have provided evidence that the effects of personality (but not role) tend to "wash-out" after the initial phases of interaction in social conflicts. The findings of Deutsch (1960), Terhune and Firestone (1966), and Gahagan and Tedeschi (1967) tend to support this conclusion. However, each of these studies used unmodified PDGs. The modified PDG is much more complex, allowing for large variations in interpretation of events and for more response alternatives by targets, and consequently may represent a less stimulus bound situation. Whatever the case may be, such structural factors as degree of conflict intensity, number of response alternatives, resource distribution between source and target, as well as many other factors, need to be specified and linked to the behaviors of the conflicting parties.

B. Media of Communications

Media may be ordered on a continuum from personal and private to social and public. Studies of persuasion have indicated that face-to-face communication is most effective in producing attitude and behavioral changes (Katz & Lazarsfeld, 1955). Merton's studies (1949) of local and cosmopolitan influentials proceeded from the hypothesis that mass media are sampled by a few and passed on to the many through face-to-face interactions. The "two-step flow" hypothesis was developed from this research. Unfortunately, few, if any, studies have been done on the differential effects of threats and promises when various media are used to communicate them. One might hazard the guess that the more personal and private a threat, the less resistance target would give to the source, all other things being equal. The rationale behind such a guess is that fewer components of the self-concept are brought into play when no one else is aware of the threat, but when the threat is publicly made, the target must "save face" in front of the audience. Thus, a soldier alone might be cowardly, but with his buddies shows fierce courage.

C. Message Content

Threats and promises vary in the purposes assigned them by sources, as well as the degree of explicitness with which they are communicated. Other content factors have to do with style, connotative meaning, type of message, context, magnitude of reward or punishment, and the credibility assigned a sequence of messages.

Schelling (1966) has distinguished between deterrence and compellence threats. A deterrent threat is meant to prevent a particular response from occurring. A compellent threat is meant to bring about a response not already occurring. A similar distinction could be made in regard to contingent promises. Rewards can be offered to a target for either making or withholding responses.

A source may use contingent threats to establish himself as a highly credible individual so as to "soften" the target for other more important and costly threat occasions. Thus, peripheral matters may be used by source as successive approximations to more central areas of concern to him. Peripheral threats may also be used to establish commitment for the benefit of allies or other potential threat targets.

Threats may also be used to counter a threat from another in a mutual deterrence system. Defensive threats may prevent an offensive threatener from carrying out his threats. On the other hand, threats and counterthreats may lead to a conflict spiral and mutual confrontation that ultimately requires that both threateners back up their words with deeds or else lose credibility for their messages. In conflict spirals, identifying the offensive and defensive individuals becomes a hopeless task, since the conflict spiral the originally offensive source may respond to the defensive source's threats with counterthreats. Each party may perceive himself as the defensive party. On the other hand, threats may act as signals to help both source and target recognize that they are in conflict and may thereby imply the need for negotiation and bargaining. Oftentimes, conflicts remain unsolved until a crisis arises and both parties stand to lose without resort to some form of conciliation.

Contingent promises are mainly directed toward reconciling conflicts of interest. Low credibility promises, however, may exacerbate conflict since they will appear as "tricks" and "bad faith" to the target who fails to gain the promised payoff when he complies. Double-contingent promises exchanged between two persons which are highly credible will lead to stable interaction patterns and take the form of contracts.

Very complicated message forms can be constructed and are probably representative of frequently used influence attempts. For example, Herman Kahn (1962) identifies a Type II deterrence threat as one meant to deter some behavior by another nation that would be short of an attack on the source nation, such as a threat by the United States to the Soviet Union that the former intends to defend Berlin against aggression. The form of the promise to West Germany would be: "A promises B that A will punish C, if C does what B doesn't want C to do." Within the promise to B is a contingent threat directed at C.

Mixing threats and promises may be more effective for source's purposes than using either alone. Classic studies in learning indicate that using reward for the correct response and punishment for the incorrect response during acquisition training was more effective than using either alone (Hall, 1966). Political scientists often refer to the carrot and stick approach to diplomacy. What mix of credibilities and intentions or other content variables maximize the effectiveness of the carrot and stick approach to influence is an empirical question yet to be answered.

The form and style which lend aesthetic qualities to a message are probably associated with connotative meaning, which in turn, is probably confounded with the noncontingent or contingent properties of the communication. Noncontingent promises from a source who clearly can gain advantages from the target may be perceived as ingratiating and cynical Jones & Davis, 1965). Stating in a PDG that "I will make choice 1" may have different connotations than stating that "I promise to cooperate on the next trial." Also, the credibility of the message should be directly related to its connotative meaning, particularly on the evaluative dimension of good–bad.

The degree of specificity in the content of the message is important to both source and target. A target may use the tactic of "ambigufying" the message sent to him. The target may attempt to convince the source that target did not understand the message and consequently could not comply with a threat. Under such conditions the source may find it cheaper not to enforce the threat, relying instead on the next influence occasion to make his threat more explicit. Where promises are ambiguous, the target may choose to act confidently so as to convince the source that target has earned a reward for complying, when in fact no such action was requested. Noise can be utilized deliberately by either source or target.

D. Rewards and Punishments

Unfortunately, neither learning theory nor motivational research in psychology is of much help when fundamental questions are asked about various qualitative types of rewards and punishments. A typology of rewards and punishments associated with promises and threats would be a first step to parametric studies comparing utilities.

The favorite punishment administered by psychologists to their animal and human Ss has been noxious stimulation. Electric shock, which varies from a tickle to a stiff jolt, is a form of punishment which varies along a continuum on which capital punishment administered by putting a man in the electric chair could be placed. Noxious stimulation can be threatened and, if noncompliance by target results from the influence attempt, can be directly delivered by source.

Another punishment often used with threats is assignment of costs. The source may deprive target of some of the latter's existing resources. Such costs may be in the form of points accumulated, candy, money, or other valuables possessed by target. Extreme forms of costs may be associated with depriving target of his automobile, bank account, or home.

Gain deprivation is clearly different from either noxious stimulation or assignment of costs. Instead of administering noxious stimuli or taking away some of his existing resources, source may deprive target of anticipated gains. Thus, points, candy, money, or other valuables which target does not possess but expects to gain may be denied to him. If a bird in hand is worth two in the bush, the utility functions associated with costs and gain deprivation should differ.

Social punishments are related to target's self-concept and his associations with other people. Expressions of dislike, name-calling, and social ostracism are clear forms of social punishment. Disagreements and key words such as "wrong" may also act as negative reinforcers. Social punishments may be more emotion laden than are noxious stimulation, costs, or gain deprivations.

Political retribution may also be used as punishment. A man may be fired from his job, incarcerated, or forcefully expatriated from his country as punishment for failing to comply with threats. In each case, there are clear repercussions to the target in terms of social punishments, but the political retribution is ordinarily more global in its application. Gain deprivation also clearly follows from political retribution. The fact that political retribution cuts across other types of punishment indicates why it has such coercive effect.

Rewards concomitant with promises can be similarly categorized. Pleasure-giving stimuli correspond to noxious stimulation and would include stimuli directly pleasurable to the body such as food, drink, and sexual stimulation. If costs can be assigned target by source, so can gains. Creating expectations of gains would be complementary to gain deprivation. Social rewards and political rewards can also be given for compliance to promises.

IV. CONCLUSION

A theory of social influence within dyads has been presented by Tedeschi (1968). The theory states the relationships between independent source–message factors and target cognitions and further presents the relationships between target cognitions and a predictor variable–the believability of the message to target. The dependent variable of interest was behavioral compliance to threats and promises.

The independent source–message factors include the role position of source, history of reward mediation (broadly defined to include notions of congruency of attitudes), the available resources and intentions of source, the degree of approval that source gains from those around him, and the credibility and magnitude of the threat or promise. The associated cognitive factors in target are status, attraction, prestige, esteem, and message utility, respectively. In the case of threats, status, prestige, and degree of negative message utility are directly related to believability and consequent compliance, while attraction and esteem are assumed to be negatively related to believability. When promises are used as a means of social influence, status, attraction, prestige, esteem, and positive message utility are directly related to believability and subsequent compliance.

The program of research reviewed in this chapter has only begun to examine the relationships stated in Tedeschi's theory. It is clear that as long as a threatener is exploitative, negative message utility is directly related to compliance. However, the negative utility of the threat must exceed the costs associated with compliance in order for utility to mediate compliance. Attraction is apparently more complexly related to compliance with threats than the Tedeschi theory suggests. When the target likes the source of threats, he will not comply with low credibility threats but will comply frequently with highly credible threats. When the target dislikes the source of threats, he will comply with threats at a moderate level of frequency irrespective of degree of threat credibility. Finally, the evidence seems to support the direct relationship between status and compliance. Greater compliance will be obtained by a high status source of threats than by a low status source, irrespective of the status of the target, as long as the latter is not of higher status than the source.

The evidence with regard to promises suggests that positive influence attempts introduce factors not relevant to coercive influence attempts. An unconditionally cooperative promisor does gain a high level of compliance and induces more cooperation from targets, but message utility does not mediate compliance. The suggestion was made that normative influences are evoked with promises that require reciprocity from the target and consequently message utility loses its power to mediate responses. Similarly, attraction failed to mediate compliance with promises in the one study that has been done.

The lack of theory or research related to a source of influence attempts was glaringly apparent. What determines a source to use coercive rather than positive influence attempts? Why will one source establish high credibility for his messages, while another will not? Why does a source pick one target rather than another? These and many other questions have their intuitive answers, but a coherent theory amenable to test by experiment has yet to be developed.

ACKNOWLEDGMENTS

Many ·individuals have participated in the formation and criticism of the ideas and research reported in this chapter. The author acknowledges his debt to Daniel Aranoff, Stephen Berger, Thomas Bonoma, Thomas Faley, James Gahagan, Raymond Hartley, Joann Horai, Len Jacobsen, Svenn Lindskold, Charles McKeown, Barry Schlenker, R. Bob Smith, Matthew Steele, Stuart Teacher, and Carl Williams. Mention in no way implies endorsement of opinions expressed.

REFERENCES

Aronson, E., & Carlsmith, J.M. Effect of the severity of threat on the devaluation of forbidden behavior. *Journal of Abnormal and Social Psychology*, 1963, **66**, 584–588.

Bazelon, D.T. *The paper economy*. New York: Vintage Press, 1965.

Berkowitz, L., & Cottingham, D.R. The interest value and relevance of fear-arousing communications. *Journal of Abnormal and Social Psychology*, 1960, **60**, 37–43.

Bixenstine, V.E., Potash, H.M., & Wilson, K.V. Effects of level of cooperative choice by the other player on choices in a PDG. Part 1. *Journal of Abnormal and Social Psychology*, 1963, **66**(4), 308–313.

Borah, L.A., Jr. The effects of threat in bargaining: Critical and experimental analysis. *Journal of Abnormal and Social Psychology*, 1963, **66**, 37–47.

Boulding, K.E. Toward a theory of peace. In R. Fisher (Ed.). *International conflict and behavioral science* New York: Basic Books, 1964. Pp. 70–87.

Brody, R.A., Benham, A.H., & Milstein, J.S. Hostile international communication, arms production and perception of threat: A simulation study. Ditto: Stanford University, 1966.

Byrne, D. Interpersonal attraction and attitude similarity. *Journal of Abnormal and Social Psychology*, 1961, **62**, 713–715.

Chu, G.C. Fear arousal, efficacy and imminency. *Journal of Personality*, 1966, **4**, 517–524.

Cohen, A.R. *Attitude change and social influence*. New York: Basic Books, 1964.

Cohen, M.R., & Nagel, E. *An introduction to logic and scientific method*. New York: Harcourt, Brace, 1934.

Coopersmith, S. *The antecedents of self-esteem*. San Francisco: Freeman, 1967.

Cruse, D.B. Socially desirable responses in relation to grade level. *Child Development*, 1963, **34**, 777–789.

Dabbs, J.M., & Leventhal, H. Effects of varying recommendations in a fear-arousing communication. *Journal of Personality and Social Psychology*, 1966, **4**, 525–531.

Demos, R. Some reflections on threats and punishments. *Review of Metaphysics*, 1957, **11**, 224–236.

Deutsch, K.W. *The nerves of government*. Glencoe, Ill.: Free Press, 1966.

Deutsch, M. Trust, trustworthiness and the F-scale. *Journal of Abnormal and Social Psychology*, 1960, **61**, 138–140.

Deutsch, M., & Krauss, R.M. The effect of threat upon interpersonal bargaining. *Journal of Abnormal and Social Psychology*, 1960, **61**, 181–189.

Deutsch, M., & Krauss, R.M. Studies of interpersonal bargaining. *Journal of Conflict Resolution*, 1962, **6**, 52–76.

DeWolfe, A.S., & Governale, C.N. Fear and attitude change. *Journal of Abnormal and*

Social Psychology, 1964, **69**, 119–123.

Evans, G. Effect of unilateral promise and value of rewards upon cooperation and trust. *Journal of Abnormal and Social Psychology,* 1964, **69**, 587–590.

Faley, T., & Tedeschi, J.T. Status and reactions to threats. Mimeographed manuscript, University of Miami, Florida, 1969.

Faucheux, C., & Moscovici, S. Self-esteem and exploitative behavior in a game against chance and nature. *Journal of Personality and Social Psychology,* 1968, **8**, 83–88.

Feshback, S., & Singer, R. The effects of personal and shared threat upon social prejudice. *Journal of Abnormal and Social Psychology,* 1957, **54**, 411–416.

Freedman, J.L. Long term behavioral effects of cognitive dissonance. *Journal of Experimental Social Psychology,* 1965, **1**, 145–155.

Gahagan, J.P., & Tedeschi, J.T. Strategy and the credibility of promises in the Prisoner's Dilemma game. *Journal of Conflict Resolution,* 1968, **12**, 224–234. (a)

Gahagan, J. P., & Tedeschi, J.T. Demographic factors in the communication of promises. *Journal of Social Psychology,* 1968, **76**, 277–280. (b)

Gahagan, J. P., Lindskold, S., Faley, T., & Tedeschi, J. T. Patterns of punishment and reactions to threats. Mimeographed manuscript, University of Miami, Florida, 1969. (a)

Gahagan, J.P., Tedeschi, J.T., Horai, J., Long, H., & Lindskold, S. Race of experimenter and the reactions of black children to threats. Mimeographed manuscript, University of Miami, Florida, 1969. (b)

Gallo, P.S., Jr. Effects of increased incentives upon the use of threat in bargaining. *Journal of Personality and Social Psychology,* 1966, **4**, 14–20.

Goffman, E. *The presentation of self in everyday life.* Garden City, N.Y.: Doubleday, 1959.

Gouldner, A.W. The norm of reciprocity: A preliminary statement. *American Sociological Review,* 1960, **25**, 161–179.

Hall, E.T. *The silent language.* Garden City, N.Y.: Doubleday, 1959.

Hall, J.B. *The psychology of learning.* Philadelphia: Lippincott, 1966.

Hermann, M.G. Testing a model of psychological stress. *Journal of Personality,* 1966, **34**, 381–396.

Holsti, O.R., & North, R.C. Perceptions of hostility and economic variables in the 1914 crisis. Stanford Studies in International Conflict and Integration, November 1963. (Mimeographed)

Homans, G.C. Social behavior as exchange. *American Journal of Sociology,* 1958, **63**, 597–606.

Horai, J., & Tedeschi, J.T. The effects of credibility and magnitude of pubishment upon compliance to threats. *Journal of Personality and Social Psychology,* 1969, **12**, 164–169.

Horai, J., Tedeschi, J.T., Gahagan, J., & Lesnick, S. The effect of threats upon a target's behavior. *Journal of Social Psychology,* 1969, **78**, 293–294.

Hornstein, H.A. The effects of different magnitudes of threat upon interpersonal bargaining. *Journal of Experimental Social Psychology,* 1965, **1**, 282–293.

Hornstein, H.A., Deutsch, M., & Benedict, B.A. Compliance to threats directed against self and against an innocent third person. Technical Report No. 6, 1966, Office of Naval Research.

Janis, I.L., & Feshback, S. Effects of fear-arousing communication. *Journal of Abnormal and Social Psychology,* 1953, **48**, 78–92.

Jones, B., Steele, M.W., Gahagan, J.P., & Tedeschi, J.T. Matrix values and behavior in the Prisoner's Dilemma game. *Journal of Personality and Social Psychology,* 1968, **8**, 148–153.

Jones, E.E., & Davis, K.E. From acts to dispositions: The attribution process in person perception. In L. Berkowitz (Ed.), *Advances in Experimental Social Psychology,* Vol.

2. New York: Academic Press, 1965, Pp. 219–266.

Kahn, H. *Thinking about the unthinkable.* New York: Horizon, 1962.

Katz, E., & Lazarsfeld, P.F. *Personal influence.* Glencoe, Ill.: Free Press, 1955.

Kelley, H.H. Threats in interpersonal negotiations. Unpublished paper presented at the Pittsburgh Seminar on Social Sciences of Organization, University of Pittsburgh, 1962.

Kelley, H.H. Experimental studies of threats in interpersonal negotiations. *Journal of Conflict Resolution,* 1965, 9, 79–105.

Kelley, H.H. Attribution theory in social psychology. In D. Levine (Ed.) *Nebraska symposium on motivation,* Lincoln, Neb.: Univ. of Nebraska, 1967. Pp. 192–240.

Kelman, H.C., & Hovland, C.I. "Reinstatement" of the communicator in delayed measurement of opinion change. *Journal of Abnormal and Social Psychology,* 1953, 48, 327–335.

Krauss, R.M., & Deutsch, M. Communication in interpersonal bargaining. *Journal of Personality and Social Psychology,* 1966, 4, 572–577.

Krech, D., Crutchfield, R.A., & Ballachey, E.L. *Individual in Society.* New York: McGraw-Hill, 1962.

Leventhal, H., & Niles, P. Persistence of influence for varying durations of exposure to threat stimuli. *Psychological Reports,* 1965, 16, 223–233.

Leventhal, H., Singer, R., & Jones, S. The effects of fear and specificity of recommendations upon attitudes and behavior. *Journal of Personality and Social Psychology,* 1965, 2, 20–29.

Lindskold, S., Bonoma, T., & Tedeschi, J.T. Compliance to a threatening simulated opponent. Mimeographed manuscript, University of Miami, Florida, 1969. (a)

Lindskold, S., Bonoma, T., & Tedeschi, J.T. Relative costs and reactions to threats. *Psychonomic Science,* 1969, 15, 205–207. (b)

Lindskold, S., & Tedeschi, J.T. Effects of contingent promises on interpersonal conflict. Mimeographed manuscript, University of Miami, Florida, 1969. (a)

Lindskold, S., & Tedeschi, J.T. Self-esteem and reactions to threats and promises. Mimeographed manuscript, University of Miami, Florida, 1969. (b)

Loomis, J.L. Communication, the development of trust and cooperative behavior. *Human Relations,* 1959, 12, 305–315.

McClintock, C.G., Harrison, A., Strand, S., & Gallo, P. Internationalism, isolationism, strategy of the other player, and two-person game behavior. *Journal of Abnormal and Social Psychology,* 1963, 67, 631–635.

McGuire, W.J. The nature of attitudes and attitude changes. In G. Lindzey & E. Aronson (Eds.) *The handbook of social psychology.* Vol. III. Reading, Mass.: Addison-Wesley, 1969. Pp. 136–314.

Marlowe, D., & Gergen, K.T. Personality and social interaction. In G. Lindzey & E. Aronson (Eds.). *The handbook of social psychology.* Vol. III. Reading, Mass.: Addison-Wesley, 1969. Pp. 590–665.

Merton, R.K. *Social theory and social structure.* Glencoe, Ill.: Free Press, 1949.

Mulder, M., & Stemerding, A. Threat, attraction to group, and need for strong leadership. *Human Relations,* 1963, 16, 317–334.

North, R.C., Brody, R.A., & Holsti, O.R. Some empirical data on the conflict spiral. *Peace Research Society (International) Papers,* 1964, 1, 1–14.

Osgood, C.E. *An alternative to war or surrender.* Urbana, Ill.: University of Illinois Press, 1962.

Parsons, T. On the concept of influence. *Public Opinion Quarterly,* 1963, 27, 37–62.

Pepitone, A., McCauley, C., & Hammond, P. Change in attractiveness of forbidden toys as a function of the severity of threat. *Journal of Experimental Social Psychology,* 1967, 3, 221–229.

Pruitt, D.G. Definition of the situation as a determinant of international action. In H.C. Kelman (Ed.). *International behavior: A Social Psychological Analysis.* New York: Holt, 1965. Pp. 391–432.

Radlow, R., & Weidner, M.F. Unenforced commitments in "cooperative" and "noncooperative" non-constant-sum games. *Journal of Conflict Resolution,* 1966, 10, 497–505.

Rapoport, A. *Strategy and conscience.* New York: Harper, 1964.

Rapoport, A. Comment on gaming. *Journal of Conflict Resolution,* 1967, 11, 196–197.

Rapoport, A., & Chammah, A.M. Sex differences in factors contributing to the level of cooperation in the Prisoner's Dilemma game. *Journal of Personality and Social Psychology,* 1965, 2, 831–838.

Robinson, J.A. *The concept of crisis in decision-making.* Series studies in social and economic sciences, No. 11. Washington, D.C.: National Institute of Social and Behavioral Science, 1962.

Robinson, J.A., & Snyder, R.C. Decision-making in international politics. In H.C. Kelman (Ed.). *International behavior: A social psychological analysis.* New York: Holt, 1965. Pp. 433–463.

Sawyer, J., & Guetzkow, H. Bargaining and negotiation in international relations. In H.C. Kelman (Ed.). *International behavior: A social Psychological analysis.* New York: Holt, 1965. Pp. 460–520.

Schacter, S., Nutton, J., de Monchaux, C., Maucorps, P.H., Osmer, D., Duyker, H., Rommetveit, R., & Israel, J. Cross-cultural experiments on threat and rejection. *Human Relations,* 1954, 7, 403–440.

Schelling, T.C. *The strategy of conflict.* Cambridge, Mass.: Harvard University Press, 1960.

Schelling, T.C. *Arms and influence.* New Haven, Conn.: Yale University Press, 1966.

Shomer, R.W., Davis, A.H., & Kelley, H.H. Threats and the development of coordination: Further studies of the Deutsch and Krauss trucking game. *Journal of Personality and Social Psychology,* 1966, 4, 119–126.

Shure, G.H., Meeker, R.J., & Moore, W.H. Computer based empirical studies. 1. The effects of threat upon bargaining. Technical Memo, System Development Corp., 1963.

Singer, J.D. Threat-perception and the armament-tension dilemma. *Journal of Conflict Resolution,* 1958, 2, 90–105.

Singer, J.D. Inter-nation influence: A formal model. *American Political Science Review,* 1963, 57, 420–430.

Steele, M.W., & Tedeschi, J.T. Matrix indices and strategy choices in mixed-motive games. *Journal of Conflict Resolution,* 1967, 11, 198–205.

Tedeschi, J.T. A theory of influence within dyads. Proceedings of the 16th International Congress of Applied Psychology, Amsterdam, August 1968.

Tedeschi, J.T., & Horai, J. Threats: A Paradigm and models. Mimeographed manuscript, University of Miami, Florida, 1968.

Tedeschi, J.T., Aranoff, D., & Gahagan, J.P. Discrimination of outcomes in the Prisoner's Dilemma game. *Psychonomic Science,* 1968, 11, 301–302. (a)

Tedeschi, J., Horai, J., Lindskold, S., & Gahagan, J. The effects of threat and conflict intensity on compliance and communication. Proceedings of the 76th Annual Meeting of the American Psychological Association, San Francisco, California. September, 1968. (b)

Tedeschi, J.T., Lesnick, S., & Gahagan, J.P. Feedback and "wash-out" effects in the Prisoner's Dilemma game. *Journal of Personality and Social Psychology,* 1968, 10, 31–34. (c)

Tedeschi, J.T., Bonoma, T.V., & Novinson, N. Retaliation vs. fixed opportunity costs: The behavior of a threatening source. *Journal of Conflict Resolution,* in press, 1969. (a)

Tedeschi, J.T., Bonoma, T.V., Schlenker, B., & Lindskold, S. Interpersonal attraction and the reaction to threats. Mimeographed manuscript, United States International University, San Diego, California, 1969. (b)

Tedeschi, J.T., Feuer, L., & Bonoma, T. Social desirability and reactions to promisor credibility. Mimeographed manuscript, University of Miami, Florida, 1969. (c)

Tedeschi, J.T., Hiester, D.S., & Gahagan, J.P. Matrix values and the behavior of children in the Prisoner's Dilemma Game. *Child Development,* 1969, **40**, 517–527. (d)

Tedeschi, J.T., Lindskold, S., Horai, J., & Gahagan, J.P. Social power and the credibility of promises. *Journal of Personality and Social Psychology,* 1969, **13**, 253–261. (e)

Tedeschi, J.T., Powell, J., Lindskold, S., & Gahagan, J.P. The patterning of "honored" promises and sex differences in social conflicts. *Journal of Social Psychology,* 1969, **78**, 297–298. (f)

Tedeschi, J.T., Schlenker, B., Lindskold, S., & Bonoma, T. Interpersonal attraction and the reaction to promises. Mimeographed manuscript, United States International University San Diego, 1969. (g)

Terhune, K.W., & Firestone, J.M. Studies of personality in cooperation and conflict. Paper read at the North American Peace Research Conference, Chicago, November 1966.

Turner, E.A., & Wright, J.C. Effects of severity of threat and perceived availability of the attractiveness of objects. *Journal of Personality and Social Psychology,* 1965, **2**, 128–132.

Chapter 6

THE EFFECTS OF PERSONALITY IN COOPERATION AND CONFLICT

Kenneth W. Terhune

I. INTRODUCTION

Would the United States history of conflict in Vietnam been any different had not an assassin's bullet found its mark on November 22, 1963? Has that history of conflict been influenced in any way by the presumed character of the American people, or at least by the character of the political elite who determine policy? These questions transfer to a grand scale the concerns of those who study personality in relation to cooperation and conflict. Many social scientists are skeptical about a possible influence of personality, of individuals or in the aggregate, on large-scale political phenomena. Their skepticism is not without foundation, for proof of the relevance of personality to cooperation and conflict in larger social domains is virtually nonexistent. Indeed, even in small-scale experimental studies, establishing the connection between personality, co-operation, and conflict has been plagued by ambiguous or negative results.

Nevertheless, the accumulation of evidence in experimental studies has reached a point where personality effects can no longer be discounted, and as we begin to understand how personality operates in lower level cooperation and conflict, there is promise that we may be able to fathom personality effects in more complex social phenomena as well.

In reviewing the extant volume of experimental studies of cooperation and conflict, one may note an apparent bias against studying the effects of personality, for the number of studies including personality variables are definitely in the minority. A likely explanation for this is the fact that many social scientists feel that situational parameters and/or factors of group dynamics are far more important influences on interactions among individuals and groups. Druckman (1967), for example, observed that Blake and Mouton (1962) and Sherif and Sherif (1965) stress the importance of group relatedness over individual motivations in intergroup relations. Blake and Mouton, in fact, use the term "psychodynamic fallacy" to denote the incorrect attribution of group behavior to personalities of individuals. Another possible reason for de-emphasizing personality factors may lie in the belief that personality effects are too ephemeral, affecting behavior in some situations but not in others. Empirical evidence lends some support to the view, as will be shown in a later section. Another reason may be that in concentrating on developing a theory on cooperation and conflict processes, researchers are reluctant to involve themselves in the messy state of affairs that is contemporary personality theory and measurement. A final reason seems to be that many researchers are discouraged by the difficulty of introducing personality into experimental studies. The difficulty stems from the fact that one may wish to test hypotheses about *particular* personality types. This approach often requires that the researcher administer personality tests to large groups of subjects, from which are selected just those individuals who exemplify the relevant types. To then exclude the remaining subjects from the experiments may seem wasteful to many researchers, especially if they have invested considerable time and money in administering and scoring tests on the original sample. Yet, it is submitted, these are insufficient reasons for avoiding the study of personality effects. If we are to develop a *comprehensive* theory of cooperation and conflict, it is necessary that personality variables be included. After all, although situational variables have been found to produce distinctive effects on cooperation–conflict behavior, there is always sufficient behavioral variance among subjects to infer that individual differences in personality must be exerting a significant influence also. The objective of this chapter is to encourage the study of personality effects by (a) considering from a theoretical perspective how personality is likely to influence cooperation and conflict; (b) suggesting improved methods for the study of personality effects; (c) indicating the domains of personality which seem most promising on the basis of past research; and (d) outlining a more sophisticated model for the operation of personality effects than is currently used in most studies on the subject. The discussion will of necessity be founded on studies in which most evidence is available, namely gaming studies of cooperation and conflict.

II. THE CONCEPTS OF "PERSONALITY" AND "SITUATION"

To begin, what do we mean by "personality," or more specifically, "personality variables?" The personality concept has been discussed at length in psychology, but reasonably satisfying is Gordon Allport's well known definition that personality is "the dynamic organization within the individual of those psychophysical systems that determine his unique adjustments to his environment (1937, p. 48)." While Allport's is an elegant definition, it is helpful to think of personality variables as the more or less enduring behavior potentials that the individual carries with him. They are his "internal programs" (to make a computer analogy) or general predispositions. The behavior potentials do not direct behavior until aroused by a particular situation, or state of the environment, in which the individual finds himself. The arousal state is a function of the behavior potentials (internal programs) and the external stimuli impinging on the individual; the arousal state is not part of personality itself. For example, personality includes *motives,* but does not refer to a particular *motivated* state, or motive-arousal. For another, personality includes attitudes, but not the condition in which a particular attitude is made salient by a specific situation.

As used here, the concept of "situation" refers to a state of the environment, by which is meant the physical environment (including other people) external to the individual. This use of the situation concept is quite common in social psychology, but Rokeach (1968) for one has rejected the idea of situation as a determinant of behavior. His argument states that psychological variables, e.g., attitudes, are from a different universe of discourse from situation variables, which are "objective" or sociological variables. "It is meaningless," Rokeach maintains, "to speak of two concepts that represent different universes of discourse as 'interacting' with one another (p. 127)." Consequently, Rokeach prefers to use the psychological concept of "attitude toward the situation" instead of situation per se.

The writer cannot accept Rokeach's argument against the situation concept, on either theoretical or methodological grounds. It seems just as reasonable to say that behavior is a function of behavior potentials and external inputs from the environment as it is to say that the "behavior" of a computer is a function of its programs stored internally and the external data fed into it. Roughly akin to the "attitude toward the situation" would be the computer's program to filter out certain kinds of information and operate on other kinds. Perhaps the computer analogy can be pushed too far, but it is presented here as a suggestive model. Furthermore, by considering the situation variables as variables external to the person, the researcher is then justified in manipulating those variables to determine their effects on behavior.

A. A Preliminary Model

The conceptual framework just described has in it the germ of Kurt Lewin's paradigm, $B = f(P, E)$. The relation to Lewin's model is only approximate, however, so to avoid confusion it would be better to write the paradigm as $B = f(P, S)$, where P = set of behavior potentials and S = characteristics of the situation. It seems preferable to expand the model further by writing $B_A = f_1(P) + f_2(S) + f_3(P \times S)$. The expanded version is provided to indicate that behavior of an actor (A) is not only an additive function of independent behavior potentials and situational influences, but also of the unique interaction between behavior potentials and particular situations, e.g., a particular external situation may tend to arouse a particular motive, resulting in motivation of the individual.

The paradigm above applies only to the behavior of the *single* individual, and it is certainly inadequate for the *interaction* behavior between two or more persons. Nevertheless, it is presented here to provide an initial orientation to subsequent discussion. Later a more appropriate model will be suggested for analyzing personality factors in social interaction, of which cooperation and conflict are particular forms.

B. Theoretical Importance of Personality Variables

On the basis of psychological theories of individual differences, there are many ways in which personality factors may influence the processes of cooperation and conflict. Using the paradigm above as a guide, personality effects may be divided into (a) behavior potentials (P factors) brought *to* the situation and (b) interactions between personality and situation, *within* the situation (P × S factors).

1. Coming to the Situation

Conflicts, almost by definition, involve an incompatibility of interests between contending parties. Exactly what the interests of the parties are will depend to a large extent on the values and motives of the actors. Each actor will set his goals and formulate plans to achieve them, such plans including the selection among alternative means. Whether or not the selection of goals and means are formulated by taking into account other actors within the social system, the actors are likely to find an interdependence of their goals and means with those of other actors. To the extent that goals or means are "promotively interdependent," cooperation may be facilitated; to the extent that they are "contriently interdependent," competition or conflict may ensue (Deutsch, 1953).

Behavior potentials may also take the form of generalized expectations about others in the form of views of human nature, general trust–mistrust of others, generalized hostilities or feelings of kinship with others, and so on. Such orientations are part of the actor's "world view," or *Weltanschauung*. They create a set or determine a posture toward the "generalized other" which are likely to determine the initial actions taken toward the other in a first encounter, and those first actions are likely to establish the general tone of the relationship.

In experimental studies of cooperation and conflict, subjects are commonly recruited and placed into a game situation without giving the subjects the option of selecting the game or choosing whether they want to play at all. In everyday life, on the other hand, personal predispositions generally lead the individual to seek out certain situations and avoid others. Some individuals, for example, may shun competitive situations, while others may throw themselves into competitions with zest. Consequently, the very situations in which individuals become involved are likely to be largely a function of their own proclivities. Yet, it is also true that entrance into many situations is not a matter of choice, because paths of individuals, groups, and nations do cross repeatedly in a world where few live in isolation. How the actors react to the situation as a function of their behavior potentials shall be considered next.

2. Within the Situation

As mentioned above, in cooperation–conflict studies using games, subjects usually have no choice regarding the game to be played. The researcher defines the situation to the subjects in terms of the rules, the behavioral options, and the payoffs, and he may even instruct the subjects on what their goals are to be. Postexperimental interviews sometimes reveal, however, that the "game" actually being played by the subjects was not as the experimenter defined. For example, subjects are sometimes told that their goal is simply to earn as much money (or other kinds of payoff) as they can; later interviews often reveal that the subjects had set their own goal to "beat" their partner. So also is it likely to be in everyday-life social encounters among actors; their definition of the situation or "the game being played" is likely to be a joint function of the objective characteristics of the situation and the actor's own general expectations. The matter is complicated by the phenomenological possibility that two or more actors in interaction may not define the situation in the same way, but will subjectively be playing different "games."

Normative game theory prescriptions of the rational strategies in various games are based on the neat layouts of "payoffs" for the actors as a function of their joint choices; such rational solutions are valid, however, only so long as the "payoff" values are at least proportional to the psychological values in the utility functions of the actors. The extent to which players deviate from "rational" strategies is likely to be partially a function of the lack of congruence between the "objective" utilities and the "subjective" utilities of the actors. In everyday life the situation is likely to be complicated further by the fact that the value systems of actors have different "currencies," in the sense that things valued by one actor may not be valued by another. Not only may there be differences among actors in this regard, but one may have different value systems that defy relative placement on a common scale (a fact that can produce indecision when an actor must choose between mutually exclusive alternatives).

While the "payoffs" at stake in "real life" interactions will be a function of the motives and value systems of actors, the complexity of the "games" being played may be expected to vary with the cognitive styles of the actors. For example, taking two actors in conflict, the one disposed toward cognitive simplicity may perceive the possible outcomes as winning or losing, victory or surrender (a zero-sum game). Therefore, the other person would be viewed as an opponent to be beaten. The "opponent," on the other hand, may be cognitively complex, perceiving a range of outcomes in which compromise or some optimal solution is possible. Depending on his motives and goals, he may, therefore, see the other person as not so much an opponent but a potential partner to be won over.

The possibilities for such P X S interactions seem endless. In the context of conflicts over racial integration, Galtung (1959) describes the phenomenon in which one actor's perception of the motives of the opponent is influenced by the actor's own prejudices. In other forms of community conflict, Coleman (1957) notes that the side to which an individual may be pulled in a controversy may depend on whether he is a "concrete" type whose allegiances are determined by personal ties or whether he is a more "abstract" type who will take sides on the basis of the issue in contention.

A major characteristic of conflict situations that make them highly susceptible to idiosyncratic influences of the actors is the fact that the intention underlying a particular act is seldom obvious. An ostensibly cooperative move may be either a genuinely cooperative act or an attempt to lure another into a vulnerable position. Similarly, an apparently uncooperative act may be either aggressive or defensive in intent. Given such ambiguities, the interpretation of one actor's actions by another is likely to be a function of the latter's predispositions, such as tendencies to be trusting or suspicious.

Although communications make it possible for actors to specify the intentions behind their actions, they certainly do not eliminate ambiguity. When messages are sent between opposing nations, there is often great care taken by the sender to use the proper words, and the receiver then scrutinizes the message in order to determine its meaning as accurately as possible. This is not to say that opponents always *try* to convey their exact meaning; they may deliberately try to deceive or "to keep the other fellow guessing." There seems almost to be a principle here—the more delicate the situation, the more extreme the tension, the greater is the importance of minor variations in messages. The message communicated will in turn be a function of (1) what the sender intends to say, (2) how he chooses to say it, (3) how the message is translated (if to a different language), and (4) how the receiver tends to interpret the message. All of these are likely to be influenced by idiosyncratic actor characteristics, such as assumptions, styles of logic, and motives.

Such then, are some theoretical reasons why personality characteristics may be expected significantly to affect behavior in cooperation and conflict. Empirical evidence on those considerations will be presented in the following sections.

III. PROBLEMS AND METHODS IN STUDYING PERSONALITY EFFECTS

In experimental studies to date, personality effects have been sufficiently elusive to render the overall results equivocal. All personality-relevant studies known to the writer are presented in Table I, which lists 30 studies using 46 personality measures. Individual differences in 16 of the 46 tests were found to be unrelated to cooperation–conflict behavior. Six tests were found to be related to behavior in some studies, but not in others. That leaves 24 tests which were found to be related to behavior, but there was insufficient replication of most of the tests to permit generalizing of the results. The picture is even less favorable than Table I indicates, for often statistically significant relations are unimpressively small, and in addition, some studies may find correlations of personality with one behavioral index, but not with others. Such results contrast with findings on situational variables, where factors such as type of game, opportunity for communication among players, and threat capabilities are found strongly to influence the development of cooperation or conflict. Therefore, it is relevant to ask: (1) are personality factors really very important in relation to situational factors, and (2) are personality factors more important in some situations than in others? The second question will be discussed first, after which evidence relevant to both questions will be considered.

The second question may be divided into two further questions: First, under what conditions are personality effects likely to operate?. Second, under

TABLE I

Personality and Attitudinal Variables
Studied in Relation to Conflict–Cooperation[a]

Personality/attitude measure employed	Studies finding relation	Studies finding no relation
California *F*-scale	Deutsch (1960): Prisoner's Dilemma; Driver (1965): Internation simulation; Bixenstine and O'Reilly (1966): Prisoner's Dilemma; Wrightsman (1966): Nonzero-sum game	Gahagan *et al.* (1967): Prisoner's Dilemma
Tolerance for ambiguity (composite)	Pilisuk *et al.* (1965): Expanded Prisoner's Dilemma; Teger (1968): Allocations Game	Nardin (1967)
Rokeach's dogmatism scale (or version thereof)	Druckman (1967): Bargaining; Gahagan *et al.* (1967): Prisoner's Dilemma	–
Cognitive abstractness– concreteness	Driver (1965): Internation simulation	–
Authoritarian nationalism vs. equalitarian internation- ism; aggressive militarism vs. nonbelligerence	Crow and Noel (1965): Internation exercise	–
Needs for achievement affiliation, dominance (EPPS)	Haythorn and Altman (1967)	–
Affiliation, self-prominence orientations	Higgs and McGrath (1965): Nonzero-sum game	–
Achievement orientation	–	Higgs and McGrath (1965): Nonzero-sum games.
Gough ACL: needs for aggression, autonomy, abasement, deference	Marlowe (1963): Prisoner's Dilemma	–
Gough ACL: needs for nurturance, dominance	–	Marlowe (1963): Prisoner's Dilemma
MMPI dominance scale	Sermat (1968): "Chicken" game	–
Allport ascendence– submission	Fry (1965): Matching game	–
Wrightsman's philosophies of human nature scale	Wrightsman (1966): Nonzero-sum game; Uejio and Wrightsman (1967): Prisoner's Dilemma	–

TABLE I (Continued)

Personality/attitude measure employed	Studies finding relation	Studies finding no relation
Lutzker's internationalism– isolationism scale	Lutzker (1960): "Chicken" game; McClintock, Harrison, Strand, and Gallo (1963): "Chicken" game; McClintock *et al.*, (1965): Nonzero-sum game	–
Internationalism scale (composite)	–	Pilisuk *et al.* (1965:): Expanded Prisoner's Dilemma
Ideology of conciliation vs. *Real politik*	Guetzkow *et al.* (1960): Internation simulation	–
Christie's Machiavellianism scale	Geis (1964): "Con Game" and "Ten Dollar Game"; Uejio and Wrightsman (1967): Prisoner's Dilemma; Teger (1968): Allocations game	Wrightsman (1966): Nonzero-sum game; Daniels (1967): Bargaining study
Bixenstine's flexibile ethicality	Bixenstein and Wilson (1963); Bixenstine *et al.* (1963): both with Prisoner's Dilemma	Bixenstine *et al.* (1964): Nonzero-sum game
Needs for achievement, affiliation, power (TAT-measured)	Terhune (1968): Prisoner's Dilemma; Terhune and Firestone (1967): Internation game	–
"Entrepreneurial" vs. "bureaucratic" types combined with level of aspiration	Crowne (1965): Prisoner's Dilemma	–
Agger's political cynacism	Uejio and Wrightsman (1967): Prisoner's Dilemma	Wrightsman (1966): Nonzero-sum game
Kogan-Wallach risk-taking propensity	Crow and Noel (1965): Internation exercise	Pilisuk *et al.* (1965): Expanded Prisoner's Dilemma
Risk-aversion propensity	–	Dolbear and Lave (1966): Prisoner's Dilemma
Gore-Rotter internal– external control test	Teger (1968): Allocations game	–

[a] In addition, all these variables found unrelated: (a) Guilford-Zimmerman Personality Test; questionnaire on "8 basic values" (Bixenstine *et al.*, 1964; nonzero-game). (b) Rogers-Dymond Self-Acceptance; Monetary Risk Preference (Pilisuk *et al.*, 1965: expanded Prisoner's Dilemma). (c) Buss-Durkee Verbal Hostility; Rehfisch Rigidity; Berkowitz Social Responsibility; Chein's Personal Optimism; Chein's anti-Police Attitudes; Crowne-Marlowe Social Desirability; Edwards' Social Desirability (Wrightsman, 1966: nonzero-sum game).

what conditions are personality effects likely to appear *if* they are operating?

To answer these questions, let us reconsider the rudimentary paradigm presented earlier. Behavior of an actor (B_A) is a function not only of his predispositions $[f_1(P)]$, but also of the physical–social environment $[f_2(S)]$, which includes the behavioral alternatives available to the actor. If the latter influences are sufficiently dominant, or if they greatly constrain the actor's behavior, there may be little freedom for the actor to behave according to his individual propensities, and personality will be only a minor influence on behavior. Another important influence on the situation is the behavior of the other actors in the social system; their behavior serves as input stimuli to the actor. For simplicity, let us consider only the dyadic (two-actor) case. The input stimuli from one actor to another is the main source of the *masking* of personality effects, because in the likely event that the two actors have different personalities, the interaction behavior between the actors will be a complex effect of their combined propensities, making it difficult to determine the influence of each actor separately. Referring again to our paradigm, the influence of the behavior of the second actor on the behavior of the first may be included in the term f_3 (P X S), in which part of the S is the behavior of the second actor. As that behavior is a function of the second actor's personality, the situation, and the behavior of the first actor, it can be seen that the determination of the social interaction behavior is a complex function of two equations, one for each actor. (An analogy can be made to two computers, each with its own program, interconnected so that the output of each computer is the input of the other. Obviously this case can be viewed as one system composed of two subsystems. We shall return to the system consideration later.)

It has been found that with continuous interaction in two-person games, partners come to behave alike. Pilisuk and Rapoport (1964), for example, reported that in long multitrial Prisoner's Dilemma games, the cooperative choice frequencies between players correlated highly (between 0.9 and 1.00). Commenting on the results, Rapoport and Chammah stated: "This result suggests that the interactions between the members of pairs rather than inherent propensities of individuals to cooperate are the dominant factors in determining a performance of a repeated Prisoner's Dilemma game (1965a, p. 832)." While Rapoport and Chammah thus seemed to rule out personality influences, they also added, "Whatever effect individual propensities may have on the performance of an individual is masked by the interaction effect (1965a, p. 832)." Thus, the input stimuli from an actor's partner *masks,* but does not necessarily *eliminate,* the influence of the actor's personality on his behavior. Undoubtedly this was the problem in several of the studies with negative results shown in Table I.

How, then, can the influence of personality predisposition in cooperation and conflict be detected? There are three appropriate experimental methods for which we are indebted in large measure to the suggestions of Rapoport and Chammah (1965b).

Method I. The first method uses simple one-trial games, such as a one-shot Prisoner's Dilemma or Chicken game. To accomplish the desired effect here, i.e., to discern personality effects free of the partner's influence, it is necessary that the subject have no prior information about his partner. Thus, the subject's behavior in this case will be determined by his own propensities and the game parameters. The latter will include such things as the behavioral choices, rewards, and costs in the game. With *no* input from the partner and with the overt situational effects constant for all subjects, the personal predispositions of the subject have a maximum chance to operate. This is a most useful technique for revealing *pre*dispositions, but by design will not show how the predispositions affect behavior over extended social interaction. For the latter purpose, the second and third methods are useful.

Method II. The second method uses multitrial games with a controlled strategy of the partner. The "partner" must, of course, be an accomplice of the experimenter, a computer, or the experimenter himself. In either case, the controlled strategy behaves in a preestablished way, and of necessity the true subject must be deceived into believing that his partner is also a genuine experimental subject. Deception, however, creates both ethical and practical problems in psychological research, as critically examined by Kelman (1967).

There are two general kinds of programmed strategies that are used. The first is a *nonreactive* strategy, which "behaves" in a fixed way regardless of what the subject does. Examples are completely cooperative ("pacifist") strategies, completely uncooperative strategies, and programs which are randomly cooperative for a fixed proportion of trials. The advantage of this method is that each experimental subject has exactly the same input from the "partner," so that the input is held constant to detect variations due to the true subject's predispositions. There is a serious deficiency in this method, however, for the very unresponsiveness of the programmed strategy may induce most subjects to behave similarly over many trials, thus minimizing the effects of subject personality. As we shall soon see, this effect is most likely if the controlled strategy is very uncooperative.

The second kind of controlled strategy is a *reactive* one, which means that the program dictates certain responses to the inputs from the true subject. Thus, the program will not respond in the same way to each subject. An example is the tit-for-tat strategy, in which the programmed "partner" responds as the subject did on the previous trial. An advantage of the method is the opportunity it gives the subject to learn that his "partner's" behavior is influenced by his own behavior, so that he (the true subject) can control the outcomes according to his own inclinations.

Method III. The third method uses experimental partners matched in personality, on the basis of prior personality tests or other indicators. Matching of personalities avoids the complex behavioral effect when different personalities play each other. Of course, no two personalities will be truly identical, so the problem is the practical one of matching as closely as possible. Obviously, matching on the basis of one personality test such as the *F*-scale (an authoritarianism measure) would be crude indeed. In principle then, several different tests would be used to create better matches. As a practical matter, however, this compounds the matching problem, for the more measures employed, the more configurations that are possible, which again makes it difficult to find sufficient numbers of subjects with similar personality profiles. A recommended solution would be to use only personality variables shown to be relevant for cooperation and conflict on the basis of experiments using Method I. Factor analysis could then be used to find the major personality types or configurations that exist within the sample, and experimental subjects would then be matched on the basis of their typal similarity. Obviously this method is cumbersome and the ideal design can only be approximated, but it is a realistic way to meet the difficult challenge inherent in the study of personality effects.

These three methods thus help to reveal the effects of personality in cooperation and conflict, if in fact the experimental situation is one that allows personality effects to be manifested. To discuss what kinds of situations reveal personality effects and which do not, empirical evidence will first be presented from studies by Terhune (1968) and Terhune and Firestone (1967), conducted at the Cornell Aeronautical Laboratory (CAL). Following that, other relevant studies will be discussed.

In the experiments, the effects of the achievement, affiliation, and power motives on behavior were studied. Without going into the theory and hypotheses that were tested, the experiments will be briefly described, and a few of the many results will be presented.

A large group of subjects was administered Thematic Apperception Tests, which were scored for presence of achievement, affiliation, and power motives. Subjects selected for experimental participation were those who were strong in one and weak in the other two motives. Thus, subjects selected were either achievement-dominant, affiliation-dominant, or power-dominant. The subjects played three types of games, in order of increasing complexity. The first were three one-trial Prisoner's Dilemma games, which varied in the rewards for successful double-cross and the costs for being double-crossed. In effect, the three one-trial games varied in their likelihood of producing cooperation among partners. The second type of game was a 30-trial Prisoner's Dilemma game in which the subjects learned of their joint outcomes after every trial. This game was played under two conditions, the first with no communication permitted between partners, the second with communication permitted via written notes.

In this experiment, the partners were matched by motivational type. The third game played was an international relations game, in which three-man groups assumed the roles of leaders of fictitious nations. All members of each group were matched by motives, so there were in effect achievement-oriented groups, affiliation-oriented groups, and power-oriented groups. All three kinds of groups participated in *each* of three experimental worlds.

Payoffs in each of the three experiments were financial. In the Prisoner's Dilemma games, the payoffs were determined by the payoff matrices, while in the international relations game, the groups were paid bonuses according to how successful they were in achieving their own freely chosen "national goals."

The results in the three experiments were as follows: In the one-trial Prisoner's Dilemma games, the three personality types exhibited clearly different kinds of behavior. The achievement-oriented types were the most cooperative in that more than the others they were found to choose cooperatively while simultaneously expecting cooperation from their partners. The affiliation-oriented subjects were the most defensive in that they tended to expect double-cross from their partners and, therefore, defected themselves. The power-oriented subjects were more exploitative in that they double-crossed their partners whom they expected to choose cooperatively. But, the important point for our purposes here was the effect of the payoff matrix on personality influences. It was found that the more threatening the game (i.e., the greater the temptation to double-cross and the greater the loss for being double-crossed), the smaller were the differences among the motive types, as they all tended to behave defensively. Furthermore, *perceived* threat had a similar effect: Among those subjects who expected their partner to double-cross them, the effects of personality were nil, while among those subjects who expected their partner to cooperate, personality differences were pronounced. Thus, both personality and situation variations distinctively influenced behavior.

Considering next the multitrial Prisoner's Dilemma games, the differences among the motive types were not so easily detected. In overall degree of cooperation, differences among the personality types were slight. This contrasts with the effects of opportunity to communicate: It was found that permitting communication more than tripled the average level of cooperation over that for noncommunication conditions. Here then, a situational factor seemed far more important than personality differences. That is not the whole story, however. On the hunch that what happened on the first trial might have affected the interaction in the subsequent 29 trials of each game, analyses of personality effects were carried out in relation to what happened on the first trial. What was found was this: When *both* partners cooperated on the first trial, effects due to personality were significant and pronounced. Consistent with results in the one-trial games, the achievement-oriented were most cooperative and the power-oriented least cooperative. If either partner defected on the first trial, there was less subsequent cooperation thereafter, and differences among the motive types were nonsignificant. Thus, in the multitrial Prisoner's Dilemma games, a threatening beginning minimized the differential effects of motives.

Turning now to the international relations game, effects due to the personality composition of the groups were hard to find. There were no overall differences in the amount of cooperation or conflict engaged in by the three types of groups. It was decided that a more appropriate analysis would determine *responsibility* for actions. For example, if two groups fought a war, it was considered important to determine which group *started* the war. Consequently, a second analysis determined which group first *initiated* the different forms of cooperation or conflict between pairs of groups. This time several distinctive differences among the groups appeared, of which the following are a few examples.

(1) Achievement-oriented groups initiated cooperation the most; affiliation groups did so the least. No significant differences were found in the initiation of conflict, although the affiliation groups were least active in this respect also. It appears that in the international relations game, where passivity and withdrawal are options not found in the Prisoner's Dilemma, the affiliation-oriented adopt this option. This indication is supported by the finding that the affiliation groups sent the fewest messages of the three types.

(2) The power-oriented groups were clearly the most active in seeking military power, while the achievement groups were least active in this respect.

(3) The power-oriented groups exhibited the most efforts to manipulate others (such as telling lies in the world newspaper and writing deceptive messages). Consistent with their passive tendencies in other activities, the affiliation groups made by far the fewest attempts at manipulating others.

In review, the CAL studies showed that personality effects were most clearly revealed in the one-trial games, less so in the multitrial Prisoner's Dilemma game, and most difficult to uncover in the international relations game. These three games are orderable by degree of complexity, suggesting that the less complex the experimental situation, the more easily are personality effects detected. From the Prisoner's Dilemma results, further, we were able to discover that personality differences actually produced substantial differences in behavior only in those situations where there was less threat, as determined either by the objective aspects of the situation or by the expectations of the players.

That threat diminishes behavioral differences due to personality has been found by other studies also. Quite a convincing demonstration of the phenomenon is found in a study comparing Prisoner's Dilemma behavior within three distinctly different samples: mental patients, prison inmates, and students (Knapp & Podell, 1968). All subjects played against a programmed strategy, although they thought they were playing with real partners. The programmed strategy consisted of 25 trials in which the partner was "cooperative" on a random basis 50% of the time. Following that, half the subjects were exposed to an 80% randomly cooperative strategy, while the other half were exposed to a 20% randomly cooperative strategy. As would be expected, there was considerably less cooperation in response to the mainly uncooperative strategy than to the cooperative one. Of special importance, however, is the finding that there were no significant differences in behavior for the three types of subjects playing against the uncooperative "partner," but there were distinctive and statistically significant differences among them when playing against the cooperative partner. The uncooperative strategy may be considered a threatening one, hence the study reaffirms the proposition that threat minimizes behavioral differences due to personality.

Dolbear and Lave (1966) studied the relation of "risk orientation" of subjects in relation to behavior in three different Prisoner's Dilemma games. The three games were equivalent in the internal differences among their payoff values, but they differed in the absolute values of their payoffs. Consequently, the first game had only positive payoff values, the second had negative "sucker's payoffs" (the loss for being exploited), while the third game had negative payoffs for joint defection as well as for being exploited. One might say that the three games differed in "situational threat" according to the number of outcomes that would yield a financial loss to the players. Dolbear and Lave did not find that risk orientation was related to behavior, but they did find that the game with the most negative payoffs produced somewhat less cooperation, and more important, it clearly produced the least variance in behavior among the subjects. It seems reasonable to interpret this as evidence that situational threat minimizes individual differences due to personality.

That such effects of threat are not limited only to two-person games is indicated by Driver's results (1965) in an internation simulation. Driver studied the intergroup behavior of three-man groups, each of which was composed of cognitively "abstract" or "concrete" individuals. In general the "concrete" groups were the more belligerent, but it was found that "abstract" groups also tended to become aggressive under the stress of situational threat, measured in such terms as presence or absence of nuclear weapons and presence or absence of mitigating treaties.

IV. PROMISING DIRECTIONS FOR FURTHER RESEARCH

Most likely some of the studies failing to find personality effects suffered by using experimental situations that depress personality effects and/or by failing to use methods which most clearly reveal those effects. Nevertheless, there is sufficient evidence now to indicate those aspects of personality that show most promise for further exploration.

Studies on the relation of personality to cooperation and conflict can be placed into two main categories—those using personality tests and those involving "known groups." By the latter is meant groups who are known to differ in one or more ways which are presumably associated with personality differences. Studies using personality tests have the advantage of testing the effects of specific personality variables, but their value is limited by not dealing with total personality and by the problems of validity and reliability of the tests used. The known group comparisons have the advantage of dealing more or less with gross personality differences, but they have inherent problems in interpreting *why* the groups differ behaviorally, i.e., they leave unanswered the question of what specific personality dimensions are the source of behavioral differences. Nevertheless, each type of study adds to our knowledge of the relation of personality to cooperation and conflict.

A. Significant Personality Dimensions

The studies listed in Table I are those involving specific personality measures. Many measures have been used in only one study, which reveals one of the problems with extant research on personality effects: Insufficient replication makes generalizing difficult. Nevertheless, patterns appear in Table I to suggest that certain aspects of personality are particularly relevant to cooperation and conflict. While specific variables such as authoritarianism and internationalism —isolationism seem to stand out, the data may also be interpreted as reflecting the importance of fundamental domains of personality. The following categories seem to be most important.

1. Motives

Earlier in the chapter the theoretical importance of motives for co-operation and conflict was noted. The empirical evidence lends support to this view, especially for motives related to power, affiliation, and possibly achievement. Not only do CAL studies by Terhune (1968) and Terhune and Firestone (1967)(discussed earlier) indicate the importance of those motives, but other studies as well. Marlowe (1963) found in his study with the Prisoner's Dilemma game that conflictive propensities were exhibited by individuals strong in the "need for aggression" and "need for autonomy," while cooperative tendencies characterized those strong in the "need for abasement" and "need for deference." Marlowe's findings overlap those of the CAL studies in that Marlowe's "needs" for aggression and autonomy seem to be variants of the "need for power." In the Terhune and Firestone (1967) study, for example, content analysis of the subjects' statements on their goals revealed a strong concern for autonomy among the power oriented.

Surprisingly, Marlowe did not find the "need for dominance" to correlate with cooperation–conflict. Nevertheless, the weight of evidence favors such a relationship. The MMPI Dominance Scale was used in a study by Sermat (1968), who found that the "highs" behaved more competitively in a "Chicken" game. Similarly, Haythorn and Altman (1967) found that isolated pairs of subjects fought and quarreled a great deal when both scored high on the EPPS "need for dominance" measure. Finally, Higgs and McGrath (1965) found that high scorers on a "self-prominence" factor tended to compete in a nonzero-sum game. Although there are unclear relationships among these various measures of "power," "dominance," and "prominence" orientations, there does seem to be an underlying personality dimension suggesting a disposition toward conflict.

An affiliation orientation also appears related to cooperation and conflict, although the nature of the relationship is not as clear as with the power –dominance measures. In the CAL studies, "need for affiliation" seemed to be more of a defensive orientation, which could lead to conflict but was more of a conflict–avoidant disposition where withdrawal was possible. So also in Haythorn and Altman's study, when pairs of subjects were dissimilar in their affiliative needs, they tended to be passive and withdrawn, an effect which may have been due to the withdrawal of the high affiliation member. In the Higgs-McGrath study, however, those scoring high on an affiliation measure generally behaved cooperatively in nonzero-sum games. At this time it can only be said that the affiliation-oriented probably prefer to cooperate, but an underlying fear of rejection may arouse defensiveness, resulting in withdrawal when possible and conflict when escape is unavailable.

While the CAL studies found need for achievement to be a cooperative disposition, little else is known about that dimension in cooperation and conflict. Higgs and McGrath found no relation between an achievement factor and behavior in nonzero-sum games, but the researchers were not satisfied with the factorial status of their achievement measure. On the other hand, Haythorn and Altman found that subjects matched in achievement needs got along well when isolated for a long period. If the CAL findings are upheld in replication, the achievement orientation may prove to be a significant one for cooperation and conflict, for evidence indicates that the orientation is that of "enlightened self-interest (Terhune, 1968)."

2. Cognitive Structure

Cognitive variables, such as abstractness–concreteness, tolerance of ambiguity, and dogmatism, definitely appear to affect cooperation and conflict. Driver (1965) found that groups comprising concrete individuals were highly prone to aggression. Driver attributed the aggressiveness of the concrete groups to their tendencies, under stress, toward perceptual simplification, their cognitive elimination of nonaggressive response alternatives, and their tendency for hostile, suspicious attitudes. Related to concreteness is intolerance of ambiguity, which Pilisuk, Potter, Rapoport, and Winter (1965) investigated in an expanded Prisoner's Dilemma game. When both players were intolerant of ambiguity, they were found more likely to enter conflict. However, Nardin (1967) failed to replicate this finding. Druckman (1967), on the other hand, found dogmatic subjects to resist compromise in a bargaining situation, for they tended to interpret compromise as "defeat." Druckman used a modified version of Rokeach's (1960) dogmatism measure, which theoretically is related to cognitive concreteness. An opposite tendency appeared in a Prisoner's Dilemma study by Gahagan, Horai, Berger, and Tedeschi (1967) where dogmatic subjects appeared more "repentant." This could have been spurious, however, for dogmatism was unrelated to other behavioral measures.

At the opposite end of the cognitive spectrum, those who are abstract, tolerant of ambiguity, or nondogmatic are more disposed toward cooperation. Theoretically, this is explained by their capability to conceive of various behavioral alternatives other than aggression and they seem capable of pursuing solutions optimal to the interests of all parties rather than view outcomes in simplistic black–white terms such as win–lose, victory-or-surrender.

3. Trust

Generalized trust–mistrust has been found related to cooperation and conflict in five studies. Shure and Meeker (1965) factor-analyzed a number of personality and attitude measures and found "trust vs. suspicion" to be a major factor. In a bargaining game, suspicious types were found to be less "generous."

The "Machiavellianism Scale" has been used in a number of experiments by Geis (1964) and others. As its name implies, the scale measures a cynical and mistrusting attitude toward others. As hypothesized by Geis, "Machiavellians" have been found adept in exploiting others. While Wrightsman (1966) did not find Machiavellianism related to cooperation or conflict in one study, in another (Uejio & Wrightsman, 1967), Machiavellianism was negatively correlated with cooperation under some conditions. Both Lake (1967) and Teger (1968) found that Machiavellians tend to respond rapidly to changes in their partner's behavior, and they severely punish another's change from cooperation to aggression. While relations are not always found with Machiavellianism, there are fairly consistent indications that Machiavellians are exploitative and react decisively to the behavior of others.

In his "Philosophies of Human Nature" scale, Wrightsman (1966) has a "trust" subscale, which correlates $-.67$ with Machiavellianism. In a Prisoner's Dilemma study, Wrightsman found that those who were "trusting" according to their scale scores were in fact more trusting and cooperative in their game behavior.

While cognition and motivation seem to be clearly distinctive domains of personality, the status of generalized trust–mistrust is not as apparent. The dimension seems to be in the domain of value-orientation or *Weltanschauung*. That is, general trust–mistrust seems to combine both cognitive elements (expectations regarding others) and motivational elements (hopes and fears). Certainly further investigation into the dynamics of generalized trust–mistrust is merited, for on theoretical and empirical grounds it seems to be central to the understanding of cooperation and conflict.

Several other studies have used personality measurements which tap combinations of motives, cognitive structure, or trust. The *F*-Scale, for example, measures "authoritarianism," a syndrome including a power orientation, proneness to concrete thinking, and a cynical, mistrusting attitude toward others (Adorno, Frenkel-Brunswik, Levinson, & Sanford, 1950). In light of the previously cited studies, such a personality would be expected to be disposed toward conflict. This is in fact the case. Deutsch (1960) found that high scorers on the *F*-scale were less trusting and less trustworthy in a Prisoner's Dilemma game; Driver (1965) found them more aggressive in his internation simulation; Bixenstine and O'Reilly (1966) found them to be competitive; and Wrightsman (1966) found Deutsch's results essentially to replicate. Only Gahagan *et al.* (1967) found the *F*-Scale unrelated to behavior in a Prisoner's Dilemma game.

Crowne (1965) compared the Prisoner's Dilemma behavior of subjects with "entrepreneurial" and "bureaucratic" family backgrounds. The former, by McClelland's theory (1961), would be expected to be achievement-oriented, while the latter, according to the Harvey, Hunt, and Schroder theory (1961), would be prone to concrete thinking. Crowne found that the entrepreneurial types were generally cooperative—consistent with the CAL findings for achievement-oriented individuals. Bureaucratic types were less cooperative, which is what would be expected of concrete individuals.

Lutzker (1960) and McClintock, Gallo, and Harrison (1965) found that those with "internationalist" attitudes were more cooperative than "isolation-ists" in experimental studies. Internationalism embodies a willingness to trust other nations, and the findings may reflect the effect of the general trust factor. Guetzkow, Brody, Driver, and Beach (1960) found that war in an internation simulation was more likely among those with a *real politik* ideology, which encompasses a power orientation.

Although studies of risk-taking propensities have not shown that variable to be very relevant for cooperation–conflict behavior, there is reason for researchers to study risk-taking further. As was noted earlier, subjects in experimental studies of cooperation and conflict rarely are given the option of choosing the game they want to play, yet in real life there is some freedom to choose one's situations. One study (Sherman, 1967) did investigate the relation of risk-taking propensity (Kogan-Wallach measure) to subject's choice of

Prisoner's Dilemma games with higher rewards for cooperation or high rewards for defecting. Subjects oriented toward risk-taking tended to choose the latter game. Here there is some evidence of the importance of personality in determining whether one will voluntarily enter into a more cooperative situation or a competitive one. The option of choosing one's situation certainly deserves more attention in studies of personality in cooperation–conflict.

In summary, there seem to be rather encouraging patterns in the extant studies incorporating personality measures into cooperation–conflict experiments. One caveat is necessary, however. In an effort to discern consistent trends, the writer may have perceived more than is actually there. Measures which *seem* similar may not in fact be correlated, and results in different studies may have not been as mutually supportive as portrayed. Different studies often use several different behavioral measures, and the writer had to judge whether results across studies were consistent. The reader should be aware, therefore, of the hazards involved in trying to detect a coherent pattern among a jumble of studies using different measures, different experimental methods, and different kinds of subjects. Consequently, the view that motives, cognitive structure, and trust are promising variables for further research should be considered as an hypothesis with some empirical support, but requiring further investigation.

B. Results on "Known Groups"

Several studies have compared cooperation–conflict behavior of samples from different subject populations. Many of these investigations merely show that the samples behave differently, providing no more enlightenment on personality effects than can be obtained from inferring personality characteristics from the behavior exhibited. Such studies can sometimes be useful, however, if either (a) there is background knowledge available on the general personality characteristics of the populations sampled, or (b) the results suggest a personality syndrome which needs further investigation.

Most of the "known group" studies compare the behavior of men and women, but inferences must be limited to sex differences within the kinds of samples studied, namely, American males and females of college age. These studies will be reviewed first, and then comparisons of miscellaneous other groups will be presented in a following section.

1. Males and Females

There is an intriguing paradox in the literature comparing males and females in cooperation–conflict situations. On the one hand, we find women portrayed as more benign in the experiments of Vinacke and his colleagues (Bond & Vinacke, 1961; Uesugi & Vinacke, 1963; Vinacke, 1959); female strategy is described as "accommodative," oriented toward equity and fairness and avoidant of ruthless competition. In contrast, masculine strategy is described as "exploitative," calculated to achieve victory over another and distinctly oriented toward maximizing self-interest. On the other hand, several gaming studies have found women to be *less* cooperative than men. Thus, Bixenstine and O'Reilly were led to observe that "there is now a strong suggestion that women have a greater tendency to respond suspiciously, resentfully, conservatively, and, thus, competitively more than do men (1966, p. 263)." The challenge here is to see whether such apparent incongruities can be resolved and whether in the process male–female differences can suggest personality constellations that enhance our understanding of cooperation and conflict.

To begin, differences between the sexes are not always found in cooperation–conflict games. Such was the case in studies by Bixenstine, Potash, and Wilson (1963), Kanouse and Wiest (1967), Lutzker (1961), Raven and Leff (1965), Sampson and Kardush (1965), and Sermat (1968), among others. In light of our earlier comments, however, it is not surprising that some studies should fail to find sex differences in behavior, because some situations can depress or mask personality effects. Most studies comparing males and females do find differences, and a review of the literature leads to the following summary of different tendencies between the sexes.

(1) Women are generally less cooperative in games where they are pitted against another, where there is some interpersonal challenge involved, where strategic coping is necessary. In such situations they tend to become involved in mutually punishing conflict deadlocks and are less "repentent" for their conflictive behavior (Bixenstine & O'Reilly, 1966; Lumsden, 1967; Oskamp & Perlman, 1966; Rapoport & Chammah, 1965a; Sermat, 1967; Steel & Tedeschi, 1967).

(2) Women prefer straightforward accommodative solutions in conflict of interest problems. They generally seek to compromise and will avoid competition. They tend to be more generous and make greater concessions than do men (Bond & Vinacke, 1961; Borah, 1963; Joseph & Willis, 1963; Pruitt, 1966, 1967; Uesugi & Vinacke, 1963; Vinacke, 1959).

(3) When placed in a vulnerable position, as when they have been exploited, women react with greater retaliation and apparent vindictiveness than do men (Bixenstine, Chambers, & Wilson, 1964; Bixenstine & O'Reilly, 1966; Rapoport & Chammah, 1965a).

(4) Men tend to use a tit-for-tat strategy more, and tend to be more cooperative in response to a tit-for-tat strategy. Women are more cooperative, if presented with cooperativeness by the other from the beginning, but once crossed, they are less responsive to cooperative gestures. In contrast, when men are presented with a highly cooperative partner from the beginning, they tend to

exploit him (Bixenstine & Wilson, 1963; Komorita, 1965; Rapoport & Chammah, 1965a).

(5) Women have difficulty in comprehending strategic situations, often failing to recognize the "optimal" or "rational" strategy. They fail, for example, to see that threats can be used as signals for establishing and coordinating cooperation (Bixenstine & O'Reilly, 1966; Kanouse & Wiest, 1967; Shomer, Davis, & Kelley, 1966).

To reconcile these diverse findings, a motivational explanation may be offered. Argyle (1967) maintains that women are more affiliative and dependent, while men are more dominant and aggressive. There is in fact a similarity between the behavior of women in experimental games and the behavior of affiliation-oriented men in the CAL studies, in that both groups seem to withdraw from competitive situations, but when that is not possible, they become engaged in conflict. If it is true that women are dependent and affiliation-oriented, then that combination, in Gough's model (1957), should lead to behavior that is acquiescing, agreeable, cooperative, and obliging. Such was the feminine behavior in the studies reported under point (2) above. It is significant that in those studies, the bargaining situations were such that cooperation could be achieved through concession and acquiescence. In most of the other studies where women were uncooperative, cooperation generally required strategic coordination between the parties. Terhune (1968) found, for example, that partners who failed to cooperate when communication was permitted were failing to use the communication opportunity to coordinate their moves. In noncommunication games, coordination is even more difficult. Now it is interesting to note that in Gough's schema, coordinating, directing, and leading are all dominance behaviors. If in fact males are more dominance motivated, then men are more likely to have the skills necessary to achieve cooperation in games like Prisoner's Dilemma, while women are handicapped. Unable to achieve cooperation, women would then be inclined to retreat or withdraw, which are also dependence behaviors in Gough's model. In Prisoner's Dilemma, the only withdrawal possible is to the defection tactic, which is usually interpreted as a conflict maneuver. It seems, consequently, that the greater conflict among women in Prisoner's Dilemma reflects not competitive orientations, but rather less ability to establish coordination in a complex problem-solving situation. To check this interpretation, men and women would have to be compared in situations with more behavioral alternatives and in which the intent behind each alternative is fairly apparent. Alternatively, comparison could be made between male and female behavior in Prisoner's Dilemma games with communication permitted prior to decisions. It is hypothesized that in such games women would be found at least as cooperative as men.

If the above interpretation is correct, the broader implication is that people who conflict are not necessarily bellicose. On the contrary, those with the best of intentions may find themselves, through ineptitude or defensiveness, locked in conflict with others.

2. Other Group Comparisons

Studies comparing the game behaviors of groups from different populations vary in their value for understanding personality effects. Thus, Lave (1965) found that students from Harvard University and Massachusetts Institute of Technology were more cooperative in playing Prisoner's Dilemma than were those from Northeastern University; Oskamp and Perlman (1966) found that students from small colleges were more cooperative than those from large universities, and McClintock and McNeel (1966) found that Belgian college students were more competitive than American college students in a "Maximizing Difference Game." While such findings demonstrate that mixed-motive games are sensitive to population differences, they do little to increase our understanding of personality effects.

Also troublesome to interpret are the results of a study by Raven and Leff (1965), in which groups differing in "collectivist ideology" were compared in their play of Prisoner's Dilemma. The researchers hypothesized that individuals indoctrinated in the kibbutz ideology of cooperative living would exhibit greater cooperativeness in a gaming situation than would those not so educated. Results did not support the hypothesis, but the researchers then suggested that the kibbutz ideology does not preclude competition in some areas of life. It is thus possible that ideological differences in groups are not indicative of more fundamental personality differences, to which the Prisoner's Dilemma game generally appears sensitive.

Contrasting with the above studies are those which compare grossly different groups, such as psychotics and normals. There can be little question of basic differences in personality of such groups, so their behavioral comparison in cooperation–conflict studies takes on special importance.

Harford and Solomon (1965) hypothesized that the suspicion and hostility characteristic of paranoid schizophrenics would be reflected in their play of Prisoner's Dilemma. Surprisingly, it was found that schizophrenics, in general, paranoid or not, were more trusting and less exploitative than were a college student comparison group. Both normals and nonparanoid schizophrenics proved responsive to variations in the strategies of a programmed "partner," but the paranoid schizophrenics were unaffected by the partner's strategies.

Travis (1965) compared the game behavior of schizophrenic and non-schizophrenic mental patients. Whether the schizophrenic group included paranoids was not indicated, but all subjects selected were of higher intellectual and educational levels. The subjects played both a Prisoner's Dilemma game, with a withdrawal option, and zero-sum games that had "rational" solutions.

Contrary to Harford and Solomon's results, Travis found the schizophrenics to be less cooperative, less "trusting," less "trustworthy," and less "forgiving" than the nonschizophrenics. [The psychological interpretations of behavior were based on measures of "state-conditioned propensities" (Rapoport & Chammah, 1965b) for the various groups.] Of particular interest is the fact that schizophrenics used the withdrawal or "escape" option more, and they tended not to use the "rational" solution in the zero-sum situation. These results were generally congruent with the hypotheses formulated on the basis of the psychodynamics of schizophrenia. Whether the results in any way contradict those of Harford and Solomon cannot be established due to insufficient descriptions of the schizophrenic samples in the two studies.

Three rather different populations were sampled and tested in a Prisoner's Dilemma game by Knapp and Podell (1968). Hospitalized mental patients of various types comprised the first sample, prison inmates of various types comprised the second, and college students constituted the third. All groups played against either highly cooperative or highly uncooperative programmed "partners." Generally, the students were most cooperative and the prisoners were least, but in addition, two findings are of special interest: (1) The cooperative programmed strategies elicited significant increases in cooperation for the normal patient groups, but not for the inmate sample; and (2) the behavior of the three groups differed considerably and significantly in reaction to the cooperative strategy, but did not differ significantly in reaction to the uncooperative strategy. Thus, both prison inmates in this study and paranoids in the Harford-Solomon study were revealed to be unresponsive to the strategies of their partners. It is important in this connection to note some related findings in two other studies. The comparison of "internationalists" and "isolationists" in the experiment by McClintock et al. (1965) revealed the isolationists to be relatively unresponsive to the cooperativeness or competitiveness of the partner. In the Terhune study (1968), while partner behavior was not varied, the power motivated group seemed least affected by variations of the payoff matrices in one-trial Prisoner's Dilemma games. Throughout all these studies, consequently, subjects with the most conflictful dispositions tended to maintain their aggressive tendencies despite situational variations. According to a study by Wolowitz and Shorkey (1966), paranoid schizophrenics exhibit more power themes than do nonparanoid subjects on Thematic Apperception Tests. If a power orientation may be presumed for isolationism also, then it is suggested that a power orientation is a disposition rather unyielding to situational variations.

As it is a recurrent problem in reviewing personality studies, it is unfortunate that the three studies using mental patients are not exactly comparable, because of different sampling procedures and experimental varia-tions. Nevertheless, the three studies provide substantial evidence that groups known to differ in important ways also exhibit distinctive differences in cooperation—conflict behavior, and some apparent consistencies with other studies suggest a line along which further inquiry is merited.

C. Hypothesized Major Orientations

Our understanding of personality effects in cooperation and conflict would certainly be facilitated if all the various personality characteristics studied to date could be reduced to a few major dispositions. That seems almost too much to hope for, but on the basis of the extant studies at least six orientations seem discernible. The validity of these types will require further research for clarification, so the propositions below are presented to encourage such research.

(1) Conflict is more likely when one or more of the actors involved has tendencies of a generally aggressive and rigid nature. (Relevant characteristics: authoritarianism, need for power or dominance, "isolationism," cognitive concreteness, dogmatism, paranoia, possibly psychopathic criminality.)

(2) Conflict is more likely when withdrawal is impossible and when one or more of the actors involved has defensive tendencies, such as fear of rejection and unwillingness to forgive; when offered unconditional cooperation, however, this type is likely to respond cooperatively. (Relevant characteristics: affiliative need involving fear of rejection, femininity, possibly nonparanoid schizophrenia).

(3) Exploitation and retaliation are likely among those who are generally mistrustful. (Relevant characteristics: Machiavellianism, possibly unfavorable views of human nature.)

(4) Cooperativeness, or at least avoidance of conflict, is likely among actors who are passive, docile, and dependent. (Relevant characteristics: needs for abasement and deference, and submissiveness.)

(5) Where cooperation is the best policy in terms of maximizing gains, a cooperative policy will be followed by those who are flexible and success oriented. (Relevant characteristics: need for achievement, cognitive abstractness, tolerance of ambiguity, open-mindedness, entrepreneurial orientation.)

(6) Cooperation is likely to be actively pursued by those who are generally trusting and egalitarian. (Relevant characteristics: "internationalism," conciliatory ideology, favorable view of human nature.)

V. RELATIVE IMPORTANCE OF PERSONALITY VS. SITUATIONAL DIFFERENCES

An important question that arises in considering personality effects on cooperation and conflict is this: Given the demonstrated effects of personality variables, are the *magnitudes* of those effects really very significant in comparison to the effects of situational variations? As stated, the question pertains to the "main effects" of personality and situation as *independent* functions in the paradigm presented earlier. Too few studies have varied both personality and situational parameters to arrive at a definitive answer to the question. Furthermore, we do not really know, and perhaps we never will, what are the full ranges of personality influences and situational influences on behavior. We can, however, at least point to the indications of three studies.

In the Knapp and Podell study (1968), the Prisoner's Dilemma behavior of three distinct groups (mental patients, prison inmates, and college students) are compared, as well as the effects of two different programmed strategies (80% cooperation and 20% cooperation). The maximum effect of personality was obtained with the 80% cooperation strategy, while the maximum effect of strategy was obtained with the student group. Personality produced a maximum difference in cooperation (proportion of cooperative responses) of roughly 20%, while the strategic variations resulted in a maximum difference of roughly 25%. Thus, the situational variations had slightly greater effects than did personality, but both factors seem quite influential.

In Terhune's study (1968), comparisons were made between situational and personality effects for both one-trial and 30-trial Prisoner's Dilemma games. In the one-trial games, the situation was varied by having subjects play three different games, ranging from one in which there was a high reward for double-crossing one's partner to one in which there was little to be gained by not cooperating. The results on four behavioral indices (cooperativeness, exploitativeness, defensiveness, apprehension) showed that, in general, the personality effects were greater than the situational effects. Quite the reverse was found in the multitrial games, however. There it was found that the opportunity for partners to communicate before making their choices vastly increased the amount of cooperation, while the differences among the motive groups was quite small. In the noncommunication condition, however, differences due to personality were fairly substantial in relation to another important situation effect, the outcome of the first trial.

In a form of internation simulation, Crow and Noel (1965) varied three classes of variables. These were: individual characteristics (militarism vs. nonbelligerence, high-risk preference vs. low-risk preference, and nationalism vs. internationalism); situation characteristics (nature of opponent and probability of winning a war); and organizational characteristics (individual-decision responsibility vs. committee-consensus responsibility). Three related experiments were conducted, and in all three, personality characteristics significantly influenced the decisions made. In contrast, situational elements were significant in only one experiment. The same was true of organizational characteristics, while in two of the experiments there was a significant interaction between situation and organization variables.

The limited conditions of these studies restrict the generalizations that may be derived from them, but at least they indicate that both personality and situational effects can assume significant proportions. One might conclude from the first two studies that situational effects have primacy in that there are certain situational conditions, generally described as "threatening," which minimize behavioral variations due to personality. One may also note the reverse, however; there are some personality types (e.g., prison inmates) who seem rather impervious to situational influences. Therefore, our conclusion must be that it makes little sense generally to assert that situational or personality variables are "more important." Conclusions must be more specific, stated in regard to *what* dimensions of personality are involved and the degree of variance along those dimensions, with similar statements regarding the variables of situations.

Some remarks on the relation of personality effects and situational complexity are in order. In the CAL studies discussed earlier, personality effects became more difficult to detect in going from simple two-person one-trial Prisoner's Dilemma games, to multitrial Prisoner's Dilemma games, thence to a multigroup international relations game. One might conclude, subsequently, that personality effects are unimportant in more complex situations. Such a conclusion seems unwarranted. It is necessary to recall a view expressed by Proshansky and Seidenberg: "It is now widely held ... that any given social phenomenon is a function not of any single sovereign determinant, but of *many interacting* determinants reflecting the influence of psychological, sociological, historical, and other kinds of factors (1965, p. 5)." The more complex the situation, the more such determinants there are likely to be. To be sure, in more complex situations personality characteristics may be less important, but only as *single* determinants of behavior. The same could be said of any single other factor as well. In other words, more complex situations necessitate the *inclusion* of more factors, but do not justify the *exclusion* of personality factors, in order to understand behavior.

A final consideration on this topic pertains to the role of atypical personalities. Generally more distinctive personality effects appear in studies that use extreme or at least unusual types. In the two studies mentioned above, Knapp and Podell used mental patients and prison inmates, while Terhune used only subjects who scored high on the achievement, affiliation, or power motive, and low on the other two. In studies where a fuller range of personalities was used (limited, of course, by the populations from which samples were selected), correlation coefficients between personality variables and behavioral indices are often low. While selection of extreme personality types generally produces more distinctive results, it is also true that situational comparisons usually involve quite different conditions. It is necessary to recognize this in assessing the strength of any relationship between behavior and either personality or situational variables. Another point to be made is that the importance of personality effects should not be belittled if a study has compared only atypical types. It seems quite likely that in cooperation–conflict situations it will be the atypical personalities who play the major roles. Leaders of groups and nations, for example, may have risen to their positions of power *because* they have atypical qualities. While based on much impressionistic evidence, the literature review by Raser (1966) indicates that political decision makers throughout the world have quite unusual personalities. Consequently, researchers would do well to study the behavior of atypical personalities, particularly if those personalities characterize influential people in the social domain of interest to the investigator.

VI. TOWARD THE ADVANCED STUDY OF PERSONALITY EFFECTS

Early in this chapter a rudimentary paradigm was presented for considering personality in relation to situational influences on cooperation and conflict. With that framework as a guide, the empirical literature was reviewed. The review has revealed the need for improved methods of study, and in addition, there is need for an improved model to replace the simple paradigm with which we began. In the sections to follow, recommendations for improved methodology will be presented and a new model for studying personality effects will be suggested.

A. Needs for Improved Study

Throughout the review of the empirical literature, the writer has felt frustrated with the difficulty of deriving any general principles from extant studies, because of their great diversity in substance and method, and because of the lack of any systematic attempt to establish certain principles so that we might have high confidence in their validity. To a certain extent the diversity of research so far may be excused—in fact, it is to be expected—because of the ground-breaking nature of research on personality effects in cooperation and conflict. Now, however, there has been sufficient exploration of the subject so that we no longer need merely to prove that personality plays an important role, so research should enter a new phase in which the nature and degree of relationships between personality and specific forms of cooperation–conflict behavior will be established. What is required then, are more sophisticated approaches and more zealous pursuit of the leads that have been established in the exploratory phase. Consequently, this section specifies some needs for improved study and some suggestions on how these needs may be met.

1. Need 1: More Complex Situations

The overwhelming reliance on the Prisoner's Dilemma game in co-operation—conflict studies is almost embarrassing. To be sure, Prisoner's Dilemma has provided a neat initial model for the study of cooperation and conflict, and it is surprising how much complexity of behavior can be studied within that simple context. But the repeated study of Prisoner's Dilemma, in all its nuances and variations, has probably reached the point of diminishing return. Prisoner's Dilemma, as well as other two-person, two-choice games, is certainly far removed from the complexities of real life cooperation—conflict situations. With but two choices for a player, the behavioral alternatives are severely limited over those encountered in most real conflict situations. And certainly, the repetition again and again of the same choices in multitrial games (which sometimes extend over hundreds of trials) does injustice to the developmental phases, including new forms of behavior, that are encountered in most conflict situations. What is needed, therefore, are more complex situations that permit a variety of behavioral alternatives, including withdrawal, and perhaps at a later stage of advancement, the use of situations that permit the actors to *create* new forms of behavior. Some new games have been developed that permit more than two behavioral alternatives, and it would behoove researchers to use them. Examples of promising games are the "Allocations Game" used by Deutsch, Epstein, Canavan, and Gumpert (1967), the expanded Prisoner's Dilemma game used by Pilisuk *et al.* (1965), and the Conflict Board developed by Swirsky (1968). It is recommended that researchers use existing games where possible, more readily to permit comparisons across different studies. Only when an existing game is inadequate for testing hypotheses should a new game be created.

More complex situations also include intergroup studies. While interpersonal conflict is of great interest within the general subject of cooperation and conflict, often the situations to which generalization is desired are intergroup and even international relations. It may be expected that the introduction of intragroup dynamics, with the phenomena of loyalty, cohesion, power relations, leadership, and so on, will likely involve new principles of cooperation and conflict beyond those found in interpersonal situations.

Along with the greater complexity of intergroup studies should be the investigation of cooperation and conflict from the longitudinal point of view. It is a big assumption to believe that the general dynamics of cooperation and conflict can be established from interactions that endure for only an hour or so. Perhaps there is some validity to the notion of time compression (an assumption involved in attempts at simulation), but certainly the decision processes within the human mind cannot be speeded up to produce the same outcome as would occur when decisions are slowly deliberated. Forcing quick decisions may be valid if one is interested only in crisis decision making, but generally researchers are interested in more than those singular phenomena. And particularly in intergroup relations, it takes time for relationships to develop, for the contending parties to "feel out" each other, and for intragroup relations to develop and stabilize. Worthy of emulation is the classic "Robber's Cave" study by Sherif, Harvey, White, Hood, and Sherif (1961), which examined intergroup conflict over a several-week period. While the study did not give special attention to personality effects, its method of studying natural conflicts longitudinally is an approach that personality studies well might follow. Another approach to intergroup relations is the use of simulated environments. However, one problem that arises with simulations, such as internation simulations, is that the subjects' interpretation of roles and general expectations of appropriate behavior in the simulated context complicate the analysis of personality effects. For example, a subject's interpretation of the role of head of state and his general understanding of international relations may govern his behavior in international simulations. Behavioral analysis is complicated when, as in the Terhune and Firestone (1967) international relations game, some subjects are found to take the simulated context seriously while others are found to interpret it as a game no more realistic than the game of Monopoly. Creation of an experimental environment that permits cooperation and conflict in intergroup relations but does not try to simulate a real life environment may obviate the problems.

The arguments for more complex experimental situations should not be construed as totally opposing further research with simple game formats. The value of simple games for revealing some of the rudiments of conflict is not questioned. What *is* questioned is the exclusive concentration of research toward developing a full blown theory about simple situations *prior* to research aimed toward a broader, general theory of conflict. Such an approach, as advocated by Rapoport (1968), runs the risk of constructing an elegant, irrelevant theory. The research strategy preferred by the writer is that which alternately uses simple and complex experimental formats in the persistent search for principles applicable across levels of complexity.

The foregoing recommendations apply to all experimental studies of cooperation and conflict, but they are specially relevant to studies of personality effects. As was shown in our empirical review, influences of personality that may stand out clearly in simply two-person games are not as readily detected in more complex situations. If personality is indeed relevant in the latter, research must demonstrate the relevance.

2. Need 2: Attention to Incentives

The impetus that game theory has given to the use of games as experimental devices has also had a deleterious effect, particularly for studying the relation of motives and values to cooperation and conflict. Game theory prescribes rational solutions in conflict-of-interest situations, based on the assumption that the numbers in payoff matrices validly reflect the utilities of the actors. Yet, it is naive to simply assume that the payoffs reflect the subjects' utilities, for the utility functions themselves will be functions of the subject's personality. For example, one subject may experience maximum utility by outwitting his partner, while another's personal utility may be maximized when he perceives an equitable distribution of rewards and costs.

Personal utilities are ignored too often in research on personality influences. A most flagrant example occurs in those studies in which the subjects play a game only for points (in which the major incentive is to win more points than the other, or perhaps to please or prove something to the experimenter) or in which the subject who earns the most points is given a tangible reward. These procedures are often used in what are ostensibly nonzero-sum games, but which by the nature of the rewards are converted essentially to zero-sum games. The use of financial payoffs seems to this writer to be preferable to point payoffs, but even with money payoffs it cannot be assumed that monetary utilities are all that are operating. More efforts should be made to discover the individual's subjective utility system in research on personality effects.

3. Need 3: Improved Measurement of Personality Variables

In studies of personality effects in cooperation and conflict, researchers have been terribly complacent about their own ignorance of what their personality tests are measuring. They often seem to assume that the label affixed to a test is a valid indicator of the variable being tapped. Yet too often it is discovered that different tests purportedly measuring similar variables are in fact uncorrelated. For example, Vannoy's factor analysis (1965) of various measures of cognitive complexity and Mitchell's factor analysis (1961) of achievement motive tests both revealed the factorial heterogeneity of tests that were ostensibly similar. There are, furthermore, different tests ostensibly measuring different personality variables, which upon investigation prove to be highly correlated. Any researcher investigating personality effects in experimental studies should be aware of these quirks in current measures of personality, and he owes it to the science to make sure he understands what he is measuring before blithely administering personality tests to subjects. Only in that way can he hope to develop a sound theory and hypotheses derived from the theory. To be sure, those interested primarily in the processes of cooperation and conflict will not wish to put everything aside while first studying personality, but this is not necessary. What is necessary is that the researcher know *in advance* as much as he can about the personality measures he is using, and after doing his experimental research, to see if his results might not contribute to personality theory and measurement as well. He can, furthermore, use multiple measures of personality, which may in concert reveal more about the dimensions under investigation than could any one test. In the process of using multiple measures, it would behoove researchers deliberately to include some personality tests from other studies, so that results across studies might be more directly compared.

4. Need 4: Conceiving Personality as Configuration

Probably few, if any, psychologists would dispute the fact that personality is multidimensional and that no single dimension is likely to be an overriding determinant of behavior. Within one social situation, however, there may be certain dimensions that are far more important than others, and many dimensions are likely to be completely irrelevant. Our earlier review of the literature suggests that a few main areas of personality stand out as relevant to cooperation and conflict, at least within the limited situations studied so far. Nevertheless, those personality dimensions that influence cooperation and conflict orchestrate to affect behavior, so that focus on only one dimension is unlikely to produce really distinctive results. Therefore, progress in research on personality in cooperation and conflict would be enhanced by studying personality configurations or types, rather than merely single dimensions of personality. This recommendation fits in with the previous recommendation for multiple measures of personality. Ideally, the researcher would use multiple measures of apparently similar variables as well as use clusters of tests tapping different aspects of personality, e.g., cognitive structure and motivational domains. If this recommendation seems too ambitious, it should be recalled that factor analytic methods may be used not only to determine underlying dimensions within several tests, but also to determine types of personalities based on the overall configuration of test scores. Use of such methods will require much effort on the part of researchers, but in the end we are likely to understand far better the behavior of personalities measured as configurations than would be our understanding based on single measures of personality.

5. Need 5: Specific Behavioral Indices

Already it has been found in Prisoner's Dilemma studies that the effects of personality become more apparent when behavior is assessed in terms of choice–expectation combinations, or by "state-conditioned propensities" as developed by Rapoport and Chammah (1965b), in contrast with such simple measures as the overall number of cooperative choices. Should the researcher follow our recommendation to study more complex situations, then the use of more specific behavioral indices becomes imperative. As the study of cooperation and conflict progresses, it may be found that cooperation and conflict can be expressed in terms of a limited number of categories, such as exploitation, violent aggression, defensive attack, withdrawal, trusting cooperation, retaliation and altruistic cooperation. Commensurate with the complexities of personality may be found propensities to indulge in particular forms of these behaviors. In any event, the researcher on personality effects in cooperation should not merely examine the correlation of personality with gross indices of cooperation and conflict (he may fail to find any significant correlations), but he should explore the relationships with specific forms of behavior as well. The Rapoport and Chammah study (1965a) is an excellent example of this approach.

6. Need 6: Studying Personality and Situation in Interaction

Personality is far too complex to expect a person to exhibit behavioral constancies across all situations. There is sufficient evidence in some of the studies reviewed to indicate that cooperation–conflict behavior is a function of both personality and situation, and furthermore, these effects are not merely additive but interact with each other. Consequently, the researcher interested in personality effects would do well to manipulate situational variables as well, not only to learn about the interaction between personality and situation, but to discover those situations in which personality differences have greater and less impact on behavior. (Crow and Noel, 1965, also argue along these lines.) At the very least, researchers should now become aware of the fact that some situations minimize personality effects, so that they can avoid falsely concluding that some personality variables are unrelated to cooperation and conflict.

These six needs are presented in the serious hope that investigators will try to meet them. The failure to remedy the needs creates vulnerabilities to which criticisms of experimental studies of cooperation and conflict are often addressed. One of the most sensitive issues is the questionable relevance of experimental studies, particularly two-person gaming studies, to actual social conflicts. While trying to remedy current weaknesses will surely make life more complicated for the researcher, he must attend to the issues raised, if he is concerned with the relevance and generalizability of his research endeavors. After all, social behavior, especially cooperation and conflict, *is* complicated.

B. A Recommended Model for Studying Personality Effects

Two important findings must be reckoned with in developing a model that accounts for personality influences in cooperation and conflict.

(1) Personality effects usually appear most clearly in those situations where there is little or no feedback on the second party's behavior. Such situations are one-trial games (e.g., Terhune, 1968), brief games (e.g., Crow &

Noel, 1965; Deutsch, 1960), and early interaction sequences (e.g., Tedeschi, Lesnick, & Gahagan, 1968).

(2) With *extended* interaction, actors generally come to behave alike toward each other. That is, actions of one party tend to be reciprocated by the other, when there are similar behavioral alternatives available to both sides. This mutuality has been observed not only in gaming studies (e.g., Rapoport & Chammah, 1965b), but also in community conflict (Coleman, 1957) and in international relations (e.g., Bronfenbrenner, 1961; Fulbright, 1967).

Imagine what goes on in any interaction sequence that has a definite beginning. The initial actions of each party are likely to be determined in large measure by their individual predispositions, i.e., their personalities. These actions set in motion a sequence of action and counteraction where each party's behavior is influenced not only by his own propensities, but also by the actions of the other. A state in which one actor is endeavoring to cooperate while the other is defecting (exploiting, aggressing) is likely to be most unstable. Hence, the *interaction* behavior will eventually reach a steady state where both actors are cooperating, involved in a conflict deadlock, or both withdraw to independent actions. The stable state that obtains will in large measure be the resultant of behaviors early in the interaction sequence (Pilisuk *et al.*, 1965; Terhune, 1968), but those behaviors in turn were partially determined by the dispositions of the actors; consequently, the stable state interaction, although both actors are behaving essentially alike, will have been influenced by the *initial joint configuration of the actors' propensities.*

Now steady states in human relationships are not interminable. There may be occasional perturbations, with a return to the steady state, or there may be an upset in the steady state which will create a set of oscillations, but which will eventually reach a new and different steady state. There may also be a slow drift in state, as in a deterioration of relations (e.g., a marriage slowly moving toward divorce). The changes away from a steady state may be caused by factors exogenous to the relationship (such as third party interference, or the appearance of new opportunities) or endogenous to the relationship, in the form of unilateral initiatives by one actor. It is the latter that is related to personality. A unilateral initiative may be a manifestation of a predisposition that had been latent all along, or the result of a new predisposition, i.e., a change in personality. In the long run our theory should be concerned with changes in personality that occur within extended interactions, but for now we will have done well if we can explain interaction behavior during those periods in which personality endures more or less unchanged.

Most experimental studies are sufficiently brief that our concern will be in understanding how a steady state is reached as a function of the initial predispositions of the actors. It should be realized, however, that we are dealing with a very special subclass of interaction situations, namely, *those in which there is a clearcut beginning to the interaction between the actors.* There are, certainly, examples of this class in real life. New acquaintances may be made, new groups may be created, a new nation may be formed, and relations established with others. Yet, there is also a class of relationships of such longevity that no clearcut "beginning" may be traced. Such would be the case among social groups whose identity and boundaries evolved only after a long prior history of diffuse interaction. In addition, there are likely to be interactions that did indeed have a specific origin, but for which records of the initial behavior between the actors are not available. In these latter instances it may not be possible for the investigator to trace personality effects in the sequence: predispositions—initial actions—counteractions . . . present state. The challenge to the researcher is to understand the effects of personality upon interaction behavior when he has data available only within a given time frame. It is submitted, therefore, that the necessary model must account for the influence of personality within that time frame even if it doesn't include the initial interactions.

Briefly, the model proposed is as follows: Behavior between two parties can be dichotomized into *initiative* behavior and *reactive* behavior. Initiative behavior is that found early in a new relationship or that which represents a change from a steady state. It is essentially unilateral and not a mere reciprocation of the other's previous behavior. Reactive behavior is involved in the transitional state (action—counteraction) following an initiation and in the steady state that emerges. The latter is characterized by reciprocity or complementarity. In reciprocity the actors are behaving similarly toward each other (such as mutual aid, trade, or mutual punishment), while in complementarity, the actors are behaving differently, but in a compatible way toward each other (such as dominance—submission, nurturance—succorance). The model to encompass the role of personality in both initiative and reactive behavior may actually be considered two models. For initiative behavior, the model is essentially the paradigm presented earlier. For reactive behavior, the model is

$$R_{1-2} = f_1(P_1 \times P_2) + f_2(S) + f_3(P_1 \times P_2 \times S)$$

where R_{1-2} = the two-party interaction behavior, which may be a form of either mutuality or complementarity; $P_1 \times P_2$ = the configuration of the personalities (behavior potentials) of both parties in the interaction; S = the situational parameters; and $P_1 \times P_2 \times S$ = the interaction between the particular set of personalities and the situation.

To illustrate the form of the model for reactive behavior, analogies from chemistry and physics may help. In chemistry, the prediction of how two elements will react to each other cannot be made by knowing only the properties of one element. The valences of each element must be known, as well as the characteristics of the physical environment, such as pressure, temperature, and the presence of a catalyst. Similarly in physics, the force of attraction between two bodies is not a function of the characteristics of either body by itself, but the mass of each and the distance between them. The resultant movement of the two bodies is a function of the attractive force between them, as well as of the attractive forces of other bodies in the environment and the physical characteristics of the medium in which the bodies are located. Similarly, reactive behaviors of two actors is a function of their joint personalities, the physical environment, the influences of third parties, and so forth. The personalities of each actor, i.e., their behavior potentials, can be considered roughly equivalent to the valences of elements in chemistry. In effect, the model for reactive behavior may be considered a sort of "social chemistry."

While we have presented only an inchoate model, it has profound implications for the way in which the search for personality effects in cooperation and conflict should be conducted. It suggests that efforts to predict the development of cooperation or conflict by focusing on the predispositions of single actors is doomed to only minor success at best. The more appropriate technique is to form theory and research on the form of *system* behavior resulting from the particular configuration of the dispositions of the two or more actors in interaction. It is hypothesized that the interaction behavior between actors with different predispositions will not as a rule be a mere average of the type of behavior toward which each is disposed. Quite possibly, for example, an actor whose defensive dispositions commonly involve him in conflict, will be as cooperative with another actor who patiently promotes mutual interests as would be the case where both actors were disposed to promote mutual interests. In essence, then, the influence of personality on behavior in a system composed of two or more actors is expected to be a complex function of their separate predispositions, not simply obtained by summing or averaging the predispositions.

An appropriate method for applying the proposed model in research is to use an expansion of Method III, described earlier. In the expanded version, opposing actors would not be only matched in personality. Instead, a $K \times K$ design would be used, in which each of K personality types under investigation would play against every personality type. [The actual number of combinations would be $K(K + 1)/2$.] If, for example, personality types A, B, and C were being studied, one type A set of subjects would interact with another type A set, a second type A set would interact with a type B set, and a third type A set would interact with type C subjects. Thus, all combinations studied would be A–A, A–B, A–C, B–B, B–C, and C–C. With such a design, the general behavioral dispositions (main effects) of each type could be discovered, as well as the forms of system behavior resulting from specific combinations of actors.

Support for the suggested design is found in a study by Fry (1965). Ascendant and submissive subjects were chosen, using the Allport A–S scale. A two-person game was played in which points were obtained when the partners matched in their independent choices among three objects. Several trials were played with feedback of the outcomes, so the problem for the subjects was to develop a coordination strategy for matching. The hypothesis that ascendant subjects, as individuals, would do better than submissive subjects was not confirmed. The hypothesis that pairs of ascendant and submissive subjects would do better than pairs of similar subjects was confirmed, however. Thus, the study demonstrated that the systemic *configuration* of personalities was the significant factor in predicting behavior, rather than the personalities of single individuals.

VII. SUMMARY AND CONCLUSION

The major points of this chapter are as follows:

(1) Personality and situation may be considered the two main influences on cooperation–conflict behavior. Personality is conceived as a configuration of behavior potentials, or internal programs, within the individual, while situation designates the physical environment (including other people) external to the individual.

(2) There are many theoretical reasons to expect that personality is an important determinant of cooperation–conflict behavior. Actors bring *to* the situation propensities to behave in a certain general way, and *within* the situation their propensities interact with situational characteristics to determine their specific behavior.

(3) While personality has a demonstrated influence on behavior in several cooperation–conflict studies, there are also many instances of negative results. While the latter may be due to the fact that some personality characteristics are simply not relevant to cooperation and conflict, there is also evidence that some experimental situations either minimize the influence of individual differences in personality, or the experimental designs and methods are such that personality effects are masked. Personality effects are generally minimized in situations describable as threatening, while the masking of personality effects results mainly from the complex interaction between actors with different personalities.

(4) Three main methods to reveal personality effects are (a) use of one-trial games, (b) use of controlled strategies of the "partner," and (c) matching interacting partners on the basis of similar personalities.

(5) Empirical evidence indicates that the more complex the situation, the more difficult are personality effects to detect. However, it does not follow that personality effects are unimportant in complex situations.

(6) A review of the empirical literature reveals such a variety of

personality measures and experimental methods that drawing generalizations is difficult. Nevertheless, indications are that the domains of personality most relevant for cooperation—conflict are (a) motives, (b) cognitive structure, and (c) an apparent value-orientation of general trust—mistrust. Differences in behavior are also well established between men and women, and between special groups such as psychotics and normals.

(7) Considering the relative importance for behavior of personality vs. situation, evidence indicates that neither is "more important" than the other. Some situations tend to minimize the differential effects of personality, but some predispositions seem impervious to variations in situation.

(8) There are several needs for improvement in studying personality effects in cooperation and conflict. The needs are for: (a) more complex experimental situations, (b) more attention to incentives, (c) improved personality measurement, (d) conceiving personality as configuration, (e) use of more specific behavioral indices, and (f) increased attention to the interaction of personality and situation.

(9) Finally, a refined model for studying personality effects was proposed. The model distinguishes initiative from reactive behavior, and attends to the systemic nature of cooperation—conflict behavior.

In conclusion, personality effects do seem influential and highly important in cooperation—conflict behavior. It is difficult to study these effects, however, and sophisticated research designs and analytic techniques are required. Certainly the researcher should not be discouraged if personality effects do not just "pop out" on first analysis, especially in complex situations. Finally, it is suggested that even minor personality effects should not be discounted. It may be the crucial "minor" differences in personalities of actors that change the course of history.

REFERENCES

Adorno, T.W., Frenkel-Brunswik, E., Levinson, D.J., & Sanford, R.N. *The authoritarian personality.* New York: Harper, 1950.
Allport, G.W. *Personality: A psychological interpretation.* New York: Holt, 1937.
Argyle, M. *The psychology of interpersonal behaviour.* Harmondsworth, Middlesex, England: Penguin, 1967.
Bixenstine, V.E., Chambers, N., & Wilson, K.V. Effect of asymmetry in payoff on behavior in a two-person non-zero-sum game. *Journal of Conflict Resolution,* 1964, 8, 151–159.

Bixenstine, V.E., & O'Reilly, E.F., Jr. Money versus electric shock as payoff in a prisoner's dilemma game. *Psychological Record,* 1966, 16, 251–264.

Bixenstine, V.E., Potash, H.M., & Wilson, K.V. Effects of level of cooperative choice by the other player on choices in a prisoner's dilemma game. Part I. *Journal of Abnormal and Social Psychology,* 1963, 66, 308–313.

Bixenstine, V.E., & Wilson, K.V. Effects of level of cooperative choice by the other player on choices in a prisoner's dilemma game. Part II. *Journal of Abnormal and Social Psychology,* 1963, 67, 139–147.

Blake, R.R., & Mouton, J.S. The intergroup dynamics of win–lose conflict and problem-solving collaboration in union–management relations. In M. Sherif (Ed.), *Intergroup relations and leadership.* New York: Wiley, 1962. Pp. 94–140.

Bond, J.R., & Vinacke, E. Coalitions in mixed-sex trends. *Sociometry,* 1961, 24, 61–75.

Borah, L.A., Jr. The effect of threat in bargaining: Critical and experimental analysis. *Journal of Abnormal and Social Psychology,* 1963, 66, 37–44.

Bronfenbrenner, U. The mirror-image in Soviet–American relations. *Journal of Social Issues,* 1961, 17(3), 45–56.

Coleman, J.S. *Community conflict.* Glencoe, Ill.: Free Press, 1957.

Crow, W.J., & Noel, R.C. The valid use of simulation results. Report, Western Behavioral Sciences Institute, June, 1965. Contract DA-49-146-XZ-110, La Jolla, California.

Crowne, D.P. Family orientation, level of aspiration, and interpersonal bargaining. Paper presented at the meeting of the Eastern Psychological Association, Atlantic City, April 1965.

Daniels, V. Communication, incentive, and structural variables in interpersonal exchange and negotiation. *Journal of Experimental Social Psychology,* 1967, 3, 47–74.

Deutsch, M. The effects of cooperation and competition upon group process. In D. Cartwright & A. Zander (Eds.), *Group Dynamics: Research and Theory.* New York: Harper & Row, 1953. Pp. 319–353.

Deutsch, M. Trust, trustworthiness, and the *F* scale. *Journal of Abnormal and Social Psychology,* 1960, 61, 138–140.

Deutsch, M., Epstein, Y., Canavan, D., & Gumpert, P. Strategies of inducing cooperation: An experimental study. *Journal of Conflict Resolution,* 1967, 11, 345–360.

Dolbear, F.T., Jr., & Lave, L.B. Risk orientation as a predictor in the prisoner's dilemma. *Journal of Conflict Resolution,* 1966, 10, 506–515.

Driver, M.J. A structural analysis of aggression, stress, and personality in an inter-nation simulation. Paper No. 97, January, 1965, Institute for Research in the Behavioral, Economic, and Management Sciences, Purdue University.

Druckman, D. Dogmatism, prenegotiation experience, and simulated group representation as determinants of dyadic behavior in a bargaining situation. *Journal of Personality and Social Psychology,* 1967, 6, 279–290.

Fry, C.L. Personality and acquisition factors in the development of coordination strategy. *Journal of Personality and Social Psychology,* 1965, 2, 403–407.

Fulbright, J.W. We must not fight fire with fire. *New York Times Magazine,* April 23, 1967.

Gahagan, J., Horai, J., Berger, S., & Tedeschi, J. Status and authoritarianism in the prisoner's dilemma game. Paper read at the meeting of the Southeastern Psychological Association, Atlanta, April 1967.

Galtung, J. A model for studying images of participants in a conflict: Southville. *Journal of Social Issues,* 1959, 15(4), 38–43.

Geis, F. Machiavellianism and the manipulation of one's fellow man. Paper presented at the meeting of the American Psychological Association, Los Angeles, September 1964.

Gough, H.G. *Manual for the California psychological inventory.* Palo Alto, Calif.: Consulting Psychologists Press, 1957.

Guetzkow, H., Brody, R.A., Driver, M.J., & Beach, P.F. An experiment on the Nth country problem through inter-nation simulation: Two case-study examples. Northwestern and Princeton Universities, November 1960. (Mimeo.)

Harford, T., & Solomon, L. The effects of game strategies upon interpersonal trust in paranoid schizophrenic samples. Paper presented at the annual meeting of the Eastern Psychological Association, Atlantic City, April 1965.

Harvey, O.J., Hunt, D.E., & Schroder, H.M. *Conceptual systems and personality organization.* New York: Wiley, 1961.

Haythorn, W., & Altman, I. Together in isolation. *Trans-action,* 1967, 4(3), 18–22.

Higgs, W.J., & McGrath, J. E. Social motives and decision-making behavior in interpersonal situations. Technical Report No. 4, September 1965, Air Force Office of Scientific Research Report AF 49 (638)-1291, University of Illinois.

Joseph, M.L., & Willis, R.H. An experimental analogy to two-party bargaining. *Behavioral Science,* 1963, 8, 117–127.

Kanouse, D.E., & Wiest, W.M. Some factors affecting choice in the prisoner's dilemma. *Journal of Conflict Resolution,* 1967, 11, 206–213.

Kelman, H.C. Human use of human subjects: The problem of deception in social psychological experiments. *Psychological Bulletin,* 1967, 67, 1–11.

Knapp, W.M., & Podell, J.E. Mental patients, prisoners, and students with simulated partners in a mixed-motive game. *Journal of Conflict Resolution,* 1968, 12, 235–241.

Komorita, S.S. Cooperative choice in a prisoner's dilemma game. *Journal of Personality and Social Psychology,* 1965, 2, 741–745.

Lake, D.G. Impression formation, Machiavellianism, and interpersonal bargaining. Unpublished doctoral dissertation, Teachers College, Columbia University, 1967.

Lave, L.B. Factors affecting cooperation in the prisoner's dilemma. *Behavioral Science,* 1965, 10, 26–38.

Lumsden, M. Social position and cognitive style in strategic thinking. *Journal of Peace Research,* 1967, 3, 289–303.

Lutzker, D.R. Internationalism as a predictor of cooperative behavior. *Journal of Conflict Resolution,* 1960, 4, 426–430.

Lutzker, D.R. Sex role, cooperation and competition in a two-person, non-zero-sum game. *Journal of Conflict Resolution,* 1961, 5, 366–368.

McClelland, D.C. *The achieving society.* Princeton, N.J.: Van Nostrand, 1961.

McClintock, C.G., Gallo, P., & Harrison, A.A. Some effects of variations in other strategy upon game behavior. *Journal of Personality and Social Psychology,* 1965, 1, 319–325.

McClintock, C.G., Harrison, A.A., Strand, S., & Gallo, P. Internationalism-isolationism, strategy of the other player, and two-person game behavior. *Journal of Abnormal and Social Psychology,* 1963, 67, 631–636.

McClintock, C.G., & McNeel, S.P. Cross cultural comparisons of interpersonal motives. *Sociometry,* 1966, 29, 406–427.

Marlowe, D. Psychological needs and cooperation: Competition in a two-person game. *Psychological Reports,* 1963, 13, 364.

Mitchell, J.V., Jr. An analysis of the factorial dimensions of the achievement motive construct. *Journal of Educational Psychology,* 1961, 52, 179–187.

Nardin, T. Communication and the effects of threat in strategic interaction. Paper presented at the Fifth North American Peace Research Conference, Cambridge, Massachusetts, November 1967.

Oskamp, S., & Perlman, D. Effects of friendship and disliking on cooperation in a mixed-motive game. *Journal of Conflict Resolution,* 1966, **10**, 221–226.

Pilisuk, M., Potter, P., Rapoport, A., & Winter, J.A. War hawks and peace doves: Alternate resolutions of experimental conflicts. *Journal of Conflict Resolution,* 1965, **9**, 491–508.

Pilisuk, M., & Rapoport, A. A non-zero-sum game model of some disarmament problems. *Peace Research Society (International) Papers,* 1964, **1**, 57–78.

Proshansky, H., & Seidenberg, B. *Basic studies in social psychology.* New York: Holt, 1965.

Pruitt, D.G. Reward structure and its effects on cooperation. *Peace Research Society (International) Papers,* 1966, **5**, 73–85.

Pruitt, D.G. Reward structure and cooperation: The decomposed prisoner's dilemma game. *Journal of Personality and Social Psychology,* 1967, **7**, 21–27.

Rapoport, A. Prospects for experimental games. *Journal of Conflict Resolution,* 1968, **12**, 461–470.

Rapoport, A., & Chammah, A.M. Sex differences in factors contributing to the level of cooperation in the prisoner's dilemma game. *Journal of Personality and Social Psychology,* 1965, **2**, 831–838.(a)

Rapoport, A., & Chammah, A.M. *Prisoner's dilemma: A study in conflict and cooperation.* Ann Arbor, Mich.: University of Michigan Press, 1965. (b)

Raser, J.R. Personality characteristics of political decision-makers. A literature review. *Peace Research Society (International) Papers,* 1966, **5**, 161–181.

Raven, B.H., and Leff, W.F. The effects of partner's behavior and culture upon strategy in a two-person game. In R.R. Eifermann (Ed.), *Scripta hierosolymitana.* Vol. 14. Jerusalem: Hebrew University, 1965. Pp 148–165.

Rokeach, M. *The open and closed mind.* New York: Basic Books, 1960.

Rokeach, M. *Beliefs, attitudes, and values.* San Francisco: Jossey-Bass, 1968.

Sampson, E.E., & Kardush, M. Age, sex, class, and race differences in response to a two-person non-zero-sum game. *Journal of Conflict Resolution,* 1965, **9**, 212–220.

Sermat, V. The effect of an initial cooperative or competitive treatment upon a subject's response to conditional cooperation. *Behavioral Science,* 1967, **12**, 301–313.

Sermat, V. Dominance-submissiveness and competition in a mixed-motive game. *British Journal of Social and Clinical Psychology,* 1968, **7**, 35–44.

Sherif, M., Harvey, O.J., White, B.J., Hood, W.R., & Sherif, C.W. *Intergroup conflict and cooperation: The robber's cave experiment.* Norman, Okl.: University of Oklahoma, 1961.

Sherif, M., & Sherif, C.W. Research on intergroup relations. In O. Klineberg & R. Christie (Eds.), *Perspectives in social psychology.* New York: Holt, 1965. Pp. 153–177.

Sherman, R. Individual attitude toward risk and choice between prisoner's dilemma games. *Journal of Psychology,* 1967, **66**, 291–298.

Shomer, R.W., Davis, A.H. & Kelley, H.H. Threats and the development of coordination: Further studies of the Deutsch and Krauss trucking game. *Journal of Personality and Social Psychology,* 1966, **4**, 119–126.

Shure, G.H., & Meeker, R.J. A personality/attitude schedule for use in experimental bargaining studies. Report TM-2543, July 1965, System Development Corporation.

Steele, M.W., & Tedeschi, J.T. Matrix indices and strategy choices in mixed-motive games. *Journal of Conflict Resolution,* 1967, **11**, 198–205.

Swirsky, L.J. Conflict and cooperation on the conflict board: A new mixed motive game. Unpublished doctoral dissertation, Stanford University, 1968.

Tedeschi, J., Lesnick, S., & Gahagan, J. Feedback and "washout" effects in the Prisoner's Dilemma game. *Journal of Personality and Social Psychology,* 1968, 10, 31–34.

Teger, A.I. The effect of early cooperation on the escalation of conflict. Technical Report No. 5, August 1968. ONR Contract No. 0014-67-C-0190, Department of Psychology, State University of New York at Buffalo.

Terhune, K.W. Motives, situation, and interpersonal conflict within prisoner's dilemma. *Journal of Personality and Social Psychology,* 1968, 8(3), Part 2 (Monograph Suppl.).

Terhune, K.W., & Firestone, J.M. Psychological studies in social interaction and motives (SIAM), Phase 2: Group motives in an international relations game. CAL Report VX-2018-G-2, March 1967, Cornell Aeronautical Laboratory, Buffalo, New York.

Travis, E.J. An investigation of the rational decision making, cooperation, greed, punishment, and withdrawal manifested by schizophrenics in several experimental conflict situations. Unpublished doctoral dissertation, University of Michigan, 1965.

Uejio, C.K., & Wrightsman, L.S. Ethnic-group differences in the relationship of trusting attitudes to cooperative behavior. *Psychological Reports,* 1967, 20, 563–571.

Uesugi, T.K., & Vinacke, W.E. Strategy in a feminine game. *Sociometry,* 1963, 26, 75–88.

Vannoy, J.S. Generality of cognitive complexity-simplicity as a personality construct. *Journal of Personality and Social Psychology,* 1965, 2, 385–396.

Vinacke, W.E. Sex roles in a three-person game. *Sociometry,* 1959, 22, 343–360.

Wolowitz, H.M., & Shorkey, C. Power themes in the TAT stories of paranoid schizophrenic males. *Journal of Projective Techniques & Personality Assessment,* 1966, 30, 591–596.

Wrightsman, L.S. Personality and attitudinal correlates of trusting and trustworthy behaviors in a two-person game. *Journal of Personality and Social Psychology,* 1966, 4, 328–382.

Chapter 7

DANGEROUS GAMES

Paul G. Swingle

I. INTRODUCTION

Without theory and an understanding of the dynamic processes of human conflict, the search for methodologies to accomplish peace, conflict resolution, or conflict management is like, as Boulding (1964) maintains, "a game of hide and seek in which we do not quite know what it is we are looking for and in which nobody is able to tell us whether we are getting 'warmer' or 'colder'." Experimental gaming, concerned with human behavior in mixed-motive bargaining situations, provides us with a microscopic view of social conflict and makes salient some of the structural variables which affect the bargaining process.

The findings of experimental gaming situations are not directly applicable to, nor do they directly reflect real life conflict situations, such as the international balance of terror or labor management disputes. The results do, however, provide us with some insight into the existence of structural dimensions in bargaining situations and provide us with an opportunity to develop terms for intellectually manipulating these dimensions toward the development of theory which should, in turn, provide intellectual levers for attempting to explore and understand interpersonal conflict in society at large.

It is disquieting to watch the mixing of different theoretical languages which occurs when theorists attempt to fill the lacuna in our knowledge about the sources and resolutions of society's conflicts. Such theorizing not only crosses the dimensions of bellicosity, but frequently ignores the distinction between the artificial and the real. To suggest that a laboratory bargaining game, for example, has any direct application to disarmament or, on the other hand, that complex international problems may be reduced not only to nonzero-sum games in which there is at least some scope for cooperative settlement, but may also be reduced still further to zero-sum games, has only to be stated to be recognized as unreasonable.

The fact that international conflicts are not pure conflict but rather nonzero-sum in character has been emphasized by many theorists inside as well as outside of government (e.g., Boulding, 1957; Coser, 1956; Hilsman, 1967; Schelling, 1963). Disagreement also exists among laboratory researchers regarding the psychological nature of the variables being studied which are labeled "weapons," "threats," etc. (e.g., Deutsch & Krauss, 1962; Kelley, 1965; Schelling, 1963). In addition, the effects of the use or even simply the availability of a punishing capability in laboratory bargaining games are so highly dependent upon the structure of the situation in which bargainers find themselves (e.g., Deutsch, Epstein, Canavan, & Gumpert, 1967; Kelley, 1965; Froman & Cohen, 1969; Geiwitz & Fisher, 1969; Komorita, Sheposh, & Braver, 1968) that generalization from the microcosm to the macrocosm must take the form of a search for common structural properties in conflict situations and the corresponding development of theory. Perhaps even this is unrealistically optimistic when one considers the disquieting semantic confusion evident in the conflict literature (Fink, 1968) and the fragility of what little theory experimental gamers have to offer.

II. THE STRUCTURE OF CHICKEN

The present chapter is an attempt to analyze some of the structural variables which distinguish dangerous games such as chicken from other types of interpersonal confrontation in which bargaining is necessary. There will be frequent references to the international situation. However, the reader is warned that the writer has installed an intellectual diode which permits the borrowing of analogies from real conflict situations for the purpose of explicating or making salient a structural variable under consideration but does not permit transfers in the opposite direction.

Basically a dangerous game, such as chicken, forces a protagonist to expose himself to risk of loss (usually substantial loss) in order to threaten his opponent. That is, although threat may be expressed unilaterally, punishment is always bilateral. Dangerous games or situations are prevalent in our society as threat of significant mutual loss is not infrequently associated with unresolved conflicts. The game of chicken as played by teenagers in their automobiles is a good example, as is two nations threatening one another with thermonuclear destruction.

The dangerous aspect of a game derives from the relationship between goal-directed behavior and threatening behavior. The most dangerous of games are those in which goal-directed behavior and threatening behavior are completely conjoined, that is, situations in which one protagonist's approaching the goal has the dual effect of increasing the probability of his obtaining the goal but also increasing the probability of substantial mutual loss.

From a structural point of view, the game of chicken played by teenagers in their automobiles is the most dangerous of games, more dangerous, in fact, than two nations threatening one another with thermonuclear destruction. In the automobile variety of the game of chicken, goal-directed behavior and threatening behavior are always completely conjoined, which may not be true of the goal directed and threatening behavior of two nations.

One critical variable distinguishing games of chicken from other bargaining situations is the punishment associated with deadlock, which is bilateral punishment. Punishment which affects only one member of the bargaining dyad is not usually characteristic of the chicken-type confrontation but rather usually characterizes situations in which one protagonist attempts to manipulate his opponent by means of superior force or, if weaker, by means of appealing to the opponent's sense of guilt, shame, or pity.

Consider, for example, two desperately hungry mountain climbers scaling a steep precipice who, at the same moment, see a chocolate bar which is equally distant from both climbers. Given the above situation, if the climbers are not tied together in the usual fashion, no threats or appeals could be made by either climber which would give the situation the structural characteristics of the game of chicken. Neither one climber's threat to jump to his certain death unless he obtains all of the chocolate bar, nor one climber's threat to push the other climber to his certain death (assuming he could do so) would characterize a chicken-type confrontation. To make this situation into a game of chicken, one need only tie the two protagonists together. Once the two climbers are linked in this fashion any threat takes the form of "If I don't get what I want, we're both going over the edge." In short, threat may be expressed unilaterally, but punishment is always bilateral in chicken-type confrontations.

It is also immediately apparent that although one outcome is of necessity bilateral in that if one climber falls, jumps, or is pushed, the other climber also falls to his death, this does not imply that all negative outcomes must be symmetrical in chicken-type confrontations. For example, if one climber "chickens-out" (i.e., allows the opponent unchallenged access to the chocolate bar), the victor eats the entire chocolate bar which results in one protagonist's having a positive outcome and the other, presumably, a negative or zero outcome.

Second, the other important characteristic of chicken-type confrontation is that either protagonist is better off being a chicken than suffering the punishment associated with deadlock. In a preemption game, one subject's firm commitment to noncooperation leaves the opponent with a choice of yielding or resisting, the latter of which results in severe mutual punishment.

As a point of departure consider the simplest form of the game of chicken represented by the 2 X 2 game matrix shown in Fig. 1.

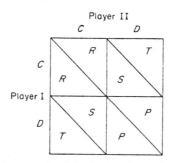

FIG. 1. An example of the simplest form of the game of chicken.

Rappoport and Chammah (1966) define a game of chicken as one which satisfies the following equations:

$$T > R > S > P \tag{1}$$

$$2R > S + T. \tag{2}$$

The simple 2 X 2 game of chicken shown in Fig. 1, although hardly representative of most actual high risk dangerous confrontations in real life, does provide a theoretical lever to help sort out some of the structural parameters of more complex situations. It seems fairly straight-forward to say that as R increases, assuming symmetry again, the proportion of C response in the dyad will increase because the self-interest of each player happens to be coincident. Raising the value of T increases the temptation for each player to preempt in an attempt to gain a larger payoff, whereas the smaller the value of S (the chicken's payoff) the less likely that unilateral cooperation will occur. Finally, the smaller the value of P (i.e., the greater the punishment), the greater is the deterrent value and, presumably, the greater the level of cooperation due to mutual desire to avoid the disastrous outcome. The evidence indicates, however, that the relationship between the magnitude of the punishment and the frequency of cooperative behavior is by no means linear or monotonic.

The matrix form of the game of chicken then is a mixed-motive situation in which the C response may be considered a cooperative, appeasing, or prudent response. The C response may be made primarily for the motive of increasing mutual joint payoff (cooperative). Choice C may also indicate appeasement in that if one player has reason to believe that the opponent has made or intends to make the D response, giving in to the opponent is the only alternative that minimizes that player's losses or maximizes his gains. Finally it may be considered the prudent response in the sense that, in the absence of any information about the opponent's intentions, a player can minimize his maximum loss by making response C.

The motive associated with making the D response is less equivocal. Assuming that the player is strategically rational, making the D response is an attempt to obtain the large payoff indicated in Fig. 1 by the letter T. The strategy associated with making the D response is usually based upon the assumption of either deterrence or appeasement. That is, if player 2 knows that player 1 has made response D, his best, and in most situations, his only response is C, that is, appeasement. In the absence of any foreknowledge of an opponent's response, either player might reasonably assume that his opponent will avoid the D response. Should either player feel safe in this assumption, he may be tempted to preempt, which if successful puts the second player in the situation of having to punish himself severely in order to punish his opponent. Dependence upon severe mutual punishment to discourage the opponent's reciprocating the D response is referred to as offensive deterrence.

Referring to Fig. 1, the structural feature which is primarily responsible for giving a game the character of a chicken-type confrontation is the severity of punishment as indicated by the letter P in the figure. As the severity of the punishment increases, the entire game changes in that, as Deutsch (1966) has maintained, the meaning of yielding is different when a person is confronted with threat than when he is not so confronted. Although as punishment increases, yielding (accepting the S payoff) becomes objectively more attractive since one gains more by avoiding P. Accepting involves a greater loss of social face in that the opponent may consider one as lacking courage. In other words, as the severity of the punishment increases, face saving motives emerge in greater strength.

It is important to note that the structural relationship which characterizes a situation as a game of chicken involves a different structural dimension from that which gives the situation the properties of a "dangerous" game. The dangerous structural aspect of a game is the relationship between goal-directed behavior and threat or punishment. Can the protagonists enjoy maximum joint payoff without flirting with disaster? In short, is there any scope in the bargaining situation for totally avoiding the potentially disastrous course of action, without reducing the joint payoff to both protagonists? Consider the automobile form of the game of chicken represented in matrix form. For the purposes of this example assume that the game is being played by young plutocrats with their fathers' brand new automobiles. The speeds of the cars have been limited to 10 mph such that deadlock results not in death or serious injury, but rather in damaged automobiles and the wrath of the fathers. In short, a *DD* outcome does not preclude repetition of the game. Although reducing the

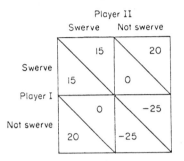

FIG. 2. A situation in which mutual avoidance of *D* maximizes the joint payoff to the dyad. The game is chicken.

game to matrix form does serious injustice to the game due to the fact that expanded response dimensions have been reduced to "Yes" or "No" alternatives, the distinction between the properties of the situation which give the game its "chicken" character and those properties which give the game its dangerous character become clear. Increasing the severity of the punishment (*P*) in the situation has the effect of increasing the relative attractiveness of the chicken's payoff (*S*). Eventually as *P* decreases, *S* will become greater than *P*, such that either player may receive a larger payoff by yielding to an opponent who has made or will make the *D* response. The only purpose of making *D* responses when the opponent makes the *D* response is to persuade the opponent, by inflicting mutual punishment, to cease making *D* responses in the future. The matrix shown in Fig. 2 represents a situation in which mutual avoidance of *D* maximizes the joint payoff to the dyad.

   If we assume, however, that both drivers swerving (a *CC* outcome) does not result in the highest joint payoff, cooperative alternation (i.e., *CD* alternating with *DC*) is the only method by which protagonists can maximize joint payoff. This means, of course, that they must coordinate their responses so as never to end up with the *DD* outcome. Such a situation is represented by the matrix shown in Fig. 3. If the game is limited to one trial, the situation becomes dangerous indeed, as cooperative settlement is precluded. Thus, the game of chicken is characterized by situations in which $S > P$, danger increasing (at any constant level of *P*) as $S + T > 2R$.

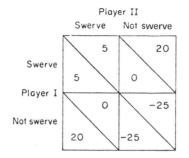

FIG. 3. Game of chicken in which cooperative alternation is the only method by which protagonists can maximize joint payoff.

The number of trials of play, then, is a critical factor in dangerous game situations. It is obvious that in the type of game shown in Fig. 3, knowledge of the fact that more than one trial is involved changes the whole character of the situation. In the one trial game, no mutually satisfactory outcome is available and a similar argument could be offered for an odd number of trials. As the number of expected repetitions of the game increases, the less critical is each individual trial.

No such dilemma exists for the game shown in Fig. 2. Although one might argue that the "subjective value" of receiving the highest available payoff is greater in single confrontation situations than in situations involving many trials, the fact remains that the *CC* outcome is a satisfactory result in a one trial game of the type shown in Fig. 2.

Repetition is also importantly related to the symmetry of punishment in the dangerous game. Although in most matrix gaming studies, $P = P$, it can be argued that P need not equal P in games of chicken. In single trial games, it is not necessary for the punishment to be equal as credibility of an opponent's threat is what influences players to yield. As Schelling (1963) states, "it is not necessary . . . that the threat promise more (*or equal*) damage to the party threatened than to the party carrying it out. The threat to smash an old car with a new one may succeed if believed . . . [p. 36 (italics added)] ."

As the number of trials increases, however, symmetry of the punishment associated with deadlock becomes more important. Over a large number of trials, inequalities in P change the character of the game to a war of attrition in which the wealthiest player must win. Just as the martingale system of doubling the size of one's bet subsequent to each loss when playing red or black in roulette is impotent when a house limit exists or when one's funds are limited, persistant exchanges of mutually destructive or harmful outcomes is tantamount to a game of attrition and the player with the greatest resources will emerge victorious. If punishment is unequal (given initially equal resources), the player suffering the greatest loss on each trial must lose if the conflict continues until resources are exhausted.

Actually one may argue that asymmetry only affects threat credibility in that the player with the more limited resources or suffering the more severe loss on each trial cannot hold out as long as his opponent, if the former goes to the limit of his resources. However, the threat to go the limit by the player with restricted resources may be sufficient to force the opponent to yield if the latter believes the former's threat to exhaust available resources in the conflict. If the threat is credible, the objective winner of any prolonged conflict is better off yielding and thereby minimizing his losses unless, of course, such losses could be recouped after one player is defeated.

A parallel is found in Kissinger's assessment (1960) of why the US did not interfere in Hungary even though the US was at the time militarily vastly superior to the Soviet Union. The US was deterred because the Soviet Union was convincing that it would run all risks to prevent intervention. Threat of defeat, therefore, did not deter intervention, but rather the probably unacceptable "price of victory."

The ratio of the payoffs to both players for unilateral cooperation is also an important source of conflict in bargaining situations. Rapoport and Chammah report (1965), for example, that as the difference between the T and the S payoff increases in the Prisoner's Dilemma game (PDG), the frequency of cooperative choice decreases. Ells and Sermat (1966), using games of the chicken type (all of which violated at least one formal property of chicken), also found that the $T–S$ difference influences cooperative behavior; increasing T has a greater effect than decreasing S when by increasing $T, R < T$. That is, when the increase in payoff for unilateral preemption results in $R<T$, the differential gain motive increases in strength with the result that C responding decreases. Increases in S, on the other hand, reduce the risk associated with C responding, which in turn enhances the level of C responding. Thus, as S approaches R, cooperation increases; as T exceeds R, cooperation decreases, and as the $T–S$ difference increases, cooperation decreases.

Swingle (1967), using a dangerous game situation which has no provision for CC type responding, found that the "win–loss" ratio (i.e., largest to smallest payoff) is curvilinearly related to the level of conflict in a game in which miscalculation or executed threat is very costly to both protagonists. This experiment involved simply increasing the T payoff while keeping the S payoff fixed at 1 unit. The level of conflict as evidenced by the overall level of mutually punishing responses, first occurrence of cooperative gestures (concession) and first occurence of a nonbelligerent settlement, was maximal at the midrange of the win–loss difference (5–1). Larger ratios (i.e., 10–1 and 15–1) resulted in more rapid establishment of cooperative responding. The data suggest that at low win–loss ratios, the prize at stake on any single trial is not sufficient to risk substantial loss, whereas at high ratios, the single trial payoff is too large to assume that the opponent will be appeasing, and hence the need to cooperate is salient to both players. In addition, the meaning of attempted dominance changes, as does the meaning of yielding when threat and the prize at stake increase. At low win–loss ratios, a show of bravado for a trivial advantage at a given level of threat suggests a fool, whereas yielding is indicative of reason. Kateb's suggestion (1966) that Krushchev's yielding during the Cuban missile crisis resulted in his emerging as the "champion of rationality" is consistent with the above notion, if one accepts the opinion of those who maintained that no change or a trivial change in the military balance of power would result from the missile placement or subsequent removal. At high win–loss ratios, attempts to dominate are met by resistance as yielding results in too great a loss of both payoff and social face.

One must avoid destroying the opponent lest one destroy oneself, an important consideration in most repeated-trial dangerous games. The labor strike is the classic example of a situation in which "familial" considerations are important. If either side holds out too long, both lose everything including the opportunity to play the game again. In single-trial dangerous games, the situation is exactly the reverse in that no compromise is possible. Failure to recognize the "familial" relationship between protagonists is one of the criticisms of "strategic thinking (Rapoport, 1964a,b; 1966)" of the "civilian militarists (Horowitz, 1963)." Complex international situations which are obviously nonzero-sum in character (i.e., compromise is possible) are reduced, for the purpose of analysis, not only to artificial (but perhaps representative) nonzero-sum matrices but are further reduced to zero-sum form which precludes cooperative settlement. Such zero-sum models are not only oversimplifications of complex situations but are actually misrepresentations. Just as the growing need to maintain face accompanies increasing levels of punishment, an important motive not usually represented by the payoff estimates, the need to preserve a rational opponent (as well as oneself) is essential if the game, indeed, if any game, is to be played again. One need only browse through the literature on deterrence to find many examples of "countercity negotiation," "negotiatory blows," "city trading," etc., which refer to thermonuclear "knockouts" of one US city and one USSR city, often being considered for the purposes of analysis as a zero payoff outcome (i.e., neither side won or lost).

The striking similarity between children's behavior in conflict situations (i.e., the tendency to resort to violence and deterrence) and international relations has also been pointed out by Boulding (1963). Boulding suggests that violence erupts because of a restricted behavioral repertoire resulting from a failure to recognize the necessity of maintaining a not too unhappy opponent. That is, given that a peaceful other is always preferable to a warlike other, the handling of conflict should take the form of rhetoric directed toward establishing the legitimacy of claims to the resources in question. Unfortunately, children and heads of state find it difficult to develop the long-sightedness necessary to suppress violent eruptions.

The most obvious question which might be asked in relation to highly dangerous games such as "chicken" is quite simply, "Why are they played?" It is not too difficult to understand why teenage males play such incredibly dangerous games. In many teenage subcultures, courage, manliness, and "guts" are highly valued characteristics in that persons assessed to possess these characteristics have greater access to the valuable resources in the group, such as females, protection, status, and admiration. Many games of chicken in such situations, then, may be considered ritualized methods for determining the proper ranking of the male members of the group. A player after a very daring performance enjoys a certain insulation in the sense that he will receive far fewer challenges. The mythology that a player is able to build up, therefore, is a source of strength due to the fact that it affects the credibility of his threat. In short, in the game of chicken you are what your opponent thinks you are.

Many will recognize this as exactly the same statement offered by President Kennedy to justify his handling of the Cuban missiles situation. Although, perhaps understandable in teenagers, comparable motives for playing far more dangerous games on the part of heads of state has quite a peculiar reaction on passive participants. Once it is realized that enormous risks are accepted for the purpose of maintaining prestige, face, and credibility, the passive players in the situation tend to have one of two types of reactions: (1) horror and disbelief, or (2) identification with the principal game player on one side, feeling that only the other side is reprehensible for playing such an incredibly dangerous game. This latter belief is usually coupled with the notion that the opposition is incorrigible and must be constantly threatened with severe punishment to deter his disturbing status quo. Heads of state may readily admit that they are accepting very large risks for what appear to be, in the first instance, trivial motives, but maintain that they are forced into such a position by the opposition due to the fact that when the ability to punish is highly developed and mutual, the individual most indifferent to the punishment enjoys a strategic advantage. The simple answer to the question "Why do heads of state play such an enormously dangerous game?" then, may simply be that the structure of the situation forces them to play the game. That is, as Deutsch maintains (1966), the availability of a punishing response encourages the threat to use such a response, so nations possessing unthinkable weapons are encouraged to threaten the use of such weapons for the purpose of establishing a bargaining advantage.

III. DETERRENCE

The availability of threat has a very peculiar reaction upon pro   ꞁnists involved in bargaining situations in that even if the structure of the situation is such that there are substantial areas for mutual cooperation, the existence of the threat encourages the opponents to issue warnings regarding reprisals for the use of threat. This leads to a spreading of threats and counterthreats which results in the paradox that both parties to the conflict may truly desire to cooperate and enjoy maximum joint outcome, but the existence of threat focuses the attention of the protagonist upon considerations of offense and defense as opposed to cooperation (Lieberman, 1964).

Deterrence is based upon the assumption that if one threatens to punish an opponent, the opponent's tendency to be disruptive is inhibited. It is also assumed that the greater the punishment, the greater the deterrent value. Although the simple-minded notion that the greater the cost the greater the deterrent value has been offered to justify such diverse practices as the heavy taxes of alcohol, hanging pickpockets, and the spending of tens of billions of dollars annually for the development and production of thermonuclear weapons and delivery systems, it has become quite clear that the relationship between the magnitude of punishment and deterrence is by no means linear and may not even be monotonic. Increasing punishment has the effect of focusing the protagonist's attention upon threat and counterthreat activity as opposed to cooperation with the result that the level of conflict remains high.

One of the problems with deterrent threat ideology is that it encourages attempts to deter what an opponent may have no intention of doing anyway. This establishes a cycle in that such threats are interpreted as attempts to limit freedom which give rise to resentment, counteraccusation, counterthreat, and provoke the opponent to do what he had no intention of doing simply to demonstrate that his freedom has not been limited.

The whole notion of deterrence is based upon the notion that if one can deliver a completely intolerable retaliatory blow at any attempt by the opponent to seriously disturb the status quo, such activity will be inhibited. Deterrence, then, depends upon the power to inflict severe punishment upon an opponent, whereas defence typically refers to the ability to prevent the enemy from inflicting punishment upon oneself. It should be noted again that deterrent threat may be used by either party to the conflict. It may be exploited by the party attempting to defend the status quo or the party attempting to change the status quo. Offensive deterrence takes the form of creating a credible threat to deliver a completely intolerable blow as a counterretaliatory strike. Thus, defensive deterrence (i.e., the threat of a defensive retaliatory strike) is itself deterred by the threat of an unacceptable counterretaliatory strike.

Capability to destroy may derive its deterrent value either objectively or subjectively. Referring again to the international situation, this distinction relates to the targeting of missiles. For example, one nation's capability to destroy the opposing nation's retaliatory capability or first strike capability would be referred to as objective or mechanistic (Kybal, 1961) deterrence, since it prevents an opponent from launching a strike of any nature. This is referred to in the strategic literature as counterforce targeting. The alternative form of deterrence which might be referred to as subjective deterrence, referred to in the literature as countervalue targeting, refers to the capability to destroy nonmilitary targets (i.e., the population and the economy). It is an effective deterrent only so long as a potential attacker chooses to avoid such destruction. The effectiveness of subjective deterrence depends upon rationality, a quality of mind rather than a mathematical fact (Kybal, 1961).

When the ability to destroy countervalue targets is highly developed between both parties to a conflict, a balance of terror exists when neither can strike first without receiving a completely intolerable retaliatory blow in return. Counterforce capability can disturb the balance when one power can, by striking first, eliminate all but a tolerable portion of the opponent's capacity to strike back (Snyder, 1961). When either side's retaliatory forces are rendered vulnerable due to improved counterforce targeting—technology or reliance upon vulnerable first-strike-only weapons (such as the Jupiter missiles the US had in Turkey)—the balance is destabilized. Several nuclear strategists have claimed, however, that the US should maintain a significant first-strike capability to prevent the opposition from behaving recklessly.

When one's ability to punish the opponent would be drastically reduced by an opponent's attack, the need to strike first or very close second is a serious aggravating factor. Vulnerability of the deterrent weapons increases the danger of both unintended attacks (i.e., responding to false alarms due to time pressures) and intended attacks (i.e., if war is imminent, to launch a preemptive or preventative strike). When weapons systems are less vulnerable, the amount of time opponents have to respond to each other's actions increases, thus reducing the probability of irrational or unintended attacks. Second, reduced vulnerability reduces or removes the inducement to launch a first strike. Even if neither opponent has any intention of striking first, the vulnerability of his retaliatory capabilities leads him to recognize the necessity of launching the attack first, if in fact weapons are to be used. Due to the fact that there is a tendency to attribute one's own motives and conclusions to an opponent in bargaining situations, one opponent cannot but become convinced that the other is coming to the same conclusion with the result that a possibility of hostility is converted into an anticipation of hostility which precipitates hostility.

Although there is little evidence as yet, it is not unreasonable to assume that increasing the magnitude of the punishment in a chicken-type confrontation would have the effect of encouraging premeditated, preventive, or preemptive attacks. A study by Pilisuk and Skolnick (1970) using a modification of the Prisoner's Dilemma game with provisions for surprise attacks and inspections designed to simulate the arms race reported "an unhappy tendency to engage in preemptive surprise attacks, out of fear of the adversary, even when there was virtually no chance of success of such an attack." It is not unreasonable to assume that increasing the severity of the punishment available to both adversaries should increase the level of fear resulting in an increased tendency to engage in premeditated attacks up to the point at which any attack results in certain bilateral destruction.

IV. THE POWER TO DESTROY

The effects of the availability of punishing capability in bargaining situations is not at all clear. If threat is used for the signaling of intentions, cooperation is usually established more rapidly (Kelley, 1965). Executed threat, however, tends to have a detrimental effect upon cooperation (Deutsch *et al.,* 1967; Geiwitz & Fisher, 1969). It should be recalled that executed threat is unsuccessful threat. A labor strike which is called, ICBM's that head for their targets, automobiles that receive damage resulting from deadlock, etc., are all indicative of unsuccessful threat. It is not unreasonable to assume, therefore, that the use of punishment in bargaining situations is not necessarily detrimental to the establishment of cooperation, but rather is indicative of a breakdown in the negotiation process related, but not causatively, to a conjunctive breakdown in cooperation. Punishing capabilities held in abeyance have been reported to increase the effectiveness of cooperative intention messages, suggesting that the availability of threat is more important than its use (Geiwitz & Fisher, 1969). The effect of the simple existence of punishment capability, however, is not at all clear. Some have reported that availability enhances cooperation (e.g., Geiwitz, 1967); others report no effect (e.g., Komorita *et al.,* 1968), which leads one to agree with Geiwitz and Fisher (1969) that the effects of the availability and use of punishment capability are highly dependent on the structure of the situation.

Referring to the figures, it is interesting to consider the effects of increasing the punishment associated with bilateral defection or preemption. Intuitively, it would seem to make sense that the less severe the punishment associated with bilateral defection, the greater will be the temptation to attempt to exploit the opponent by responding to his cooperative gestures with defection. One might also expect a greater tendency for dyads to lock-in on the mutually punishing outcome (*DD*) at lower levels of punishment. The *DD* lock-in is not unusual in games such as the PDG. As the punishment associated with deadlock increases, however, one might expect bargainers to avoid preemptive responding, fearful of the very large risks associated with such a response.

The literature suggests that there are several consequences of increased punishment associated with mutual noncooperation. As punishment increases, protagonists tend to depend upon deterrence which takes the form of threats *not* to avoid the mutually disastrous outcome. In addition, as the severity of the punishment increases, the probability of successfully blackmailing the opponent increases, if one can get a slight edge. This in turn gives rise to a striking advantage going to the first player who is able to make a preemptive response, making known, of course, the fact that he has preempted. The magnitude of the punishment also affects the credibility of the threat of the use of the punishing response. That is, if the punishment, particularly bilateral punishment, is extremely severe, an opponent may not believe a threat to use such punishment due to the fact that it is not in the interests of the threatener to execute the threat at any time. This, in turn, gives rise to a policy of encroachment in which each infraction is not large enough to justify execution of the threat. Finally, and most importantly, severe threat tends to put a premium upon antagonists acting as though they are irrational, since the appearance of irrationality increases the credibility that the threat might actually be executed. Each one of the above consequences of increase of bilateral destructive power will be discussed in greater detail in the following sections.

One study which addressed itself to the effects of increasing the magnitude of the punishment associated with the deadlock was conducted by Rapoport and Chammah (1966) in which the punishment (P) was varied from -3 to -40 payoff units, whereas the mutually cooperative payoff was $+1$ unit for each player. The results of this study indicate that the relationship between punishment and deterrence, as evidenced by cooperative responding, is by no means linear or monotonic. That is, percent cooperative responding and percent cooperative lock-ins increase as punishment increases at both low levels and high levels of punishment, but dip in the center. This effect maintained for both male and female dyads and was observed in a number of different measures such as the percent cooperative responding and the frequency of CC and DD outcomes. The reduced level of cooperative outcomes appeared to be due almost entirely to an increased tendency on the part of both males and females to preempt, that is, defect from a CC outcome at moderate levels of punishment. In the female dyads, the reduced frequency of cooperative choice seemed to result principally from their reduced tendency to respond cooperatively to cooperative gestures of the opponent. It is also noted that skewness (persistence of appeasement respond-ing) tends to increase as the magnitude of P increases which indicates that retaliation for preemption becomes more difficult as the mutual punishment increases. In chicken-type games, the frequency of observed C responding is higher than in the PDG which seems to be due primarily to increases in the asymmetrical outcomes, CD and DC, indicating an avoidance of the DD outcome. It is also reported that the conditional frequencies for forgiveness (a C response following CD outcome), repentance (C following DC), and trust (C

following *DD*) are higher in the chicken matrix than in the PDG for both men and women, which again indicates that there is a strong pressure to escape from the larger punishment associated with mutual deadlock in the game of chicken.

One of the most interesting findings is that in the game of chicken the magnitude of punishment for mutual deadlock appears to be a more effective deterrent than the certainty of the punishment. The findings indicate a greater frequency of repentance in the game of chicken. The potential retaliator hesitates to use the punishing response in the chicken game due to the large punishment that he must expose himself to. Even though subjects enjoy greater reinforcement for *D* responding in chicken (retaliation is less certain), there seems to be a greater tendency on the part of the players to stop misbehaving (to stop *D* responding) in the game of chicken than in the PDG, presumably resulting from fear of more severe but less certain punishment. Thus, severe punishment seems to be more effective than certain punishment.

A second study on the effects of various magnitudes of threat and punishment is reported by Hornstein (1965). Hornstein made use of a bargaining situation which has some features of chicken-type confrontations in that there was an imposed time limit. If no agreement was reached within the time limit, neither player received any points (no money was involved in this study). The threat potential available to subjects was either equal or unequal and varied from weak (reduction of 10% of the other player's profits) up to very severe (90% reduction in the opponent's profit). In the equal power dyads, the results indicated a curvilinear relationship between the frequency of threat initiation and magnitude of punishing power. A similar curvilinear relationship was also reported between the execution of the threat and magnitude of punishing power. Hornstein argues that very large punishment may be considered too severe to use, whereas weak punishment may be considered too insignificant to be used as a successful deterrent threat. Bargainers in the middle ranges (50% reduction in opponent's profits) were in a position in which the punishment was not too powerful to preclude use, nor too insignificant to be deemed ineffective. This group was, therefore, tempted to threaten to use the punishment both to deter and to retaliate.

One of the most interesting findings in Hornstein's study was that when threat potential was not equally distributed, the frequency of threat initiation by the weaker bargainer is curvilinearly related to the magnitude of the difference in threat potential between the powerful and the weak bargainer, that is, fewer threat initiations at the middle ranges than at the extremes. It is possible that a weaker bargainer was encouraged to initiate more threats when the discrepancy between power was great, due to the fact that he anticipated the stronger bargainer to be reticent about executing such a massively punitive response in retaliation for a trivial threat. The data on the frequency of execution of the threat supports the notion that subjects who only have massive retaliatory force available to them will hesitate in the use of such force. In the unequal power distribution conditions, the stronger bargainer executed the threat far less frequently when the disparity was great than when it was moderate or low. This suggests that when a protagonist must rely upon a single massively punishing response, he is relatively helpless against a strategy of escalation. One hesitates to use punishment which is too severe for the crime and when such punishment is bilateral, one can never rationally punish an opponent's minor infractions.

Hesitancy to exercise power, either unilateral or bilateral, may encourage exploitative behavior by an opponent. There is an increasing amount of evidence coming from game research which indicates that unreserved cooperation in situations in which threat is available invites exploitation. Solomon (1960), for example, found that when subjects were involved in the PDG, significantly greater exploitation (subject increases own payoff at partner's expense) was obtained when the simulated partner was unconditionally cooperative than when the partner's cooperation was conditional. Similar results are reported by Bixenstine and Wilson (1963) who found that initially highly cooperative partners fared less well than initially uncooperative partners.

Tendency to exploit partners whose strategies should presumably be perceived as well intentioned is further supported by the studies of Bixenstine, Potash, and Wilson (1963) and McClintock, Harrison, Strand, and Gallo (1963) who report that highly cooperative partners (83% and 85% cooperative choice, respectively) do not result in any greater cooperative choice by the subject than when the partner is highly uncooperative.

Several hypotheses have been advanced to account for this phenomenon, all of which revolve around the central notion that subjects expect partners to respond guardedly in bargaining situations which involve risk of exploitation. When their opponent's strategy does not indicate the expected caution or self-interest, subjects perceive the partner as intending to trick them or, conversely, as not understanding the purpose nor the mechanics of the game situation. Perceived in this way, the partner's cooperative behavior is responded to with enhanced caution or exploitation on the part of the subject.

A study by Shure, Meeker, and Hansford (1965) leads one to suspect that the crucial factor which increases the subject's exploitative behavior is the opponent's disuse of available power. They had subjects involved in a game situation in which the partner was a simulated pacifist. The game situation was structured so that the subject could continually dominate the situation and receive the lion's share of the payoff if he chose not to reciprocate the pacifist's initial cooperative gestures. The pacifist, although he had a "violent" means (electric shock) at his disposal, never used it but rather made his claim to a fair division of the payoff by blocking the subject's goal responses and forcing the subject to use his violent means to acquire the payoff.

Several different conditions were included in the above study in an attempt to enhance the effectiveness of the pacifist's attempts to establish cooperation. The pacifist's nonviolent intentions were communicated to the subject, the pacifist's background (i.e., a Quaker morally committed to nonviolence) was communicated, and the pacifist, in one condition, even disarmed himself to guarantee no reprisal. The results were clear: The pacifist's strategy *enhanced* the subject's exploitative behavior. Neither clarification of the pacifist's intentions nor disarmament were effective in increasing the total number of subjects who cooperated. It is also interesting to note that the subject's opinion of the pacifist was more positive after receiving the additional information with respect to the pacifist's intentions and moral commitments. which indicates that the exploitation results from the partner's strategy and not from any misconception of the pacifist's intent nor any disliking resulting from subject's perceiving pacifism as weakness.

It is possible that a contributing cause for this unhappy tendency may be that the severe punishment available to one player reduces the credibility that he will in fact use the punishing response. That is, power encourages challenges to power based upon the supposition that an opponent with a powerful option will be disinclined to execute the punishing response, if he has initiated the interaction in a conciliatory fashion. Studies in the author's laboratory have indicated that subjects tend to exploit powerful opponents who are unconditionally cooperative (i.e., 98% cooperative) more than they exploit equally powerful opponents. Unconditionally cooperative weak opponents are exploited least of all. Slight reductions in the level of cooperative behavior (i.e., 94% cooperative) tend to reduce the frequency of noncooperative responding when the opponent is in power and increase the level of noncooperative responding when the subject is in power. When the opponent is conditionally cooperative (i.e., tit-for-tat), subjects confronted with a powerful opponent quickly reduce their level of noncooperative responding, whereas subjects confronted with a weak opponent maintain a high level of exploitative behavior. Subjects in the equal power condition demonstrate the usual reduction in frequency of noncooperative behavior when confronted with a conditionally cooperative opponent.

The tendency to exploit unconditionally cooperative opponents is also found in games of chicken. Sermat (1964), for example, found that subjects are more uncooperative when the opponent is 100% cooperative than when he is 0% cooperative, a tendency which increases as the subjects gain evidence that the opponent will not retaliate. This result was replicated by the present author with the opponent's unconditional strategy set at 90% cooperation. Since people expect other people to behave with restraint in the use of punishing capabilities, particularly when such punishment is bilateral, the greater the severity of the punishment, the less credible is the threat.

The tendency to exploit unreservedly cooperative but powerful opponents may simply reflect an increase in exploitive behavior resulting from perceived reduced risk. That is, very powerful opponents who are initially cooperative may be considered less likely to use their punishing capabilities than are less powerful opponents. Kissinger's discussion of the "nuclear age dilemma" (1957) is based upon a similar notion: "The greater the power, the greater the inhibitions against using it except in the most dire emergencies." This in turn reduces the probability that any encroachment will be deemed important enough to risk the use of the power and the "smaller the risks, the more likely they are to be accepted" by the preemptor.

It is interesting to note that the structure of the situation may place protagonists in the position of having only massive retaliatory potential. Even though protagonists have no intention of using massive punitive power, nonuse of capability at minor infringements may lead to overconfidence that a highly destructive capability would not be used, when, in fact, the triggering process may be a threshold phenomenon. Nonuse of massive retaliatory capabilities at low levels of infringement might also simply reflect ignorance of the infringement. In short, being caught in the dilemma of having only a few response alternatives available, those perceived to be conciliatory and those perceived to be highly destructive, may put the protagonist in the unhappy position of encouraging exploitative or disruptive behavior due to an unwillingness to make use of highly punishing capabilities.

One study which directly manipulated the precision of power available in a two-person bargaining situation is reported by Smith and Leginski (1968). Subjects in this study were provided with a punishing response which was either flexible (precise) in that level of punishment, up to the limit available, was up to the discretion of the punisher, or imprecise in that the punisher could only choose to administer the full punishing magnitude available (i.e., a punish or not punish option). High precision subjects increase the frequency of threat with increasing magnitude of power, whereas subjects with inflexible power decrease the frequency of threat with greater power. Low precision subjects punish less frequently and are less likely to follow threat with punishment as compared with high precision subjects. This suggests that one effect of increased magnitude of available power when not flexible is to reduce the willingness to use the capability and hence adversely affect threat credibility.

Unfortunately, a highly cooperative strategy by an extremely powerful protagonist may not be viewed as a desire to cooperate but rather as hesitancy resulting from fear (or perhaps guilt) of the effects of the use of available power. An opponent perceived as hesitant to use power may be exploited or blackmailed since the potent punishment has, due to reduced credibility of use, lost its value as a deterrent. Magnitude of punishment, then, affects the credibility of the use of the punishment, whether the punishment is unilateral or bilateral. When the punishment is in fact bilateral, a policy of massive retaliation has only to be stated to be recognized as ridiculous and completely without credibility. It is extremely difficult to establish a credible threat in a situation involving the infliction of severe mutual punishment that neither protagonist has any intention, nor the incentive, to carry out either before or after the occurrence of the event the threat was designed to deter. As Kissinger (1957) notes, "massive retaliation strategy is rather like threatening suicide to prevent eventual death." The more severe the punishment, the less credible is the threat of the deterrer. The policy of massive retaliation is, of course, impotent against a policy of escalation, due to the fact that a rational threatener naturally hesitates to execute the threat for minor infractions (Etzioni, 1962). Unchallenged minor encroachments then in turn invite further infractions. The policy is not only foolish, but dangerous because it leads the opponent to question the threatener's resolve to execute the threat which may in fact be a threshold phenomenon such that four minor infractions might go unchallenged or unpunished, whereas the fifth releases the full fury.

Although the structure of the situation may put one in a position of having to rely only upon massive punishment, it is surprising that heads of state inadvertently put themselves in this position, either structurally or strategically. For example, the policy of massive retaliation during the Eisenhower administration is a perfect example of heads of state setting themselves up for nuclear blackmail. Having ordered most of the conventional systems adapted for nuclear weaponry, Eisenhower found himself in the position of not being able to respond to minor encroachments. Just as one is not likely to cut off one's own arm to reduce the irritation of mosquito bites, so one is not likely to use nuclear weapons for minor disturbances, or the loss of insignificant territories. Reaction to the massive retaliation policy gave rise to notions of measured response (McNamara, 1963), limited war (Kissinger, 1957, 1960), and escalation (Kahn, 1965). These techniques are designed to provide the United States with the opportunity to meet a threat with an appropriate threat or, when desired, to influence others by confronting them with a reasonable (and therefore credible) threat. Kahn's escalation strategy is an attempt to enunciate a large number of steps between that of nations making rude remarks at one another and nations firing their entire stockpiles of thermonuclear weapons at one another's cities (spastic war).

Escalation and measured response are attempts to attenuate the advantage and the extraordinary danger associated with preemption, that is, the advantage of being first to encroach, first to threaten, and in the event of war, first to strike. About the best example of the pressure toward preemption or preventative strike is the early stages of nuclear weapon technology and delivery systems. In the early stages, the delivery systems were vulnerable to attack, and, therefore, were most effective as a first strike capability, or at very worst, a very close second. This obviously created a situation in which enormous advantage went to the first nation to launch the attack, and should an attack be in process it was imperative that the threatened nation get its warheads off the ground, so to speak. When one side recognizes the advantage of going first, it cannot avoid attributing the same reasoning to the opponent, with the result that nations seriously consider launching preventative wars. Vulnerability also forces nations to maintain a state of super alert which has the effect of further intimidating the opponent, due to the fact that it is very, very difficult to distinguish between defensive and offensive activities when decisions must be made in a matter of minutes. Now that delivery systems are far less vulnerable, the situation is considerably more stable, such that less advantage accrues to a nation's being first to strike. It is interesting to note, however, that if one relies upon massive retaliatory strategies, there still is an advantage in being the first one to encroach, as this has the effect of placing the responsibility upon the opponent as he has the last clear chance to avoid mutual disaster. The placing of the naval blockade around Cuba during the Cuban missile crisis had the effect of returning the initiative to the Soviet Union in that they had the last clear chance to avoid further hostilities (i.e., the decision to run the blockade). Similarly, the stationing of US troops in Western Europe has the effect of guaranteeing the involvement of the US in any Soviet advance which, by reducing the element of choice, attenuates the advantage of a preemptive move.

The strategy of escalation (Kahn, 1965) is a refinement of the game of chicken in which protagonists, finding themselves at any particular stage of hostility, may threaten to increase the level of hositilty in their attempt to persuade or dissuade the opponent. One of the problems with the escalation strategy is that the advantage of preemption is, of course, retained. That is, if hostility starts, there are advantages in being the first one on a particular rung. In addition, there is some pressure to escalate the level of hostility just to demonstrate to the opponent that one is willing to do so. Fortunately, there are salient thresholds such as that of the nuclear threshold which tend to reduce the tempo of escalating hostility. Brodie (1966) states that the tradition of nonuse of nuclear weapons can serve as an escalation limiter, provided the threshold is placed high up the scale of conventional violence so that the pressure to pass the threshold will not be too great. For example, using tactical nuclear warheads for artillery may place the nuclear–nonnuclear threshold too low on the scale of violence such that nations readily cross the threshold, thereby reducing the constraints against the use of larger nuclear weapons. Both parties to the conflict will likely be very grateful for the existence of the limiter to stop further increases in violence, particularly when the steps at the upper end of the escalator tend to be quite large. As the distinction between conventional and nuclear weapons is salient, if the threshold is placed high enough on the scale, nations may attempt to outbid one another in violence up to the threshold, but then tend to stop at that point. Many strategists have suggested that it may be advantageous for a country to actually use a nuclear device, that is to cross the nuclear threshold, primarily to make the opponent aware of the obvious fact that one is not overly constrained by the tradition of nonuse. Unfortunately, without such limiters, it is difficult to see how the escalation process may be stopped or slowed down once it has started to pick up momentum. It should be noted that the nuclear–nonnuclear threshold is not the only threshold which might serve to limit the escalation of violence. Other thresholds exist or may be established such as the use of nuclear weapons only in battle zones, only outside of the opponent's homeland, for exemplary strikes as opposed to counterforce or countervalue strikes, and for counterforce strikes as opposed to countervalue strikes and so on, which could serve to slow down the escalation process at various levels of violence (Kahn, 1965).

The distinction between war and nonwar is not a sharp precipice, but is rather a slope, and a slippery slope at that (Schelling, 1963). Nations do not figuratively stand on the edge of a cliff and threaten to jump into war. Rather, the brink is more like a slope in which the two combatants, who are tied together, keep advancing out on the slope in an attempt to threaten each other with destruction. Thus, despite their best efforts, they might slip and plunge into war, unless one or both agree to back off. Escalation is much the same sort of situation in which attempts to outbid one another in violence involve ever greater steps with the result that the process may accelerate to what Kahn refers to as insensate war. With limiters, however, escalation may decelerate once it approaches one of the agreed upon (agreement in the terms of a shared norm) thresholds, such as the threshold between nuclear and nonnuclear weapons, although as Kissinger (1960) maintains since war cannot really be limited, danger of escalation to all out war should deter encroachments.

A. Strategy

As the ability to inflict mutual punishment becomes highly developed, the major problem facing each protagonist in the situation is that of how to deter the opponent with threatened use of punishment which the threatener has no incentive at all to carry out. A threat is truly successful only if it is never challenged. A successful threat of strike on the part of labor is one which is never carried out, a successful doomsday machine never goes off, and a successful threat of willingness to play chicken is one which prevents an opponent from accepting the challenge. The problem then is how to make credible an essentially incredible threat. Curiously, in the game of chicken, the more potent the punishment available to both opponents, the less credible becomes the threat of use of such capabilities. The subject of threat credibility is covered in some detail in Chapter 5, so the present discussion will be limited to the relationship between the severity of punishment and threat credibility, as well as the strategies used by the protagonists in dangerous game situations to increase the credibility of their threats.

In dangerous situations, credibility may be altered in essentially three different ways. First, it can be altered experientially. In a situation in which there is a salient threshold, such as the international situation in which the use of nuclear weapons represents a salient threshold, crossing the threshold should obviously have the effect of increasing the credibility of one's willingness or resolve to go the limit. Kahn (1965), for example, suggests that it might be strategically advantageous for a country to cross the nuclear threshold since the mere fact that a nuclear weapon has been used cannot fail to impress the opposition that the situation is grave, and it obviously has the effect of enhancing the credibility of one's willingness to go to the limit since one has, in fact, used a nuclear weapon.

Second, protagonists may use different forms of committal strategies (Kahn, 1961). Basically, all committal strategies are designed to impress upon the opponent, before the fact, that one has committed oneself irrevocably to do something in a certain eventuality even though it may not make sense to carry out the committal, if the eventuality occurs. Committal can be accomplished by relinquishing one's ability to stop the punishing response. This kind of commitment is difficult to arrange. About the closest approximation to relinquishing control is the example of a nation's going to a full alert. This has the effect of increasing the probability of accidental war, primarily due to misperception of the opponent's actions on the part of the nation in a state of super alert. Another approach to the committal strategy is binding oneself with extra situational considerations. For example, the United States finding itself in an eyeball to eyeball confrontation with mainland China over one of the offshore islands may indicate to the Chinese that failure to go the limit to protect the island would result in a serious loss of prestige to the United States in the eyes of its enemies and its allies. The loss of prestige would in turn increase the probability of confrontation with other enemies and loss of support of allies and, therefore, represents a general threat to the security of the United States.

Finally, the most disturbing of all strategies is the rationality of irrationality. If one can appear a little mad or out of contact with reality in almost any bargaining situation involving some degree of threat, one stands a better chance of receiving a more favorable settlement. As Schelling (1963) has maintained, a beggar who appears at one's door is likely to be somewhat more successful if he is bleary-eyed and desperate looking as opposed to submissive and placatory. Kahn (1965, p. 11) has suggested that in the automobile variety of the game of chicken played by teenagers:

The "skillful" player may get into the car quite drunk, throwing whiskey bottles out the window to make it clear to everybody just how drunk he is. He wears very dark glasses so that it is obvious that he cannot see much, if anything. As soon as the car reaches high speed, he takes the steering wheel and throws it out the window. If his opponent is watching, he has won. If his opponent is not watching, he has a problem; likewise if both players try this strategy.

The reason that high risk games put a premium on irrationality is the fact that although it may be rational to irrevocably commit oneself to an irrational act, if the other side still refuses to back down after the irrevocable committal has been made, it would be irrational to carry out the punishment. Thus, to preclude the possibility of the opponent's not fully believing one's irrevocable commital to the act, one's appearing irrational or mad reduces the opponent's confidence that one will act in one's own self-interest. Irrationality is an advantage, as the protagonist perceived by the opponent to be most willing or likely to carry out the threat enjoys a significant bargaining advantage. That is, due to the structure of chicken-type confrontations, the more conservative or rational opponent has no option but to back down.

Reducing one's control over mutual destruction can, of course, be overdone with the result that an opponent will strike out of fear in an attempt to prevent or preempt a mutual interchange. Take, for example, Khrushchev's relinquishing an obvious strategic advantage by assuring the United States that the missiles being constructed in Cuba would not be under the control of the Cubans, but rather would be under the control of "responsible Soviet officers."

When the response opportunities in a situation are limited, such that a protagonist must rely upon a single and severe mutually punishing response to threaten or deter, the situation becomes one in which one player may blackmail the other player with the latter's own weapons, if the former is able to obtain a slight advantage. An advantage in this kind of situation is usually based upon experience, that is, previous conflicts in which one player has backed down. The blackmail paradigm is quite simple and often quite effective. Rather than say to an opponent "If I don't get what I want, I'm going to blow us both up" the successful blackmailer simply takes what he wants and says to his opponent "If you don't like it, blow us both up." The blackmailed protagonist is relatively powerless against this type of approach because he obviously has no incentive to carry out the threat, and second each successful repetition of the process decreases the credibility of the threat to retaliate. Preemption is, of course, offensive deterrence (Gallois, 1961) in that the preemptor is utilizing the opponent's desire to avoid mutual disaster to force the opponent to appease. The blackmail model was studied in the laboratory using the train game (Swingle, 1967, 1968).

Figure 4 is a schematic drawing of the entire game situation. Two players are seated in separate sound-resistant isolation cubicles and can view the game

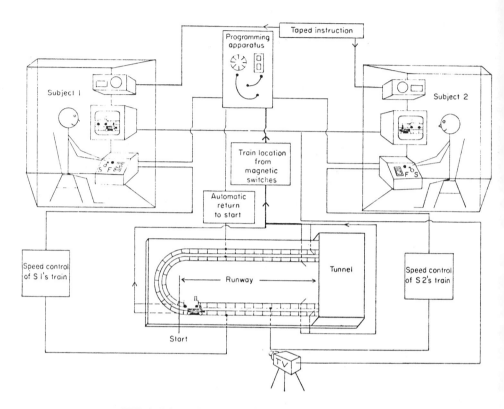

FIG. 4. Schematic drawing of the entire train game situation.

board (situated in another room) from individual TV monitors. The game board consists of a 4-foot by 12-foot board upon which two circular model train tracks are mounted. One model train engine is situated on each track facing the tunnel shown at the right of the game board.

The game is played in trials. When a trial starts, the trains are situated at "start" as shown in the figure and the subject's "Go" light, mounted on the control panels, goes on. When this light is on, each subject has control of the speed of his train on the 6-foot section of track labeled "runway" in the drawing and may vary the speed of the train from a dead stop to about 2.3 feet per second.

The rules of the game are quite simple: (1) get into the tunnel first, and (2) get out the other side of the tunnel before the opponent enters the tunnel.

A different number of points is usually given to the first and second train into the tunnel. The first train in, for example, might receive 10 points, whereas the second train receives only one point. The points won are accumulated automatically on the electric impulse counters mounted on each subject's control panel. Points are redeemable at the rate of 2 cents per point for subjects randomly drawn in a lottery.

In the game of chicken, if neither subject backs down, both subjects lose a considerable amount. That is, either player is better off being a chicken than suffering mutual loss. In the laboratory situation, this is simulated by either a loss of points (or electric shock) and occurs whenever both trains are in any part of the tunnel at the same time. Loss of points is accomplished by a resetting of the counters to zero, whereas electric shock is delivered to the second and third fingers of the left hand. (Electrode placement is assured by means of a contact relay connected to a signal audible only to the experimenter.) No points are accumulated by either player on reset or shock trials. It is apparent, then, that the longer play continues without reset, the greater is the threat available to each player in the point loss conditions in that a greater number of points may be lost. By starting either or both subjects with some number of points, the pregame "wealth" which can be lost is variable.

The train game duplicates all of the essential structural characteristics of dangerous games. That is, the basic moves of the game have the effect of advancing a subject toward his goal while at once threatening the opponent; failure to cooperate results in substantial loss to both players: The interaction necessitates a "head-on" confrontation which heightens competitiveness and the subject's concern lest he appear weak in the opponent's eyes; the game situation is exceedingly simple.

To examine the blackmail strategy, the subject operated one train and the experimenter operated the opponent's train. In the first instance, cooperative alternation (taking turns going first) was established rather rapidly by the experimenter for the purpose of building up a reasonable point score for both players, so that threat of reset would be a meaningful threat. The experimenter then started the manipulation attempt which involved demanding two first unchallenged entries for every one unchallenged entry permitted the opponent. This was followed by a 3:1 ratio, then 4:1, and so forth. In a situation of this nature, allowing the opponent into the tunnel unscathed and unchallenged may be considered the reinforcer for the immediately preceding submissive or appeasing response. Once a subject has permitted an unfavorable distribution to take place (e.g., 4:1), he finds himself in a position in which it is difficult not to back down, due to the fact that tradition, in the context of the game, dictates that his opponent will never submit so that the choice of either appeasement or mutual loss is all his. Due to the fact that mutual punishment is quite costly, the subject's best response on any particular trial is submission. Exploratory work indicated that it is not difficult to establish distribution ratios as high as 15:1, once subjects have accumulated a fair number of points. Several attempts have been made to study the effect of the number of repetitions of a particular distribution process upon a subject's tolerance of an opponent's attempts to increase the distribution ratio. Subjects are typically brought to a state in which they receive one free entry for every two free entries of the experimenter. The 2:1 distribution may then be reiterated once, twice, five times, ten times, and so on, followed by the experimenter's attempt to increase the ratio to 3:1. It is very difficult to conduct a study of this nature due to lack of randomness of subject assignment in each one of the conditions. That is, in the higher reiteration conditions there is a greater tendency to lose subjects who would be unwilling to tolerate a 2:1 distribution reiterated say, five times which, of course, is never put to the test in the 2:1 reiterated once situation. However, several pilot studies have indicated that the longer training has continued, the less tolerant is the subject of attempts on the part of the experimenter to increase the distribution ratio. One might expect just the reverse due to the fact that the larger the number of reiterations the greater the point score of the subject and hence the more hesitant one might expect him to be in the use of the punishing (point reset) capability. On the other hand, however, the subject may assume that his opponent is in a somewhat more vulnerable position due to the fact that whatever point accumulation the subject has, the opponent has exactly twice as many points, and presumably the more points the opponent has to lose, the greater is the threat available to the subject. It appears, however, as though the number of reiterations develops a salient threshold for the subject, and the more salient the threshold, the more ritualized the distribution system, and the greater the probability of the subject going to the limit any time the opponent attempts to make further encroachments.

Two similar studies were conducted to determine the effects of the length of cooperative experience with an opponent upon a subject's tolerance of the opponent's attempts to disturb the status quo. That is, following the development of cooperation in the dyad and some exposure to a stable cooperative settlement, the opponent attempts to change the reward distribution by unilaterally defecting on every trial. Subjects were involved in the train game situation with the win–loss ratio set at 5:0. In the first study, the reset contingency was always in effect, while in the second study deadlock resulted in a painful electric shock presented to the index and middle finger of the left hand. In the shock condition, the subject's counter did not reset when both trains were in the tunnel at the same time. In both studies, points had a redemption value of 2 cents each for those subjects selected in the day's lottery.

The experimental manipulation involved varying the number of iterations of cooperative alternation. Three conditions were included in each study: group 1 in which the subject experienced one cooperative alternation (2 trials) with the opponent, group 5 in which the subject experienced five successful cooperative alternations (10 trials) with the opponent, and group 10 in which the subject experienced ten successful cooperative alternations (20 trials) with the opponent. After the pretraining, the opponent's train was left consistently in the "On" state and at no time during the next 30 test trials did the opponent's train ever stop to allow the subject first access through the tunnel.

The measures of interest in the present studies are, first, the average number of test trials subjects will tolerate before resisting (i.e., entering the tunnel and resetting the counters or exposing both players to electric shock); second, the total number of cooperative gestures made during the 30 test trials (the number of free access trials given to the unconditionally uncooperative opponent); and, third, the proportion of cooperative responses made following the first instance of resistance. The latter is a better measure (than the total number of cooperative responses) of the subject's attempts to reinitiate cooperative alternations in that it eliminates concessions made prior to the mutual punishment trial. (Concessions made prior to the punishment may reflect fear of loss of points or fear of electric shock as opposed to being indicative of cooperative intent.) The results indicate that when loss of points is at stake, the subject's tendency to reset the counters decreases as the number of pretraining trials increases. However, since the number of points to be lost increases directly with number of pretraining trials, it is, of course, possible that it is the loss of points and not the extent of the cooperative experience which results in the hesitancy to reset the counters. The same measure for the shock condition indicates no reliable difference in subject's tendency to resist as a function of length of initial cooperative experience. This indicates, of course, that fear of loss of points and not the extent of cooperative experience was responsible for differences in subject's tendency to resist. A similar situation exists with respect to the total number of cooperative responses measure in that, in the point reset condition, subjects make a greater number of cooperative responses as the length of pretraining on cooperative alternation increases but no such difference exists for the electric shock group.

The best measure of the effects of length of cooperative experience upon subject's tendency to make cooperative gestures when exposed to an unconditionally uncooperative opponent is the proportion of cooperative responses made following the first instance of resistance (i.e., point reset or electric shock). The data indicate that there was a reliable tendency for subjects in the shock condition to make more cooperative gestures following the first resistance as compared with the subjects in the point condition which, of course, is not surprising given that the level of punishment is constant across all trials in the shock condition but varies depending on point accumulation in the point reset condition. The data also indicate a curvilinear relationship between the extent of cooperative experience with the opponent and the tendency to make cooperative gestures. The data for subjects in the point reset condition demonstrated a similar curvilinear relationship. This indicated that the tendency to attempt to reestablish cooperative alternation was maximal after a moderate level of exposure to cooperative alternation and gave some evidence of decreasing at higher levels of exposure. Subjects in shock group 1 appear to be considerably more cooperative (relative to group 5) as compared with similar conditions in the point reset condition. Further, the decrease in cooperative tendencies at the higher levels of exposure drops precipitously in the shock group as compared with the point loss conditions.

The above studies indicate that in the game of chicken, such as the automobile variety, it is difficult for either protagonist to make a concession without thereby forcing himself to further capitulate to the opponent. As soon as one player gives clear evidence of reducing his speed, presumably expecting the second driver to reciprocate the concession, the concession may establish an expectancy on the part of the unyielding opponent that the concession maker is weak and will make further concessions and eventually yield. The problem is one of yielding in a situation involving extraordinary danger to both protagonists which establishes an expectation on the part of the unyielding player that any concession is simply a prelude to further concession and final capitulation (Schelling, 1963). The problem may be that such concession-making may not be interpreted as a cooperative gesture but rather as evidence of the opponent's weakness or lack of resolve to maintain an unyielding position. Players, therefore, are in a dilemma in which unyielding behavior can preclude the establishment of cooperation which in turn may have disastrous results, whereas making a cooperative gesture may encourage the opponent to press for further concessions and, in dangerous games of chicken, to press for final capitulation. Negotiators (e.g., in labor–management disputes) face much the same sort of problem, that of offering concessions while at the same time preventing increased pressure for further concessions. Many writers have commented on the problem of controlling the adversary's expectations and the techniques for making a concession without seeming to yield (Ilke, 1964; Kerr, 1954; Knowles, 1958; Peters, 1958; Schelling, 1963; Stevens, 1963; Walton & McKersie, 1965). Several of the above writers have also indicated that making concessions through a mediator may be a means for controlling an adversary's expectations. Such mediated offers may control an adversary's expectations in that the concession may have been elicited by the mediator, or that a mediated offer may be tentative and, therefore, not likely a prelude to total capitulation (Podell & Knapp, 1969).

B. Cost of Punishment

When two drivers are jockeying for position and one car is a brand new expensive model while the second is a well-worn old junk, we tend to believe that the driver of the older car has a distinct advantage in that deadlock would be far less costly for him as compared with the costs to the new car driver. Since the driver of the older car may execute the threat at least cost to himself, his threat is, other things equal, more credible than his opponent's. Thus, asymmetries in costs associated with threat, assuming fully knowledgeable opponents, affects the credibility of threat.

An obvious but nonetheless interesting empirical question is whether or not subjects capable of executing threat at less cost than their opponent in bargaining situations do in fact have a greater tendency to execute the threat or to succeed in forcing the opponent to give in. The method used to vary the cost of executing threat was to provide one subject of a pair in the dangerous train game with pregame "wealth." That is, prior to the start of the game, subjects were told that one member of the dyad, selected by chance, was going to receive a specific number of points which would be recorded on his counter. The game was structured so that only one subject could win a cash prize to heighten competitiveness, but the game was mixed-motive since high scores were required to qualify for the prize. The win—loss ratio was 3:1 with the reset contingency always in effect, and five practice trials were given. Four conditions were included in the study: Three conditions of unilateral wealth in which one player received either 25, 50, or 100 points on his counter, and one control condition in which both players started with no points on their counters. The results support the expectation that players without pregame wealth are more likely to use the reset capability or to force the opponent to back down. During the first ten trials, experimental group dyads, on the average, reset more frequently than control group dyads. No differences in frequency of reset were observed among experimental groups.

Subjects without pregame point advantage in the experimental groups did tend to utilize a more aggressive strategy on the first trial of the game in that exactly twice as many of these players (80%) were allowed through the tunnel first or were primarily responsible for resetting the counters as compared with subjects in control group dyads, matched on the basis of playing position (i.e., subjects operating the same train). This indicates that subjects are less likely to yield when they can execute a threat at less cost to themselves than to their opponent.

Schelling (1963) has stated that the cost of threat and punishment to the executant need not be symmetrical. The threat to smash an old car with a new car is effective as long as it is believed. When the cost to the threatener for executing the threat is exorbitantly high, however, it may have the effect of reducing the credibility of the threat and encouraging the threatened player to resist. An interesting question, given a repeated trial game with a chicken-type structure is: What is the effect of such asymmetries which are equalized in the early part of the game situation? Two drivers competing for the right of way at an intersection every morning on their way to work provides a useful analogy. If one driver has a very expensive automobile and the other an old junk, one tends to think that the individual who is able to execute the threat at the least cost to himself has a bargaining advantage. This situation might be compared with a situation in which both drivers have very expensive automobiles or both have very inexpensive automobiles. After the first deadlock or dual preemption, both automobiles, let us assume, become equally worthless. The question, of course, is: What residual effect does initial loss to one or both protagonists have upon the bargaining process? One might expect, for example, that in the unilateral case (i.e., one player loses pregame wealth whereas the second does not), the bargainer sampling the poor outcome in the interpersonal situation might be reluctant to make cooperative gestures or to respond cooperatively to an opponent's trusting gestures. In short, angered by his unilateral loss, a person may be reluctant to make concessions with the result that a high level of conflict maintains over the course of the interaction. One could argue, on the other hand, that if both protagonists experience an initial loss at the beginning of the bargaining session, the need for establishing a bargaining norm would be made salient. One might also argue that the same effect would be observed in unilateral loss conditions. That is, the bargainer experiencing initial loss may realize that cooperation is essential for either bargainer to benefit. This player would be encouraged to attempt to establish cooperation with his opponent.

To research this problem, the train game was again used. The win–loss ratio was set at 5 points for the first train and 0 points for the second train through the tunnel on no reset trials. Subjects were told that a lottery was to be held each day and the person selected in the lottery would have his points redeemed at 2 cents each. Three pregame wealth values were included: 25 points, 50 points, and 100 points, which were either unilateral (only one subject received pregame points) or bilateral (both subjects received pregame points). Thus, subjects who had points started with either 50 cents, 1 dollar, or 2 dollars potential value. A control condition was also included in which both players started with no pregame wealth. With the above reward structure one could argue that any loss, be it unilateral or bilateral, should have the effect of increasing the speed with which cooperation is established, since loss should lead subjects to realize that cooperative alternation is the only method by which a substantial payoff can be realized, assuming, of course, that the opponent will not be submissive and the initial loss of points is evidence that the opponent is not likely to be submissive.

The results indicate that both unilateral and bilateral loss of points give rise to fewer deadlocks during the first 10 trials of the game and earlier instance of a punishment-free trial, as compared with the control condition. The above data also reflect an ordering effect in that fewer resets occur and the first no punishment trial appears earlier in the game as the pregame wealth, bilateral or unilateral, increases. With the possible exception of the 50 point bilateral group, all measures of the occurrence and stability of cooperative settlement indicate that point loss enhances earlier settlement as compared with control. As the settlements in the dangerous train game tend to be unstable due to the increasing threat (i.e., accumulating points available for reset), the enhancing effect of point loss seems to be limited to the early trials of the game. Subjects in point loss pairs show greater evidence of attempted dominance over the entire 100 trial game and are more likely to arrive at an inequitable settlement (i.e., one subject enjoying more than 50% entries *after* the last reset trial) as compared with control subjects. Frequency and extent of inequitable settlement appear directly related to magnitude of point loss in the unilateral conditions and curvilinear (most prominent in the 50 point group) in the bilateral conditions. Average joint payoff data indicates no reliable difference between groups by the end of the game although the payoff was more evenly divided between subjects in control group dyads.

V. SAVING FACE

One of the major problems with chicken-type games is the effect of mutual punishment which is twofold. Although it may be assumed to have a deterrent effect in that neither protagonist dares run a risk of suffering the severe penalty, it unhappily encourages protagonists to behave in ways which should suggest courage or at least not weakness in the face of the substantial mutual punishment. Thus, a protagonist gets some added satisfaction in forcing the opponent to back down, but feels a greater necessity not to allow himself to be intimidated when the punishment associated with deadlock is exceedingly high.

One of the principal factors maintaining a high level of conflict in chicken-type confrontations emerges from the implications of not going the limit in such head-on confrontations. Even the name of the game derives from the label attached to the player who chooses to initiate the deescalation process by giving evidence that he is not resolved to carrying out the severe mutual punishment. Such gestures are not generally regarded as salubrious acts, but rather as indications of weakness, cowardliness, or being a chicken. Thus, although one might assume that the relationship between magnitude of the punishment and deterrence (*ceterus paribus*) is positive and monotonic, the relationship between magnitude of punishment and "loss-of-face" may also be positive and monotonic and, therefore, should protagonists ever find themselves in an eyeball-to-eyeball situation, further hostility may be the only tolerable course of action.

Bertrand Russell likening the automobile variety of the game of chicken to the international balance of terror suggests that loss-of-face could become so intolerable to heads of state that nuclear exchange is the only way out of the conflict (1959, p. 30).

> The game may be played without misfortune a few times, but sooner or later it
> will come to be felt that loss of face is more dreadful than nuclear annihilation.
> The moment will come when neither side can face the derisive cry of "Chicken!"
> from the other side. When that moment has come, the statesmen of both sides
> will plunge the world into destruction.

There is, unfortunately, no paucity of examples of contemporary heads of state behaving in a manner which suggests that fear of loss of reputation was prepotent over reducing the risk of unimaginable horror to millions of people. The popular example is the Cuban missile crisis in which the "odds that the Soviets would go all the way to war . . . seemed to [President Kenndey] . . . between one out of three and even (Sorensen, 1965, p. 705)"—odds that were acceptable to force a confrontation to remove not so much a military threat[1] as a threat to the reputations of the United States, the Democratic Party, and President Kennedy (see Eisner, 1967; Horelick, 1946; Kateb, 1966; R.F. Kennedy, 1968). Offers by Khrushchev to negotiate mutual withdrawal of missiles from Cuba and Turkey were refused (Stevenson suggested a similar tradeoff) by President Kennedy even though the United States only had about 15 Jupiters in Turkey, one-third the number of medium range missiles known to have been shipped to Cuba, not counting the preparations which were being made for longer range missiles (Horelick, 1964). A face-saving confrontation was deemed preferable to the trade despite the fact that the Jupiters were vulnerable (and therefore provocative) and had actually been ordered removed by President Kennedy several months before the missile crisis (Hilsman, 1967; R.F. Kennedy, 1968). The missiles in Turkey would not be removed in return for removal of the missiles from Cuba, since it would look to the world as though President Kennedy was responding to Chairman Khrushchev's threat. It should also be noted that some of President Kennedy's advisors during the crisis felt that the blockade was a more dangerous course of action than a "surgical strike" against the missile installations (Acheson, 1969).

---

[1] Opinions differed as to the actual extent of the military threat (see Hilsman, 1967; R.F. Kennedy, 1968; Sorenson, 1965;), although it appears as though President Kennedy, at the time, did not consider missiles in Cuba as substantially changing the balance of military power and, of course, it is the protagonist's perception of the payoff matrix which is the central issue. It should also be noted that President Kennedy may have had reliable information that the Soviet Union's nuclear missile capability was not ready for immediate use so he could act as tough as he wanted (Penkovskiy, 1965).

Neither side wanted war over Cuba, we (JFK, RFK, Sorenson, and O'Donnell) agreed, but it was possible that either side (U.S.A. or U.S.S.R.) could take a step that—for reasons of "security" or "pride" or "face"—would require a reponse by the other side which, in turn, for the same reasons of security, pride, or face, would bring about a counter-response and eventually an escalation into armed conflict (R.F. Kennedy, 1968).[2]

The work of Deutsch (1966) and his students among others has suggested that the maintenance of face is an important motive in mixed-motive bargaining situations, particularly in those having a chicken-type head-on confrontation structure. Deutsch argues that the very existence of punitive response alternatives in bargaining situations changes the meaning of yielding. To yield in the face of threat is to suffer a loss of social face and self-esteem. Maintenance of social face in such situations involves a struggle for power to intimidate, and "courage" (as well as madness) in the use of threat is a source of power.

If saving face, or not appearing weak in the opponent's eyes, is a strong motive in chicken-type confrontation, then the anticipated future interaction with the opponent should directly influence the strength of the face saving motive. Expecting to meet one's opponent in the future or having to interact with him in a situation in which he may play the victor's role may intensify the need to appear strong and courageous, or conversely, to avoid initiating a relaxation of a head-on confrontation lest one be labeled a coward or a chicken. If, on the other hand, a person could be assured of anonymity following chicken-type confrontations, this assurance might mollify the need to appear courageous.

Consider a situation in which a person was put in a position of being a professional but anonymous negotiator, charged with the responsibility of negotiating a settlement or detente under conditions in which the negotiator was never personally exposed to his counterpart. Although under such conditions one would certainly expect the negotiator to make use of the threats inherent in chicken-type structures, the use of such threatening responses would be based upon strategic considerations for maximizing the returns to the negotiator's constituents, as opposed to demonstrating the negotiator's courage since fear of loss-of-face has been minimized as neither negotiator may play the victor's role.

There have been a number of bargaining studies which have addressed themselves to the anonymity and expected future interaction variables. Preliminary work was done by Marlowe, Gergen, and Doob (1966) using the PDG. The experimenters led some subjects to believe that they would confront their opponents after the bargaining session, whereas control subjects received no such induction. Results of this study indicated that in the absence of

---

[2]The need to allow the Soviets a face-saving way out of the Cuban missile crisis was stressed by several of Kennedy's advisors (Hilsman, 1967).

definitive information about the opponent, subjects were more cooperative when they expected to confront their opponents in the future. However, when the opponent was characterized as having personality dispositions which might lead him to be intolerable as a victor, anticipated future interaction did not enhance cooperation.

Brown (1968) using a variation of the Deutsch and Krauss (1960) trucking game attempted to manipulate the face-saving motive by exposing the subjects' behavior to the scrutiny of a (bogus) group of peers who were not dependent on the outcome of the bargaining session. Brown found that subjects who believed that the audience assessed their preliminary bargaining behavior as foolish retaliated against the opponent at a cost to themselves during the ensuing game. The use of costly retaliatory responses was attenuated when subjects believed that the opponent knew the cost of using the punishing response. In addition, humiliated subjects soon discovered alternative means of retaliating against the opponent, spreading, as Brown states, the conflict beyond the limits set by the rules of the game. Brown's results are consistent with the notion that the use of retaliatory responses may be an attempt to save face in head-on confrontations between protaganists.

If face-saving is an important motive in interpersonal bargaining situations involving high risk alternatives which lead negotiators to believe that their courage is subject to public scrutiny, being guaranteed anonymity should attenuate the face-saving motive because the opponent is deprived of the privilege of playing the victor's role. Subjects can, then, more rationally determine an optimal strategy, safe in the knowledge that the utilization of less risky alternatives or initiating cooperative gestures is only tangentially, if at all, related to one's courage in high risk situations. For, after all, the utilization of dangerous courses of action in chicken-type confrontations should be a matter of attempting to maximize the probability of realizing desirable outcomes. Not wishing to appear weak in the eyes of the opponent becomes a relevant and presumably desirable outcome only insofar as the protagonists in dangerous situations have an opportunity to engage in the interpersonal comparison process after negotiations have been completed.

A recent study by the author (Swingle, 1969) using a PDG situation compared subjects who had been guaranteed anonymity following the bargaining situation vs. those who were led to believe that they would meet with their opponents following the experimental session. The subjects were exposed to a programmed opponent which played a tit-for-tat strategy with a 90% probability. The results suggested that subjects expecting to meet with their opponent after the experimental session are generally less cooperative, less trustworthy, and less repenting than subjects who have been guaranteed anonymity. Although these findings seem to be at variance with the first study reported by Marlowe *et al.*, (1966), it will be recalled that in the Marlowe *et al.*

study, subjects in the no-future-interaction conditions were simply not given the future interaction induction, whereas in the present study, subjects in the anonymity condition were actually told that they would remain anonymous.

It is possible that in bargaining situations, the effect of anonymity is one of allowing subjects to relax their guarded responding, secure in the knowledge that, if beaten, the opponent will not be able to play the victor's role. If concern regarding loss-of-face is an important motive in bargaining situations, guaranteed anonymity may have the effect of relaxing interpersonal conflict by reducing the importance to the subject of maximizing the difference between his score and that of the opponent.

The effect of anonymity may be reversed for subjects who, by virtue of the social environment, are in a weak social position such as being a member of a minority group or in an insecure social position. If they need not be concerned about crimination for their behavior by the opponent after the bargaining session, such socially disadvantaged subjects' desire to harm plenipotentiary group opponents or to be disruptive should find greater expression than if future confrontation is anticipated.

The latter study was concerned with a PDG-type situation which, although it incorporates risky response alternatives, does not have the structural characteristics of the game of chicken which involves a payoff structure such that either member of the bargaining dyad would be, in an objective sense, better off being a chicken than persevering in the mutually destructive state.

Other data also lend support to the notion of reduced conflict in situations in which the protagonists have been guaranteed anonymity. In a study by Gruder (1968)—using a somewhat different bargaining situation which has some of the properties of the game of chicken in the sense that deadlock resulted in an outcome which was objectively worse than that which the subject would obtain by accepting the programmed opponent's offer—one variable under investigation was the effect of leading some subjects to believe they would meet the opponent after the experimental bargaining situation whereas other subjects were assured that they would not be confronting their opponent. Although the data suggest that the proportion of offers which were concessions tended to be smaller for subjects not expecting to confront their opponent, the average size of all concessions was greatest for subjects guaranteed anonymity. Although Gruder interprets this as support for the notion that anticipated future interaction increases the subject's cooperativeness due to the fact that a larger number of concessions are made, the overall size of the concession was reliably greater for subjects guaranteed anonymity even when total number of offers was covaried. The latter strongly suggests that the effect of anonymity was one of permitting subjects to relax their guarded responding by making substantial concessions, a response which may be suggestive of weakness should the subject have to meet with, and justify, his bargaining behavior to the opponent after the experimental session. The fact that a greater number of offers did in fact involve concessions for subjects expecting to confront their opponent also may be interpreted in support of the latter argument due to the fact that subjects apparently make a greater number of minor concessions when they expect to interact with their opponent, but a fewer number of major concessions when anonymity has been assured. It is not unreasonable to argue that a large number of small concessions is a tougher policy than a few large concessions.

Experimental evidence demonstrating the existence of the face saving motive in a chicken game is provided by Sermat (1967a). Subjects in this study, involved in the game shown in Fig. 5, were exposed to a 0% cooperative opponent for 50 trials followed by 20 trials during which the opponent's strategy drastically switched to 100% cooperation.

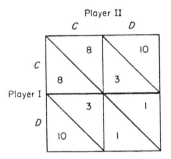

FIG. 5. Face-saving motive in a chicken game.

Some subjects were led to believe that they were actually playing against another person; others believed that they were playing against opponents who had committed themselves to a strategy and were not at liberty to modify their strategy. Committed opponents were either present, informed of each trial's outcome, or absent and, therefore, would not be informed of each trial's outcome. One final group of subjects was told that they were playing against a machine which had a fixed series of choices unresponsive to the subject's own choices. Subjects playing against the unconditionally uncooperative machine were highly cooperative (over 90% appeasing responses during last 30 trials), thus maximizing their scores, as opposed to minimizing the score difference between themselves and the machine by locking in on the *DD* outcome. The data for the assumed real opponent condition was exactly reversed. Subjects were initially less cooperative (approximately 40% cooperative choice) and became increasingly less cooperative over the course of the 50 trials. Subjects confronted with committed opponents were, in terms of cooperativeness, about halfway between the "free" and the "machine" groups' averages. The results indicate that in the absence of the social implications of appeasement, subjects will maximize their outcomes, accepting a payoff which is smaller than that obtained by a machine. Although the committed absent opponent was responded to more cooperatively than the committed but present opponent, the difference was not reliable. A replication of the study with military personnel paid at the rate of 1 cent per point, however, indicated that subjects playing against a committed but absent opponent maximized significantly more than subjects playing against a committed but present opponent.

The trend of the entire series of studies reported in Sermat (1967a) indicates that the greater the social implications of differential loss to the subject, the less willing subjects are to maximize their own payoffs by making C responses in the chicken game. Subjects exposed to similar experimental treatments in the PDG showed no significant differences in frequency of C responding, since maximization of payoff, when confronted with an unconditionally uncooperative opponent in the PDG, is accomplished by D responding.

In a similar study with male High School student subjects, Sermat (1964) found that players maximize more against an unconditionally uncooperative opponent when they believe the opponent is not being informed of each trial's outcome than when the opponent is informed. In addition, subjects tended to exploit an unconditionally cooperative opponent and exploitative responding was most pronounced when the opponent was not informed of each trial's outcomes.

The above series of experiments indicate that the social implications of accepting a lesser payoff than the other in a chicken game affects the subject's tendency to maximize his own returns. Although attempting to modify the behavior of an opponent free to change his strategy is, of course, an important factor encouraging subjects to punish the opponent at a cost to themselves, the tendency for subjects to maximize more when a committed opponent is absent rather than when the opponent is present suggests that depersonalization of the situation removes the appeasement implications of the subject's maximizing his own payoff.

It should be noted that the effects of anticipated future interaction v. anonymity in a game which satisfies all of the formal characteristics of chicken have not, however, been determined empirically. As chicken is a preemption game, it is not unreasonable to assume that anonymity might have the effect of encouraging preliminary preemptive moves. Initial preemption might result should each player assume that his opponent will concede (i.e., maximize his score), since the pressure to maintain social face by resisting is reduced as the players expect to remain anonymous. One could, of course, argue the reverse that reduced pressure to maintain face will encourage cooperative gestures leading to an earlier and more stable cooperative settlement.

A major challenge to game researchers is determining appropriate measures for the payoffs in bargaining situations. Such measures or indices must incorporate not only the tangible payoffs (e.g., the redemption value of points accumulated during the game) but also must reflect the intangible (Gallo, 1968) payoffs inherent in any bargaining situation. Honor, prestige, social face, victory, respect, and so on are terms recognizable by anyone as imprecise labels for the intangible payoff(s) in even the most trivial of bargaining situations. The focusing of protagonists' attention on such intangibles may preclude cooperative settlement, since such payoffs may not be divisible. There can be but one winner. Unfortunately, heads of state seem to have a propensity for defining negotiable situations in nonnegotiable terms: Rusk to John Scali (State Department correspondent for ABC), "Remember when you report this (Cuban missile situation), that eyeball to eyeball, they blinked first. (Hilsman, 1967, p. 219)."

Even when tangible payoffs (i.e., money) are exceedingly high, subjects still state that "not chickening out," "beating the other guy," "winning," or "getting more" (money) than the opponent was important to them. Fortunately, not all intangible payoffs in conflict situations reflect bellicose and/or competitive motivation. Many subjects express satisfaction when they enjoy a high joint payoff which was "fairly" or "evenly" divided.

An exciting challenge to "polemological" (Boulding, 1968) researchers will be to determine the nature of the scarce resources that protagonists compete for in conflict situations and to explore the effects of the structure of the conflict situation upon the emergence of the protagonists' need for such intangible payoffs.

VI. CONCLUSIONS

This chapter analyzed some of the structural variables which distinguish games of chicken from other mixed-motive bargaining situations and explored some of the behavioral consequences of manipulations of these dimensions. Variations in the form of chicken-type games is limited only by the ingenuity of the protagonists in the situation. Practically any social situation which involves some degree of threat of financial loss, pain, embarrassment, additional effort, loss of social face, and so on, may be restructured by the protagonists so that it satisfies the essential formal characteristics of chicken-type confrontations. Any situation may be given the character of the chicken-type confrontation when either protagonist is capable of reducing the response alternatives of the opponent, such that a continuous dimension is reduced to a Yes or No type of response, and the threat or implied threat takes the form of do "X" or I will do "Y," even though "Y" is painful to us both.

Small children accompanying their parents in public places appear to be very adept at the game of chicken. By threatening to create a substantial disturbance, embarrassing to the parent, the child gains a marked strategic advantage while negotiating for favors with the parent. Very young children, however, enjoy an asymmetry in cost due to the lack of super-ego development, whereas with adults, threat credibility must be built-up experientially or circumstantially (e.g., demonstrated willingness to make a scene or over-indulgence in alcoholic beverages). The varieties of chicken-type confrontations are legion. Two examples should suffice to demonstrate the range of possibilities.

> Denver—Security patrols are being stepped up at Stapleton International Airport to prevent teenagers from playing chicken with airplanes on the runways. Officials said youngsters had been found at night on the runways, daring each other to stand in the paths of approaching planes.
> *Toronto Globe and Mail,* November 15, 1968.

A most curious game of chicken described by Schelling (1967) involves a situation in which there is a jointly valued capability. Assume that two nations with nuclear capabilities jointly share the desire to avoid accidental nuclear war. If one can be sure of the intensity of the adversary's desire to prevent accidental war, rendering his warning system less reliable could force him to divert resources from other military efforts into the warning system.

An interesting area for future research is dynamic process games in which protagonists may acquire or purchase punishment or penalty capability. Such "arms race" simulations may help us to isolate those structural and pre-dispositional variables which encourage the acquisition of deterrent capabilities and whether they are obtained for offensive or defensive purposes. It should also be fascinating to explore the behavioral consequences of the transition from an essentially cooperative situation to a game having a chicken-type structure, which results from the acquisition of punishing capability by both protagonists.

REFERENCES

Acheson, D. Dean Acheson's version of Robert Kennedy's version of the Cuban missile affair. *Esquire,* Feb. 1969, p. 76.
Becker, G.M., & McClintock, C.G. Value: Behavioral decision theory. *Annual Review of Psychology,* 1967, 18, 239–286.

Bixenstine, V.E., Potash, H.M., & Wilson, K.V. Effects of level of cooperative choice by the other player on choices in a prisoner's dilemma game. Part I. *Journal of Abnormal and Social Psychology,* 1963, **66**, 308–313.

Bixenstine, V.E., & Wilson, K.V. Effects of level of cooperative choice by the other player on choices in a prisoner's dilemma game. Part II. *Journal of Abnormal and Social Psychology,* 1963, **67**, 139–147.

Boulding, K.E. Organization and conflict. *Journal of Conflict Resolution,* 1957, **1**, 122–134.

Boulding, K.E. The role of law in the learning of peace. *Proceedings of the American Society of International Law,* 1963, 92–103.

Boulding, K.E. Toward a theory of peace. In R. Fisher (Ed.), *International conflict and behavioral science.* New York: Basic Books, 1964. Pp. 70–87.

Boulding, K.E. Preface to a special issue. *Journal of Conflict Resolution,* 1968, **12**, 409–411.

Brodie, B. *Escalation and the nuclear option.* Princeton, N.J.: Princeton University Press, 1966.

Brown, B. The effect of need to maintain face on interpersonal bargaining. *Journal of Experimental Social Psychology,* 1968, **4**, 107–122.

Coser, L.A. *The functions of social conflict.* Glencoe, Ill.: Free Press, 1956.

Deutsch, M. Bargaining, threat and communication: Some experimental studies. In Kathleen Archibald (Ed.), *Strategic interaction and conflict.* Berkeley: Institute of International Studies, University of California, 1966. Pp. 19–41.

Deutsch, M., Epstein, Y., Canavan, D., & Gumpert, P. Strategies of inducing cooperation: An experimental study. *Journal of Conflict Resolution,* 1967, **11**, 345–360.

Deutsch, M., & Krauss, R.M. The effect of threat on interpersonal bargaining. *Journal of Abnormal and Social Psychology,* 1960, **61**, 181–189.

Deutsch, M., & Krauss, R.M. Studies of interpersonal bargaining. *Journal of Conflict Resolution,* 1962, **6**, 52–76.

Eisner, R. Comment on strategy and resource allocation. In R.N. McKean (Ed.), *Issues in defense economics.* New York: Columbia University Press, 1967. Pp. 153–161.

Ellis, J.G., & Sermat, V. Cooperation and the variation of payoff in non-zero-sum games. *Psychonomic Science,* 1966, **5**, 149–150.

Etzioni, A. *The hard way to peace.* New York: Collier, 1962.

Fink, C.F. Some conceptual difficulties in the theory of social conflict. *Journal of Conflict Resolution,* 1968, **12**, 412–460.

Frank, J.D. *Sanity and survival.* New York: Knopf, 1968.

Froman, L.A., & Cohen, M.D. Threats and bargaining efficiency. *Behavioral Science,* 1969, **14**, 147–153.

Gallo, P. Prisoners of our own dilemma? Paper presented at the meeting of the Western Psychological Association, 1968.

Gallois, P. *The balance of terror: Strategy for the Nuclear Age.* Boston: Houghton, 1961.

Geiwitz, P.J. The effects of threats on prisoner's dilemma. *Behavioral Science,* 1967, **12**, 232–233.

Geiwitz, P.J., & Fisher, Sandra, J. Threats, statements of intentions, and interpersonal conflict. Unpublished manuscript, Stanford University, 1969.

Gruder, C.L. Effects of perception of opponent's bargaining style and accountability to opponent and partner on interpersonal, mixed-motive bargaining. Unpublished doctoral dissertation, University of North Carolina, 1968.

Hilsman, R. *To move a nation.* Garden City, N.Y.: Doubleday, 1967.

Horelick, A. The Cuban missile crisis. *World Politics,* 1964, **16**, 363–389.

Hornstein, H.A. Effects of different magnitudes of threat upon interpersonal bargaining. *Journal of Experimental Social Psychology,* 1965, **1**, 282–293.

Horowitz, I.L. *The war game.* New York: Ballantine Books, 1963.

Ilke, F. *How nations negotiate.* New York: Harper, 1964.

Kahn, H. *On thermonuclear war.* Princeton, N.J.: Princeton University Press, 1961.

Kahn, H. *On escalation.* New York: Praeger, 1965.

Kateb, G. Kennedy as statesman. *Commentary,* 1966, **41**, 54–60.

Kelley, H.H. Experimental studies of threats in interpersonal negotiations. *Journal of Conflict Resolution,* 1965, **9**, 80–107.

Kennedy, R.F. My brother's secret ordeal. *London Times,* October 27 through November 2, 1968.

Kerr, C. Industrial conflict and its mediation. *American Journal of Sociology,* 1954, **60**, 230–245.

Kissinger, H.A. *Nuclear weapons and foreign policy.* New York: Harper, 1957.

Kissinger, H.A. *The necessity for choice.* New York: Harper, 1960.

Knowles, W.H. Mediation and the psychology of small groups. *Labor Law Journal,* 1958, **34**, 780–784.

Komorita, S.S., Sheposh, J.P., & Braver, S.L. Power, the use of power, and cooperative choice in a two-person game. *Journal of Personality and Social Psychology,* 1968, **8**, 134–142.

Kybal, D. The role of stabilized deterrence. In D.H. Frisch (Ed.), *Arms production: Program and issues.* New York: Twentieth Century Fund, 1961. Pp. 135–153.

Lieberman, E.J. Threat and assurance in the conduct of conflict. In R. Fisher (Ed.), *International conflict and behavioral science.* New York: Basic Books, 1964. Pp. 110–122.

Marlowe, D., Gergen, K.J., & Doob, A.N. Opponent's personality, expectation of social interaction, and interpersonal bargaining. *Journal of Personality and Social Psychology,* 1966, **3**, 206–213.

McNamara, R.S. Remarks before the economic club of New York, November 18, 1963. In R. Perrucci and M. Pilisuk (Eds.), *The triple revolution.* Boston: Little, Brown, 1968. Pp. 66–76.

McClintok, C.G., Harrison, A., Strand, S., & Gallo, P. Internationalism-isolationism, strategy of the other player, and two-person game behavior. *Journal of Abnormal Social Psychology,* 1963, **67**, 631–635.

Penkovskiy, O. *The Penkovskiy papers.* Garden City, N.Y.: Doubleday, 1965.

Peters, E. The mediator: A neutral, a catalyst, or a leader. *Labor Law Journal,* 1958, **34**, 764–769.

Pilisuk, M., & Skolnick, P. Experimenting with the arms race. *Scientific American,* 1970, in press.

Podell, J.E., & Knapp, W.M. The effect of mediation on the perceived firmness of the opposing negotiator. Unpublished manuscript, San Francisco State College, 1969.

Rapoport, A. *Fights, games and debates.* Ann Arbor, Mich.: University of Michigan Press, 1960.

Rapoport, A. Critique of strategic thinking. In R. Fisher (Ed.), *International conflict and behavioral science.* New York: Basic Books, 1964. Pp. 211–237.

Rapoport, A. *Strategy and conscience.* New York: Harper, 1964.(b)

Rapoport A. Strategic and non-strategic approaches to problems of security and peace. In Kathleen Archibald (Ed.), *Strategic interaction and conflict.* Berkeley: Institute of International Studies, University of California, 1966. Pp. 88–102.

Rapoport, A. Prospects for experimental games. *Journal of Conflict Resolution.* 1968, 12, 461–470.

Rapoport, A., & Chammah, A.M. *Prisoner's dilemma.* Ann Arbor, Mich.: University of Michigan Press, 1965.

Rapoport, A., & Chammah, A.M. The game of chicken. *American Behavioral Scientist,* 1966, 10, 10–28.

Russell, B. *Common sense and nuclear warfare.* London: Unwin Brothers, 1959.

Schelling, T.C. *The strategy of conflict.* Cambridge, Mass.: Harvard University Press, 1963.

Schelling, T.C. The strategy of inflicting costs. In R.N. McKean (Ed.), *Issues in defense economics.* New York: Columbia University Press, 1967. Pp. 105–127.

Sermat, V. Cooperative behavior in a mixed-motive game. *Journal of Social Psychology,* 1964, 62, 217–239.

Sermat, V. The possibility of influencing the other's behavior and cooperation: Chicken versus prisoner's dilemma. *Canadian Journal of Psychology,* 1967, 21, 204–219.(a)

Sermat, V. The effect of an initial cooperative or competitive treatment upon a subject's response to conditional cooperation. *Behavioral Science,* 1967, 12, 301–313.(b)

Sermat, V. Dominance - submissiveness and competition in a mixed-motive game. *British Journal of Social and Clinical Psychology,* 1968, 7, 35–44.

Sermat, V., & Gregovich, R.P. The effect of experimental manipulation on cooperative behavior in a chicken game. *Psychonomic Science,* 1966, 4, 435–436.

Shure, G.H., Meeker, R.J., & Hansford, E.A. The effectiveness of pacifist strategies in bargaining games. *Journal of Conflict Resolution,* 1965, 9, 106–117.

Smith, W.P., & Leginski, W.A. Magnitude and precision of punitive power as determinants of bargaining behavior. Paper presented at the meeting of the Eastern Psychological Association, Washington, 1968.

Snyder, G.H. *Deterrence and defense.* Princeton, N.J.: Princeton University Press, 1961.

Solomon, L. The influence of some types of power relationships and game strategies upon the development of interpersonal trust. *Journal of Abnormal Social Psychology,* 1960, 61, 223–230.

Sorenson, T.C. *Kennedy.* New York: Harper, 1965.

Stagner, R. *Psychological aspects of international conflict.* Belmont, Calif.: Brooks, Cole, 1967.

Stevens, C.M. *Strategy and collective bargaining negotiation.* New York: McGraw-Hill, 1963.

Swingle, P.G. The effects of the win-lose difference upon cooperative responding in a "dangerous" game. *Journal of Conflict Resolution,* 1967, 11, 214–222.

Swingle, P.G. Illusory power in a dangerous game. *Canadian Journal of Psychology,* 1968, 22, 176–185.

Swingle, P.G. Ethnic factors in interpersonal bargaining. *Canadian Journal of Psychology,* 1969, 23, 136–146.

Walton, R.E., & McKersie, R.B. *A behavioral theory of labor negotiations.* New York: McGraw-Hill, 1965.

Chapter 8

DETERRENCE GAMES:
FROM ACADEMIC CASEBOOK TO MILITARY CODEBOOK

Irving Louis Horowitz

I. INTRODUCTION

The outrage traditional scholars exhibit at the work done by war game strategists, be they of civilian or military affiliation, is closer to the anguish of men concerned with professional status than to that of men compromised by poor social science. In part, this chapter is an attempt to redress this set of concerns. This is the problem: No amount of theoretical assault on war gaming as a strategy has discouraged raising the use of this technique of analysis to the level of theory. Perhaps one solution is to look more soberly and seriously at the consequences such a strategy has in the real world and for actual men.

First, I shall examine the social structural components entailed in war game strategies that facilitate its use by military leaders. Second, I will examine the theory of war gaming in the light of military practice. Only by examining empirical events which claim to have employed game strategies to advantage can we move beyond the arguments over the actual worth of the theory. If I eschew the usual criticisms of war game theory it is not because of ignorance of them—indeed, I feel partially responsible for having collated these arguments in the first place (Horowitz, 1962, 1963)—but simply because the test of any theory must ultimately be its use. One unnerving missile crisis may not constitute a definitive rebuke, but at least it opens up the possibility of counterfactualizing statements in an area thus far held sacrosanct by at least some portion of the social scientific community connected to military decision-making.

War game theorists' reactions, when confronted by the military use of their findings, customarily vary from amusement to disaffiliation. Some maintain that the work of war gamers is of great therapeutic value in replacing old-fashioned horror stories, but has no more and no less validity. Others claim that war game concepts are radically distinct from and even contradictory to basic game theorems derived from probability theory. My own belief is that these disclaimers are much like the one made by the original founding members of the Royal Academy of Science when they discovered that atheists and agnostics were attempting to obtain membership on the basis of the principles of mechanics: to reaffirm, against all empirical information, that the principles of mechanics demonstrably prove the existence of Providential Will and, therefore, that nothing but good can come of such principles.

The assumption herein made is that however proximate or distant the relationship between war games and other games, there is such a connection. Further, however amusing or frightening these games are to participants or victims, game theory represents genuine empirical as well as metaphorical elements which, translated into operational terms through federal agencies, become part of the foreign policy of the United States.

This chapter is not to be a history or a chronicle of the relationship between war games and federal policy, but rather an attempt to understand the most general relations between national policy and military behavior by testing a specific theory about the influence of strategy expertise in policy matters, using deterrence theory as a model and testing it against the Cuban missile crisis as an empirical event of major consequence. In its specifics, this is an attempt to understand some of the general relations between politics and militarism through a test of a specific theory about the influence of war game theory on United States foreign policy.

II. THE GAME OF DETERRENCE: A MILITARY CODEBOOK

The theory of military deterrence through games of strategy is contained in an article by Colonel Wesley Posvar, former Chairman of the Air Force Academy Political Science Department, entitled "The Impact of Strategy

Expertise on the National Security Policy of the United States" (Posvar, 1964). His theory beings with a definition of strategy (Posvar, 1964, p. 38):

> In the present context strategy pertains to the systematic development and employment of national power, particularly military power, to secure national aims . . . The constituents of national power which are relevant . . . include military power and other instruments to the extent that they are closely linked to military power, including economic (foreign assistance, trade, discrimination), psychological (propaganda, terror), and in limited degree, ideological and political.

This definition is one that is generally accepted by the strategy experts and is suitable to this context; so I see no reason not to accept it.

Part of Posvar's theory concerns how strategic policy is created: "Policy is formulated not only in the way usually understood, that is, by a body at the center of government, drawing the information it needs." Strategy is also formed by the cumulative action of subordinate and outlying elements, "in the sense that the weapons chosen for development today determine national strategy ten years from now . . . Although the making of strategy is a function of government . . . it is possible for this function to be performed to a great extent completely outside the structure of government (Posvar, pp. 39–40)." Here he is describing a process which many others have observed—policy by lack of decision, by default. Insofar as decisions could be made but are not, Posvar feels that decisive influence (he would not use the word "power") passes to the strategy experts, insofar as they invent or define available options.

Posvar next describes the system of games of strategy: "Strategy expertise is the product of men, organizations, and methods." It is not the product of a statistical aggregate, for the strategy experts make up a community "with a degree of coherence that seems to exceed the bonds of common organization and shared technique (1964, p. 43)." Strategy expertise is produced in two organizational contexts, research corporations and university research centers (cf., Lyons & Morton, 1965). The most highly organized strategy expertise is concentrated in half a dozen research corporations: RAND (working primarily for the Air Force), Research Analysis Corporation (successor to ORO, working mostly for the Army), the Institute for Defense Analyses (performing contract studies for the Department of Defense at large), the Hudson Institute, the Operations Evaluation Group (working for the Navy), and the Stanford Research Institute (working for industry as well as government).

Strategy expertise is produced by distinctive methods of analysis, such as economic theory, e.g., mathematical models of war used for computer simulation, or informal games of decision-makers in conflict situations simulated by individual role-playing, and, of course, that amalgamation of everything—and, therefore, particularly attractive to some social scientists—systems analysis, which is the "result of associating experts from various disciplines together under favorable circumstances of organization and communication, experts who share attention to common tasks (Posvar, 1964, p. 52)." Posvar's description of the organization and methods of the system of game strategy is brief but fairly accurate, though the coherence he ascribes to it has implications far beyond his own considerations.

Posvar finally describes several ways in which game strategy can be implemented in actual policy. One way is "the reverse of the dispersal of the strategy-making function . . . the problem of assembling and using the output of the system . . . This step involves the whole decision-making process of the United States government. So we are forced to limit our present observations to the difficulties which are encountered in attempting to place recommendations and studies in the right hands." Here Posvar observes that in order to maintain their institutional autonomy, the game strategy experts try to maintain the principle of nonadvocacy. This factor, combined with the position of the experts outside the government, tends "to obstruct the entry of important ideas and findings into the decision-making process." What happens to the specific policy recommendations once they are in the proper hands is a separate question which Posvar (1964, pp. 56–57) does not consider.

> The pattern of influence works another way, too, as strategic analysis is solicited by high government offices for specific tasks . . . There is little wonder that the "celibate mistress" (i.e., the RAND Corporation, kept but ignored by the Air Force) has become the object of flirtation by the Office of the Secretary of Defense, which now includes former members of the strategic community who fully appreciate her charms.

His theory provides another way in which strategic analysis has influence on policy; of greater importance is the direct and objective influence upon the whole policy echelon provided by a massive outpouring of scholarship. The system provides an ever-larger volume of published works plus myriad briefings of policy officials and staff officers. This is the process by which game strategy experts are able to influence the decisions in the subordinate and outlying elements.

This is the foundation of Posvar's theory of game strategy. However, Posvar raised other important issues which it is necessary to consider. First, there is the question of an evaluation of the system. At this point Posvar's theory turns into celebration: "RAND appears to be one of the best investments the United States government has made since the Louisiana Purchase. Secretary McNamara, who is not prone to make such extravagant statements as this, does acknowledge that the Air Force gets 'ten times the value' of the cost of the RAND contract." Posvar illustrates this evaluation with seven examples in which strategic analysis was implemented successfully, but presents no examples of failure. He explains (Posvar, 1964, pp. 61 and 64–65),

> We are unable to perceive a failure in a weapon system, so long as the goals of policy are being adequately served. Who can say now whether our decision to rely on the B-47 plus aerial tanker force, and on the B-36 force before it, were the best decisions? Who, indeed, cares? The presumption is in favor of success inasmuch as the policy of deterrence of general war was fulfilled.

This explanation has the same sophistication as that of the compulsive urbanite when asked why he continually snaps his fingers: "To keep the elephants away. Works pretty well, doesn't it?" Be that as it may, Posvar's theory of how the system works can be judged independently of his evaluation of the system.

A second issue is the relationship of civilian strategy experts to military professionals. Some people feel that the strategy experts undermine the older military professions by preempting their essential functions. Posvar feels that "this complaint masks a need for further strengthening the professional bureaucracy itself" by learning the methods and techniques of strategy expertise so that the military can better judge and use it.

A third issue is whether strategy experts constitute a power elite, whether they are part of the military–industrial–academic "complex." Posvar considers this question just long enough to dismiss it, though it crops up again later in a different form:

> We may therefore state the basis of our concern explicitly as a displacement of power relative to responsibility . . . We refer to the power (or authority) to make or decisively to influence strategic decisions, and the responsibility (or account-ability) to a superior political object for the consequences of those decisions. They should reside in the same place.

Posvar feels that the solution is clear: "The dissociation of power and responsibility which is a deficiency of the strategy-making process could be largely remedied by raising the qualifications of professional bureaucrats, both military and civilian (Posvar, 1964, pp. 63–64)." The military in this country has long had an ideology of being professional and apolitical. Military profession-alism, of course, puts an emphasis on expert judgment. Posvar is a military man, and he seems to assume that the professional quality of game strategy, or its "scientific" status, assures its pervasive implementation at all levels of government. When management fails to put into effect the research findings it contracts for, Posvar thinks it is a failure of understanding, to be corrected by education. To think that this can be changed through education is to fail to perceive political reality. Expert judgment may be correct, but correctness alone is not enough. There is also the question of interests, of who benefits.

Finally, Posvar specifically mentions the Cuban missile crisis. He writes (Posvar, 1964, pp. 66–67):

> There is a new awareness of the utility and also the limitations of strategic striking power in situations involving limited national objectives, like Cuba. Herman Kahn's Type II Deterrent [which "guards against major aggression against a vital area other than the U.S. (e.g., Europe) by the threat of retaliation directly against the U.S.S.R."], and Thomas Schelling's Threat That Leaves Something to Chance [which "deters lower scale actions by the danger that somebody might inadvertently start a big war"], have contributed to this awareness . . . When one reflects on these new perceptions in strategic thought, and the likelihood that a president would be familiar with them as President Kennedy evidently was in the Cuba crisis, the conclusion is inescapable that the strategists have made a vital contribution.

The difficulty is the failure to note whether the Kahn-Schelling framework is as "familiar" to either Castro or Khrushchev—those directly involved and in power at that time. This is said only partially in jest. In point of fact, both Kahn and Schelling imply an explicit level of mutual rationality in order for the deterrent and threat mechanisms to be made operational. In a sense, too, this is the Achilles' heel of such gaming strategies, since if shared rationality is a requirement for the conduct of politics by military means, there is no way of avoiding the counterproposal: the conduct of military activities by political means. However, the reason this logical equivalent is not developed by Posvar and his fellow new civilian militarists is if such a high decree of rationality can be assumed in the pursuit of self-interest, one should be able to claim, in good Adam Smithian terms, that this same rationality would point up the futility of brinkmanship games to begin with, and hence reinforce the notion of settlement through accommodation rather than victory through fear.

III. THE GAME OF DETERRENCE: AN ORGANIZATIONAL NETWORK

Doubtless, the Cuban missile crisis fits Posvar's definition of war game strategy. The United States government had at the time of the missile crisis (and still has) three basic national aims with respect to Cuba. These main goals were to prevent the spread of communism, to overthrow the Castro government, and to crush communism in Cuba. These sentiments were expressed in a joint resolution of Congress passed on September 20 and 26, 1962 (Pachter, 1963, p. 179):

> The United States is determined: (a) to prevent by whatever means may be necessary, including the use of arms, the Marxist–Leninist regime in Cuba from extending, by force or by the threat of force, its aggressive or subversive activities

to any part of this hemisphere; (b) to prevent in Cuba the creation or use of an externally supported military capability endangering the security of the United States; and (c) to work with the Organization of American States and with freedom-loving Cubans to support the aspirations of the Cuban people for self-determination.

By military power and by other instruments of national power such as trade discrimination, Cuba was to be isolated, to make the maintenance of communism in Cuba costly to the Soviet Union (McNamara, 1963a, p. 274). Since it fits his definition, the missile crisis is a test case relevant to Posvar's theory.

The next question is how game strategy policy was formulated in the Cuban case. In formal terms, the answer is simple. An executive committee of the National Security Council, appointed *ad hoc* by President Kennedy, formulated and recommended a course of action, and the President approved it. But the real issue is how game strategy came to be implemented, if it was, in the actual policy followed. This is the crux of the problem and a much more difficult question to answer.

There are several modes of influence to be considered. First is the assembly and use of specific recommendations or studies dealing with the introduction of offensive weapons into Cuba. Whether the analysis is solicited by higher or lower government offices makes a difference only after the recommendations exist; the first problem is to establish their existence. Bruce Smith pointed out, however, that the effective advisory group usually goes to great pains to conceal its impact on policy (Smith, 1966, p. 231). For example, the RAND strategic bases study, *Selection and Use of Strategic Air Bases*, R-266, was put into effect in 1953, but remained classified until 1962, nine years later. In establishing his case for the influence of this study over Air Force policy, Smith relied extensively on personal interviews, which might have been difficult to obtain, if his dissertation advisor had not been a member of RAND's board of trustees. (Smith's study was a Ph.D. dissertation. His faculty advisor, Don K. Price, was both a Harvard Dean and a RAND trustee.) The RAND Corporation made a number of studies after the crisis, but if any studies were made before the crisis they are still classified (cf., Graham & Brease, 1967). Because any such study would be extremely politically sensitive in nature, it would be unlikely to be declassified in the near future. Second, specific policy recommendations are atypical; most RAND strategy analysis deals with more abstract questions. Information analysis directed toward specific policy is the responsibility of the intelligence branch. Although on the Cuban question, the theoretical distinction between research and intelligence fades, the institutional distinction remains clear—research and intelligence functions are performed by different bureaus. By all accounts, only the intelligence experts were involved in the executive committee council of war. According to Wohlstetter, no one thought the Cubans and Russians would install the missiles (1965). One must infer, lacking any other evidence, that no specific policy recommendations relating to the Cuban situation were produced by the RAND Corporation. Since RAND's influence seems out of the question in this case, there is no point in speculating about methodological problems such as communication and distortion of policy recommendations or the merits of systems analysis.

The other mode of influence is the pervasive frame of reference contained in the "massive outpouring of scholarship" in support of the new politics based on behavioral psychology. The early sixties were characterized by the emergence of war game theory as the basic form of macroscopic social science. This occurred in part as a metaphorical displacement of the "historical" orientations of previous periods characterized by the writings of such men as Hans Morgenthau and Arnold J. Toynbee, and in part as a commonly held belief that the results of experimental psychology, particularly of reinforcement, exchange, and balance theories, could be extended to cover political behavior between nations. The concurrence of circumstances (i.e., the emergence of a group of war gamers such as Alain Enthoven and Adam Yarmolinsky in positions of advisory power, the professional demands by men like Bernard Brodie and Ethiel de Sola Pool to "test" behaviorist assumptions in a broadened context, the coalescence of "systems" designers with engineering backgrounds such as Seymour J. Deitchman, and "social" designers with behavioral backgrounds such as Henry J. Kissinger): All of these factors served as a fulcrum for organizing a new view of "relevance"–a new faith in a social science of political "meaning."

At the same time the inner organizational requisites of war game theory were being met, the outer political requisites of real conflict were also being met in the Cuban missile crisis. This crisis had the perfect scenario dimensions: (a) It was a simple two-person struggle between major powers (or so it seemed to the protagonists at the time); (b) it had a stage setting of showdown proportions that revealed relatively clear-cut and unambiguous dimensions; and (c) it was a situation in which victor and vanquished would be readily determined by the behavior shown. That all of these assumptions were radically in error was either disbelieved or discounted at the time. It was not a simple two-person struggle, but one interpreted by Cuba–and much of the Third World–as a struggle between big powers acting arrogantly and a small power acting with principles to preserve its autonomy and sovereignty. There was nothing unambiguous about the showdown, since in fact the resolution was such as to convince all combatants and parties to the dispute that they had in fact been the winner. It was a showdown without losers, in fact. Indeed, this really made peace possible under the circumstances, since no one was willing to accept responsibilities for any defeat, or any outcome perceived by each people as a defeat.

According to the *New York Times'* account of the Committee's October 19 meeting, there were some second thoughts about the blockade, some renewed interest in an air attack. "The reason was what the group called a 'scenario' [a phrase originating in the strategy community] —a paper indicating in detail all the possible consequences of an action (1962)." Elie Abel pointed out that "Bundy prepared the air-strike argument; and Alexis Johnson with Paul Nitze's assistance, drafted what came to be called the blockade scenario (Abel, 1966, p. 86)," indicating that the frame of reference of the Executive Committee was game strategy analysis.

Bruce Smith noted that "Gaming and simulation had important uses as a training device for government officials to help them understand what kinds of behavior to be prepared for in various crisis situations. Crisis games became widely used by high State and Defense Department officials early in the Kennedy Administration (Smith, 1966, p. 112)." In addition, many high level civilian executives were formerly members of the game strategy community: Charles Hitch, Assistant Secretary of Defense (Comptroller), Henry Rowen and Alain Enthoven, Deputy Assistant Secretaries of Defense, Walt W. Rostow, Assistant Secretary of State, and Paul Nitze, Secretary of the Navy (Posvar, 1964, p. 48). At the time of the crisis Paul Nitze was Assistant Secretary of Defense for International Security Affairs and a member of Kennedy's *ad hoc* crisis committee.

Political gaming as a special subfunction of military policy is a procedure for the study of foreign affairs which the RAND Corporation began developing in 1954. A RAND report, referring to the State Department's interest in gaming, noted that: "Even before the first four games had been completed RAND began to receive requests for information about its political gaming procedures, and staff members have by now taken part in a substantial number of discussions about it (Spier & Goldhammer, 1959, p. 80)." As witness to this interest, "three senior Foreign Service Officers from the Department of State participated in the fourth political game, along with specialists from RAND's Social Science, Economics, and Physics Divisions (Spier & Goldhammer, 1959, p. 74)."

There is scant doubt that gaming and simulation were widely used in the Executive Committee of the President. Nearly all higher echelon figures knew immediately what games were referred to. Although State Department officers like George W. Ball may have doubted that political games were of greater value than a similar amount of involvement in ordinary reading and study, many senior officers even of the "traditional" State Department no less than the "modern" Defense Department participated in the fourth round. Although only a minority of Kennedy's war council came from the Departments of State and Defense, the rest were seemingly also familiar with strategy analysis.

The chilling degree to which a game of showdown proportions had been arranged around the Cuban missile crisis is reported by Schlesinger (1965, p. 830). "Saturday night was almost the blackest of all. Unless Khrushchev came through in a few hours, the meeting of the Executive Committee on Sunday night might well face the most terrible decisions." In a revealing metaphor, Schlesinger then notes, "At nine in the morning Khrushchev's answer began to come in. By the fifth sentence it was clear that he had thrown in his hand." And it is finally made clear that this unwillingness to risk all-out war on the Soviet Union's part came "barely in time." Schlesinger concludes by drawing out the option. "If word had not come that Sunday, if work had continued on the bases, the United States would have had no real choice but to take action against Cuba the next week. No one could discern what lay darkly beyond an air strike or invasion, what measures and countermeasures, actions and reactions, might have driven the hapless world to the ghastly consummation." It should be noted that this account is made not simply from a writer, but from a member of the President's inner group of advisors; and that the differences between hard-liners and soft-liners over the missile crisis concerned the character of the response, not the necessity for playing the game of showdown poker. Thus, at a critical point in United States foreign policy, traditional methods of accommodation were abandoned in favor of a military definition of the situation—a definition made intellectually palatable by the "science" of game theory.

Game strategy analysis also played an influential role through the Joint Chiefs of Staff. Although Senator Sparkman of Alabama, in the September hearings, remembered "General LeMay, Chief of Staff of the Air Force, stating that there would be no difficulty in knocking out those missile sites (Sparkman, 1962, p. 75)," only the Chairman of the Joint Chiefs, Maxwell Taylor, actually sat on the Executive Committee. When Kennedy met separately with the Joint Chiefs, they would not guarantee that a so-called "surgical strike"—one that would destroy all the missiles and bombers yet inflict few casualties on the general population—was feasible (cf., Sorenson, 1965). In any case, such feasibility studies are the proper responsibility of the military profession and are not farmed out to research corporations. Posvar's argument about the influence of strategy analysis thus has little value. The final executive committee recommendations actually emerged from a political bargaining process which involved not only the military factors and strategic analysis, but also considerations of morality (e.g. Robert F. Kennedy argued against the air strike position, saying it would be another Pearl Harbor) and international political consequences.

Many questions arise to make even the hardiest political man uneasy over this concept of the "surgical strike." For people like Wohlstetter and Kahn, the problem of defense begins with the military issues surrounding a first strike strategy and proceeds to conditions for a second strike situation. The uses of war game theory thus serve to limit options and deepen ambiguity in the military situation as well. Under such circumstances, it is small wonder that even those who in the past were close to systems design would raise serious questions as to the efficacy of war gaming. The following remarks by Robert Boguslaw well illustrate the source of much fear that arose both during and after the Cuban missile crisis (Boguslaw, 1967, p. 57).

To what extent does the Wohlstetter solution introduce more uncertainty into the international situation and thereby increase the probability of a first strike? To what extent does the effort to confuse an enemy so that he can "never be sure" about the destination of a flight of American bombers serve to make his radar crews and "first strike" forces more jumpy? What are the implications of the analyses and the fail-safe procedures for increasing the probability of unintended nuclear war? Where are the spectacles to correct the consumer-oriented analytic myopia of contemporary systems analysis?

The fact that neither Posvar nor any of his colleagues at RAND addressed themselves to these issues means that a basic aspect in a true gaming situation is constantly violated—namely, the existence of sufficient equilibrium in the situation designed so as to prevent an artificial resolution of the problem, or a termination of the game due to bias and misinformation. Yet, it was precisely the increase in ambiguity that decreased rather than increased chances for making accurate predictions as to the outcome of the Cuban missile crisis. It ultimately came down to the "rationality" of the "other player," rather than a science of game theory, since all the moves of the United States had been telegraphed well in advance, whereas only the Soviet response remained truly problematic (cf., Brodie, 1964, p. 53; Horelick, 1963, p. 26).

IV. DETERRENCE GAMES: THE POLITICAL CONTEXT

The military emphasis on how a game strategy system molds future decisions outside the government ignores the political aspects of decisions made inside the government. According to such a view, no central body tries to "understand" problems of government; instead, a number of partially conflicting factions tries to promote particular interpretations and emphases favorable to their own interests. There are at least three interest groups in government: the top civilian office-holders of the national security apparatus, the military professionals of the various armed services, and the civilian strategy experts.

Interservice rivalry is an important aspect of this political context. Interservice competition is a post-World War II phenomenon resulting from new technology of war—atomic bombs and missiles—and the changed military requirements of the Cold War balance of power.

The transition from civilian—service controversy to inter-service controversy as the main focus of service political activity was graphically illustrated in the struggle over Universal Military Training between 1945 and 1948. The lines of battle were initially drawn between the Army and certain patriotic and veterans groups on the one hand, and various civilian educational, religious, pacifist, and farm groups on the other.

Huntington, 1965, p. 453

This issue was resolved by the convergence of two factors: the relative persuasiveness of Air Force vs. Army strategy doctrine, and the relative political costs of an $822 million hardware appropriation vs. universal conscription. This provides only one illustration of how political forces on the Congressional battlefield are deployed.

The military services can mobilize several kinds of political forces. The fist of these is voluntary associations, such as the Navy League or the Association of the US Army. These can engage in political tactics and activities traditionally denied to active servicemen by the restraint of civilian control and the prohibition of military politics. Patriotic groups still support the military generally, but not always the viewpoint of one service over another. In cultivating grass roots support, the services face a difficult problem (Huntington, 1965, pp. 463–464):

> Unlike many private associations and a fair number of governmental agencies, the services could not easily mobilize sentiment across the country in support of a national program. The problem which they faced was not dissimilar from that confronted by the large industrial corporations. Both the corporation and the services are national and highly centralized institutions. Political power in America, however, is to a large extent channeled through local organs. Individual political influence depends on prolonged local residence and participation; the employees of the corporation and the service are continually on the move. On the one hand, the economic health of the local community may depend upon decisions by a General Staff in Washington or a board of directors in New York. On the other hand, the small community normally possesses direct access to state and local governing bodies, and frequently to Congress, in a way that is denied to the national organization.

Since national organizations cannot guarantee serving local *interests,* they try to influence local power through appealing to local *values.* The corporations play upon their ideology of free enterprise; the military services emphasize their ideology of anticommunism. The Cold War has made it possible to outmaneuver the traditional antimilitarism of isolationists, pacifists, and religious and educational groups by playing upon their fear of communist subversion and aggression.

Political support is also available for industry. The Air Force used to be able to rely on the aircraft industry and the Navy on the shipbuilding industry for political lobbying and support,but the shift of demand to missiles and electronics—often manufactured by companies holding contracts with two or more services—means that industrial interests no longer take sides in interservice competition.

A final type of political support is provided by doctrine. Productive enterprise needs no justification save its product; military expenditures are wasteful and thus require intellectual rationale. The armed services explicitly justify all their activities as essential for the achievement of national goals. The bureaucratic rigidity of the military made it incapable of doctrinal innovation; so it hired outside consultants to rethink strategy. Because technical questions about what strategies best serve national ends have political consequences for the military, game strategy experts became part of the fray.

> It is a rare man in Washington who does not suffer from the "Edifice Complex," a tendency which directs his work toward building up his own agency or service whenever possible. Thus, experts associated with the Army or the Navy have developed arguments supporting stabilized deterrence combined with a buildup of conventional forces. Air Force-linked experts have countered with a strategy based on overwhelming superiority in missiles and bombers, buttressed with schemes such as civil defense and studies that prove that *under certain conditions*, we could win a thermonuclear war without destroying our society.
> Maccoby, 1963, p. 106

The class of civilian strategy experts originated when the Air Force set up the RAND Corporation. At this time, "the mission of the Air Force was almost equivalent to the whole of the national defense effort. The Air Force was secure in its possession of the atomic bomb and the means of its delivery, and had little reason to fear either foreign enemies or a competing sister service (Smith, 1966, p. 49)." In the early days of the RAND Corporation, loyalties to the theory of scientific strategy and to doctrine supporting the Air Force position coincided perfectly; game strategy experts felt they could work for a single service without sacrificing their scholarly autonomy. As the other services obtained bombs and missiles of their own, this confidence changed. RAND began to diversify its sponsorship contracts and strategic theory, as it elaborated and took cognizance of the international and interservice strategic situation. Thus, RAND deviated from its support of Air Force interests. The Air Force attempted to bring RAND back into line. "It was the cumulative effect of various RAND–Air Force differences that led to RAND's budget for the fiscal year 1961 being cut in half to $7,000,000 in the initial round of budget preparation (Smith, 1966, p. 134)." The RAND management acknowledged that its primary loyalties lay with the Air Force and agreed that Air Force sources should supply most of its research funds. This political resolution was not without scientific cost. RAND had "the problem of continuing to attract first-rate staff at a time when Air Force concerns no longer are the central focus of the nation's defense policies (Smith, 1966, p. 138)." The strategy community's ambiguity on policy questions is a political strategy of self-preservation which only half succeeds.

Top civilian office-holders are in a quite different position. As the bureaucratic superordinates of the professional military men, they are limited only by what political pressures the military can indirectly bring to bear upon them through Congress.

> They have assigned themselves the task of presiding over a vast military bureaucracy—and its supporting institutions—in a period in which changes in technology have forced revolutionary changes in the military art . . . They generally lack military training and yet somehow must try to maintain direction over the efforts of their always restive military technicians. Under such circumstances they have become the most ideological of men. Without the presumed superiority of an almost infallible conception of the National Interest they could not hope to force grudging acquiescence from their more technically skilled military subordinates.

John McDermott's description (1967, p. 5) of the "crisis managers" ignores the role of the civilian strategy experts and overestimates the military bureaucracy's ability to adjust to the revolutionary developments in war technology. In founding the RAND Corporation, the Air Force admitted its own inflexibility. It could neither pay high enough salaries nor provide enough intellectual freedom to attract to its own ranks men capable of coping theoretically with the new technology. The civilian managers, realizing that the services bought their expertise from the civilian strategy experts, did likewise. When RAND wanted to diversify its sponsorship the Defense Department was ready. "The Air Force, seeing RAND develop an intimate advisory relationship with the agencies at the level of the Office of the Secretary of Defense, has had second thoughts about its confidential lawyer–client tie with RAND (Smith, 1966, p. 129)." In addition, the Defense Department is in a position to monitor all research. In April 1962, the Secretary of Defense directed the secretaries of the Air Force, Army, and Navy to forward to his office copies of each study received from RAND, ORO, and the other advisory corporations (Horowitz, 1968). And while such periodic reviews of research are not proof that such research is actually used, the distinct impression was instilled—in part as a consequence of Kahn's inordinate influence on many Presidential advisors—that game theory was the operational codebook, and not just an intellectual curiosity, of the new administration.

V. THE GAME OF DETERRENCE: A CUBAN CASEBOOK

Given the general context of the political situation of the defense establishment, it is time to examine the Cuban missile crisis in its specifics. The services and the Defense Department expressed different strategic interpretations of the Cuban crisis in the Congressional appropriations hearings in 1965. General

Curtis LeMay, Chief of Staff of the Air Force, expressed the Air Force position (1963, pp. 888–896):

> We must maintain a credible general war force so that lesser options may be exercised under the protection of this general war deterrent. It is the general war strength of aircraft and missile forces which place an upper limit on the risks an aggressor is willing to take, and which deter escalation into an all-out conflict. In the Cuban crisis, this limit was tested.
>
> I am convinced that superior U.S. strategic power, coupled with obvious will and ability to apply this power, was the major factor that forced the Soviets to back down. Under the shelter of strategic power, which the Soviets did not dare challenge, the other elements of military power were free to exercise their full potential.

This version of strategic theory is clearly beneficial to the long-run interests of the Air Force. The Air Force answer to the problem of how to deter minor "aggression" is to play "chicken" with the Air Force-delivered general war force. Posvar's above comments on the Cuban crisis, though brief, seem quite consonant with the Air Force position. General Earle Wheeler, Army Chief of Staff, expressed the Army position in his statement (1963, p. 507):

> In my opinion, the major lesson for the Army in the Cuban situation lies in the demonstrated value of maintaining ready Army forces at a high state of alert in order to equip national security policy with the military power to permit a direct confrontation of Soviet power. As Secretary McNamara pointed out to the NATO ministers recently, " . . . the forces that were the cutting edge of the action were the nonnuclear ones. Nuclear force was not irrelevant, but it was in the background. Nonnuclear forces were our sword, our nuclear forces were our shield." I wholeheartedly agree with this statement. In the Cuban situation, the Army forces were alerted, brought up to strength in personnel and equipment, moved and made ready for the operations as part of the largest U.S. invasion force prepared since World War II.

The Air Force interpreted limited war and limited "aggression" as capable of being deterred by strategic nuclear forces and the credibility of its threatened use, while the Army Defense Department views strategic nuclear forces alone as insufficient.

A circumstantial argument for the influence of strategy expertise could be made if the position of the RAND Corporation coincided with the strategic interpretation of the Air Force, its sponsor. A staff-initiated RAND study, however, as early as 1957 noted that "in the case of a sharply limited war in Europe, tactical forces have renewed utility, with strategic air forces complementing tactical forces as the necessary enforcers of weapons limitations (Hoag, 1957, p. 13; 1961, p. 26)." In at least a dozen other studies of limited war before the crisis, the RAND Corporation developed the same theme. Because of the strategic balance of power, "neither side could expect to use its strategic capabilities to enforce a level of violence in the local area favorable to itself." A limited war capability was needed because "we shall not be able to rely on our strategic forces to deal with limited aggressions (DeWeerd, 1961, p. 17)." These studies clearly supported the Army doctrine on limited warfare and contributed to the above mentioned estrangement of RAND and the Air Force. The Defense Department, on the other hand, became quite interested (Smith, 1966, p. 127):

> In early 1962, a large contract was consummated between the RAND Corporation and the Office of the Assistant Secretary of Defense for International Security Affairs (ISA). The ISA contract involved analytic studies of a variety of defense problems, including counterinsurgency and limited war questions, and the annual funding under the ISA contract for a two-year period amounted to over $1,000,000. The ISA contract frightened the Air Force . . . because many Air Force officers felt that some of the civilians in the ISA were contemptuous of military professionalism.

The standard interpretation of this complaint by the New Civilian Militarists (NCM) is the masking of a lack of understanding and competence in strategic theory. However, the Air Force officers correctly perceived a threat to their position in the defense establishment—a more plausible explanation. The NCM theory would similarly attribute the Air Force's failure to implement the RAND-generated expertise on limited war to a lack of understanding. This theory would not explain why bureaucratic incompetence was limited to the Air Force, and not to the Army or Defense Department. The NCM theory of expertise equates lack of enthusiasm with ignorance and incompetence. One might argue that the Air Force neglected RAND's contribution because they did not know about it; Smith's account of the implementation of the strategic bases study showed that the communication of research findings is a long and complicated process. Furthermore, this NCM objection does not explain how the Army and the Defense Department positions coincided with the RAND position—they knew about RAND's work. The Air Force refused to understand because RAND's expert judgment benefited the Army to the detriment of the Air Force.

Implementation of policy depends not only on the validity of game theory, but also on the question of who benefits. The above emphasis on conflicts within the defense establishment neglects the consensus on two articles of faith: ideological anticommunism which divides the world into communists and anticommunists and coercion as the only mode of intercourse between the two.

The careful perusal of the military definition of game theory reveals that gaming strategy is the "science" of coercion. Anything which is not coercive is irrational from a strategic frame of reference. Anticommunism, too, is deeply rooted in strategic analysis. A RAND study notes that if limited wars occur, "they should be looked at as a local and limited manifestation of the global struggle between Communism and the Non-Communist World (DeWeerd, 1967, p. 17)." These two articles of faith pervade not only the strategy community and the defense establishment but also the rest of the government involved in the crisis, so that even if the strategy community had no influence over anyone else, it is questionable whether there would be any substantial difference in policy (cf., Commager, 1968).

While this analysis has emphasized the political and sociological aspects of gaming analogies, experts themselves often emphasize the truth and rationality of war games. As de Sola Pool (1967, p. 268) puts matters: "That is essentially the choice that we face, the choice between policy based on moralisms and policy based on social science." Traditional political concerns vanish in this hygienic version of social science. The claim of truth is a powerful way to legitimate authority, but it is also an exclusive way. The claim to social science expertise illegitimates other decision criteria. The illegitimation inherent in the claim for expertise is reflected in the NCM belief that the neglect of expert recommendations is a function of ignorance and bureaucratic incompetence. Further, they claim that the failure to perceive the role of expertise as a weapon in the political conflict within the defense establishment and between the defense establishment and civilian groups against militarism weakens the United States military "posture" abroad. Thus, game theory serves as an organizational weapon of military terror—even when its strategies may go awry—as in the Cuban missile crisis.

One might conclude by noting that the United States used the war game strategies, while the Soviet Union used conventional rhetoric of Marxism—and yet the latter managed to walk away with at the very least a stalemate, and in some interpretations the full victory. For in exchange for the withdrawal of long-range missiles, the Soviet Union guaranteed the long-range survival of Cuba's socialist regime, and no less, a long-term Soviet presence in the Western Hemisphere. It might be argued that conventional diplomacy might have netted the United States far greater results: the maintenance of diplomatic ties between Cuba and the United States. Direct negotiations with Castro rather than negotiations with the Soviets about Castro would have had the result of preventing the Soviets from maintaining a long-range presence and done nothing more to strengthen Cuba's sense of sovereignty than it already has. But, of course, this would make the military subject to pressures of an historical, geographic, and cultural variety that they reject almost instinctively. War game theory is a model of simplicity. It supplies a two-person situation, even if it does sometimes select the wrong players. It structures outcomes, even if it does leave out of the reckoning the optimal sort of outcome. It resolves problems, even if it does so by raising the ante of the problem beyond its initial worth.

What I have attempted to do is provide a sociological explanation of the functional role of war game theory for the military. Only a final word needs to be said about the symbolic role of war game theory—namely, the comfort provided by a world of psychological neatness—a world in which the behavior of large-scale nations is reducible to the decisions of a single man or small group of men. In this sense, war game theory is the ultimate expression, not only of the military ethic, but of the elitist and *étatist* mentality. But it remains the case that the management of political crises is made more complex, not more simple, by the new military technology. The danger is that military leaders have chosen to ignore this, and respond simplistically precisely as the world of politics and ideology grows more problematic and complicated.

It is important to appreciate the fact that we have been describing a conventional war game built on coercion and threat, and not a model of a game premised on a mechanism of positivist reinforcement built on consensus and compromise. Nor am I prepared to argue the merits of those who claim that ultimately consensual game models reduce to conflictual models anyhow, thus eliminating the need to study "milder" forms of game theory. Indeed, one might point out that the consensual models only seem to penetrate the literature when some sort of stable equilibrium was in fact reached between the Soviet Union and the United States in the postmissile crisis period. Hence, war game theory is not so much an independent input in decision-making as it is a sophisticated rationaliziation of decisions already taken (cf., Green, 1966; Horowitz, 1967).

Beyond the clear sets of objections other analysts of war game theory and I have pointed out over the years, there is one that has seemingly escaped everyone's attention in the past (including my own)—namely, the role of war game theory as a legitimation device for whatever crude military strategy has been decided upon. A tautological aspect thus emerges: If the decision to blockade Cuba is taken, war game theory is appealed to as ultimate arbiter; if the decision to lift the blockade is taken, the same appeal to war gaming is made; and since any complete holocaust would "terminate the game" and "eliminate the players," there is no real possibility of disconfirming the "theory" on which the decision is ostensibly reached.

Under such a wonderful protective covering of *post hoc* legitimation, and with every strategic decision confirming anew the worth of war game theory, it is extremely difficult to reach any final estimate of the theory as such; for this reason, the examination of real events—particularly military fiascos such as the Bay of Pigs landing or the Gulf of Tonkin retaliations—may be the clearest way open to analysts for evaluating the potency, or as is more usually the case, the paucity, of war game strategies.

In part, what has been described in this paper belongs to history rather than to politics. And this is as it should be, since when a particular strategy becomes elevated to the level of military theology, the clear and present danger to human survival soon becomes apparent. And in the shock surrounding the

Cuban missile crisis—the delayed awareness that the world stood still for a week while games of strategy were permitted to run their course—war game theory had its proudest moment and yet its last moment.

It was not long after the Great Missile Crisis that the "game of chicken" was abandoned in favor of conventional forms of political accommodation. This came about through the mutual realization of the Soviet Union and the United States (especially the latter) that Cuba was not a pawn or an ace-in-the-hole, but a sovereign power in its own right. The Castro Revolution was both national and hemispheric; it evolved its own brand of socialism to meet the challenges of a single-crop island economy. Thus, the Cuban regime was a system that had to be dealt with in traditional political terms of how sovereign states with differing social structures relate to each other. When this dawning took place the Cuban "crisis" was really solved, precisely by surrendering the notion that this was a behavioral situation reducible to the moves and countermoves of the world's big two military powers. Yet, as long as such repudiation of strategic thinking remains informal and unthinking, the dangers in a repetition of such forms of crisis management through games of chance remain ever present. And what first appeared as tragedy may return not so much as comedy, but rather as absurdity—in this instance, the absurdity of total mutual annihilation.

REFERENCES

Abel, E. *The missile crisis.* New York: Bantam Books, 1966.

Boguslaw, R. RAND in retrospect. *Trans-Action* 1967, **4**, 56–57.

Brodie, B. The American scientific strategists. P-2979, October, 1964 The RAND Corporation.

Commager, H.S. Can we limit presidential power? *New Republic* 1968, **158**, 15-18.

DeWeerd, H.A. Concepts of limited war: An historical approach. P-2352, November, 1961, The RAND Corporation.

DeWeerd, H.A. Political-military scenarios. P-3535, February, 1967, The RAND Corporation.

Graham, I.C.C., & Brease, E. Publications of the Social Science Department, RM-3600-4, May, 1967, The RAND Corporation.

Green, P. *Deadly logic: The theory of nuclear deterrence.* Columbus, Ohio: Ohio State University Press, 1966.

Hearings before the Committee on Armed Services, United States Senate, 88th Congress, First Session, 1963.

Hoag, M.W. NATO deterrent vs. shield. RM-1926-RC, June, 1957, The RAND Corporation

Hoag, M.W. On local war doctrine. P-2433, August, 1961, The RAND Corporation.

Horelick, A.L. The Cuban missile crisis: An analysis of soviet calculations and behavior. P-2433, August, 1963, The RAND Corporation

Horowitz, I.L. *Games, strategies and peace.* Philadelphia: American Friends Service Committee, 1962.

Horowitz, I.L. *The war game: Studies of the new civilian militarists.* New York: Ballantine, 1963.

Horowitz, I.L Social science and public policy: Implications of modern research. In *The rise and fall of project Camelot: Studies in the relationship between social science and practical politics.* Cambridge: M.I T. Press, 1967, Pp. 339–376.

Horowitz, I.L. America as a conflict society. In H.S. Becker (Ed.), *Social problems: A modern approach.* New York: Wiley, 1968. Pp. 695-749.

Huntington, S.P. Inter-service competition and the political roles of the armed services. In H. Kissinger (Ed.). *Problems of national strategy,* New York: Praeger, 1965. p. 453.

LeMay, C. Hearing before the committee on Armed Services, United States Senate, 88th Congress, First Session, 1963.

Lyons, G.M., & Morton, L. *Schools for strategy: Education and research in national security affairs.* New York: Praeger, 1965.

McDermott, J. Crisis manager. *New York Review of Books,* September 14, 1967, 4-10.

McNamara, R.S. Hearings on Military Posture. Committee on Armed Services, House of Representatives, 88th Congresss, First Session, 1963 (a).

McNamara, R.S. Hearings before the Committee on Armed Services, United States Senate, 88th Congress, First Session, 1963 (b).

Maccoby, M. Social scientists on war and peace: An essay review. *Social Problems* 11, 1963, 106-116.

Military Procurement Authorization, Fiscal Year 1964. 1963 Hearings before the Committee on Armed Services, United States Senate, 88th Congress, First Session (Esp. statements by Zukart: 874-886; LeMay: 887-898; Wheeler: 504-517; and McNamara: 398-406).

New York Times. Cuban crisis: A step-by-step review. November 13, 1962.

Pachter, H. *Collision course:* The Cuban missile crisis and coexistence. New York: Praeger, 1963.

Posvar, W.W. The impact of strategy expertise on the national security policy of the United States. In J. Montgomery and A. Smithies (Eds.), *Public Policy 13.* Cambridge, Mass.: Harvard School of Public Administration, 1964.

Schlesinger, A.M., Jr. *A thousand days: John F. Kennedy in the White House.* Boston: Houghton, 1965.

Smith, B. *The RAND Corporation: Case study of a non-profit advisory Corporation.* Cambridge, Mass.: Harvard University Press, 1966.

de Sola Pool, I. The necessity for social scientists doing research for government. In I.L. Horowitz (Ed.), *The rise and fall of project Camelot.* Cambridge, Mass.: M.I.T. Press, 1967, Pp. 267-279.

Sorenson, T. *Kennedy.* New York: Harper, 1965.

Sparkman, J. Situation in Cuba. Hearings before the Committee on Foreign Relations and the Committee on Armed Services, United States Senate, 87th Congress, Second Session, September, 1962.

Speier, H., & Goldhammer, H. Some observations on political gaming. The RAND Corporation, RM-1679-RC, June, 1959 (Reprinted: World Politics, 1960, 12).

Wheeler, E. Hearings before the Committee on Armed Services, United States Senate, 88th Congress, First Session, 1963.

Wohlstetter, Alberta, Cuba and Pearl Harbor: Hindsight and foresight. RM-4320-ISA, April, 1965, The RAND Corporation.

AUTHOR INDEX

Numbers in italics refer to the pages on which complete references are cited.

A

Abel, E., 285, *295*
Acheson, D., 266, *273*
Adorno, T.W., 209, *228*
Allport, G.W., 195, *228*
Altman, I., 207, *230*, 233
Aranoff, D., 173, *190*
Argyle, M., 212, *228*
Arkoff, A., 128, *154*
Aronson, E., 167, *187*
Arrowood, A.J., 128, *153*
Aumann, R.T., 33, 34, *42*

B

Bass, B.M., 122, *152*
Bartos, O.J., 57, 66, 67, *68*
Bazelon, D.T., 156, *187*
Beach, P.F., 209, *230,* 234
Becker, G.M., *273*
Beckman, L.L., 135, *153*
Bem, D.J., 82, *105*
Benedict, B.A., 170, *188*
Benham, A.H., 157, *187*
Berger, S., 208, 209, *229,* 233
Berkowitz, L., 75, 85, 88, *105, 106, 107,* 163, *187*
Bixenstine, V.E., 173, *187,* 209, 211, 212, *228, 229,* 233, 234, 250, *274*
Blake, R.R., 194, *229*
Boguslaw, R., 287, *295*
Bond, J.R., 127, 128, *152,* 210, 211, *229*
Bonoma, T., 166, 171, 172, 173, 174, 178, 180, *189, 190, 191*
Borash, L.A., Jr., 131, 133, *152,* 166, *187,* 211, *229*
Boulding, K.E., 156, *187,* 235, 236, 243, 272, *274*
Braithwaite, R.B., 39, *42*
Braver, S.L., 236, 247, *275*
Brease, E., 283, *295*
Brehm, J.W., 78, *106*

Brock, T.C., 85, *106*
Brodie, B., 254, *274,* 287, *295*
Brody, R.A., 157, 165, *187, 189,* 209, *230,* 234
Brown, B.R. 85, 91, *106,* 126, 143, *152,* 268, *274*
Burdick, E., 98, *107*
Buss, A.H., 85, *106*
Byrne, D., 173, *187*

C

Canavan, D., 219, *229,* 236, 247, *274*
Caplow, T.A., 126, *152*
Carlsmith, J.M., 167, *187*
Carlson, E.R., 99, *106*
Cartwright, D., 70, 78, *106*
Chambers, N., 211, *228,* 234
Chammah, A.M., 122, *153,* 172, 173, *190,* 200, 201, 211, 212, 214, 222, 223, 224, 231, 238, 242, 248, *276*
Chertkoff, J.M., 126, 128, *152*
Chu, G.C., 163, *187*
Chun, N., 96, *109*
Cohen, A.R., 181, *187*
Cohen, M.D., 236, *274*
Cohen, M.R., 157, *187*
Coleman, J.S., 198, 224, *229*
Collins, B.E., 72, 78, 81, 99, *106*
Commager, H.S., 293, *295*
Condry, J.C., Jr., 94, *107*
Coopersmith, S., 175, *187*
Coser, L.A., 71, 86, *106,* 236, *274*
Cottingham, D.R., 163, *187*
Crow, W.J., 216, 223, 224, *229,* 233, 234
Crowne, D.P., 209, 234, *229*
Cruse, D.B., *187*

D

Dabbs, J.M., 163, *187*
Dahlke, A.E., 94, *107*

SUBJECT INDEX

A

Anonymity, 123-126, 131, 267-271
Appeasement, 239, 271
Arms race simulations, 246, 273
Attacks
    preventative, 246, 254
    premeditated, 246
    preemptive, 246-248, 254
    surgical, 266, 286
Attraction, 114
Attribution theory, 82, 83

B

Balance of power, *see* Power
Bargaining set solution, 32-35
Bargaining tradition, 255, 256
Behavior control, 114, 115, 120, *see also* Fate control
Bilateral threat, *see* Threat

C

Chance, 2, 3, 5
Characteristic function of game, 21
Chicken, game of, 132, 201, 207, 235-273, 291, 295, *see also* Dangerous games
Civilian militarists, 243, 292
Coalition, 3, 21-26, 31-34, 40ff, 126-129
Coercive power, *see* Power
Cold war, 287, 288
Collective rationality, principle of, 33
Communication, 49, 89-92, 104, 120ff, 160, 182ff, 199, 212
Comparison level, 113
    for alternatives, 113, 117-119, 134, 136, 145
Concession, 47, 48, 262, 267, *see also* Yielding
Conflict, types of, 70-72, 196, 236
Conservative utility, 19
Constant-sum games, 3, 37

Cooperative games, 3
Counterforce targeting, 246, 255
Countervalue targeting, 246, 255
Cuban missile crisis, 244, 254, 266, 267, 272, 277-295

D

Dangerous games, 235-273, *see also* Chicken
Dependence, 114, 117
Deterrence, 156, 158, 161, 183, 238, 239, 242-248, 252, 255, 265, 277-295, *see also* Threat
Differential gain motive, 242
Differential games, 36

E

Elementary bargaining problem, 10-13
Escalation, 103, 104, 253, 254, *see also* Strategy
Ethics, 39
Exemplary strikes, 255
Experimental gaming, 235
    relevance of, 235, 236
Expert power, *see* Power
Exploitation, 250-253, 271

F

Face saving, 124, 239, 243, 244, 265-272
Fate control, 114-116, 120, *see also* Behavior control
First strike capability, 245, 246, 253, 254, 286, 287
Foreign policy, influence of game theory upon, 278

G

Game
    core, 27, 28, 31, 32
    matrix, 7